Edward Whalen a
Mitchell Schroete

C000143246

Oracle Performance Tuning

Addison-Wesley

Boston • San Francisco • New York • Toronto • Montreal
London • Munich • Paris • Madrid
Capetown • Sydney • Tokyo • Singapore • Mexico City

Many of the designations used by manufacturers and sellers to distinguish their products are claimed as trademarks. Where those designations appear in this book, and Addison-Wesley were aware of a trademark claim, the designations have been printed in initial capital letters or in all capitals.

The author and publisher have taken care in the preparation of this book, but make no expressed or implied warranty of any kind and assume no responsibility for errors or omissions. No liability is assumed for incidental or consequential damages in connection with or arising out of the use of the information or programs contained herein.

The publisher offers discounts on this book when ordered in quantity for special sales.

For more information, please contact:

Pearson Education Corporate Sales Division

201 W. 103rd Street

Indianapolis, IN 46290

(800) 428-5331

corpsales@pearsoned.com

Visit AW on the Web: www.awl.com/cseng/

ISBN 0-672-32146-7

05   04   03   02   4   3   2   1

First printing, April 2002

Acquisitions Editor
Kevin Howard

Managing Editor
Charlotte Clapp

Project Editor
Carol Bowers

Copy Editor
Karen Gill

Indexer
Bill Meyers

Proofreader
Leslie Joseph

Technical Editor
Jim Kotan

Team Coordinator
Pamalee Nelsen

Media Developer
Dan Scherf

Interior Designer
Gary Adair

Cover Designer
Alan Clements

Page Layout
Ayanna Lacey

Contents at a Glance

Introduction 1

Part I   Instance Tuning

1   Tuning Fundamentals 5

2   Using the Oracle Configuration Parameters 23

3   Tuning the Oracle Instance 35

4   Performance-Enhancing Features 67

5   Tuning Workloads 103

6   The Oracle Performance Views 115

7   Using UTLBSTAT and UTLESTAT 125

Part II   Oracle Hardware Topics

8   Oracle and System Hardware 163

9   I/O Concepts 179

10   Oracle and I/O 207

Part III   Application and SQL Tuning

11   Using EXPLAIN PLAN and SQL Trace 237

12   Index Tuning 255

13   The Oracle Optimizer 267

14   Tuning SQL 293

15   Using Hints 309

Part IV   Advanced Topics

16   Oracle9i Real Application Clusters 331

17   Tuning Backup and Recovery 343

18   Creating a High-Performance Disaster Survival System 365

19   Oracle Networking Performance 377

Index 387

Table of Contents

Introduction   **1**

Part I   **Instance Tuning**

1   **Tuning Fundamentals**   **5**

Tuning Concepts 6
     What Is Tuning? 6
     Do You Need to Tune? 7
     When Have You Tuned Enough? 7
Tuning Goals 7
     Tuning for Throughput 7
     Tuning for Response Time 8
     Tuning for Large Numbers of Users 9
     Tuning for Fault Tolerance 9
     Tuning for Load Time 9
Tuning Methodology 10
     Examine the Problem 10
     Determine the Problem 12
     Determine the Solution and Set Goals 14
     Test the Solution 15
     Analyze the Results 15
What Affects Oracle Server Performance? 16
     System Bottlenecks 17
     System Tuning 18
     System Limitations 19
Sizing and Capacity Planning 19
     Sizing Versus Capacity Planning 20
     Sizing Steps 20
     Capacity Planning Steps 21
Summary 21

2   **Using the Oracle Configuration Parameters**   **23**

Starting the Oracle Instance 24
     Connect to Oracle 25
     Using the STARTUP Command to Start the Instance 25

Starting the Instance 26
Troubleshooting the Instance Startup 26
Stopping the Oracle Instance 28
The Initialization Parameters 31
Instance Tuning Parameters 32
Resource Limiting Parameters 32
Summary 33

3 Tuning the Oracle Instance   35

Initialization Parameters Used in This Chapter 36
SGA Parameters 37
Program Global Area and User Memory Parameters 37
Undo Parameters 38
Miscellaneous Parameters 39
Tuning the SGA 39
Tuning the Operating System 40
Tuning the Private SQL and PL/SQL Areas 41
Tuning the Shared Pool 42
Tuning the Buffer Cache 47
Managing Rollback Segments and Undo Information 52
Tuning Undo in SMU Mode 53
Tuning Undo in RBU Mode 54
Summary of Undo Tuning 61
Checking for Redo Log Buffer 62
Redo Log Buffer Contention 62
Tuning Checkpoints 62
Optimizing Sorts 63
Tuning the Sort Area 64
Tuning the Sort Area Retained Size 64
Tuning the Temporary Tablespace 64
Minimizing Free List Contention 65
Summary 66

4 Performance-Enhancing Features   67

Parameters That Are Used in This Chapter 68
Indexes 69
Index Concepts 70
Index Types 70
B*-Tree Indexes 70

How the Oracle Bitmap Index Works 73

What to Index 74

How to Index 76

Parallel Execution in Oracle 77

Parallel Query Processing 78

Parallel Index Creation 84

Parallel Loading 84

Parallel Recovery 85

Clusters 86

Hash Clusters 89

When to Hash 89

Multiblock Reads 91

Partitioning 91

Partitioning Concepts 92

Range Partitioning 93

List Partitioning 94

Hash Partitioning 95

Composite Partitioning 95

Benefits of Partitioning 97

Partitioning and Indexes 97

Plan Stability 98

Multithreaded Server 98

Dedicated Server 98

Multithreaded Server 99

Summary 101

5   Tuning Workloads **103**

Parameters Used in This Chapter 104

Using Resource Consumer Groups 104

Overview of Resource Consumer Groups 105

Configuring Resource Consumer Groups 105

Adding Users to the Plan 109

Monitoring the Consumer Groups 110

Tuning User Resources 110

OLTP Systems 111

Response Time 112

Relocating Functions to Different Systems 112

Distributing Historical Reports 112

Distributing Online Reports 113

Application Support for Distributed Systems 114

Summary 114

6 The Oracle Performance Views 115

The V$ Views Versus the G$ Views 116

Overview of the Dynamic Performance Views 117

Using the Dynamic Performance Views 122

Using Queries to Access the Dynamic Performance Views 122

Using UTLBSTAT/UTLESTAT and Statspack 123

Using Performance-Monitoring Tools 123

Summary 124

7 Using UTLBSTAT and UTLESTAT 125

UTLBSTAT/UTLESTAT 126

Running UTLBSTAT/UTLESTAT 126

The UTLBSTAT/UTLESTAT Output File 127

Interpreting BSTAT/ESTAT Statistics 127

Statspack 142

Installing Statspack 142

Running Statspack 142

Administering Statspack 144

Statspack Results 144

Summary 160

Part II Oracle Hardware Topics

8 Oracle and System Hardware 163

Parameters Used in This Chapter 164

Overview of the Oracle Instance 164

The Oracle Memory Structure 165

Processes 168

System Architecture Overview 170

CPUs and Caches 170

CPU Design 171

32-Bit Versus 64-Bit Processors 174

System Memory Architecture 175

Bus Design 176

I/O Bus 177

Network 177

To Cluster or Not to Cluster 177

Summary 177

9 I/O Concepts   **179**

The Disk Drive 180

Overview 180

Disk Drive Performance 184

RAID Disk Subsystems 187

Hardware Versus Software RAID 188

Striping 189

RAID 0 189

RAID 1 190

RAID 10 191

RAID 2 192

RAID 3 192

RAID 4 193

RAID 5 194

Parity Overview 195

RAID Performance Overview 197

RAID Controller Performance Features 199

Elevator Sorting 199

Controller Caches 200

Hardware XOR Engines 201

Stripe Size 201

Internal Versus External RAID Systems 201

Internal RAID Systems 202

External RAID Systems 202

SAN Systems 203

Network Attached Storage (NAS) Systems 206

Summary 206

10 Oracle and I/O   **207**

Parameters Used in This Chapter 208

Oracle's Dependency on I/O 209

Why Read Latency Is Important 209

Write Latency 211

Fault Tolerance 212

Configuring the I/O Subsystem for Oracle.........................212
   Performance Versus Fault Tolerance Versus Cost.........212
   Protecting Your Investment.........................213
Tuning I/O...215
   Understanding Disk Contention.........................215
   Identifying Disk Contention Problems.........................216
   Solving Disk Contention Problems.........................218
Reducing Unnecessary I/O Overhead.........................222
   Migrated and Chained Rows.........................222
   Dynamic Extensions.........................224
   PCTFREE and PCTUSED Command Options.........................225
   A Review of I/O Reduction Techniques.........................228
Block Size.........................229
   Using Multiple Block Sizes.........................230
Fragmentation.........................231
Summary.........................234

Part III   Application and SQL Tuning

11   Using EXPLAIN PLAN and SQL Trace   237

SQL Trace.........................238
   SQL Trace Initialization.........................239
   Controlling SQL Trace.........................239
   SQL Trace Functionality.........................240
   TKPROF Functionality.........................241
   Interpreting SQL Trace.........................243
The EXPLAIN PLAN Command.........................248
   EXPLAIN PLAN Initialization.........................249
   Invoking EXPLAIN PLAN.........................250
   Extracting EXPLAIN PLAN Results.........................250
Registering Applications.........................251
Summary.........................252

12   Index Tuning   255

Parameters Used in This Chapter.........................257
Index Types.........................257
Using the B*-Tree Index.........................258
   What Should Be Indexed.........................259
   Maintaining the Index.........................261

The Index Organized Table (IOT) 262
The Bitmap Index 262
    When to Use a Bitmap Index 263
Function-Based Indexes 264
Using Hints 264
Monitoring and Analyzing Indexes 265
    ALTER INDEX MONITORING USAGE 265
Summary 265

13 The Oracle Optimizer   267

Understanding the Optimizer 268
    How the Optimizer Works 269
    Optimizer Initialization Parameters 269
    Optimization Methods 271
Using the DBMS_STATS Package 273
    Creating a Statistics Table 274
    Gathering Table Stats 274
    Deleting Statistics 275
    Restoring Statistics 276
    Other DBMS_STATS Package Functions 276
    Working with Statistics 277
Using the ANALYZE Command 277
    How to Run the ANALYZE Command 278
    Data Dictionary Statistics 280
Transaction Processing 282
SQL Statement Processing 284
    Cursor Creation 284
    Statement Parsing 284
    Query Processing 286
    Bind Variables 286
    Statement Execution 286
    Parallelization 287
    Fetch Rows to Be Returned 287
Analyzing SQL Statements 288
Designing New SQL Statements 290
    Packages, Procedures, and Functions 290
Using Hints 290
Summary 292

14   Tuning SQL   **293**

Optimal SQL Statements 294

How to Identify Poorly Tuned SQL Statements 294

Join Types 295

    Nested Loops Join 295

    Merge Join 296

    Hash Join 296

Tuning SQL Statements 297

    Tuning an Existing Application 298

    Designing a New Application 303

Summary 306

15   Using Hints   **309**

Implementing Hints 311

    Hint Syntax 311

    Hint Errors 311

    Using Multiple Hints 312

Hints 313

    Optimization Approaches 313

    Access Methods 315

    Join Orders 319

    Join Operations 319

    Parallel Query Hints 321

    Query Transformation 323

    Miscellaneous Hints 325

Summary 328

Part IV   Advanced Topics

16   Oracle9i Real Application Clusters   **331**

Overview of RAC 332

    Computer Systems 333

    Shared Disk Subsystem 333

    Server Interconnect 334

    Locking 334

    Cluster Configuration 336

When to Use RAC 341

Tuning RAC 341

Configuration and Sizing 342

Instance and Lock Tuning 342

Application Tuning 342

Summary 342

17   Tuning Backup and Recovery   343

Parameters Used in This Chapter 345

Oracle Operational Review 345

Backup Process 346

Recovery Process 346

Characteristics of the Oracle Backup Process 347

Cold (Offline) Backup Using User-Managed Backups 347

Hot (Online) Backup Using User-Managed Backups 347

Hot (Online) Backup Using the RMAN Utility 348

Hot (Online) Backup Using Storage Area Network Features 348

Data Access Patterns During User-Managed Backups 349

Data Access Patterns During RMAN Backups 349

System Load During Backup 350

Backup Goals 350

System Design Considerations 350

Cold Database Backup 351

Hot Database Backup 352

Tuning Considerations Using User-Managed Backups 355

Tuning Considerations Using RMAN Backups 356

The RMAN Buffers 356

Asynchronous Versus Synchronous I/O 356

RMAN Tuning Parameters 357

Monitoring RMAN 357

System Enhancements to Improve Backup Performance 358

CPU Enhancements 358

I/O Enhancements 358

Network Enhancements 359

Split Up the Backup 359

Performance Verification 361

What to Test in the RDBMS 361

What to Test in the OS 361

Summary 364

18   Creating a High-Performance Disaster Survival System   **365**

Parameters Used in This Chapter 366

Why Plan for a Disaster? 366

Disaster Survival Concepts 367

    Remote Mirroring 367

    Oracle9i Data Guard 368

    Replication 370

Planning for a Disaster 371

    Planning Steps 371

    Documentation 372

    Scenarios 372

Recovering from a Disaster 373

Tuning Standby Systems 374

Summary 375

19   Oracle Networking Performance   **377**

Network Architecture 378

    Hardware Components 378

    Network Protocols 381

Tuning the Network Components 382

Software Tuning 383

    Oracle Tuning 383

Network Design 383

    Bandwidth Considerations 384

    Segmenting the Network 384

    Bridges, Routers, and Hubs 385

Summary 385

Index   **387**

About the Author

Edward Whalen is vice president of Performance Tuning Corporation (www.perftuning.com), a consulting company that specializes in database performance, administration, and backup/recovery solutions. Prior to Performance Tuning Corporation, Edward worked at Compaq Computer Corporation in the capacity of OS developer, and then as database performance engineer. He has extensive experience in database system design and tuning for optimal performance. His career has consisted of hardware, operating system, and database development projects for many different companies. Edward has published two other books on the Oracle RDBMS: *Oracle Performance Tuning and Optimization* and *Teach Yourself Oracle 8 in 21 Days*. He has also written four books on Microsoft SQL Server. In addition to writing, Edward has worked on numerous benchmarks and performance-tuning projects with both Oracle and MS SQL Server. He is recognized as a leader in database performance tuning and optimization.

Mitchell Schroeter is a senior consultant with Performance Tuning Corporation (www.perftuning.com) and has worked in the field of database performance tuning for five years. Prior to Performance Tuning Corporation, Mitchell worked at Dell Computer Corporation as a systems analyst in the systems performance analysis group, specializing in database technologies and high-performance storage systems. He has extensive experience with developing client-server and multitiered applications on both Oracle and Microsoft SQL Server in a variety of programming languages. Mitchell specializes in tuning database systems and application code, storage area networks, and Oracle 9i Real Application Clusters.

Acknowledgments

Edward Whalen:

It is not easy acknowledging all the people who have made this book possible. Not only is there the work that went into the book, but the support and encouragement of friends and family also moved the book forward.

I would like to thank Mitchell Schroeter for his part in making this book happen. I would also like to thank Kevin Howard, Angela Kozlowski, Karen Gill, Carol Bowers, and Rosemarie Graham for all their help in the development of the book. This book would not be what it is without the help of a great team of editors from both Sams and Addison-Wesley.

I would also like to thank Larry Ellison. Without him, Oracle would not be what it is today. Thanks also to Ken Jacobs, whom I have had the pleasure of knowing and from him gaining a new appreciation of Oracle's RDBMS.

I would especially like to thank Susan Georgson for her work on Chapter 7. This chapter was derived from a presentation that she gave at the IOUG conference last year. Thanks, Susan.

Writing a book involves a lot of time and effort. I would like to thank my wife, Felicia, for putting up with the sacrifices necessary to write this book.

The acknowledgments for a book are difficult to write because I am always afraid I have missed someone. If I have, I deeply regret it and apologize.

Mitchell Schroeter:

I believe it goes without saying that this book would not have happened without the dedication and hard work of my good friend, Ed Whalen, who presented me with an amazing opportunity to assist him with this project. He is an experienced author and a great teacher. I learned a lot from him during this process, and I can only hope I lived up to his expectations. Thanks again, Ed.

I would like to thank Kevin, Angela, Carol, Karen, and the countless folks at Addison-Wesley who dedicated their time and effort in putting forth this project. I can assure you that your contributions did not go unnoticed or unappreciated.

A very special thank you goes to my good friend and co-worker, Marci Garcia, who set me back on track several times and made me see the light at the end of the tunnel.

Thanks to Phil (no, the *other* Phil), who taught me Oracle in three days some years ago. Without that knowledge, I wouldn't be where I am today.

Thanks to Laurie and Domino, who gave me the space and quiet time when I needed it, and for the support and patience it takes to be a part of something like this.

To Mom, Dad, Brad, Jill, Jakob, and Jonathan: Thanks for being there.

Introduction

Each year, computer systems become faster. At the same time, memory and disk storage are becoming more plentiful and less expensive. Because of this, the means and the budget are now available to store vast amounts of information at relatively inexpensive prices. This has allowed users to increase the amount of data stored as well as increase the amount of processing that is done with that data. Because of this, society cannot simply solve performance problems by throwing more hardware at the problem. It's necessary to analyze, size, and properly configure systems to perform optimally.

For us, performance engineers, one of the problems that we see in the industry today is the introduction of large disk drives. At one time, it would have been necessary to configure 10 disk drives to hold the data that you have generated; you can now store the same data in 1 disk drive. What many people don't know is that this 1 disk drive is 10 times slower than 10 smaller disk drives. In this book, concepts such as this will be explained and explored.

Our philosophy in writing this book is that tuning must be done holistically. You cannot focus on one part of the system and achieve optimal performance. It is necessary to look at the application, the Oracle instance, the operating system, and the hardware and I/O subsystem to achieve optimal performance. In this book, we explore all areas of the system from SQL statements down to the operation of the disk drive.

We hope that you will use this book not only as a guide for learning Oracle performance tuning, but as a reference as well.

How to Use This Book

To keep the book interesting, we have added some personal anecdotes relevant to the subject matter. We hope we have conveyed some of the excitement that comes when you push systems to their limits. Those of us who work in the database performance field constantly push the envelope of technology to achieve new levels of performance previously thought impossible. This kind of experimentation can be satisfying when everything works well, but frustrating when it doesn't.

Our hope is that, having read this book, you will have a basic understanding of how the components of the system work together to form the whole. If you have this foundation, you should be able to tackle a performance problem, know what to look for, and know how to fix it. Not all performance problems are alike, and solutions aren't either. It is important that you have a basic understanding of what to look for and what the possible solutions are.

If we have done our jobs correctly, you should finish this book with the ability to analyze the problem, hypothesize a solution, test that solution, and understand the result. We hope this book gives novices an idea of what performance engineering is all about. Seasoned professionals should receive new insight and ideas. By applying this newly acquired knowledge, you will find that tackling even the most complex performance problems can be broken down into simple, manageable tasks.

PART I

Instance Tuning

IN THIS PART

1 Tuning Fundamentals

2 Using the Oracle Configuration Parameters

3 Tuning the Oracle Instance

4 Performance-Enhancing Features

5 Tuning Workloads

6 The Oracle Performance Views

7 Using UTLBSTAT and UTLESTAT

TUNING FUNDAMENTALS

This chapter covers the basic concepts behind performance tuning. It starts by introducing the concepts of performance tuning. The next part of this chapter covers tuning goals. It then covers tuning methodology, which is the manner in which you analytically determine what it is you want to tune and for what ends. Next is a section on the types of things that affect Oracle performance. Finally, the chapter has an introduction to sizing and capacity planning.

At the conclusion of this chapter, you should have an understanding of a simple tuning methodology and the basic concepts of performance tuning. You should also be exposed to the fundamentals of system sizing and capacity planning.

Tuning Concepts

Before getting into tuning details, this chapter will discuss some basic tuning concepts. My philosophy has always been to cover the basics first, and then move on to details. By understanding the basics, you will more easily understand the more complex concepts and techniques that are covered in this book. You will start by learning what tuning is and when you need to do it.

What Is Tuning?

Tuning is the act of making a modification to hardware or software to change system properties. I have intentionally avoided using the term *performance* in this definition because you might not necessarily be tuning your system for performance. In fact, you might tune your system for any of the following reasons:

- Tuning for Throughput. This involves tuning to accomplish the largest amount of work in the least amount of time.

- Tuning for Response Time. This occurs when you are tuning in order so that data can be returned quickly.

- Tuning for Large Numbers of Users. Here the system is tuned to support the greatest number of users.

- Tuning for Load Time. This involves tuning to make database loads perform optimally.

- Tuning for Back Up and Recovery Performance. Here the system is tuned to back up and restore the database quickly.

You might have many different tuning goals. Tuning goals are covered later in this chapter.

Do You Need to Tune?

Before beginning a tuning exercise, you might want to determine whether you need to tune. How do you determine this? Following are some of the ways to determine if you need to tune:

- Listen to your customers. Your customer might be a different department in your company or might be the user community. Listen to what they have to say.

- Monitor the system. Regular system monitoring is a must. Look for trends such as increasing CPU utilization, I/O utilization, and so on.

- Requirements have changed. You might need to tune your system if your requirements have changed, such as number of users, load time, and so on.

- Response times are increasing. It is a good idea to monitor response times of certain well-known functions. This data can be used to determine trends.

You can't determine whether you need to tune your system in any single way. The best way is to be aware of the system and system requirements.

When Have You Tuned Enough?

In addition to determining whether you need to tune, it is also important to determine when to stop tuning. The best way to do this is with goals. When you have achieved your goals, you are finished. If your goal is to have the most optimally tuned system possible, then your job is never ending.

System requirements often change. It is also common for the load on the system to change. Thus, tuning is an ongoing process, but individual projects should end whenever you have achieved your goals. The next section discusses how to determine these goals.

Tuning Goals

Set tuning goals for your system. Each system has different characteristics depending on the needs of the users. You must determine why you are tuning a particular system. The desired goals often influence the kind of changes made and whether those changes are successful. People tune their systems for different reasons; the following sections examine a few of them.

Tuning for Throughput

Throughput is defined as the amount of work done divided by the time it takes to do that work. Work to be done is usually defined in terms of transactions. Therefore, the throughput of the system is defined as follows:

Throughput = #transactions / time

The time in this equation is usually some measurement interval during which a large amount of work is done. Consider, for example, a company that takes reservations. If the reservation office is open eight hours a day and the number of tickets sold for an event must be 25,000 for the first day of sales, the required throughput for this system must meet or exceed 3,125 transactions per hour:

Throughput = (25,000 transactions / 8 hours) = 3,125 transactions per hour, or 52.1 transactions per minute

Of course, it is not realistic to base required transaction rates on an eight-hour interval because not all requests come in at a steady rate. When we are sizing a system and determining a system's capacity, we base our calculations on the busiest time interval. This is known as sizing for the worse case.

Depending on the complexity of the transaction and the granularity of your measurements, you can express throughput in transactions per hour, transactions per minute, or transactions per second. For some large Decision Support System (DSS) applications, you might even measure throughput in transactions per day.

For your particular configuration, the most important tuning goal might be system throughput. In some environments such as OLTP (On-Line Transaction Processing), it might be vital to achieve the highest throughput possible, thus getting the most possible work through the system in the shortest possible time.

To achieve the highest possible throughput, you might have to make sacrifices in some areas, such as response time and perhaps fault tolerance and recovery time.

Tuning for Response Time

Response time is the time from when you press the last key for an input form until all the data has been displayed on the display device. Response time is essentially the time the end user spends waiting for the behind-the-scenes processing of the job.

Although some installations require the highest throughput possible, others might have strict response time criteria. In such an environment, slow response times usually mean customers waiting on a phone line, thus keeping other customers on hold. Because this can mean lost business, it is essential to reduce this hold time.

For installations that have strict response time criteria, you might have to tune the system differently. It might be necessary to run the system at a much lower throughput rate than it can handle or to delay batch jobs until off-hours.

Tuning for Large Numbers of Users

Connectivity, or the ability to support connections to other systems or clients, might be an important factor in configuring and tuning your system. It might be necessary to configure and tune your system to support large numbers of users in an effective manner. Additionally, it might be necessary to incorporate the additional capacity necessary to support additional users. Such a system might be used for a business that requires additional employees at various peak times during the year.

To tune for large numbers of connections, memory can be a special concern. You must carefully plan for the memory requirements of these users and make sure that you don't exceed available resources during peak periods. This might mean that you have to configure extra memory into the system that is on standby for user connections. Operating system resources associated with network and user connectivity must be closely monitored.

The resources associated with these users can be determined experimentally. Try running the application with a specific number of users and monitor system resource usage. Increase the number of users and monitor the system again. This should give you a fairly good idea of the amount of resources that are associated with each user.

When performing these types of tests, good note taking is critical. By logging configuration changes and their results, you can get a good idea of how those changes have affected the system.

Tuning for Fault Tolerance

For some installations, it is of the utmost importance that *fault tolerance* be employed in every aspect of the system. Any down time in such a system might be devastating. A site with high fault tolerance requirements might require frequent checkpoints and frequent backups.

Several tuning considerations come into play when fault tolerance is the highest priority. The disk subsystem should use some type of hardware RAID (Redundant Array of Inexpensive Disks) to protect against disk failures. The memory should be protected with advanced ECC memory. In some cases when up-time is critical, you might even consider a redundant system, which can be used if the primary system were to fail.

Tuning for Load Time

Some systems have a requirement that a certain amount of data be loaded each night to be available for the next day's processing. Usually, the load time is limited, and it is essential that a specific amount of data be loaded within a certain time. Although the load time requirement can be met, doing so might be costly in terms of additional hardware that might be required.

In this situation, you might have to tune the I/O subsystem for load time. Configuring for load time might affect the general performance of the system. By tuning for both load time and run time, this affect can be minimized.

ANALYZE EACH SITE INDIVIDUALLY

It is important to realize that your tuning goals and my tuning goals might not be the same. Depending on your installation, differences in configuration might be drastic. Each site is different and serves a unique function; each site must be analyzed individually.

Tuning Methodology

This section explains why it is important to follow a structured, goal-oriented methodology in your tuning efforts if you want to achieve optimal results. The methodology I use involves these five steps, as shown in Figure 1.1.

1. Analyze the system. Decide if there is a problem; if there is a problem, what is it?

2. Determine the problem. What do you think is causing the problem? Why?

3. Determine a potential solution and set goals. Decide what you want to try and what you think will result from your changes. What is it you want to accomplish? Do you want higher throughput? Faster response times? What?

4. Test the solution. See what happens.

5. Analyze the results. Did the solution meet the goals? If not, you might have to go back to step 1, 2, or 3.

The following sections describe each of these steps individually and explain why each step is important to the final outcome. Sometimes, you don't have an answer to the problem or perhaps you don't even know what the problem is. Over time, however, a little analysis is worth more than considerable trial and error.

Examine the Problem

The first phase in tuning the system should always be the determination phase. First, see whether you even have a problem. You might just be at the limits of the configuration. To make sure, examine the system, look for problems, and make this determination logically.

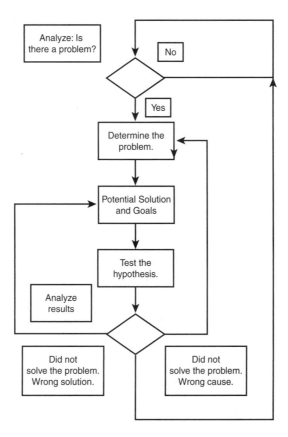

FIGURE 1.1
The tuning methodology flowchart.

The determination phase consists of examining the system as it currently is, looking for problems or bottlenecks, and identifying areas with more activity than the rest of the system, or "hot spots." Keep in mind that performance problems might not always be obvious. Here is a partial list of some areas you should examine:

- Application code. The problem might consist of an application that executes excessive code or performs table scans when it is not necessary.

- Oracle database engine. The problem might be an improperly sized SGA (System Global Area) or another tuning parameter.

- Operating system parameters. The operating system might not be configured properly and might be starving Oracle of needed resources.

- Hardware configuration. The layout of the database might not be efficient and might be causing a disk bottleneck.

- Network. The network might be overloaded and causing excessive collisions and delays.

I prefer to categorize performance issues into the following three classes:

- It's broken. Performance is severely handicapped because of a configuration error or an incorrect parameter in the operating system or Relational Database Management System (RDBMS). I consider problems that fall into this category to cause a performance swing of 50% or more. Problems in this category are usually oversights during the system build (such as incorrectly building an index or forgetting to enable asynchronous I/O).

- It's not optimized. Performance is slightly degraded because of a small miscalculation in parameters or because system capacity is slightly exceeded. These types of problems are usually easily solved by fine-tuning the configurations.

- Not a tuning problem. Don't forget that sometimes a problem doesn't exist—you have just reached the capacity of the system. Upgrading or adding more capacity can easily solve this situation. Not all problems can be solved with tuning.

In the case of the first class of problem, you might need to take drastic action. With the second class of problem, tuning might solve it. With the third class of problem, no action needs to be taken.

Following are some questions to ask yourself when examining the system and searching for problems:

- Are you getting complaints from the user community?

- Are some operations taking much longer than the same operations did in the past?

- Is CPU usage low but I/O usage high?

- Are you seeing excessive response times?

- Does the system seem sluggish?

If you answer *yes* to any of these questions, you might be seeing some performance problems that can be fixed. In some cases, you have reached the limitations of your hardware and should add an additional CPU or perhaps more disks.

If you answer *no* to all these questions, your system might be running well. However, you should still periodically monitor the performance of the system to avoid future problems.

Determine the Problem

After you have decided that the system does have a problem, make a careful analysis to determine the cause of the problem.

At first glance, it is not always obvious what the problem is. You might see excessive disk I/O on a certain table that might lead you to believe you have an I/O problem when, in fact, you have a cache hit problem or an index problem that is causing excessive I/Os.

Take a few minutes to think about the problem. Decide what area you believe the problem to be in. Thinking through the problem can help you avoid a long trial-and-error period in which you randomly try different things without positive results.

At this stage, note taking is a must. By writing down your ideas and thoughts, you can better organize them. If you have to go back and rethink the problem, these notes will be useful.

Look at the chief complaint and try to understand how that component works and what can be affecting it. Suppose that you are having a client/server response time problem. The following sidebar analyzes this problem.

RESPONSE TIME EXAMPLE

The user response time is measured from when the data is input and submitted until the results are displayed on the user's display device. To analyze a response time problem, start by considering the components. The problem can be broken into three major areas:

- Client. The problem could be with the client application code.
- Server. The problem could be with the database engine.
- Network. Some problem in the network could be delaying processing.

You can use analysis tools to help determine the area to which you can isolate the response time problem. By putting debug statements into the application code, you can determine whether the delays are part of the client component. By using EXPLAIN PLAN, you might see that you are not taking advantage of an index and are causing excessive table scans.

I have heard of several examples in client/server systems in which the end user complains about the server causing 10-second or greater response times. After analysis, it was determined that the database was giving subsecond response times but was spending more than 9 seconds in the GUI (Graphical User Interface).

Be open-minded and look at every component of the system as a potential for bottlenecks. You might be surprised to find that the problem is something simple and in an area you would not normally think would cause problems.

Following are some questions to ask yourself when trying to determine the cause of the performance problem:

- What are the effects of the problem: Response times? Throughput? What?
- Does every user see the same problem or does the problem affect just a few users? If the latter, what are those few users doing differently?
- What does the system monitor tell you? Are you 100% CPU bound? What about I/Os: Are you exceeding I/O limits?
- Is only a certain type of transaction a problem? What about other transaction types? Are they okay?
- Is it a client problem or a server problem?

By asking yourself these questions and making up your implementation-specific questions, you will get more insight into how the application operates and where the potential bottlenecks are.

Determine the Solution and Set Goals

Regardless of the type of problem you have, you must determine a course of action. In many cases, determining the problem has already pointed you to a solution. In other cases, more analysis is necessary. After the problem has been determined, you must set some goals about what you want the solution to accomplish. When you set specific goals, not only can you measure success, but specific goals might also sometimes point you to specific solutions.

The solution might consist of changing a parameter in the operating system or in Oracle; the solution might consist of a rewrite of a section of application code. With packaged applications, you might have to tune the operating system and database to overcome a problem in the application.

The determination of a solution should include some expectation of what results you expect to see. Changing a parameter without at least knowing what it is supposed to do might provide the desired results or might instead mask the true problem.

Goal Setting

After you determine the problem (or at least have a pretty good idea about the area causing the problem), set some goals. Your ultimate goal is always optimal performance, but here I want you to think more specifically.

Your goals should be specific and achievable. Following are some examples of realistic and achievable goals:

- Increase the cache hit ratio in the buffer cache.

- Reduce the number of I/Os.

- Increase the number of connections supported.

- Tune your queries.

Goals such as these might or might not be achievable in your system, but at least they give you an area on which to focus your tuning efforts. Unachievable goals end in disappointment. Smaller, more specific goals can help you achieve the larger goal more effectively.

Here are some questions to ask yourself when you are determining the solution and setting result goals:

- What will this solution do? What do you expect the result of your changes to be?

- How will your changes affect performance? For example, does a better cache hit rate mean fewer I/Os?

- Will this solution directly or indirectly affect the problem?

- How will your idea of the problem change if this solution doesn't fix the problem?

These are just a few examples of the kind of things to think about when determining the solution and setting goals.

Test the Solution

After you put the solution in place, you must test it to see whether you have achieved the desired results. Although you might be able to test the results in a test configuration by setting up an emulated load, your only choice might be to put the system into the production environment for analysis.

At this stage, it is important to take notes. These notes can be extremely valuable in the future when similar problems arise and you are looking for solutions.

AVOID USING TEST CONFIGURATIONS IN PRODUCTION

I don't recommend putting test configurations into production unless you completely understand the changes that have been made and have assessed the risks.

In most cases, you will have the test programs and user-emulation facilities you used in the development phase. You can use these to test the new configuration against already-known performance results.

Analyze the Results

The final step is to analyze the results of any changes you have made. If the desired results have not been achieved, go back to the analysis stage to determine whether more tuning is necessary. You should always ask the question "Why?" It is possible that the problem has been incorrectly identified or that you have not chosen the correct solution for that problem.

Following are some questions to ask yourself during the analysis phase:

- Did the change have the desired results?

- Did the overall system performance change?

- Do you now think that the problem is different from what you first thought?

- Do you think more changes are necessary?

These are some examples of the types of questions you should ask yourself to determine whether the problem has been solved or even affected by the changes. You might have to reanalyze the problem and try different things. Maybe you did not understand the problem correctly and have to add some additional debug code to the application to track down the problem.

This five-step methodology leads to an analytical, logical way of viewing performance data. Using this or any methodology should lead you to the proper solution.

What Affects Oracle Server Performance?

Many factors contribute to the performance of Oracle on the server: the tuning of the Oracle instance, the operating system, the hardware, and the load generated by the users. In tuning the system, you have some control over almost all these factors.

As mentioned earlier in this chapter, I like to break down the performance of a system into three categories: things that are broken, things that need to be optimized, and things that aren't a problem. The first category can cause significant performance loss; the second can cause minor degradation. Sometimes, a significant gray area exists between the first two categories of problems, but the solutions are the same.

Many different situations can cause performance loss. Examples of these situations include the following:

- An I/O subsystem that is overloaded. This can cause the entire system to slow down waiting on disk requests to return.

- Not enough memory. This can cause additional I/O usage by reducing the memory that is available for Oracle to cache recently accessed data, and by causing the operating system to swap or page.

- Lack of Oracle resources. A shared pool that is too small can cause performance problems, as described in Chapter 3, "Tuning the Oracle Instance."

- A slow network. Network performance problems can reduce throughput and cause user response times to rise.

These problems can be caused by any part of the system that consists of the following:

- Hardware. This might consist of defective hardware or just an insufficient amount of some resource, such as memory or disk.

- Operating system. This includes tuning as well as operating system resources that Oracle uses.

- Oracle. It is essential to properly tune Oracle for your configuration to provide for optimal performance. A poorly tuned Oracle instance can drastically affect performance.

A significant performance loss caused by a limiting factor in the system is known as a *bottleneck*.

System Bottlenecks

The term *bottleneck* comes from the shrinking in size of the neck of a bottle. This constriction causes a reduction in flow, limiting the amount of liquid coming out of the bottle. In a similar fashion, this term describes something that is constricting system performance. Over the years, this term has grown to represent any sort of major limiting factor in a computer system.

A bottleneck can significantly reduce the performance of a system while leaving some resources, such as the CPU, completely underutilized. It is the job of the performance engineer to reduce or eliminate bottlenecks.

Finding the Bottleneck

As you will see in the next few chapters, it is not always easy to determine where a bottleneck is and what is causing it. In some cases, it is almost impossible to determine exactly where the problem is.

If the bottleneck is internal to the operating system or to Oracle, you can't do anything about it. The developers of Oracle as well as developers of most operating systems are constantly testing new releases to eliminate all the bottlenecks they can.

If the bottleneck is in the hardware, you often have an easier time eliminating it. Solving a hardware limitation usually involves simply adding more disk drives or increasing the amount of RAM in the system. If an inherent bottleneck is in the system's cache design or memory bus, you usually can't do much about it. Most hardware vendors concentrate on reducing system bottlenecks as quickly as they can. For hardware companies that do significant benchmarking, it is especially important that they have optimal performance.

BUYER BEWARE ——

This is a case where the buyer should beware. Many small "clone vendors" do no work to optimize their hardware for RDBMS performance. You might find that the money you save on hardware is spent buying additional components or systems to make up for the deficiency in the original hardware.

Removing the Bottleneck

How do you get rid of a system bottleneck? The solution involves analysis, tuning, and hard work. The next few chapters discuss the particulars of how to get rid of specific bottlenecks.

The goal is to remove the bottleneck as a limiting factor in the performance of your system. If disk I/O is causing a bottleneck, tuning the I/O subsystem, by either redistributing your database or by adding additional capacity, should remove I/O as a limiting factor. After this is done, I/O is no longer an issue in tuning your system. You have moved the limiting factor somewhere else.

System Tuning

How well the system is tuned is also a major factor in the overall performance. For the most part, tuning the system involves resource allocation. Adding or removing a resource in the RDBMS, the operating system, or even the hardware can drastically affect performance.

The next few sections briefly introduce some of the tuning factors that can alter system performance. Details on how to determine whether these factors are a real problem and how to find them are scattered throughout this book.

Tuning RDBMS Resources

The RDBMS takes up many system resources; it uses these resources to serve the user requests. If Oracle does not have enough of a particular resource, you can see vast reductions in performance.

Memory is of particular importance to Oracle. If Oracle does not have enough memory resources allocated for the block buffer cache, the data dictionary cache, or even the log buffer, Oracle can be out of tune. If enough memory isn't allocated for the buffer cache or the data dictionary cache, you might see low cache hit rates. If enough memory isn't allocated for the log buffer, you might experience inefficient access to the redo log.

Increasing the value of some of the Oracle resources, such as the buffer cache, the shared pool, or the log buffer, can improve cache hit rates and reduce system I/O, resulting in improved performance. Careful analysis should be done to ensure that you are increasing the correct resource the right amount. This is discussed in more detail in Chapter 2, "Using the Oracle Configuration Parameters."

You can use other Oracle tuning parameters to take advantage of special operating system features. For example, in the UNIX operating system, you might have to tell Oracle that you have Asynchronous I/O (AIO) available and that it should use it.

Tuning Operating System Resources

The operating system is typically tuned to allow Oracle to allocate needed resources. Many operating systems have limitations on how much memory or CPU time a single process or user can consume. Because Oracle is not a regular user—it is a server process—these resources must be increased to allow Oracle to consume vast system resources.

You might have to turn on other operating system features to allow Oracle to use them. Some features such as AIO (mentioned in the preceding section) are not turned on by default in some operating systems. Other new features are just coming available.

Sometimes, you must reduce operating system parameters to make room for Oracle getting resources. For example, you might have to reduce the amount of memory that the operating system uses to buffer files because Oracle bypasses any buffering that the file system might use. This additional and possibly unused memory could be beneficial to Oracle performance.

Tuning Hardware Resources

Hardware cannot be tuned in the same manner as the RDBMS and the operating system. Although you can think of hardware tuning as more of a resource-balancing act than a tuning exercise, the methodology is the same.

After analyzing the system, you might discover that it is necessary to add hardware resources such as more disks, disk controllers, RAM, cache, CPUs, and so on. Adding hardware resources is all part of the tuning game and requires the same analysis and testing as RDBMS and operating system tuning.

Other Tuning Factors

Other factors might be limiting the performance of your system, such as inefficiencies in the application code that cause unnecessary table scans or network limitations.

Other processes running concurrently on the system might be stealing badly needed CPU cycles from Oracle. These processes might be using memory that could be allocated for Oracle; they could be causing contention on the same disk devices that Oracle is using.

When analyzing the performance of your system, remember not to focus so much on the RDBMS that you miss something external to it. Many factors contribute to the database's performance, and these factors might not all be within the database.

System Limitations

Finally, the performance of the system is limited by how fast the system can go. Even with the most optimally tuned system, you are limited by the speed of the system's CPUs. In this case, you have done everything possible to reduce bottlenecks; the system performance relies on the speed of the CPUs, as it should.

When the speed of the computer limits you, your job as a performance engineer is done. If you still need more performance, you need more CPUs or more systems (perhaps clusters). Many factors make it unwise to constantly run your system at its performance limits; it is better to leave a little capacity available for peak activity.

Sizing and Capacity Planning

One of the major problems that you run into in the field is a system that does not have sufficient hardware or software to support the required tasks. The best way to avoid this is to properly size your system and regularly perform capacity planning exercises. In this section, you will be introduced to sizing and capacity planning.

Sizing Versus Capacity Planning

You have probably heard of the terms *sizing* and *capacity planning* before. I will provide my definition of sizing and capacity planning and a little bit of information on how these tasks are accomplished.

Sizing is the art of determining how much hardware or software is required in a new system that you are building. *Capacity planning* is the art of determining when the capacity of your current system will run out. As you might imagine, these tasks are similar—if not identical—in many respects.

THE CAR ANALOGY

The main differences between sizing and capacity can be summed up in a simple analogy of a car. When you're sizing a system, it's like buying a car and making sure it has enough horsepower or the right fuel efficiency for your needs. Capacity planning is like determining how many people the car can hold or how far it can go on a tank of gas.

In sizing the system, you're determining the performance needs of the system today. With capacity planning, you're determining what you'll need in the system down the road.

Because each system has unique needs, no exact formula for sizing or capacity planning exists. It's more art than science, and it involves interpretation, guessing, and sometimes even just a gut feel. What this book hopes to accomplish is to help you identify those areas that affect the sizing and capacity planning processes the most. Combined with this and good data going into the process from the start, you will achieve better results than before.

Sizing Steps

Both sizing and capacity planning involve essentially the same steps. However, the steps are different enough to necessitate making two separate lists. The following are the steps involved in sizing a system:

1. Data collection. Find out as much information as possible about the system. Try to find a similar system or one that runs in a similar function.

2. Data analysis. Take the data that you have collected in step 1 and analyze it by looking at things like CPU utilization, I/Os per second (IOPS), and memory utilization.

3. System determination. Based on whatever data you can find, try to find hardware or software that will satisfy the needs that have been determined in step 2.

4. System test (optional). If possible, benchmark a few systems that meet the requirements and see which performs better. You can never have too much data.

5. Implement. After you have done all the analysis and planning, all you can do is put it into production and hope you did the right thing.

As you might imagine, a fair amount of guesswork is involved in sizing. You might not actually have a similar application, you might not really know the number of users, and other necessary information might be missing. Do your best and gather as much data as possible.

Capacity Planning Steps

The steps involved in capacity planning are slightly different because you currently have the hardware and software in place. Thus, much more information is available. The steps involved in capacity planning on a system are as follows:

1. Data collection. Find out as much information as possible about the system. Because you have the system at hand, monitor things like CPU utilization, I/Os per second (IOPS), memory, and so on. Consider long-term statistics as an example. Weeks or months of data make trend analysis easier.

2. Data analysis. Take the data that you have collected in step 1 and analyze it by looking at things like CPU utilization, IOPS, and memory utilization. Create formulas and graphs where you can do forward projections.

3. Capacity determination. Because you know what the current configuration and current utilization are, interpolate data by projecting forward from historical data.

4. Implement. After you have determined the capacity, you can plan for reaching limitations and make adjustments, such as system upgrades, the addition of new hardware, and so on.

As you might imagine, a fair amount of guesswork is involved in capacity planning as well. Because more information is available, the task might be easier than sizing. Do your best with the data at hand.

Summary

In this chapter, you have been introduced to tuning concepts. The chapter began with an introduction to performance tuning concepts followed by goals and goal setting. Setting goals is important for several reasons. Without goals, you don't really know what problem you are trying to solve. In addition, without tuning goals, it is difficult to determine if you have met those goals. If you have tuning goals, you will know when you can stop tuning.

Another concept covered in this chapter is tuning methodology. I have introduced you to my methodology, which might or might not work for you. Develop a scientific approach to tuning and follow it. I prefer this five-step method:

1. Analyze the problem. Determine whether something is broken, whether it is not tuned well, or whether you are at the limits of the system.

2. Determine specifically what you think the problem is. Don't look just at the superficial; try to determine the root of the problem or bottleneck.

3. Develop a solution. Decide what you want to change and what you believe the result of these changes will be. Set realistic goals, but aggressive goals. Don't expect enormous results from fine-tuning.

4. Test the solution. You have to test the solution to determine whether or not the change is effective.

5. Analyze the results. See whether you achieved the desired results. If not, what went wrong and why?

This methodology might or might not work for you. If you prefer a different system, use what works best for you. Do use some sort of system or methodology for tuning. When following a tuning methodology like this, it is important that you take careful notes. If several iterations are done without careful notes, you might not be able to reproduce the results.

You were also introduced to sizing and capacity planning. Many of the chapters in this book fall into the category of sizing and capacity planning as well as tuning. These topics are intertwined and must be done together.

USING THE ORACLE CONFIGURATION PARAMETERS

To tune the instance, you need to know a little bit of how Oracle starts up and uses the initialization parameters. The primary mode of tuning the Oracle instance is via the configuration parameters. These parameters are commonly known as the init.ora parameters because they are modified and configured within the initialization file. You will use the knowledge gained of initialization parameters in this chapter to further explore the concepts of Chapter 3, "Tuning the Oracle Instance."

Whereas all of the configuration parameters can be set within the initialization file, a number of parameters can be set dynamically using ALTER SYSTEM and ALTER SESSION commands. Using these commands causes the change to take place immediately. The difference is the initialization file that is only read on instance startup and tells the Oracle instance several things, such as the following:

- How to start up. This is information about where the control file is and what the database name is.

- Instance tuning parameters. These parameters specify how the System Global Area (SGA) is to be built. This information tells the instance how much memory to use, among other things.

- Limits on resources. Here the initialization file contains limits on resources such as processes, users, and so on.

This chapter begins with an overview of how the Oracle instance is invoked and how the Oracle initialization parameters take effect. This chapter does not provide an exhaustive look at all of the Oracle initialization parameters, yet it will introduce you to the main areas of the parameter file and will touch on some of the important parameters. The individual parameters will be discussed throughout this chapter and the rest of the book.

Starting the Oracle Instance

Starting the Oracle instance is somewhat dependent on which operating system you are running. In general, Oracle is started from SQL*Plus. Those of you who are familiar with Oracle8 were probably used to starting up Oracle using the console command "svrmgrl" (Server Manager). In addition, some operating systems like Microsoft Windows NT include an application called the Service Manager that can be used to start up and shut down the Oracle instance.

STARTING ORACLE INSTANCE FROM SQL*PLUS

Before Oracle9i, you could not start up an Oracle instance from SQL*Plus. It was necessary to use "svrmgrl". Now, starting or shutting down Oracle instances is down from within SQL*Plus. The "svrmgrl" command has been dropped.

CREATE A BACKDOOR ————————————————————————————————

If you are using Multithreaded Server (MTS) processes, it is always a good idea to create an Oracle service that uses dedicated server processes for administrative use. This service will have a different name from the main "user service" so you're not confused about which service you are using.

Although the general user population is connected to Oracle via the shared server processes, you can still connect into the instance via your backdoor. This is extremely useful if the system is busy and MTS processes are running slow. With this backdoor, you should always be able to connect into the Oracle instance (assuming that it is running properly).

Connect to Oracle

To cover the most common denominator, we will focus on using SQL*Plus to start up and shut down the Oracle instance. It is important that you connect into SQL*Plus using the SYSDBA role. This is accomplished by invoking SQL*Plus and issuing the following command:

```
CONNECT username/password AS SYSDBA
```

CONNECT VIA A DEDICATED SERVER PROCESS ——————————————————

It is important that you be connected via a dedicated server process to start the Oracle instance. You cannot start the instance via a shared service connection because MTS relies on the Oracle instance to work.

After you have connected, you are ready to start the Oracle instance. If the listener is not running or the network services are not set up correctly, you will not be able to connect and start up the Oracle instance.

Using the STARTUP Command to Start the Instance

After you are connected, you can start up Oracle using the STARTUP command. The STARTUP command must be passed the initialization parameter filename as part of the command, as follows:

```
SQL> STARTUP PFILE = /u01/oracle/dbs/initorcl.ora
```

The initialization filename usually contains the instance name within the filename. This makes it easier to keep track of multiple initialization files for multiple instances.

BOOTSTRAP INSTANCE MUST BE STARTED ————————————————————

Oracle on Microsoft Windows requires a bootstrap process to be running before the regular instance can be started. This is done to allow the Oracle instance to run as a service. If the Oracle bootstrap process has not started, you will not be able to start the Oracle instance. The bootstrap process must be started from the service manager.

Starting the Instance

After the STARTUP command has been invoked, the Oracle startup begins. The startup contains the following set of events:

1. The parameter file is parsed and checked for errors.

2. The database name and the name of the control file are determined.

3. The control file is opened and read. The control file contains information on the files that make up the Oracle instance, such as the redo log files and data files.

4. The database is optionally mounted to the instance but not opened for general use. Mounting can be avoided by using the keyword NOMOUNT with the STARTUP command.

5. The database is opened. To mount the database and avoid opening it, use the keyword MOUNT with the STARTUP command.

Startup can go wrong in several places:

- If incorrect parameters are in the init.ora file, the startup will abort in step 1.

- If problems exist with the control file or files, the startup will abort in step 3.

- If the data or redo log files have a problem, the startup process will abort in step 4.

If you are lucky, you will get an error message that you will be able to decipher. More than likely, you will not have a good indication on why the Oracle instance failed to start. This is especially true in an operating system like Windows NT.

Troubleshooting the Instance Startup

You find out what went wrong by analyzing the alert log. The Oracle alert log is a place where status information on the Oracle instance is kept. Where this file is found is somewhat operating-system dependent, but it is usually found in the $ORACLE_HOME/rdbms/log directory and is called alrtORCL.log (where ORCL is your instance name).

After you have located the alert log, you can analyze it to see what—if anything—went wrong. Because the alert log is written to every time the state of the instance changes or an error occurs, the file can become quite large. It isn't a bad idea to copy it off and start a new log whenever it gets too large.

The following is a sample alert log. What is it telling you?

```
Sun Jul 1 15:47:01 2001
Starting ORACLE instance (normal)
LICENSE_MAX_SESSION = 0
```

```
LICENSE_SESSIONS_WARNING = 0
LICENSE_MAX_USERS = 0
Starting up ORACLE RDBMS Version: 9.0.0.0.0.
System parameters with non-default values:
  processes               = 150
  timed_statistics        = TRUE
  shared_pool_size        = 54525952
  large_pool_size         = 1048576
  java_pool_size          = 4194304
  control_files           = /u01/app/oracle/oradata/orcl/control01.ctl,
  [ccc]/u01/app/oracle/oradata/orcl/control02.ctl,
  [ccc]/u01/app/oracle/oradata/orcl/control03.ctl
  db_block_size           = 4096
  db_cache_size           = 41943040
  compatible              = 9.0.0
  undo_management         = AUTO
  undo_tablespace         = UNDOTBS
  remote_login_passwordfile= EXCLUSIVE
  instance_name           = orcl
  background_dump_dest     = /u01/app/oracle/admin/orcl/bdump
  user_dump_dest          = /u01/app/oracle/admin/orcl/udump
  core_dump_dest          = /u01/app/oracle/admin/orcl/cdump
  sort_area_size          = 524288
  db_name                 = orcl
  open_cursors            = 300
PMON started with pid=2
DBW0 started with pid=3
LGWR started with pid=4
CKPT started with pid=5
SMON started with pid=6
RECO started with pid=7
```

The best thing to do when looking at an alert log is to jump down to the end of the file and then back up to when the last time the instance was started. The instance startup can be found by looking for the keywords "Starting ORACLE Instance." From here, you can follow the alert log forward. In the previous example, the beginning of the alert log was truncated to avoid having 10 pages of this book devoted to it.

Following are a few of the components of the alert log that are especially useful:

- Date. The date when the log message was initiated is the first thing written to the alert log. This indicates when the alert happened.

- Version. The Oracle version number is extremely important if you need to debug a problem.

- Parameters. The non-default parameters that the init.ora file has set are provided. This can also be useful in the event of a problem.

- Process IDs. For some operating systems, the process IDs of the Oracle background processes are provided.

This information can be used to help you debug problems, determine how long the system has been up, and other useful information. During normal operation alerts, DDL information and checkpoint information might be written to the alert log. The alert log can be quite useful.

KNOW YOUR ALERT LOG

The alert log should be the first place that you look in the event of an Oracle problem. Over the years, I have had many problems that are easily solvable by just consulting the alert log. It is surprising to me how many people don't realize that the alert log exists and what value that it has.

Stopping the Oracle Instance

As with starting the Oracle instance, you can stop the Oracle instance in several ways. The way you choose to stop the instance really depends on the circumstances. You have several options:

- SHUTDOWN NORMAL. For normal operational shutdowns.

- SHUTDOWN TRANSACTIONAL. For quicker shutdowns in which you still have time to preserve some of the user's work.

- SHUTDOWN IMMEDIATE. The instance must be shut down as quickly as possible.

- SHUTDOWN ABORT. All hope is lost and you have no other options but to abort any pending transactions.

These options are listed in order of preference as well as in order of desperation, where SHUT-DOWN ABORT is a command of last resort.

As with starting up the Oracle instance, you cannot shut down the Oracle instance if you are not connected into a dedicated server process.

DO YOU KNOW WHERE YOU ARE? ────────────────────────────────

Before shutting down an Oracle instance, double-check the instance into which you are connected. Shutting down the wrong instance can cause unnecessary grief. It only takes a few seconds to double-check into which instance you are connected by using the following query:

```
SELECT * FROM V$INSTANCE
```

This query shows to which instance and host you are connected. It is easy to run.

Several years ago, I worked at an engineering firm in the engineering software department. One day when I was deleting some files, I went to get a drink of water. Unknowingly while I was gone, the guy in the cube next to me used my terminal to change directories to where some software was kept to check on something. When I returned the directory looked similar (because I was just getting rid of object and library files). A few minutes after I deleted some of these files, the support calls started coming in. Little did I know that I had deleted production code. The chain of events caused a serious problem that could have been avoided if the following conditions existed:

1. People did not use other people's systems.

2. I had double-checked the files that I was deleting.

The moral of this story is that you should make sure that you are actually connected into the instance that you intend to shut down before issuing the SHUTDOWN command.

I didn't use a screen lock because the event happened in the days of VT100 terminals, in which it took a significant amount of time to log into the system.

Using SHUTDOWN NORMAL

With a SHUTDOWN NORMAL command, the Oracle instance politely waits on all users to disconnect from the instance before it shuts down. During this time, no new users are allowed to connect into the Oracle instance. Because Oracle waits for all users to disconnect, the users have time to finish their work and are not inconvenienced much.

The downside to SHUTDOWN NORMAL is that you might be waiting a long time for the instance to shut down. Some people do not disconnect from the instance until they are forced to. Unfortunately, this might cause you to escalate to the next level of shutdown.

The SHUTDOWN NORMAL command should be used whenever possible because it causes the least amount of grief on the user community. If conditions change, you can perform a SHUTDOWN TRANSACTIONAL after the SHUTDOWN NORMAL has already started.

Using SHUTDOWN TRANSACTIONAL

The SHUTDOWN TRANSACTIONAL command signals the Oracle instance to terminate the user connections as soon as they have finished the transactions that they are in. As with the SHUTDOWN NORMAL command, as soon as SHUTDOWN TRANSACTIONAL is issued, no more new connections are allowed. In addition, new transactions are not allowed to be started.

Unfortunately, SHUTDOWN TRANSACTIONAL also has the problem of misbehaving users and applications. If the application allows a user to begin a transaction and then go to lunch without closing the transaction, it might be quite a long time before the instance is actually shut down. Again, this might mean escalating to the next level.

Use SHUTDOWN TRANSACTIONAL when you still have some time, but you cannot count on the users to relinquish the system without some prompting. This is still a fairly friendly way of shutting down the instance.

Using SHUTDOWN IMMEDIATE

The SHUTDOWN IMMEDIATE command is more drastic than the previous two options. Upon this command being issued, all currently open transactions are rolled back. All of the user processes connected into the instance are terminated. As with the previous two options, no instance recovery is required.

Because SHUTDOWN IMMEDIATE performs rollbacks on all of the currently running transactions, it might take some time to complete. In fact, if the transaction has been running for a long time, this might be a significant amount of time.

Use SHUTDOWN IMMEDIATE whenever the instance must be shut down in a fairly quick timeframe. If you lose main power and are running on a limited UPS, it's a good time to use SHUTDOWN IMMEDIATE. This command is your best bet for shutting down quickly without causing an instance recovery.

Using SHUTDOWN ABORT

The SHUTDOWN ABORT command terminates the Oracle instance immediately. This is the equivalent of pulling the plug on the instance. The only case when SHUTDOWN ABORT should be used is when the instance is having a problem, no other shutdown methods are working, or a catastrophe is imminent. If the building where the database system is located has caught fire, SHUTDOWN ABORT is probably better than nothing; however, I do not recommend sticking around to shut down the Oracle instance if the building is on fire. Never risk your life for data.

SHUTDOWN ABORT
The SHUTDOWN ABORT command is a measure of last resort. Try the other options first.

As you can see, you have several options for shutting down. I recommend trying them in order and escalating if you need to.

The Initialization Parameters

The initialization parameters are used so that the Oracle engine can start the instance. If the following parameters are incorrect, the instance will not start up:

- CONTROL_FILES. Specifies one or more names of control files, separated by commas. Every database has a control file, which contains entries that describe the structure of the database (such as its name, the time stamp of its creation, and the names and locations of its datafiles and redo files).

- COMPATIBLE. This parameter specifies the release with which the Oracle server must maintain compatibility. COMPATIBLE allows you to use a new release, while at the same time guaranteeing backward compatibility with an earlier release.

- BACKGROUND_CORE_DUMP. BACKGROUND_CORE_DUMP is primarily a UNIX parameter. It specifies whether Oracle includes the SGA in the core file for Oracle background processes.

- BACKGROUND_DUMP_DEST. BACKGROUND_DUMP_DEST specifies the pathname (directory or disc) where debugging trace files for the background processes (LGWR, DBWn, and so on) are written during Oracle operations.

- DB_NAME. DB_NAME specifies a database identifier of up to eight characters. If specified, it must correspond to the name specified in the CREATE DATABASE statement. It is required for Oracle Real Application Clusters.

- IFILE. Use IFILE to embed another parameter file within the current parameter file. You can have up to three levels of nesting.

- LOG_ARCHIVE_DEST. Defines up to 10 archive log destinations when the database is in ARCHIVELOG mode. If you have installed Oracle Enterprise Edition, use LOG_ARCHIVE_DEST_n instead.

When starting up the Oracle instance, this initialization file must be specified. If any of the parameters are incorrect, the instance might not start (depending on the parameter). To find out what the problem is, consult the alert log. This log will be named alrtORCL.log, in which ORCL is replaced by the instance name.

KNOW THE INITIALIZATION FILE

When I worked in the database performance group at a major computer company, I was called upon to help a customer with a seemingly straightforward problem. The customer was running into performance problems that seemed memory related. Before traveling to the customer site, we decided to try to solve the problem remotely.

After several attempts at modifying the initialization parameters to increase the memory used by Oracle, we were having no success. Finally, I asked the customer to send me the Oracle alert log. Because the Oracle alert log prints the non-default parameters, I was immediately able to diagnose the problem.

The customer was modifying one init.ora file, and starting up the Oracle instance with another one. No wonder none of the changes made a difference—they were not applied!

Therefore, be sure which init.ora file you are modifying. If things are acting strange, check out the alert log.

These parameters are important for starting up the Oracle instance, but they have no effect on the performance of the running instance. The next section contains some of the important performance parameters.

Instance Tuning Parameters

The instance tuning parameters are really what the next few chapters—in fact, what the entire book—is about. These parameters will be covered in the chapters to which they pertain. In the beginning of each of these chapters is a section on the initialization parameters (where applicable).

Resource Limiting Parameters

Many parameters are designed to set limits on certain resources. These parameters include the following:

- DB_FILES. DB_FILES specifies the maximum number of database files that can be opened for this database. The maximum valid value is the maximum number of files, subject to operating system constraint, that will ever be specified for the database, including files to be added by ADD DATAFILE statements.

- INSTANCE_GROUPS. INSTANCE_GROUPS is an Oracle9i Real Application Clusters parameter that you can specify only in parallel mode. Used in conjunction with the PARALLEL_INSTANCE_GROUP parameter, it allows you to restrict parallel query operations to a limited number of instances.

- LICENSE_MAX_SESSIONS. LICENSE_MAX_SESSIONS specifies the maximum number of concurrent user sessions allowed. When this limit is reached, only users with the RESTRICTED SESSION privilege can connect to the database.

- LICENSE_MAX_USERS. LICENSE_MAX_USERS specifies the maximum number of users you can create in the database. When you reach this limit, you cannot create more users. You can, however, increase the limit.

- MAX_DUMP_FILE_SIZE. MAX_DUMP_FILE_SIZE specifies the maximum size of trace files (excluding the alert file). Change this limit if you are concerned that trace files might use too much space.

- OPEN_LINKS. OPEN_LINKS specifies the maximum number of concurrent open connections to remote databases in one session. These connections include database links, as well as external procedures and cartridges, each of which uses a separate process.

- OPEN_LINKS_PER_INSTANCE. OPEN_LINKS_PER_INSTANCE specifies the maximum number of migratable open connections globally for each database instance.

- PROCESSES. PROCESSES specifies the maximum number of operating system user processes that can simultaneously connect to Oracle. Its value should allow for all background processes, such as locks, job queue processes, and parallel execution processes.

- SESSIONS. SESSIONS specifies the maximum number of sessions that can be created in the system. Because every login requires a session, this parameter effectively determines the maximum number of concurrent users in the system. If this parameter is not set, Oracles derives a value based on PROCESSES where SESSIONS = (1.1 * PROCESSES) + 5.

- TRANSACTIONS. TRANSACTIONS specifies the maximum number of concurrent transactions. Greater values increase the required memory in the SGA and can increase the number of rollback segments allocated.

Summary

In this chapter, you learned a little bit about the Oracle initialization parameters and how to use them. You also learned the basics of the startup and shutdown processes of Oracle and how to identify associated problems. In the next chapter, you will begin to see when and how these parameters should be used. The rest of the book will contain chapters discussing the initialization parameters. This introduction to these parameters has been designed to allow you to take that information and apply it to the init.ora file.

TUNING THE ORACLE INSTANCE

This chapter looks at the various areas of the Oracle instance (such as memory usage and I/O) that you can affect and what you can change. To effectively tune the instance, you must know what is affected by your changes. This chapter looks at some specific areas within the instance, describes how to know if you have a problem, and tells you how to make a change.

FIRST THINGS FIRST

Usually, it is best to tune the Oracle instance after you tune the application code because the access patterns into the database and memory usage might change after you tune the application. Because of the flow of this book, however, it was decided to focus on the server first. However, you should still tune the server after you tune the application.

You should do Oracle instance tuning in conjunction with application tuning. Because much of the instance tuning is based on the data access patterns and memory usage of the application, changes to the application might result in the opportunity to re-tune the instance for greater optimization. A perfectly optimized Oracle instance cannot make up for a poorly tuned application.

As with the remaining chapters in this book, this chapter begins with an overview of the pertinent Oracle initialization parameters that will be covered in this chapter. This overview will list the parameters with a brief description of these parameters and why they are important. These parameters will then be used later in this chapter.

The chapter begins with memory usage within the Oracle System Global Area (SGA) and then looks at latch contention, tuning checkpoints, archiving, sorts, and free list contention. These are the areas where the most bottlenecks occur and where you can most effectively tune.

In a computer system, the fastest storage component is the level two (L2) CPU cache, followed by the system memory. I/O to disk is thousands of times slower than access to memory. This fact is the key for why you should try to make effective use of memory whenever possible and defer I/Os whenever you can. The majority of the user response time is actually spent waiting on a disk I/O to occur.

By making good use of caches in memory and reducing I/O overhead, you can optimize performance. The goal is to retrieve data from memory whenever you can and to use the CPU for other activities whenever you have to wait for I/Os. This chapter examines ways to optimize system performance by taking advantage of caching and effective use of the system's CPUs.

Initialization Parameters Used in This Chapter

This chapter includes the use of many Oracle initialization parameters. Chapter 2, "Using the Oracle Configuration Parameters," introduced you to these parameters and explained how to use them. This chapter looks at a number of parameters that fall outside of the core and affect the performance over the functionality of Oracle.

SGA Parameters

The following parameters affect the shared memory allocation of the Oracle instance:

- DB_CACHE_ADVICE. DB_CACHE_ADVICE enables and disables statistics gathering used for predicting behavior with different cache sizes through the V$DB_CACHE_ADVICE performance view.

- DB_CACHE_SIZE. DB_CACHE_SIZE specifies the size of the DEFAULT buffer pool for buffers with the primary block size (the block size defined by the DB_BLOCK_SIZE parameter).

- DB_KEEP_CACHE_SIZE. DB_KEEP_CACHE_SIZE specifies the number of buffers in the KEEP buffer pool. The size of the buffers in the KEEP buffer pool is the primary block size (the block size defined by the DB_BLOCK_SIZE parameter).

- DB_RECYCLE_CACHE_SIZE. DB_RECYCLE_CACHE_SIZE specifies the size of the RECYCLE buffer pool. The size of buffers in the RECYCLE pool is the primary block size defined in DB_BLOCK_SIZE.

- LARGE_POOL_SIZE. LARGE_POOL_SIZE allows you to specify the size (in bytes) of the large pool allocation heap. The large pool allocation heap is used in shared server systems for session memory, by parallel execution for message buffers, and by backup processes for disk I/O buffers.

- LOCK_SGA. LOCK_SGA locks the entire SGA into physical memory. It is usually advisable to lock the SGA into real (physical) memory, especially if the use of virtual memory would include storing some of the SGA using disk space. This parameter is ignored on platforms that do not support it.

- SHARED_POOL_RESERVED_SIZE. SHARED_POOL_RESERVED_SIZE specifies (in bytes) the shared pool space that is reserved for large contiguous requests for shared pool memory. You can use this parameter to avoid performance degradation in the shared pool in situations where pool fragmentation forces Oracle to search for and free chunks of unused pool to satisfy the current request.

- SHARED_POOL_SIZE. SHARED_POOL_SIZE specifies (in bytes) the size of the shared pool. The shared pool contains shared cursors, stored procedures, control structures, and other structures. Larger values improve performance in multiuser systems. Smaller values use less memory.

Program Global Area and User Memory Parameters

The following are parameters that affect the Program Global Area (PGA) and session-specific user memory allocation:

- ENQUEUE_RESOURCES. ENQUEUE_RESOURCES sets the number of resources that the lock manager can lock concurrently. An *enqueue* is a sophisticated locking mechanism that permits several concurrent processes to share known resources to varying degrees.

- HASH_AREA_SIZE. HASH_AREA_SIZE is relevant to parallel execution operations and to the query portion of DML or DDL statements. It specifies the maximum amount of memory, in bytes, to be used for hash joins. Oracle does not recommend using the HASH_AREA_SIZE parameter unless the instance is configured with the shared server option.

- HASH_JOIN_ENABLED. HASH_JOIN_ENABLED specifies whether the optimizer should consider using a hash join as a join method. If set to FALSE, then hashing is not available as a join method. If set to TRUE, then the optimizer compares the cost of a hash join with other types of joins, and chooses hashing if it gives the best cost.

- SORT_AREA_RETAINED_SIZE. SORT_AREA_RETAINED_SIZE specifies (in bytes) the maximum amount of the user global area (UGA) memory that is retained after a sort run completes. Oracle does not recommend using the SORT_AREA_RETAINED_SIZE parameter unless the instance is configured with the shared server option.

- SORT_AREA_SIZE. SORT_AREA_SIZE specifies in bytes the maximum amount of memory that Oracle will use for a sort. After the sort is complete but before the rows are returned, Oracle releases all of the memory allocated for the sort, except the amount specified by the SORT_AREA_RETAINED_SIZE parameter. After the last row is returned, Oracle releases the remainder of the memory. Oracle does not recommend using the SORT_AREA_SIZE parameter unless the instance is configured with the shared server option.

Undo Parameters

These parameters dictate how the Oracle instance will manage undo space:

- UNDO_MANAGEMENT. UNDO_MANAGEMENT specifies which undo space management mode the system should use. When set to AUTO, the instance starts in Automatic Undo Management mode. In Manual Undo Management mode, undo space is allocated externally as rollback segments.

- UNDO_TABLESPACE. UNDO_TABLESPACE specifies the name of the tablespace used for undo information. This parameter is used if running in System Managed Undo (SMU) mode. This tablespace can only be used for undo information.

- UNDO_RETENTION. UNDO_RETENTION specifies how long undo information is kept in the undo tablespace before it is aged out.

- UNDO_SUPPRESS_ERRORS. UNDO_SUPPRESS_ERRORS allows you to suppress errors when performing manual undo operations in SMU mode.

- TRANSACTIONS_PER_ROLLBACK_SEGMENT. TRANSACTIONS_PER_ ROLLBACK_SEGMENT specifies the number of concurrent transactions you expect each rollback segment to have to handle. The minimum number of rollback segments acquired at startup is TRANSACTIONS divided by the value for this parameter.

Miscellaneous Parameters

These parameters affect various aspects of the SGA and not one specific area:

- LOG_BUFFER. LOG_BUFFER specifies the amount of memory in bytes that Oracle uses when buffering redo entries to a redo log file. Redo log entries contain a record of the changes that have been made to the database block buffers. The LGWR process writes redo log entries from the log buffer to a redo log file.

- OPEN_CURSORS. OPEN_CURSORS specifies the maximum number of open cursors (handles to private SQL areas) a session can have at once. You can use this parameter to prevent a session from opening an excessive number of cursors.

- SESSION_CACHED_CURSORS. SESSION_CACHED_CURSORS allows you to specify the number of session cursors to cache. Repeated parse calls of the same SQL statement cause the session cursor for that statement to be moved into the session cursor cache. Subsequent parse calls can find the cursor in the cache and do not need to reopen the cursor.

Tuning the SGA

In the Oracle instance, data is stored in two places: in memory and on disk. Memory has by far the best performance, but it is also the most in demand and the most limited in terms of space. Disk, on the other hand, can store vast amounts of data cost effectively; however, it has slow performance relative to memory.

Because memory is the better performer, it is desirable to use memory to access data whenever possible. But because of the vast amounts of data usually accessed and the number of users who need this data, this resource has much contention. To make the most effective use of memory, you must achieve a balance between the memory used for Oracle caching and the memory needed by the users.

Tuning memory in the Oracle instance involves tuning several major areas:

- The OS (to provide these resources)

- Private SQL and PL/SQL areas

- The shared pool
- The redo log buffer
- The buffer cache

Tuning the Operating System

The first step in tuning memory for the Oracle instance is to make sure that sufficient resources are available in the operating system. You cannot allocate memory to Oracle that doesn't exist. Giving Oracle additional memory at the expense of causing paging or swapping is ineffective and hurts performance. Some operating systems handle this automatically, and other operating systems require manual intervention. What you need to do depends on the OS on which you are running.

The goal of tuning the operating system for Oracle is to provide enough resources so that Oracle can function. The operating system must provide for the following:

- Enough memory for the SGA to fit into main memory. In most operating systems, this involves allocating a special type of memory structure called *shared memory*. The operating system provides shared memory to allow multiple processes to access the same memory through special system calls. In many operating systems, the shared memory is locked into place and cannot be swapped or paged.

- Enough memory for the user processes to fit into main memory. Remember that each shadow process, or dispatcher, also consumes memory. For user processes, the amount of memory consumed depends on the number of users connected and whether they are dedicated or shared server processes.

- Avoidance of paging and swapping. Although it is not uncommon for some paging or swapping to occur, if it occurs frequently, you should take steps to reduce it. After paging and swapping occur, performance is so far degraded by these tasks that most other tuning changes do not make a difference.

- Enough memory for operating system activities. Remember that other OS activities might become active at various times and allocate memory. In most cases, you will want to limit other OS activities on the system that is used as your Oracle database server.

- Enough memory to accommodate Oracle operations, such as archiving, loading, backing up online, and so on. These critical functions might require significant resources. If these resources are not available, you might experience severe performance problems.

In the OS, the main function of tuning memory is to allocate it for Oracle. As you see in the following section, Oracle can take advantage of this memory in several ways.

Tuning the Private SQL and PL/SQL Areas

A *private SQL area* is an area in memory that contains binding information and runtime buffers. Every session that issues SQL statements has a private SQL area; reducing these resources can be effective when many users are involved. A private SQL area is further segmented into a persistent area and a runtime area.

The *persistent area* contains binding information used during the query for data input and retrieval. The size of this area depends on the number of binds and the number of columns specified in the statement.

The *runtime area* contains information used while the SQL statement is being executed. The size of the runtime area depends on the complexity and type of SQL statements being issued and the size of the rows being processed. The runtime area is freed after the statement has been executed. In a query operation, the runtime area is freed only after all the rows have been fetched.

In a dedicated server, the private SQL area is located in the user's PGA. In the case of a multi-threaded server, the persistent areas and (for SELECT statements) the runtime areas are kept in the SGA.

It is important to make sure that users can allocate enough memory for their private SQL area; in the case of the multithreaded server, sufficient space must exist in the SGA to connect the required number of users.

Cursors can be used in precompilers to improve performance by reducing the frequency of parsing. To take advantage of cursors, it might be necessary to increase the value of the Oracle parameter OPEN_CURSORS. The reduction of parsing increases performance because it does not have to perform the parsing operations as frequently, but this is done at the expense of memory. To determine how often parsing is being done in relation to executions, you can perform the following query:

```
SELECT SQL_TEXT, PARSE_CALLS, EXECUTIONS FROM V$SQLAREA;
```

From the results of this query, you can determine how often parsing is occurring in relation to the number of executions. If these values are close to each other, excessive parsing might be occurring. Increasing OPEN_CURSORS and using Oracle precompiler directives can reduce parsing by allowing Oracle to cache more cursors in the cursor cache. This generally avoids excessive reparsing of statements.

The application and tunable parameters such as OPEN CURSORS determine the size of memory needed for each user. This memory is allocated automatically. In some operating systems, the amount of memory that can be allocated per user is controlled by system parameters. If your application or tuning changes the amount of memory for each user process, it might be necessary to increase the value of those O/S parameters. It might also be necessary to increase the amount of system RAM or reduce the Oracle instance memory usage to avoid swapping or paging.

In systems where memory is abundant and cursor performance is important, the parameter CURSOR_SPACE_FOR_TIME can improve cursor performance at the cost of more memory used.

Tuning the Shared Pool

To tune the shared pool, you must look at the individual parts of the shared pool. The *shared pool* contains both the library cache and the data dictionary cache. In a multithreaded server, the shared pool is also used to store session information.

Library Cache

The *library cache* contains the shared SQL and PL/SQL areas. Performance can be improved by both increasing the cache hit rate in the library cache and by speeding access to the library cache by holding infrequently used SQL statements in cache longer.

A cache miss in the shared SQL area occurs when a parse statement is called and the already parsed statement does not already exist in the shared SQL area. It also occurs if an application tries to execute a SQL statement and the shared SQL area containing the parsed statement has been deallocated from the library cache.

For a SQL statement to take advantage of SQL or PL/SQL statements that might have already been parsed, the following criteria must be met:

- The text of the SQL statement must be identical to the SQL statement that has already been parsed. This includes whitespace.

- References to schema objects in the SQL statements must resolve to the same object.

- Bind variables must match the same name and data type.

- The SQL statements must be optimized using the same approach; in the case of the cost-base approach, the same optimization goal must be used.

At first glance, you might think that many of these conditions make it difficult to take advantage of the shared SQL areas; however, users sharing the same application code can easily take advantage of already parsed shared SQL statements. It is to the advantage of the application developer to use the same SQL statements to access the same data and thus ensure that SQL statements within the application can also take advantage of this caching.

Using stored procedures wherever possible guarantees that the same shared PL/SQL area is used. Another advantage is that stored procedures are stored in a parsed form, eliminating run-time parsing altogether.

STANDARDIZED NAMING CONVENTIONS

A standardized naming convention for bind variables and spacing conventions for SQL and PL/SQL statements also increases the likelihood of reusing shared SQL statements. It only takes a single character difference in a SQL or PL/SQL statement to produce a shared SQL area cache miss.

The V$LIBRARYCACHE table contains statistics on how well you are utilizing the library cache. The important columns to view in this table are PINS and RELOADS.

PINS	The number of times the item in the library cache was executed.
RELOADS	The number of times the library cache misses and the library object must be reloaded.

A low number of reloads relative to the number of executions indicates a high cache hit rate. To get an idea of the total number of cache misses, use this statement:

```
SELECT SUM(reloads) "Cache Misses",
  SUM(pins) "Executions",
  100 * ( SUM(pins - reloads) / SUM(pins) ) "Cache Hit Percent"
  FROM v$librarycache;


Cache Misses Executions Cache Miss Percent
------------ ---------- ------------------
          9       2017         .44620724
```

The sample output shown here indicates that a total of 2,017 SQL statements, PL/SQL blocks, and object definitions were accessed, with only nine having to reload because they had aged out of the library cache. This means that only .44% of these statements resulted in reparsing.

To look at the cache hits based on the types of statements, you can use the following statement:

```
SELECT namespace,
  reloads "Cache Misses",
  pins "Executions"
  FROM v$librarycache;


NAMESPACE       Cache Misses Executions
--------------- ------------ ----------
SQL AREA                   4       1676
TABLE/PROCEDURE            5        309
BODY                       0          0
TRIGGER                    0          0
INDEX                      0         21
CLUSTER                    0         15
```

```
OBJECT                    0          0
PIPE                      0          0
```

8 rows selected.

The total amount of reloads should be near zero. If you see more than 1% library cache misses, take action. You can reduce the number of cache misses by writing identical SQL statements or by increasing the size of the library cache with the SHARED_POOL_SIZE initialization parameter.

You might also have to increase the number of cursors available for a session by increasing the Oracle parameter OPEN_CURSORS.

Do not increase the amount of memory you require beyond that set aside by the operating system. Any paging or swapping caused by over-allocating memory offsets any advantage you get from the library cache.

If you have plenty of memory, you might be able to speed access to the shared SQL areas by setting the Oracle initialization parameter CURSOR_SPACE_FOR_TIME equal to TRUE. When this parameter is TRUE, it specifies that a shared SQL area cannot be deallocated until all the cursors associated with it are closed.

If CURSOR_SPACE_FOR_TIME is TRUE, it is not necessary for Oracle to check whether the SQL statement is in the library cache because this parsed statement cannot be deallocated as long as the cursor is open. If memory is scarce on your system, do not set this parameter. If the value is TRUE and no space is available in the shared pool for a new SQL statement, an error will be returned, thus halting the application.

Data Dictionary Cache

The *data dictionary* contains a set of tables and views Oracle uses as a reference to the database. Oracle stores information here about both the logical and physical structure of the database. The data dictionary contains information such as the following:

- User information such as user privileges
- Integrity constraints defined for tables in the database
- Names and data types of all columns in database tables
- Information on space allocated and used for schema objects

Oracle frequently accesses the data dictionary for the parsing of SQL statements. This access is essential to the operation of Oracle; performance bottlenecks in the data dictionary affect all Oracle users.

You can check the efficiency of the data dictionary cache. Statistics for the data dictionary cache are stored in the dynamic performance table V$ROWCACHE. (The data dictionary cache is sometimes known as the *row cache*.) The important columns to view in this table are GETS and GETMISSES:

GETS	The total number of requests for the particular item
GETMISSES	The total number of requests resulting in cache misses

A few number of cache misses are expected, especially during startup when the cache has not been populated. To get an idea of the total number of cache misses, use the following statement:

```
SELECT SUM(getmisses) "Cache Misses",
  SUM(gets) "Requests",
  100 * ( SUM(gets - getmisses) / SUM(gets) ) "Cache Hit Percent"
  FROM v$rowcache;
```

```
Cache Misses  Requests Cache Miss Percent
-----------  --------- ------------------
       277      2185         12.677346
```

The output shown here indicates that 2,185 requests were made to the data dictionary cache with 277 data dictionary cache misses. This means that 12.68 percent of these requests caused a cache miss.

To get the cache miss statistics on the individual elements of the data dictionary, execute this SQL statement:

```
SELECT parameter,
  getmisses "Cache Misses",
  gets "Requests"
  FROM v$rowcache;
```

```
PARAMETER                           Cache Misses  Requests
--------------------------------    ------------  ---------
dc_free_extents                                4         92
dc_used_extents                                0          0
dc_segments                                    1          7
dc_tablespaces                                 0          0
dc_tablespaces                                 0          0
dc_tablespace_quotas                           0          0
dc_files                                       0          0
dc_users                                       8         90
dc_rollback_segments                           4        122
```

```
dc_objects                         44        378
dc_constraints                      0          0
dc_object_ids                       0          0
dc_tables                          20        318
dc_synonyms                         5          9
dc_sequences                        1          6
dc_usernames                        4         71
dc_database_links                   0          0
dc_histogram_defs                   0          0
dc_profiles                         0          0
dc_users                            0          0
dc_columns                        153       1028


PARAMETER                Cache Misses  Requests
-------------------------------- ------------ ---------

dc_table_grants                    14         18
dc_column_grants                    0          0
dc_indexes                         12        176
dc_constraint_defs                  7          7
dc_constraint_defs                  0          0
dc_sequence_grants                  0          0
dc_user_grants                      7         62


28 rows selected.
```

In frequently accessed dictionary caches, the miss rate should not rise above 10–15%. If the percent of misses continues to increase during runtime, increase the amount of memory allocated for the data dictionary cache. Use the same parameter as for the library cache: SHARED_POOL_SIZE.

Using the Reserved Area in the Shared Pool

A few special areas within the shared pool can be tuned for different types of requests and activities. These are the reserved area and the large pool.

Using the reserved area allows you to break the shared pool into an area for large requests for contiguous memory. With this setup, large requests for memory are fulfilled from one part of the shared pool and smaller requests from another part. This reduces fragmentation, thus allowing large requests to more readily be fulfilled.

The size of the reserved area can range from 5% of the shared pool to 50% of the shared pool. The size is set by specifying the value of SHARED_POOL_RESERVED_SIZE in the initialization parameters. In general, Oracle recommends setting the SHARED_POOL_RESERVED_SIZE to 10% of SHARED_POOL_SIZE.

You can see how well the shared pool reserved space is working by viewing data from V$SHARED_POOL_RESERVED. The goal is to have REQUEST_MISSES and REQUEST_FAILURES as small as possible. If failures of either of these are increasing, increase the values of SHARED_POOL_RESERVED_SIZE and SHARED_POOL_SIZE. This should reduce the failures or at least the rate of failures. It might take several attempts before these failures stabilize.

An example of the query is as follows:

```
SELECT * FROM V$SHARED_POOL_RESERVED
```

Shared Session

In the multithreaded server (MTS) configuration, the session information is also stored in the shared pool. This information includes the private SQL areas as well as sort areas. It is important to make sure that you do not run out of space in the shared pool for this information.

One way of assuring that you do not run out of space for MTS sessions as well as making sure that the shared pool does not run out of space is by allocating space in the large pool for MTS sessions. Using and tuning MTS is covered in more detail in Chapter 4, "Performance-Enhancing Features."

Using the Large Pool

The large pool is an area in the shared pool that is reserved for large requests for memory by MTS processes, parallel execution message buffers, and backup operations. Unlike earlier versions of Oracle where this memory was taken from the general allocation of the shared pool, now it is taken from its own area defined by the initialization parameter LARGE_POOL_SIZE.

Tuning the Buffer Cache

Probably the most important Oracle cache in the system is the buffer cache. The *buffer cache* makes up the majority of the Oracle SGA and is used for every query and update in the system.

Each time a data block is read, it is copied into the buffer cache. Each time a modification is made, it is done in the buffer cache. Remember that each server process accesses the buffer cache directly.

In a read operation, the server process first checks to see whether the requested data is already in the SGA. If it is, the data is accessed directly from the SGA. If the data is not already in the SGA, the server process copies the data from the data file into the SGA where it is accessed.

In an update operation, the server process modifies the data block buffer(s) in the SGA only. It is up to the DBWR to write these dirty buffers out to disk. With the exception of the CKPT process, only the DBWR writes to the data files.

Because the buffer cache is accessed so frequently, it is important that the buffer cache has sufficient size to get a good cache hit rate. The statistics for the buffer cache are kept in the dynamic performance table V$SYSSTAT. The important columns to view in this table are as follows:

PHYSICAL READS   This is the total number of requests that result in disk access; this is a *cache miss*.

DB BLOCK GETS   DB BLOCK GETS are normal requests for data.

CONSISTENT GETS   CONSISTENT GETS are requests for data in consistent mode. The sum of the two values DB BLOCK GETS and CONSISTENT GETS represents the total number of requests for data.

To see how well the block buffer cache is doing, use this query:

```
SELECT name, value
  FROM v$sysstat
  WHERE name IN ('db block gets', 'consistent gets', 'physical reads');
```

NAME	VALUE
db block gets	155
consistent gets	5293
physical reads	334

To calculate the cache hit ratio, use this formula:

```
Cache Hit Ratio = 1 - ( PHYSICAL READS / ( DB BLOCK GETS + CONSISTENT GETS))
Cache Hit Ratio =
1 - (334 / ( 155 + 5293) ) = 1 -(334 / 5448) = 1 - 0.0613 = 0.938
```

This example shows a cache hit rate of 93.8%.

OFF TO A FRESH START

A freshly started instance produces skewed results when measuring cache hit ratios. When the instance is first started, all the caches are empty, and most database queries generate cache misses. As a result, it's best to wait until the system has run a period of time for caches to fill and the cache hit ratio to stabilize.

If the cache hit rate is lower than 70 or 80%, you might need to increase the database buffer cache to improve performance. You can increase the size of the buffer cache by tuning the Oracle initialization parameter DB_CACHE_SIZE. The initialization parameter DB_BLOCK_BUFFERS is retained for backwards compatibility, but the newer parameter is recommended.

DON'T BANK ON CACHE HIT RATIOS

Be careful about investing too much time in achieving extremely high cache hit ratios. You might be moving in the wrong direction. Can a 90% cache hit ratio be better than a 99.99% cache hit ratio? Absolutely.

If you have a query that performs 10,000 logical reads (gets), and of those, one misses and results in a physical read, you end up with a 99.99% cache hit ratio.

If you took that same query and tuned the SQL or some index on a table, and now it only did 10 gets, and of those, one misses and results in a physical read, you have a 90% cache hit ratio.

Is it worse simply because the cache hit ratio is lower? Absolutely not. You've made great progress in reducing contention in other areas of the system—namely, memory in the SGA—by reducing logical reads by a thousandth.

The initialization parameter DB_CACHE_SIZE specifies the size of the buffer cache. The DB_CACHE_SIZE parameter is specified in Kilobytes, Megabytes, or Gigabytes.

If you prefer to use the initialization parameter DB_BLOCK_BUFFERS, the total amount of space utilized by these buffers is calculated as follows:

```
Buffer Size = DB_BLOCK_BUFFERS * DB_BLOCK_SIZE
```

TOO MUCH OF A GOOD THING

Be careful not to configure DB_CACHE_SIZE or DB_BLOCK_BUFFERS to use more memory than the system has allocated. Doing so can cause swapping or paging to occur in some systems or a failure of the Oracle instance to start up in other systems.

Because the data files and the db block buffers make up the majority of the I/Os in the system, it is important to have a sufficiently large buffer cache. Don't increase your db block buffers at the expense of the shared pool. Although the shared pool is not as large or as heavily used, it serves a critical purpose in the execution of SQL statements.

Any time you make a significant change in DB_CACHE_SIZE or DB_BLOCK_BUFFERS or any Oracle parameter, go back and check the OS for different I/O rates. Also check within Oracle to see whether the cache hit rates and the I/O rates have changed.

Using Multiple Buffer Pools

Starting with Oracle 8, several different buffer pools can be used. These are the Default Buffer Pool, the Keep Buffer Pool, and the Recycle Buffer Pool. These buffer pools, although essentially constructed the same, serve different purposes. The Keep Buffer Pool is designed to keep things in cache longer before they get ejected. The Recycle Buffer Pool is designed to keep large non-cacheable items from ejecting other objects from cache. Finally, the Default Buffer Pool is for what is left over.

After the multiple buffer pools feature has been enabled, you allocate memory for those buffer pools by using the initialization parameters. This chapter now looks at these caches in a little more detail.

Using the Keep Buffer Pool

The Keep Buffer Pool is designed to keep things in cache by providing an area of cache where only other objects assigned to the Keep Buffer Pool can eject other Keep Buffer Pool objects from this cache. By carefully sizing the Keep Buffer Pool, you can make this happen. The Keep Buffer Pool should be used for lookup tables or indexes that require quick response times and might not be continually accessed. Using the Keep Buffer Pool increases performance on these objects if done correctly.

The Keep Buffer Pool is allocated by using the Oracle initialization parameter DB_KEEP_CACHE_SIZE, which specifies the number of buffers in the Keep Buffer Pool. The size of these buffers is the same size as the primary database blocks.

Analyzing the Keep Buffer Pool Cache Hit Ratio

To determine how effective the Keep Buffer Pool is at caching data, you can use the same formula that was used previously:

```
Cache Hit Ratio = 1 - (PHYSICAL READS / (BLOCK GETS + CONSISTENT GETS))
```

In this case, however, instead of selecting these values from V$SYSSTAT as before, the values should be selected from V$BUFFER_POOL_STATISTICS where you are only selecting for the KEEP name as shown here in this example:

```
SELECT physical reads, block_gets, consistent_gets
  FROM v$buffer_pool_statistics
  WHERE name name = 'KEEP';
```

This provides the buffer pool cache hit ratio specifically for the Keep Buffer Pool. The Keep Buffer Pool cache hit ratio should be high. If possible, keep the Keep Buffer Pool hit ratio above 99%.

Analyzing the Keep Buffer Pool for Latch Contention

It is important to make sure that the buffer pool has a sufficient number of lru latches. To determine the ratio of times when latch contention is occurring, look at the ratio of sleeps to gets. As with general latch contention problems as described later in this chapter, a request for a latch that cannot be fulfilled causes the process to sleep waiting for the latch. For more details on latch contention, read on.

```
SELECT child#, sleeps / gets ratio
FROM v$latch_children
WHERE name = 'cache buffers lru chain';
```

Using the Recycle Buffer Pool

The Recycle Buffer Pool is designed to keep objects out of cache by providing an area of cache where objects quickly age through. For example, tables where huge table scans are common often only look at this data while it is being read to search for a specific piece of data. By sizing the Recycle Buffer Pool properly, this data can be quickly aged out here, rather than ejecting more important (and cacheable) data from the main buffer pool. If the Recycle Buffer Pool is used correctly, it can make the other buffer caches more efficient.

The Recycle Buffer Pool is allocated by using the Oracle initialization parameter DB_RECYCLE_CACHE_SIZE. Just like the DB_KEEP_CACHE_SIZE, this parameter specifies the number of buffers to allocate to the Recycle Buffer Pool. The size of the buffers is the same as the primary database block size.

Analyzing the Recycle Buffer Pool Cache Hit Ratio

To determine how effective the Recycle Buffer Pool is at caching data, you can use the same formula that was used previously:

```
Cache Hit Ratio = 1 - (PHYSICAL READS / (BLOCK GETS + CONSISTENT GETS))
```

In this case, however, instead of selecting these values from V$SYSSTAT as before, the values should be selected from V$BUFFER_POOL_STATISTICS, where you are only selecting for the RECYCLE name as shown here in this example:

```
SELECT physical reads, block_gets, consistent_gets
  FROM v$buffer_pool_statistics
  WHERE name name = 'RECYCLE';
```

This provides the buffer pool cache hit ratio specifically for the Recycle Buffer Pool. The Recycle Buffer Pool cache hit ratio should be high. If possible, keep the Recycle Buffer Pool hit ratio above 99%.

Analyzing the Recycle Buffer Pool for Latch Contention

Make sure that the buffer pool has a sufficient number of lru latches. To determine the ratio of times when latch contention is occurring, look at the ratio of sleeps to gets. As with general latch contention problems as described later in this chapter, a request for a latch that cannot be fulfilled causes the process to sleep waiting for the latch. For more details on latch contention, read on.

```
SELECT child#, sleeps / gets ratio
FROM v$latch_children
WHERE name = 'cache buffers lru chain';
```

Using the Default Buffer Pool

The Default Buffer Pool is essentially what is left over. The amount of blocks allocated to the Default Buffer Pool is determined by the following formula:

```
Default Cache_Size = DB_CACHE_SIZE - DB_KEEP_CACHE_SIZE - DB_RECYCLE_CACHE_SIZE
```

The Default Buffer Cache should be used for objects that require a fairly good cache hit ratio, but not immediate access.

Analyzing the Default Buffer Pool Cache Hit Ratio

To determine how effective the Keep Buffer Pool is at caching data, you can use the same formula that was used previously:

```
Cache Hit Ratio = 1 - (PHYSICAL READS / (BLOCK GETS + CONSISTENT GETS))
```

In this case, however, instead of selecting these values from V$SYSSTAT as before, you should select the values from V$BUFFER_POOL_STATISTICS, where you are only selecting for the DEFAULT name, as shown here in this example:

```
SELECT physical reads, block_gets, consistent_gets
  FROM v$buffer_pool_statistics
  WHERE name name = 'DEFAULT';
```

This provides the buffer pool cache hit ratio specifically for the Default Buffer Pool. The Default Buffer Pool cache hit ratio should be high. If possible, keep the Default Buffer Pool hit ratio above 99%.

Managing Rollback Segments and Undo Information

Read consistency allows a long-running transaction to obtain the same data within the query. During the transaction, the data is consistent to a single point in time and does not change. Even though the data might have changed, and perhaps the DBWR might even have written it out, other transactions do not see those changes until a COMMIT has occurred. In fact, only transactions that start after this transaction has been committed see those changes.

Read consistency has traditionally been handled in Oracle via the use of rollback segments. An addition to Oracle9i is the use of SMU. This is a new way of handling read consistency, rollbacks, and recovery.

With Oracle9i, the recommended method of managing undo information is using the SMU scheme. Using this method of undo, you do not need to put the level of effort into configuring and tuning rollback segments that you do when using the Rollback Segment Undo (RBU) scheme.

The SMU scheme is enabled by setting the initialization parameter UNDO_MANAGEMENT to AUTO, and by setting the initialization parameter UNDO_TABLESPACE to be the name of the tablespace to be used. This, in conjunction with creating an undo tablespace, will enable SMU.

For those of you who still want configure rollback segments by hand, you can do so by setting the initialization parameter UNDO_MANAGEMENT to MANUAL. In this mode, the following information applies to you. For those of you opting to use the SMU scheme, you have little to tune. To properly configure a system's rollback segments, you must create enough rollback segments and they must be of a sufficient size.

Tuning Undo in SMU Mode

As mentioned previously, setting the UNDO_MANAGEMENT parameter to AUTO enables SMU mode. In SMU mode, few initialization parameters need to be adjusted. An undo tablespace must be created and then that tablespace assigned to undo information. With this new scheme of managing undo information, you can now specify how long undo information is retained. This, in conjunction with sizing the undo tablespace, is all that is required to manage undos.

Creating an Undo Tablespace

Undo tablespaces are created with the CREATE UNDO TABLESPACE command. The undo tablespace is created just like any other tablespace and requires you to specify the location and the size of the tablespace. It can be made up of one or more data files and is similar to the temporary tablespace in that it can serve only one function.

In addition to setting the UNDO_MANAGEMENT parameter to AUTO, you must also assign the tablespace to undo by using the UNDO_TABLESPACE initialization parameter.

You should create the undo tablespace large enough to hold the required amount of undo information. This can be roughly calculated using the UNDO_RETENTION parameter as discussed later in this section. That parameter specifies how long undo information is retained.

If you know how long the undo information is retained, along with how much undo information per second is being generated, you can calculate how much undo tablespace is needed. Use the formula:

```
Undo space needed = Undo retention time * Undos/time
```

For example, if the undo retention is 300 seconds and the system generates 1000 undo blocks per second, the number of blocks required is as follows:

```
Undo blocks required = (300 seconds) * (100 undos blocks/sec) = 30,000 blocks
```

Thus, the space needed is 30,000 times the block size.

Monitoring the Undo Tablespace

You might be wondering from the last section how to find out what the undo rate is. This and other information can be found in the performance view V$UNDOSTAT. Some of the data that is of particular interest is as follows:

BEGIN_TIME	This is the time when the measurement interval began.
END_TIME	This is the time when the measurement interval ended.
UNDOBLKS	This is the number of undo blocks that were consumed during the measurement interval.
SSOLDERRCNT	This is the number of OER (snapshot too old) errors that have occurred during the measurement interval.
NOSPACEERRCNT	This specifies the number of OER (snapshot too old) errors that have occurred for this instance.

If you are seeing non-zero values for the error counts, you can do one of two things: lower the retention period, or increase the size of the undo tablespace.

Tuning the Retention Period

The retention period allows you to specify how long undo information is retained. The parameter UNDO_RETENTION is specified in seconds. The length of time that undo information is retained is 30 seconds by default. This should be sufficient for OLTP systems, which usually don't have long-running queries. If you feel that undo information needs to be retained longer, you can increase this value.

Increasing the retention periods allows undo information to be kept longer so that long-running transactions that require a consistent view of data have a better chance of finishing. If you receive the error message "snapshot too old" (referred to as an OER), increase the undo retention period.

Tuning Undo in RBU Mode

Rollback segments record transactional information that can be used if the transaction should be rolled back. Rollback segments are also used to provide read consistency and are used for database recovery.

Rollback segments must be carefully watched and can be tuned in several ways. It is important not only to size the rollback segments correctly, but also to create the proper number of rollback segments and properly distribute them according to the number of user processes that require them. The next section discusses how the rollback segments operate.

Understanding How Rollback Segments Work

As a transaction is being processed, rollback segments constantly record the old values of data as they are being changed. It is important that this information be saved because a rollback requires that all data be restored to its original condition.

The original, unchanged data written by the transaction to the rollback segments are called *rollback entries*. Depending on the length of the transaction and the amount of changes to data, each transaction might have more than one rollback entry. These entries are linked together so that they can easily be used in the event of a rollback.

One or more transactions concurrently use rollback segments. You can tune the rollback segments to provide for optimal efficiency and space usage. More transactions sharing rollback segments cause more contention and use space more efficiently. Fewer transactions per rollback segment cause less contention and waste more space.

Oracle maintains what is called a *transaction table* for each rollback segment. The transaction table stores information about what transactions use that rollback segment and the rollback entries for each change done by these transactions.

Each time a new transaction begins, it is assigned to a rollback segment. This can happen in one of two ways:

Automatic	Oracle automatically assigns the transaction a rollback segment. The assignment takes place when the first DDL or DML statement is issued. Queries are never assigned rollback segments.
Manual	The application can manually specify a rollback segment by using the SET TRANSACTION command with the USE ROLLBACK SEGMENT parameter. This arrangement allows the developer to choose the correct size rollback segment for a particular task. The rollback segment is assigned for the duration of the transaction.

At the end of each transaction, when the COMMIT has occurred, the rollback information is released from the rollback segment but is not deleted. This provides read-consistent views for other queries that started before the transaction was committed. To retain this information as long as possible, the rollback segments are written as a circular buffer, as described next.

You can think of rollback segments as a sort of circular buffer. A rollback segment must have at least two extents (usually more). When a transaction fills up one extent, it starts using the next extent in sequence. When it gets to the last extent, the transaction continues with extent 1 again, if it is available (see Figure 3.1).

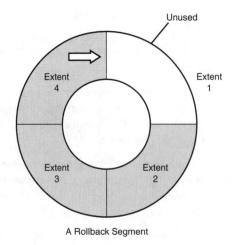

FIGURE 3.1
A rollback segment.

If the transaction uses the last extent in the segment, it looks to see whether the first extent is available. If it is not, another extent is created (see Figures 3.2 and 3.3).

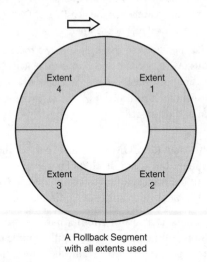

FIGURE 3.2
A rollback segment with all extents used.

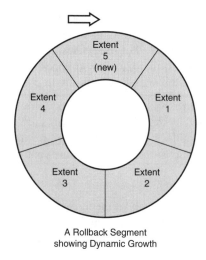

A Rollback Segment
showing Dynamic Growth

FIGURE 3.3
A rollback segment showing dynamic growth.

The number of extents used for the rollback segments is determined in the definition of the rollback segments when you create them. Rollback segments are created with the following command:

```
CREATE PUBLIC ROLLBACK SEGMENT rsname
TABLESPACE tsname
STORAGE (
INITIAL 100K
NEXT 100K
OPTIMAL 1500K
MINEXTENTS 15
MAXEXTENTS 100);
```

In this example, the user specifies the following values:

INITIAL	This is the initial size of the extent.
NEXT	This is the size of the second extent. With rollback segments, it is always a good idea to make all extents the same size because no distinction exists between different extents.
OPTIMAL	This value specifies what you think the optimal size for the rollback segment should be. When extents are no longer needed, they are eliminated until this size is reached.
MINEXTENTS	This is the minimum number of extents. This is also the number allocated when the segment is created.
MAXEXTENTS	This is the maximum number of extents that can be dynamically allocated.

Initially, MINEXTENTS number of extents are in the rollback segment. As extents fill up, they are used in a circular fashion, returning to the first extent when all others are filled. If a rollback segment has used all the space in all of the extents, and MAXEXTENTS has not been reached, another extent is created. If the size of the rollback segment is larger than OPTIMAL and unused extents are available, the unused extents are dropped from the rollback segment.

The creation and destruction of rollback segment extents cause overhead in the system. In addition to the overhead created by the addition of extents to a rollback segment, the transaction needing to write into that rollback segment must wait for the extent to be created before it can continue. The following sections explain how to tune your use of rollback segments.

Number of Rollback Segments

You can determine the number of rollback segments by the number of concurrent transactions in the database. Remember: The fewer transactions per rollback segment, the less contention. A good rule of thumb is to create one rollback segment for every four concurrent transactions.

Rollback contention occurs when too many transactions try to use the same rollback segment at the same time and some of them have to wait. You can tell whether you are seeing contention on rollback segments by looking at the dynamic performance table, V$WAITSTAT. V$WAITSTAT contains the following data related to rollback segments:

UNDO HEADER	The number of waits for buffers containing rollback header blocks
UNDO BLOCK	The number of waits for buffers containing rollback blocks other than header blocks
SYSTEM UNDO HEADER	The same as UNDO HEADER for the SYSTEM rollback segment

The SYSTEM rollback segment is the original rollback segment that was created when the database was created. This rollback segment is used primarily for special system functions, but it is sometimes used when no other rollback segment is available. Typically, the SYSTEM rollback segment is not used and you do not need to be concerned about it.

You can view these values with the following SQL statement:

```
SELECT class, count
  FROM V$WAITSTAT
  WHERE class IN
  ('undo header', 'undo block', 'system undo header', 'system undo block');


CLASS                 COUNT
-----------------  ---------
system undo header       0
system undo block        0
undo header              0
undo block               0
```

Compare these values with the total number of requests for data. Remember that the number of requests for data is equal to the sum of DB BUFFER GETS and CONSISTENT GETS from V$SYSSTAT. Also remember that you can extract that information with the following query:

```
SELECT SUM(value) "Data Requests"
  FROM v$sysstat
  WHERE name IN ('db block gets', 'consistent gets');


Data Requests
- - - - - - - - - - - -
        5105
```

If the number of waits for any of the rollback segment blocks or headers exceeds more than 1% of the total number of requests, you should reduce the contention by adding more rollback segments.

Size of Rollback Segments

Create several different sizes of rollback segments. The application developer should use each type of rollback segment based on the type and length of the transaction:

Transaction Type	Comments
OLTP	OLTP transactions are characterized by many concurrent transactions, each modifying perhaps only a small amount of data. These types of transactions benefit from a reduction of contention and quick access from cached rollback segments. Try to create many small rollback segments of perhaps 10–20K in size, each with 2–4 extents optimally with a rollback segment available for each transaction.
	The small size of the rollback segments provides for a better chance of being cached in the SGA. The extents probably have little dynamic growth.
Long Queries	For long queries where read consistency calls for quite a bit of rollback information to be accessed, use a larger rollback segment. A good rule of thumb is to create rollback segments approximately 10% the size of the largest table. (Most SQL statements affect only about 10% of the data in a table.)
Large Updates	For transactions that update large amounts of data, you should also use a larger rollback segment. As is the case with the long queries, it is appropriate to create rollback segments approximately 10% of the size of the largest table.

Size and Number of Extents

In general, you can obtain the best performance of rollback I/O performance when approximately 10–20 extents of equal size exist per rollback segment. To determine the size and number of extents, use the following formula:

```
Rollback Segment Size (Rsize) = Size of largest table / 10
Number of Extents (NE) = 10
Size of Extents (Esize) = Rsize / NE
```

When creating the rollback segments, use the value of Esize for INITIAL and NEXT; use the value of NE for MINEXTENTS. Even when using these rules, you might not achieve the most effective size for your rollback segments. If dynamic growth is occurring, you might be losing performance.

Avoid Dynamic Growth

As stated previously, avoid the dynamic space management that causes additional overhead and transactional delays. To determine whether rollback segments are a problem, look in the dynamic performance table, V$ROLLSTAT. The following columns are of particular interest:

EXTENTS	The number of rollback extents.
RSSIZE	The size in bytes of the rollback segment.
OPTSIZE	The size to which OPTIMAL was set.
AVEACTIVE	The current average size of active extents. *Active extents* are defined as extents with uncommitted transaction data.
AVESHRINK	The average number of bytes deallocated per shrink (see the second item following).
EXTENDS	The number of times the rollback segment added an extent.
SHRINKS	The number of times the rollback segment shrank. Each shrink might be one or more extents at a time.
HWMSIZE	The high water mark of rollback segment size. This is the largest that the segment size ever grew to be.

You can look at these statistics by using a SQL statement such as this one:

```
SELECT substr(name,1,40), extents, rssize, aveactive, aveshrink, extends,
➥shrinks
  FROM v$rollname rn, v$rollstat rs
  WHERE rn.usn = rs.usn;
```

SUBSTR(NAME,1,40)	EXTENTS	RSSIZE	AVEACTIVE	AVESHRINK	EXTENDS	SHRINKS
SYSTEM	4	202752	0	0	0	0
RB_TEMP	53	540672	23929	0	0	0
RB1	2	202752	0	0	0	0
RB2	2	202752	55193	0	0	0

If the average size is close to the size set for OPTIMAL, then OPTIMAL is set correctly. If either extends and shrinks are high, you must increase the value for OPTIMAL.

Review of Rollback Segment Tuning in RBU Mode

To optimize rollback segments, remember the following rules:

- Avoid using the default rollback segments in the SYSTEM tablespace. Create your own tablespace for rollback segments.

- Create approximately one rollback segment for every four concurrent transactions you expect to have.

- Create 10–20 extents for each rollback segment (except for short-running OLTP transactions).

- Assign large rollback segments to long-running queries. These queries might need a large rollback to reconstruct a read-consistent version of the data. This data must be available for the entire length of the transaction. The size of the rollback segments should be approximately 10% of the size of the largest table.

- Assign large rollback segments for long transactions that modify much data. These transactions create large amounts of rollback information. The size of the rollback segments should be approximately 10% of the size of the largest table.

- Avoid dynamic expansion and reduction of rollback space by monitoring rollback information.

Rollback segments should be monitored periodically because the applications and user activity change. What is optimal for rollback segments today might degrade over time because of an increase in user activity or changes in application code.

Summary of Undo Tuning

As you have seen, using SMU mode is much less work and tuning effort than using the traditional rollback segments found in RSU mode, but it's up to you whether you stick with RBU mode or try SMU mode.

Checking for Redo Log Buffer

For a transaction to be completed, redo information must be written to the redo log. Until this write has occurred, it's possible that the transaction could be lost if some sort of instance failure occurred. To avoid this condition, a COMMIT is not completed until the redo record has been written.

Any kind of bottleneck in the redo log can cause performance problems for every process on the system. To make sure that this does not happen, check for contention on the redo log buffers.

Redo Log Buffer Contention

To check for contention on the redo log buffer, simply check the dynamic performance table, V$SYSSTAT, for redo allocation buffer retries. If this number is not 0, a process had to wait for space in the redo log buffer and the size of the redo log buffer should be increased. Check for this condition with the following SQL statement:

```
SELECT name, value
  FROM v$sysstat
  WHERE name = 'redo buffer allocation retries;
```

```
NAME                                                              VALUE
-------------------------------------------------------------- ---------
redo buffer allocation retries                                        0
```

If this value is not 0, increase the initialization parameter LOG_BUFFER by 5–10% until your system runs with redo log space requests close to 0.

Tuning Checkpoints

Checkpoints occur in the Oracle database to ensure that all "dirty blocks" in the SGA are eventually written to disk. Because the DBWR works on a Least Recently Used (LRU) algorithm, data that has been untouched in the SGA for the longest time is flushed out first. This has the side effect that often-used data blocks might never be flushed out or written to disk.

A checkpoint causes all the dirty blocks for committed transactions in the SGA to be written to disk. The following situations can cause a checkpoint:

- Every log switch causes a checkpoint. If a checkpoint is in progress, the log switch overrides it and the checkpoint restarts.

- The number of redo blocks written has reached a threshold that causes the recovery time to exceed the number of seconds to recover specified by the initialization parameter FAST_START_MTTR_TARGET.

- The number of redo blocks written has reached a threshold that causes the recovery I/Os to exceed the number of I/Os to recover specified by the initialization parameter FAST_START_IO_TARGET.

- The initialization parameter LOG_CHECKPOINT_INTERVAL can be set to force a checkpoint when a certain number of redo log blocks have been written relative to the last checkpoint. This is useful when you are running with large log files and want several checkpoints between log switches.

- The initialization parameter LOG_CHECKPOINT_TIMEOUT can be set to cause a checkpoint to occur a specific number of seconds since the beginning of the last checkpoint. This parameter can be used for large redo log files that have a desired checkpoint frequency. This is the default method of operation.

- A checkpoint is forced at the beginning of a tablespace backup only on the affected data files. The checkpoint also overrides any other checkpoint that is in progress.

- A checkpoint is forced on the data files of a tablespace that is brought offline.

- A checkpoint is forced on an instance shutdown. If the administrator shuts down the instance with SHUTDOWN NORMAL or SHUTDOWN IMMEDIATE, a checkpoint occurs.

- An administrator can manually cause a checkpoint. This checkpoint overrides any in-progress checkpoints.

If you are not as interested in recovery time as you are in throughput, you can set the checkpoint frequency so that a checkpoint is performed only when the redo log switch occurs. To further increase the checkpoint interval, increase the size of the redo log files. If you are interested in quick recovery, set the checkpoint frequency more often.

Optimizing Sorts

The default sort area size is sufficient for most applications. If your application often does sorts that do not fit into memory, you might want to adjust the size of the sort area. One way to determine whether your sorts are occurring in memory or on disk is to look at the dynamic performance table, V$SYSSTAT. The statistics of interest are given here:

Sorts (memory)	The number of sorts that were able to fit in the in-memory sort area
Sorts (disk)	The number of sorts that required temporary space on disk

You can look at these parameters by using the following SQL statement:

```
SELECT name, value
  FROM v$sysstat
  WHERE name IN ('sorts (memory)', 'sorts (disk)');
```

NAME	VALUE
sorts (memory)	22
sorts (disk)	0

Tuning the Sort Area

If you have a lot of sorts that use temporary space on disk, you might see a performance improvement by increasing the size of the sort area in memory. Do this by increasing the Oracle initialization parameter, SORT_AREA_SIZE. By increasing the sort area size, you see a benefit from faster sorts and fewer disk I/Os.

MEMORY REQUIREMENTS FOR SORTING

Sorts occur in user memory, not in the SGA. Be careful that multiple simultaneous sorts do not cause paging and swapping in your system. Be sure that enough free memory is available for your sorting activities.

Tuning the Sort Area Retained Size

If you increase the value for SORT_AREA_SIZE, you might want to decrease the value of SORT_AREA_RETAINED_SIZE (the amount of session memory retained for sorts). When Oracle performs sorts, it uses the amount of memory defined by SORT_AREA_SIZE. When the sort is completed, Oracle deallocates the memory, leaving as much as it can of the sort output in memory. Oracle deallocates memory until it reaches the value defined by SORT_AREA_RETAINED_SIZE.

If the sort cannot fit into SORT_AREA_SIZE, the sort is broken into smaller pieces, which are sorted individually. These individual sorted pieces are known as *runs*.

Tuning the Temporary Tablespace

In addition to tuning the memory sort areas, it is also a good idea to tune the temporary tablespace for sorts. Because large sorts use the temporary tablespace for storage, having optimal storage behind the temporary tablespace improves performance. You can tune the temporary tablespace in several ways.

The most effective way to tune the temporary tablespace is by using extremely fast storage, such as solid state devices. New solid state devices have made this type of storage much more affordable. By using a solid state device, access to the temporary tablespace can be greatly improved.

Another way to improve sort performance on the temporary tablespace is to configure extents to be in a multiple of the SORT_AREA_SIZE. This reduces extent creations. Set PCTIN-CREASE to 0 and set the INITIAL and NEXT values to a multiple of SORT_AREA_SIZE. Be sure to make it sufficiently large, so if SORT_AREA_SIZE is 10MB, try setting INITIAL and NEXT to 50MB. This reduces extent allocation overhead.

Minimizing Free List Contention

Another area of possible contention is in the free list. The *free list* is maintained to provide a faster mechanism to get free data blocks from the buffer cache. The free list contains a linked list of blocks in the segment that has space available.

You can determine contention on the free list by looking at the dynamic performance table, V$WAITSTAT. Use the following SQL statement to obtain this information:

```
SELECT class, count
  FROM v$waitstat
  WHERE class = 'free list'


CLASS                COUNT
----------------- ---------
free list                0
```

If the free list number is greater than 1% of the total number of requests, add more free lists. Remember that the total number of requests is determined from the sum of database block gets and consistent gets from V$SYSSTAT, as shown here:

```
SELECT SUM(value) "Data Requests"
  FROM v$sysstat
  WHERE name IN ('db block gets', 'consistent gets');


Data Requests
------------
        5105
```

You can add more free lists by re-creating the table with a larger value for the FREELISTS storage parameter. You might want to increase this parameter to the number of concurrent INSERT transactions that you expect to see.

Although there usually is not a problem with free lists, monitoring them periodically will alert you if the system load has increased to where free lists are a problem.

Summary

This chapter looked at several areas you can improve in the Oracle instance. Most of these areas have a general theme; this theme relates to the fact that disk I/O is many times slower than memory.

If you can optimize an instance to take advantage of this fact, you can achieve optimal performance. Following is a summary of the goals discussed in this chapter:

- Tune for cache hits. By sizing DB_CACHE_SIZE or DB_BLOCK_BUFFERS and SHARED_POOL_SIZE to get good cache hit rates, I/Os are reduced.

- Minimize contention. This is true for rollback segments, free lists, and redo log buffers.

- Sort in memory. If you have memory available, allow sorts to occur in memory, thus increasing sort performance and reducing I/Os.

- Tune checkpoints. Adjust the checkpoint interval based on your needs. (Remember the performance versus recovery interval issue here.)

These areas of instance tuning can help the overall performance of the system. The next chapter looks at some additional areas where you can change the system to increase performance.

PERFORMANCE-ENHANCING FEATURES

4

This chapter continues where the last chapter left off. This chapter continues to look at the Oracle server and additional things you can do to improve system performance. Even though these topics are a part of the Oracle server, they can be thought of as performance-enhancing features. This is because they are objects or features that are not automatically run, but features that must be enabled to take advantage of them.

This chapter covers indexes. Indexes are objects that can be created on Oracle data to improve performance of accessing data. Indexes require careful planning and an understanding of data access patterns. In some cases, poorly designed indexes can cause performance degradation.

Parameters That Are Used in This Chapter

This chapter includes the use of many Oracle initialization parameters. Chapter 1, "Tuning," introduced you to these parameters and explained how to use them. In this chapter, the following initialization parameters are covered:

- MAX_DISPATCHERS. MAX_DISPATCHERS specifies the maximum number of dispatcher processes that are allowed to run simultaneously.

- MAX_SHARED_SERVERS. MAX_SHARED_SERVERS specifies the maximum number of shared server processes that are allowed to run simultaneously. If artificial deadlocks occur too frequently on your system, you should increase the value of MAX_SHARED_SERVERS.

- PARALLEL_ADAPTIVE_MULTI_USER. PARALLEL_ADAPTIVE_MULTI_USER, when set to true, enables an adaptive algorithm that is designed to improve performance in multiuser environments that use parallel execution. The algorithm automatically reduces the requested degree of parallelism based on the system load at query startup time.

- PARALLEL_AUTOMATIC_TUNING. When PARALLEL_AUTOMATIC_TUNING is set to true, Oracle determines the default values for parameters that control parallel execution.

- PARALLEL_BROADCAST_ENABLED. PARALLEL_BROADCAST_ENABLED allows you to improve performance of hash and merge join operations, in which a large join result set is joined with a small result set. (Size is measured in bytes rather than number of rows.)

- PARALLEL_EXECUTION_MESSAGE_SIZE. PARALLEL_EXECUTION_ MESSAGE_SIZE specifies the size of messages for parallel execution (formerly referred to as parallel query, PDML, Parallel Recovery, replication).

- PARALLEL_MAX_SERVERS. PARALLEL_MAX_SERVERS specifies the maximum number of parallel execution processes and parallel recovery processes for an instance. As demand increases, Oracle increases the number of processes from the number that is created at instance startup to this value.

- PARALLEL_MIN_PERCENT. PARALLEL_MIN_PERCENT operates in conjunction with PARALLEL_MAX_SERVERS and PARALLEL_MIN_SERVERS. It allows you to specify the minimum percentage of parallel execution processes (of the value of PARALLEL_MAX_SERVERS) that is required for parallel execution.

- PARALLEL_MIN_SERVERS. PARALLEL_MIN_SERVERS specifies the minimum number of parallel execution processes for the instance. This value is the number of parallel execution processes that Oracle creates when the instance is started.

- PARALLEL_THREADS_PER_CPU. PARALLEL_THREADS_PER_CPU specifies the default degree of parallelism for the instance and determines the parallel adaptive and load balancing algorithms. The parameter describes the number of parallel execution processes or threads that a CPU can handle during parallel execution.

- PARTITION_VIEW_ENABLED. PARTITION_VIEW_ENABLED specifies whether the optimizer uses partition views. Oracle Corporation recommends that you use partitioned tables (available starting with Oracle8) rather than partition views. Partition views are supported for backward compatibility only.

- RECOVERY_PARALLELISM. RECOVERY_PARALLELISM specifies the number of processes to participate in instance or crash recovery.

Indexes

An *index* is an optional structure that is designed to help you achieve faster access to data. Just like the index in this book, an Oracle index is logically and physically independent of the data in the associated table or cluster. You can use the index to speed access to the data or you can retrieve the data independently from the index by searching the tables for it. When indexes are optimally configured and used, they can significantly reduce I/O to the data files and greatly improve performance.

The presence of an index is transparent to the user or application and requires no application changes. However, if you are aware of an index, you might be able to take advantage of it when forming SQL. The only indication of an index might be improved access time to data.

After an index has been created for a table, Oracle automatically maintains that index. Inserts, updates, and deletions of rows in the table automatically update the related indexes.

A table can have any number of indexes, but the more indexes that it has, the more overhead that is incurred during table updates, inserts, and deletions. This overhead is incurred because all associated indexes must be updated whenever table data is updated.

Index Concepts

Before getting into the specifics on how an index works, you need to learn a few of the fundamentals and concepts. An index is built on one or more columns in a table. The usefulness of this index usually depends on the selectivity of that column or set of columns. The selectivity refers to how well the index can reduce the data set. A unique index has good selectivity because each value on which the index has been created has only one row of data associated with it. An example of bad selectivity would be a true/false column, where each value exists many times. You will see later on in this section that the selectivity will help you determine what type of index to create.

The index might only help you reduce the data that is selected and might not totally isolate just one row. For example, if an index is created on the Last Name field of a table and you are searching for John Smith, the index will return all of the Smiths and you will still have to search each of them for John. The better the selectivity, the more the index will help narrow the results and speed up access.

Index Types

Two major types of indexes can be used within an Oracle database, with several different subtypes of indexes. These major types of indexes are B*-Tree indexes and bitmap indexes. A B*-Tree index is one in which the index is shaped like a tree, where the search condition traverses the tree to find the desired data.

A bitmap index is different in that it creates a bitmap of the data file for each unique value on which the bitmap index is created and uses that to find certain values. Bitmap indexes are useful in certain situations, as you will see later in this section.

The B*-Tree index can have several subtypes, whereas the bitmap index does not have variations. A B*-Tree index can be limited to one column value or can consist of several columns. An index can be either unique or nonunique.

The index should be created based on the values that are accessed in the application; the application should be developed to take advantage of these indexes. Having knowledge of and influence over these indexes can be useful to the application developer.

B*-Tree Indexes

B*-Tree indexes are the most common type of index. The B*-Tree index uses a tree-type search to find the data that this index references. Data is stored in an inverted tree; thus, the term B*-Tree index was born. The Oracle index is actually called a Balanced Tree Index. The top level of the index (where the search starts) is referred to as the *root node*. The end (where the ROWIDs are kept) is referred to as the *leaf nodes*. In between are the branch nodes.

When an index is created, an index segment is automatically allocated. This index segment contains information that speeds access to data by determining the location of indexed data with as few I/Os as possible. Oracle indexes data by using an index structure known as a B*-Tree index.

A B*-Tree index is designed to balance the access time to any row. A B*-Tree index is a tree of descending comparison values (see Figure 4.1). As you traverse down the index, you compare the desired value with the values in the upper-level index blocks, called *branch blocks*. Based on the outcome of the comparison with the branch blocks, you compare the desired value with more branch blocks until you reach the lowest-level index blocks. The index blocks on the lowest level, called leaf blocks, contain every indexed data value and the associated ROWID of that data.

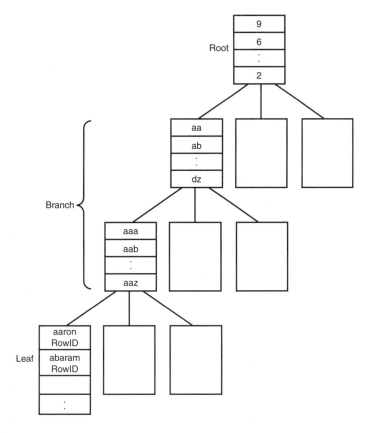

FIGURE 4.1
The B*-Tree index structure.

With a unique index, one ROWID exists per data value in the leaf block. With a nonunique index, several values might be associated with the data value. In the case of the nonunique index, the data values are sorted first by the index key and then by the ROWID.

With a B^*-Tree index, all the leaf blocks are at the same level. Access of index data takes approximately the same time regardless of the value of the data. B^*-Tree indexes provide quick access to data whether it is an exact match or a range query. In addition, B^*-Tree indexes provide good performance regardless of the size of the table, and the performance does not degrade as the table grows.

Within the B*-Tree index are several subtypes of indexes. These subtypes are described next.

Unique and Nonunique Indexes

A unique index is an index value that has the additional constraint of not being able to be duplicated. Although this constraint might be specified, it is usually better to associate this constraint with the table rather than with the index. Oracle enforces UNIQUE integrity constraints by automatically defining a unique index on the unique key.

A nonunique index does not impose the constraint that the index value must be unique. Such an index can be quite useful when quick access is desired on a nonunique value. However, a unique index is better for finding a specific piece of data because the index resolves down to only one value. With a nonuninque index, after the index has been traversed to its lowest level, all of the values that match the requested data must be retrieved.

Simple Versus Complex Indexes

Another type of index is a composite index, an index that indexes several columns in a table. These column values can be in any order, and the columns do not have to be adjacent in the table.

A composite index is useful when SELECT statements have WHERE clauses that reference several values in the table. Because the index is accessed based on the order of the columns that are used in the definition, it is wise to base this order on the frequency of use. The most-referenced column should be defined first, and so on.

A composite index is also good for making several nonunique columns into a unique set of columns. You can then use this composite index to create a unique composite index.

Function-Based Indexes

A function-based index is one in which the system designer or DBA creates a specific function that is used to index the data. The function can either be an arithmetic function or a PL/SQL function. A function-based index is only useful when the function on which the index is based is used within a WHERE clause of a SELECT statement.

Perhaps Company A wants to send a letter of appreciation to all customers whose purchases have increased in the last year. A query to determine which customer IDs to select might look something like this:

```
SELECT cust_id
FROM customers
WHERE this_years_sales - last_years_sales > 0
```

A function-based query can be created on the c_id column that looks like the function shown here:

```
CREATE INDEX idx ON customers (this_years_sales - last_years_sales)
```

Having this index both reduces load on the system and improves performance of this query.

Index-Organized Tables

An Index-Organized Table (IOT) is an object that looks like an index, yet the data is stored within the index. The IOT is good for tables that are only accessed via an index. With a normal index, when the index has been resolved, a ROWID is used to find the data. In an IOT, the data is stored in the leaf block, rather than a ROWID.

In cases where the data in this table is always accessed through this index, using an IOT saves you the I/O operation that would be required to retrieve it via the ROWID. In addition, because the data is stored within the index, it is guaranteed to be stored in sorted order. This might be useful, depending on how this data is accessed.

How the Oracle Bitmap Index Works

The Oracle bitmap index is formed in a completely different manner. A bitmap is created for each unique value that exists on the indexed column. This bitmap contains information on which ROWIDs contain that value. An advantage of bitmap indexes is that several bitmap indexes can be joined; thus, the indexes are combined. An illustration of a bitmap index is shown in Figure 4.2.

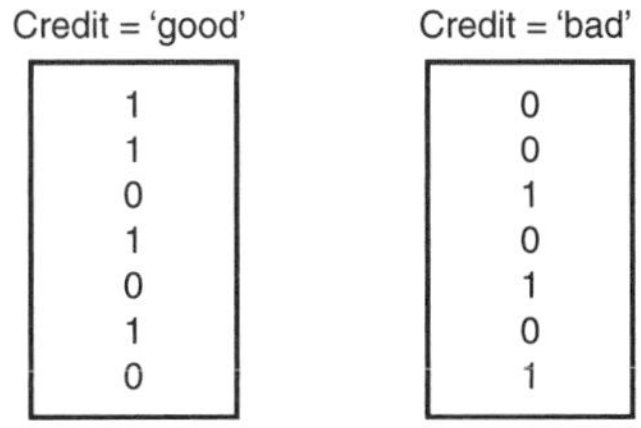

FIGURE 4.2
The bitmap index.

Whereas B*-Tree indexes work best on columns or sets of columns that are unique or have a good selectivity, bitmap indexes are the opposite. A bitmap index is good for yes/no values, true/false values, and so on. A B*-Tree index is traversed until it gets to the point in which many values meet the specified criteria, and then those values are selected. With a bitmap index, those rows are found immediately without having to traverse the index.

If the data represented by the column does not have good selectivity because it does not have an adequate distribution of values, a bitmap index is appropriate. A bitmap index is especially good when you are combining several values whose combined bitmaps perform significant data reduction, as illustrated in Figure 4.3.

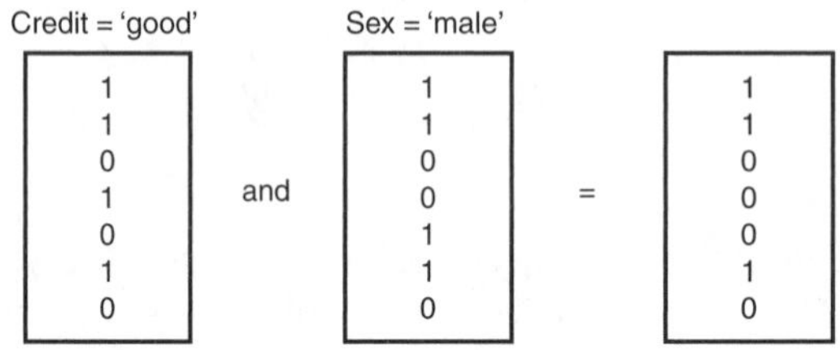

Credit = 'good'		Sex = 'male'		
1		1		1
1		1		1
0		0		0
1	and	0	=	0
0		1		0
1		1		1
0		0		0

FIGURE 4.3
Using a bitmap index for data reduction.

As you can see, a bitmap index can be useful in certain situations.

What to Index

An index is effective only when it is used properly. The use of the index is determined primarily by the column values that are indexed. Remember that the more indexes you have on a table, the more overhead that is incurred during updates, inserts, and deletes. Therefore, it is important to index selectively.

The next few sections are tips and guidelines for creating and using indexes effectively.

Indexes and Data Reduction

One of the primary uses of indexes is the reduction in the amount of data processed. I/O operations are expensive, both in CPU usage and time waiting on the I/O to complete. By reducing I/Os, performance improves, as well as the capacity of the system. Without the use of indexes, all of the data in the table would have to be read to find the data that is requested.

For example, look at the following query:

```
SELECT *
FROM emp
WHERE employee_id = 10290
```

Without the use of an index, the entire emp table must be scanned and each row examined for the value of employee_id. If the emp table is large, this could mean significant I/O operations and processing time.

If an index were placed on the emp column, the index would be traversed, a ROWID would be found for the row in question, and after the ROWID were known, one additional I/O would be used to retrieve the data.

The best case is one in which one row of data is retrieved. Something like the employee_id is probably a unique value. This returns only one row and is quite efficient.

Sometimes the index must return a large amount of data, as in the following example:

```
SELECT *
FROM customers
WHERE region = 'North'
```

This most likely returns a large amount of data. Because the index operations return a large number of ROWIDs and these ROWIDs must be accessed independently, it might be more efficient not to use an index in this case. A table scan might be more efficient. The better method depends largely on the number of rows and the organization of the data in the table.

A bitmap index might be useful in some cases and not useful in others depending on the data. An example might help illustrate the point.

Assume that a column in the customer table is used to indicate good credit or bad credit. Further assume that 99% of the customers have good credit.

If you are looking for customers with good credit, it will probably be more efficient to perform a table scan. On the other hand, if you are looking for customers with bad credit, it will be more efficient to access that data via an index because only 1% of the customers fit into this category. Because the selectivity is low, a bitmap index is recommended.

Indexes and Updates

Updates, inserts, and deletes incur extra overhead when they are indexed. Before the commit of these operations can be completed, all of the associated indexes must be updated. This can be quite time consuming and can add quite a bit of overhead to the system.

Indexing When Selectivity Is Poor

Sometimes you might have tables in which selectivity is poor on some columns. It is not always necessary to index a table; in fact, in some cases, the index causes more problems than it solves. Determining whether an index can help is sometimes a case of trial and error.

In some cases, however, a bitmap index can work well with poor selectivity. The bitmap index can be combined with other bitmap indexes to reduce the data set that is retrieved.

Data such as TRUE/FALSE, YES/NO, and other types of small-range values can be bitmapped effectively. Remember: The amount of space that is taken up by bitmap indexes increases based on the number of distinct values that the column holds.

How to Index

If you decide to use an index, it is important to decide the columns on which to put the index. Depending on the table, you might choose to index one or more columns.

Use the following guidelines to decide which columns to index:

- Choose columns that are most frequently specified in WHERE clauses. Frequently accessed columns can benefit the most from indexes.

- Columns that are commonly used to join tables are good candidates for indexing.

- Remember the trade-off between select improved performance and possible degradation of update performance.

- Frequently modified columns probably should not be index columns because of the overhead involved in updating the index.

In certain situations, the use of composite indexes might be more effective than individual indexes. Following are some examples of when composite indexes might be useful:

- When two columns are not unique individually but are unique together, composite indexes might work well. For example, although columns A and B have few unique values, rows with a particular combination of columns A AND B are mostly unique. Look for WHERE clauses with AND operators.

- If all values of a SELECT statement are in a composite index, Oracle does not query the table; the result is returned from the index.

- If several different queries select the same rows with different WHERE clauses based on different columns, consider creating a composite index with all the columns used in the WHERE statements.

Composite indexes can be useful when they are carefully designed. As with single-column indexes, they are most effective if applications are written with the indexes in mind.

After you have created the index, periodically use the SQL Trace facility or EXPLAIN PLAN to determine whether your queries are taking advantage of the indexes. It might be worth the effort to try the query with and without indexes and then compare the results to see whether the index is worth the space it uses.

Remove indexes that aren't often used. Use ALTER INDEX MONITORING USAGE to track index usage. Look in the system tables ALL_INDEXES, USER_INDEXES, and DBA_INDEXES to determine how often indexes are accessed.

Indexing an inappropriate column or table can actually reduce performance. Indexing appropriately can greatly improve performance by reducing I/Os and speeding access times.

Careful planning and periodic testing with the SQL Trace feature or EXPLAIN PLAN can lead to an effective use of indexes, with optimal performance as the outcome.

Parallel Execution in Oracle

Parallel execution of operations within Oracle is formerly known as the Oracle Parallel Query option. Because this feature is built into the Oracle RDBMS and is no longer an option, the Oracle Parallel Query designation has been dropped. The feature is much enhanced since its introduction in Oracle7, but the idea is the same.

Parallel execution makes it possible for some Oracle functions to be processed by multiple server processes. These functions are queries, index creation, data loading, and recovery. In each of these functions, the general principle is the same: Keep the CPUs busy.

Why does this matter? Most RDBMS operations fall into three categories:

- Operations that are CPU bound. These operations run as fast as one CPU can run. By parallelizing the operation, multiple CPUs can handle the load, thus finishing the operation more quickly.

- Operations that are I/O bound. These operations spend most of the time waiting for an I/O to complete. As you will see in Chapter 9, "I/O Concepts," most RAID controllers operate better when multiple I/Os are requested simultaneously. In addition, the CPUs can be kept busy handling the CPU portion of one thread while another thread is waiting for I/Os to complete.

- Operations that are slowed by contention. Those operations that are bound by contention for resources will not be aided by parallelism.

For table scans, the time spent waiting for the data to be retrieved from disk usually overshadows the amount of time actually spent processing the results. With parallelism, you can compensate for this by using several server processes to execute the query. While one process is waiting for I/Os to complete, other processes can be executing. If you are running on a Symmetric Multiprocessor (SMP) computer, a cluster, or a Massively Parallel Processing (MPP) machine, you can take maximum advantage of the parallelism.

Parallel Query Processing

Parallel Query Processing allows certain Oracle statements to be run in parallel by multiple server processes. The Oracle server can process the following statements in parallel:

- SELECT statements

- Subqueries in INSERT, UPDATE, and DELETE statements

- CREATE TABLE tablename as SELECT statements

- CREATE INDEX and ALTER INDEX REBUILD statements

Parallel queries are effective on large operations such as table scans and sorts.

Parallel Query Operation

With traditional queries such as table scans, the server process reads the data sequentially (see Figure 4.4). Much of the time spent in this query is spent waiting for I/Os to complete.

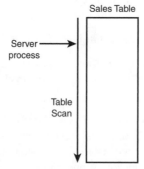

FIGURE 4.4
A table scan without parallel query.

A parallel query splits the query into several different pieces, each one processed by a different server process. These processes are called *query servers*. A process known as the *query coordinator* dispatches the query servers.

The query coordinator dispatches the query servers and coordinates the results from all the servers to send back to the user. The result of this arrangement is that many smaller table scans take place under the hood (transparent to the user). From the user's standpoint, it is simply a much faster table scan. Figure 4.5 shows a parallel query.

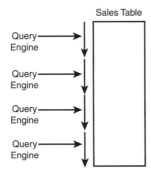

FIGURE 4.5
A table scan with parallel query.

The query coordinator is given a SQL statement and a degree of parallelism and is responsible for dividing the query among the query servers and integrating the individual results into one result. The *degree of parallelism* is the number of query servers that is assigned to the particular query.

The Oracle server can make parallel the following operations:

- Joins
- Sorts
- Table scans

Each of these operations has requirements that determine how the query is parallelized. The performance that the parallel query achieves is determined both by the size of the data to be accessed and the degree of parallelism achieved.

The query coordinator determines the way that the query is parallelized (if at all). The decision is made in this order:

1. The optimizer determines the execution plan of the statement.

2. The query coordinator determines which operations can be performed in parallel.

3. The query coordinator determines how many query servers to enlist.

4. The query coordinator enlists query servers that perform the query.

5. The query coordinator reassembles the resulting data and passes it back to the user.

The degree of parallelism is determined by using the following precedence:

1. Query hints. User-defined hints that are included in the SQL statement have the highest precedence.

2. Table definition. The default degree of parallelism that is defined for the table has second precedence.

3. Initialization parameters. The Oracle initialization parameters have the lowest precedence.

Regardless of what these values are set to, the number of query servers cannot exceed the number of query servers that is available in the query server pool. This number is specified by the Oracle initialization parameter, PARALLEL_MAX_SERVERS.

Hints for the degree of parallelism are set within a comment string in the SQL statement. The syntax of this comment is as follows:

```
PARALLEL ( alias_or_tablename , [ integer/DEFAULT ] [ , integer/DEFAULT ] )
```

The parallel hint specifies the table or alias that is being scanned, followed by a value for the number of query servers to be used (or the DEFAULT). The final optional value specifies how the table is to be split among different instances of a parallel server. These hints are described in detail in Chapter 15, "Using Hints." Here is an example using the emp table:

```
SELECT /*+ FULL(emp) PARALLEL(emp, 4) */
Employee_name
FROM emp;
```

By adding the FULL and PARALLEL hints to this statement, the Oracle optimizer creates an execution plan that uses a full table scan. Furthermore, this table scan is executed with a parallel degree of four if the query servers are available. This statement overrides both the degree of parallelism that is specified in the table definition and the default Oracle initialization parameters.

The hint NOPARALLEL disables parallel scanning of a table and overrides the specified degree of parallelism. The NOPARALLEL hint has the following syntax:

```
NOPARALLEL ( alias_or_tablename )
```

Parallel Query Tuning

Parallel query operations can be effective on multiprocessor or parallel-processing computers; they can also be effective on uniprocessor systems where much of the time is spent waiting on I/O operations to complete. Systems with sufficient I/O bandwidth and especially systems with disk arrays benefit from parallel query operations.

If your system is typically processing at 100% of your CPU utilization and you have a small number of disk drives, you will probably not benefit from parallel query operations. If your system is extremely memory limited, you also will probably not benefit from parallel query operations.

The two areas that can be tuned for parallel queries are I/O and parallel servers. By properly configuring your data files, you can help parallel queries be more effective.

I/O Configuration

The function of a parallel query is to split up query operations so that they more effectively take advantage of the system. One of the ways that a parallel query does this is by allowing the processing of the query to continue while pieces of the query operation are stalled waiting on I/Os to complete. Parallel queries are not effective if the entire table is limited to one disk drive.

By striping the table across many drives, I/Os can be distributed and a higher level of parallelism can occur. Striping can be done with OS striping, with Oracle striping, or (better yet) with a hardware disk array.

Large contiguous extents can also help performance in parallel query operations. During scan operations, the query coordinator splits contiguous ranges of blocks into large, medium, and small groups of blocks. Each query server is given a large group of blocks with which to start, progressively working its way down to the small group of blocks until the scan is completed. This is done to try to balance the load by each query server. If a table has several large extents, the query coordinator can find blocks to dispatch to the query servers much more easily.

TUNING TEMP

Remember that your temporary tablespace should contain several large extents on a striped volume. This arrangement helps sorting performance.

Degree of Parallelism

Properly distributing I/Os and the degree of parallelism are the two most important things to tune in the Parallel Query option. Tuning the degree of parallelism is partially trial and error and partially analysis. It is important to take notes when you are experimenting with the degree of parallelism. Your first guess should be based on the following factors:

- The CPU capacity of your system. The number and capacity of CPUs has an effect on the number of query processes that you should run.

- The capacity of the system to handle large numbers of processes. Some OSes can handle many simultaneous threads; others are more limited.

- The system load. If the system is already running at 100% capacity, the degree of parallelism doesn't have much effect. If the system is running at 90%, too many query processes can overload the system.

- The amount of query processing on the system. If most operations are updates, but a few critical queries exist, you might want many query processes.

- The I/O capacity of the system. If your disks are striped or if you are using a disk array, you should be able to handle many parallel queries.

- The types of operations. Are you performing many full-table scans or sorts? These operations benefit greatly from parallel query servers.

These parameters should have some influence on the degree of parallelism you set up for your system. Remember that the preceding points are just guidelines to help with your best guess as a starting point. Following are a few other suggestions:

- CPU-intensive operations such as sorts should indicate a lower degree of parallelism. CPU-bound tasks are already taking advantage of the CPUs and tend not to wait on I/O.

- Disk-intensive operations such as full-table scans should indicate a higher degree of parallelism. The more operations that are waiting on I/O, the more the system can benefit from another query server.

- Many concurrent processes should indicate a lower degree of parallelism. Too many processes can overload the system.

SHOULD YOU PARALLELIZE THE SYSTEM?

When I am speaking of parallel query, I often have to make sure that I say parallelize rather than paralyze. After all, you don't want to paralyze the system. Sometimes, however, parallel operations can do just that.

I recently worked on a system that performed mainly OLTP-type operations, but also concurrently ran several reporting-type functions. These reporting functions took advantage of parallelism well. The result was that these reporting functions consumed all the system CPU time.

By disabling parallelism, the system behaved in a more polite manner, letting each job get a chance at the CPUs. Not all cases can benefit from parallelism.

After you determine your starting point, you can monitor your system by querying the dynamic performance table, V$PQ_SYSSTAT. You can do this with the following query:

```
SQL> select * from v$pq_sysstat;

STATISTIC                          VALUE
------------------------------- ----------
Servers Busy                          0
Servers Idle                         12
Servers Highwater                    16
Server Sessions                     380
Servers Started                       4
```

```
Servers Shutdown                       4
Servers Cleaned Up                     0
Queries Initiated                     21
DML Initiated                          9
DFO Trees                             77
Session active                        12
Local Msgs Sent                  2459361
Distr Msgs Sent                        0
Local Msgs Recv'd                2459318
Distr Msgs Recv'd                      0

15 rows selected.
```

When you look at the output from this query, the following statistics are quite useful:

Servers Busy	This is the number of servers that are busy at any one time. Check this statistic several times to get a good idea of the average value. If the value is equal to the initialization parameter, PARALLEL_MIN_SERVERS, you have probably configured too many query servers.
Servers Idle	This is the number of servers that are idle at any one time. If you always have many idle servers, consider reducing PARALLEL_MIN_SERVERS.
Servers Started	This is the number of query servers that have started up in this instance. If the value for Servers Busy is low but you see a large number of Servers that have Started, you might be using query servers sporadically.
Servers Shutdown	This is the number of query servers that have been shut down because they are idle. This value is most likely similar to the Servers Started value.

After you determine your degree of parallelism, begin testing; evaluate the information you get from V$PQ_SYSSTAT and from your operating system monitoring facilities. Keep an eye out for CPU usage and excessive waiting on I/O. If the CPU usage is too high, try reducing the degree of parallelism. If the CPU usage is too low and significant waiting on I/O occurs, try increasing the degree of parallelism.

Remember that the degree of parallelism is determined by SQL hints, table definitions, and initialization parameters. The total number of query servers is determined by the initialization parameter, PARALLEL_MAX_SERVERS; the number that is started up initially is determined by the initialization parameter, PARALLEL_MIN_SERVERS.

The total number of query servers in use is the number of queries executed in parallel multiplied by their degree of parallelism. If you try to use more than PARALLEL_MAX_SERVERS, you will not be able to parallelize your query.

Parallel Index Creation

Another feature of the Parallel Query option is its ability to create indexes in parallel. With the parallel index creation feature, the time it takes to create an index can be greatly reduced.

Similar to parallel query processing, a coordinator process dispatches two sets of query servers. One set of query servers scans the table to be indexed to obtain the ROWIDs and column values that are needed for the index. Another set of query servers performs the sorting on those values and passes off the results to the coordinator process. The coordinator process then puts together the B*-Tree index from these sorted items.

When creating an index, the degree of parallelism follows the same precedence as it does in parallel query processing. The first value used is an optional PARALLEL clause in the CREATE INDEX statement, followed by the table definition, and finally the initialization parameters.

SPEEDING UP INDEX CREATIONS

You can speed up the creation of indexes in several ways. Those of you who have created indexes on large tables know how long the index creation process can take. The use of parallel index creation helps speed up the index creation process, but the NOLOGGING option can also enhance performance of this process. Using the NOLOGGING option, the index creation steps are not logged to the redo log files. In the event of a system failure, all of the work is lost; however, in the event that indexes are frequently rebuilt, this might not be a problem.

Databases that are reloaded every night often require the indexes to be dropped before the load and re-created afterwards. In this type of environment, the NOLOGGING option in conjunction with the parallel index creation might be ideal.

Creating an index in parallel can be several times faster than creating an index by normal means. The same conditions apply for index creation as were given for parallel query processing. A system that has been configured to take advantage of parallel query processing will also see good performance from parallel index creation.

Parallel Loading

Loading can be done in parallel by having multiple concurrent sessions perform a direct path load into the same table. Depending on the configuration of the system, you can see excellent load performance by loading in parallel. Because loading is both CPU and I/O intensive, in an SMP or MPP environment with a high bandwidth I/O subsystem, you should see positive results.

Parallel loads are performed by multiple direct loader processes, each using the PARALLEL=TRUE and DIRECT=TRUE options. When you specify PARALLEL=TRUE, the loader does not place an exclusive lock on the table that is being loaded as it would otherwise.

During the parallel load, the loader creates temporary segments for each of the concurrent processes and merges them on completion.

Although parallel loading performs best when each temporary file is located on a separate disk, the increased performance of the load does not usually justify the complexity of the manual striping needed to do this. It is recommended that you stripe the tables on an OS level or preferably on a hardware disk array. You can improve performance by putting each of the input files on a separate volume to take advantage of the sequential nature of the reads.

Parallel loading can be beneficial, especially if load time is critical in your environment. By putting each of the input files on separate disk volumes, you can increase performance. Overall, the general tuning principles used in parallel query processing are also valid in parallel loading.

Parallel Recovery

Parallel recovery is a great feature of the Parallel Query option. When benchmarking Oracle and testing hardware and software, it is often necessary to intentionally crash the system to prove recoverability. With the Parallel Recovery option, the time it takes to perform and instance recovery can be dramatically reduced.

Recovery time is significantly reduced when the system that is being recovered has many disks and supports asynchronous I/O. For a small system that has few drives or for an operating system that does not support asynchronous I/O, it might not be wise to enable parallel recovery.

In traditional recovery, one process both reads from the redo log files and applies changes to the data files. This operation can take a significant amount of time because the recovery process must wait for disk I/Os to complete.

With the Parallel Recovery option, one process is responsible for reading and dispatching redo entries from the redo log files and passing those entries on to the recovery processes that apply the changes to the data files.

Because the dispatcher process reads from the redo log files sequentially, the I/O performance is much higher than that of the recovery processes that are writing random data throughout the data files. Because writing the data is seek intensive, it is a good idea to have one or two recovery processes for each data disk in the system.

By having more recovery processes, you can have more outstanding I/Os and use all the data drives simultaneously. Because recovery is done at instance startup, this arrangement reduces dead time when no other database processing can be done.

The number of concurrent recovery processes is set with the initialization parameter RECOVERY_PARALLELISM. The value of this parameter cannot exceed the value that is specified in the initialization parameter PARALLEL_MAX_SERVERS.

By specifying a sufficient number of recovery servers, you will see an immediate improvement in instance recovery time. Do not use parallel recovery if your system does not support asynchronous I/O or if you are limited to a small number of disk drives. If your I/O subsystem is high bandwidth and your data is properly striped (either through software or hardware), you should notice improvement.

In summary, the Parallel Query option is useful in distributing processing loads so that CPUs are kept busy processing while other processes are waiting for I/Os to complete. With multiprocessor machines, the Parallel Query option can be quite beneficial; this is not to say that the option is not beneficial on uniprocessor machines as well.

STRENGTH IN NUMBERS

Probably the biggest performance problem I have come across is a lack of disk drives, or disk spindles. As larger disks are produced at lower prices, many installations end up with I/O problems caused by a lack of disk drives, even though they have enough storage space. As drives double in size, each drive will be responsible for searching though twice the data to find what you need if the drive is always packed with data. The Parallel Query option can help only in systems where I/O is not a bottleneck. When I/O is not a problem, you will see significant gains from parallel queries.

If you have processes waiting for queries to complete and a sufficient number of disk drives, you will see an improvement with parallel queries, regardless of whether you are on a multiprocessor or uniprocessor system. Many smaller disks typically outperform fewer larger disks.

Clusters

A *cluster*, sometimes called an *index cluster*, is an optional method of storing tables in an Oracle database. Within a cluster, multiple related tables are stored together to improve access time to the related items. Clusters are useful only when the related data is often accessed together. The existence of a cluster is transparent to users and to applications; the cluster affects only how data is stored.

Using clusters can be advantageous in certain situations and disadvantageous in others. Be careful when determining whether a cluster can help performance in your configuration. Typically, clusters are advantageous if the related data that is clustered is primarily used in joins.

If you have two tables with related data that are frequently accessed together, using clusters can improve performance by preloading the related data into the SGA. Because you frequently use the data together, having that data already in the SGA greatly reduces access time.

Clusters are beneficial in joins, where the join occurs on the cluster data because the data is all retrieved in one I/O operation. Following is an example of where a cluster would be beneficial.

Suppose that you are keeping a sales database. To reduce the amount of duplicate data in the database, you have created two tables. The first is a salesperson table. This table has the following columns:

ID

Name

RegionID

In addition, you have a table that keeps information on the region. The region table keeps the following information:

RegionID

RegionName

RegionManager

The only reason that the region table has been created is as a lookup so that the region name is not duplicated throughout the salesperson table. This way, if the RegionManager changes, you don't have to make major updates in the salesperson table. This is shown in Figure 4.6.

Salesperson Table

ID	Name	Region ID
1	Smith	1
2	Jones	2
3	Todd	3
4	Garcia	1
5	Burns	2
6	Whalen	4
7	Wilson	1

Region Table

Region ID	Region Name	Region Manager
1	North	Ford
2	Northwest	Carter
3	Northeast	Simms
4	East	Able

FIGURE 4.6
The salesperson and region tables.

Furthermore, all accesses to the salesperson table are via a join on the region table in a query like this:

```
SELECT Name, RegionName, RegionManager
FROM salesperson, Region
WHERE salesperson.RegionID = Region.RegionID
```

This is a perfect example of when a cluster would be beneficial. These two tables should be clustered on the RegionID columns. The common column(s) of the cluster is called the *cluster key*, and it must be indexed.

Figure 4.7 shows what the table looks like as a cluster. Note that the cluster key is the RegionID.

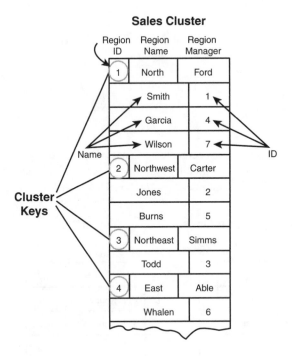

FIGURE 4.7
The salesperson and region tables as a cluster.

If this information is frequently used together, this cluster arrangement is a performance win. The cluster has the ease of use of individual tables but the additional performance of the cluster.

If you do not typically use information together, then using a cluster won't benefit performance. A slight disadvantage actually exists because additional SGA space is taken up by the extra table information.

An additional disadvantage of clusters is a reduction of the performance of INSERT statements. This performance loss is caused by the further complexity of the use of space and the fact that multiple tables are in the same block. The clustered table also spans more blocks than the individual tables, which causes more data to be scanned.

In summary, a cluster can be useful for tables in which data is primarily accessed together in a join. The reduced I/O that is needed to bring the additional data into the SGA and the fact that the data is already cached can be a definite advantage.

If the tables have a large number of INSERT statements or if the data is not frequently accessed together, a cluster is not useful and should not be used.

Do not cluster tables if full-table scans are often performed on only one of the tables in the cluster. The additional space that is required by the cluster and the additional I/O reduce performance.

Hash Clusters

A hash cluster is similar to a cluster, but it uses a hash function rather than an index to reference the cluster key. A hash cluster stores the data based on the result of a hash function. The hash function is a numeric function that determines the data block in the cluster based on the value of the cluster key.

To find the data block in an index cluster, one or more I/Os to the cluster index must exist. In a hash cluster, the cluster key tells Oracle where the data block is, an arrangement that can reduce to one the number of I/Os that is needed to retrieve the row.

In contrast to the index cluster, which stores related data together based on the row's cluster key value, the hash cluster stores related rows together based on their hash values.

The number of hash values is determined by the HASHKEYS value parameter of the CREATE CLUSTER command. The number and size of the cluster keys are important and should be carefully calculated.

Do not use hash clusters on tables where table scans are often performed on only one of the tables in the cluster. The additional space that the cluster requires and the additional I/O can reduce performance.

Do not use a hash cluster on a table in which the application frequently modifies the cluster key or when the table is constantly being modified. Because the cluster key is based on a calculation, significant overhead is involved in constantly recalculating the key.

When to Hash

Although hash clusters can be used in a similar fashion to index clusters, you do not have to cluster the tables. In fact, it is frequently useful to create a single table as a hash cluster to take advantage of the hashing feature. By using hashing, you might be able to retrieve your data with only one I/O rather than the multiple I/Os required to retrieve data using a B*-Tree index.

Because hashing uses the value of the data to calculate the data block in which the desired data is located, hashing is best used on tables that have unique values for the cluster key and where the majority of queries are equality queries on the cluster key. For equality queries, the data is usually retrieved in one read operation; the cluster key does not have to be a single column. If the typical query uses an equality on a set of columns, use these columns to create a composite key.

Hashing is also most optimal when the table or tables are fairly static in size. If the table stays within its initial storage allocation, hashing usually does not cause performance degradation. However, if the table grows out of its initial allocation, performance can degrade because overflow blocks are required.

Hashing might degrade the performance of table scans because the hashing process reads blocks that might not have much data in them. Because the table is originally created by laying out the data into the cluster based on the value of the cluster key, some blocks might have few rows.

Hashing can also degrade performance when the value of the cluster key changes. Because the location of the block in which the data resides is based on the cluster key value, a change in that value can cause the row to migrate to maintain the cluster.

A good candidate for hashing has the following properties:

- The cluster key value is unique.

- The majority of queries are equality queries on the cluster key.

- The size of the table is static; little growth occurs.

- The value of the cluster key does not change.

An example of a good hashing candidate is a table used for storing parts information. By using a hash cluster keyed on the part number, access can be extremely efficient and fast. Any time you have a somewhat static table with a unique column value or set of column values, consider creating a hash cluster.

Just as with index clusters, using hash clusters has both advantages and disadvantages. Hash clusters are efficient in retrieving data based on equality queries on the cluster key. If you are not retrieving data based on that key, the query is not hashed. As with the index cluster, you see a performance decrease when executing INSERT statements in a hashed table.

With both index clusters and hash clusters, make a careful determination about whether a cluster can help performance based on the access patterns on the tables. As with many aspects of RDBMS, tuning based on a wrong decision can end up costing performance.

If you can take advantage of hashing by meeting somewhat strict criteria, you can see good performance. Hashing is extremely efficient if you can meet the criteria described previously.

Multiblock Reads

When performing table scans, Oracle has the ability to read more than one block at a time, thus speeding up I/O. By reading more than one block at a time, Oracle reads a larger block from the disk and eliminates some disk seeks. By reducing disk seeks and reading larger blocks, both I/O and CPU overhead are reduced.

This feature is called *multiblock reads*. Multiblock reads are beneficial but take advantage of only contiguous blocks. Blocks in an extent are always contiguous. If your data is in many small extents, the effect of multiblock reads is reduced.

The Oracle initialization parameter, DB_FILE_MULTIBLOCK_READ_COUNT, specifies the amount of data that is read in a multiblock read. The value for this parameter should always be set high because rarely does a disadvantage result from doing so. The size of the I/Os depends on both DB_FILE_MULTIBLOCK_READ_COUNT and DB_BLOCK_SIZE.

To take advantage of multiblock reads, try to configure your system so that the database blocks are as contiguous as possible. To do this, try to create your database with optimally sized extents. The extent size should be significantly larger than the size of the multiblock reads.

Creating these extents might not be a straightforward process, however. By creating extents too large, Oracle might have a difficult time finding enough contiguous space to create these extents. On the other hand, creating extents that are too small not only adversely affects multiblock reads, but also causes more dynamic extensions. Knowing what your initial data and growth patterns will be might help in sizing your extents.

Partitioning

Partitioning is a feature that Oracle added in Oracle8. Partitioning is designed to allow large tables or indexes to be broken down into smaller, more manageable pieces, or *partitions*. Because these partitions are smaller, they can be accessed more quickly and more efficiently, yet presence of the partitions is transparent to the user. You can think of partitions as dividing table or index data into several smaller tables or indexes. These smaller tables or indexes can be accessed individually, in groups, or as a whole.

Partitions are created on specific keys, similar to indexes. The key column or columns are used to partition data into the proper partition. Each partition is its own Oracle segment. The sum of these segments makes up the table or index.

Partitions can be created using several different partitioning schemes. These schemes are used to determine how the data is divided into the partitions. These schemes are as follows:

Range Partitioning	Range partitioning takes table data and divides it based on ranges of data such as month, year, and so on.
List Partitioning	List partitioning is similar to Range Partitioning except that specific values are used rather than ranges of values.

| Hash Partitioning | Hash partitioning uses a hash function to automatically partition the data. |
| Sub-Partitioning | Also known as composite partitioning, sub-partitioning allows you to use multiple partitioning schemes simultaneously. |

In the next few sections, you will learn which partitioning scheme is right for you.

Partitioning Concepts

Partitioning is designed for large tables where it is impossible to effectively index the data. This ineffectiveness of indexes is primarily due to the use of aggregates in that data. In cases where reports are being run on large amounts of data, where some data reducing predicates are in the WHERE clause, yet indexes are not effective due to the large amount of data retrieved, partitioning can be quite effective.

Think of the case where aggregation of data is done on data but only for the last month's worth of data at a time. For example:

```
SELECT region, sales_person, SUM(sales)
FROM sales_data
GROUP BY region, sales_person
WHERE date >= TO_DATE('2001-01-01', 'YYYY-MM-DD')
AND date < TO_DATE('2001-02-01', 'YYYY-MM-DD');
```

Here you are selecting all of the sales data from January 2001. Indexes would be ineffective on the date field, because so many values will be selected because of the number of sales in January. Therefore, a table scan will be done on the sales_data table, as shown in Figure 4.8.

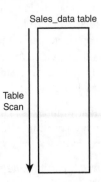

FIGURE 4.8
A table scan on the sales_data table.

By partitioning the table by months, the same table scan will still occur, but the Oracle optimizer will detect that the table is partitioned and that the query contains the partitioning key in the WHERE clause. Thus, the same table scan will occur, but only on the necessary partition, as shown in Figure 4.9.

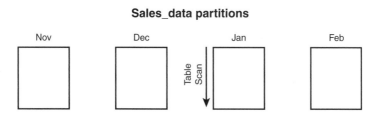

FIGURE 4.9
A partition scan on the sales_data January partition.

Thus, the amount of data that has been read from memory, the CPU processing of that data and the I/Os have all been reduced. This improves performance as well as conserves system resources. The Oracle optimizer accomplishes all this automatically.

The example given here uses Range Partitioning. In the next section, Range Partitioning is covered, and following that, the other partitioning types are covered.

Range Partitioning

Range partitioning allows data to be partitioned into ranges of values (hence the name "range partitioning"). When creating a partitioned table using range partitioning, the table is defined as well as the partitions in the following manner:

```
CREATE TABLE rangetable (
id1 number,
id2 number,
name1 varchar2(40),
name2 varchar2(40),
name3 varchar2(40) )
PARTITION BY RANGE ( id1 )
    ( PARTITION part1 VALUES LESS THAN (2501)
      TABLESPACE rangets1,
    PARTITION part2 VALUES LESS THAN (5001)
      TABLESPACE rangets2,
    PARTITION part3 VALUES LESS THAN (7501)
      TABLESPACE rangets3,
    PARTITION part4 VALUES LESS THAN (MAXVALUE)
      TABLESPACE rangets4);
```

As with the example shown previously, it is quite common to partition by date, as shown here:

```
CREATE TABLE sales_data
(region  VARCHAR2(10),
sales_person INT,
sales_amount NUMBER(10)
sales_date    DATE)
PARTITION BY RANGE(sales_date)
(
PARTITION jan2001 VALUES LESS THAN(TO_DATE('02/01/2001','DD/MM/YYYY')),
PARTITION feb2001 VALUES LESS THAN(TO_DATE('03/01/2001','DD/MM/YYYY')),
PARTITION mar2001 VALUES LESS THAN(TO_DATE('04/01/2001','DD/MM/YYYY')),
PARTITION apr2001 VALUES LESS THAN(TO_DATE('05/01/2001','DD/MM/YYYY')),
PARTITION may2001 VALUES LESS THAN(TO_DATE('06/01/2001','DD/MM/YYYY')),
PARTITION jun2001 VALUES LESS THAN(TO_DATE('07/01/2001','DD/MM/YYYY')),
PARTITION jul2001 VALUES LESS THAN(TO_DATE('08/01/2001','DD/MM/YYYY')),
PARTITION aug2001 VALUES LESS THAN(TO_DATE('09/01/2001','DD/MM/YYYY')),
PARTITION sep2001 VALUES LESS THAN(TO_DATE('10/01/2001','DD/MM/YYYY')),
PARTITION oct2001 VALUES LESS THAN(TO_DATE('11/01/2001','DD/MM/YYYY')),
PARTITION nov2001 VALUES LESS THAN(TO_DATE('12/01/2001','DD/MM/YYYY')),
PARTITION dec2001 VALUES LESS THAN(TO_DATE('01/01/2002','DD/MM/YYYY')),
PARTITION maxval VALUES LESS THAN(MAXVALUE)
);
```

In this case, each month has its own partition. Data that is inserted into the sales_data table is automatically routed to the correct partition.

PARTITIONING WITH THE MAXVALUE RANGE

It is always a good idea to include the MAXVALUE range. If you do not and a value exceeds the values that are assigned to the partitions, the INSERT or UPDATE statement fails.

List Partitioning

List partitioning is similar to range partitioning except that a list is used rather than a range of values. This list contains distinct values that are used to route data to the proper partition. An example of a list partition is shown here:

```
CREATE TABLE sales_data
(region  VARCHAR2(10),
sales_person INT,
sales_amount NUMBER(10)
sales_date    DATE)
```

```
PARTITION BY LIST(region)
(
PARTITION office1 VALUES IN (1, 2, 3, 4),
PARTITION office2 VALUES IN (5, 6),
PARTITION office3 VALUES IN (7, 8, 9, 10)
);
```

With list partitions, you cannot specify a MAXVAL, so be careful that all of the possible values are contained in the list.

Hash Partitioning

Hash partitions use a hashing function to decide in which partition to store data. This type of partition is good for tables, where it is unclear how to properly partition the data, but where you feel that partitioning might be useful. For example, take the sales_data table example that was used earlier.

If a large amount of data in that table is accessed by the sales_person column, but it is unclear of the distribution of the salespersons, you could create a hash cluster on it. Queries that use the sales_person column in the WHERE clause would benefit from a hash partition. Hash partitions are good here because you might not know the distribution of the data. Many rows could contain the same sales_person identifier and dilute any possible uniqueness.

A hash partition can be created with the following syntax:

```
CREATE TABLE sales_data
(region  VARCHAR2(10),
sales_person INT,
sales_amount NUMBER(10)
sales_date    DATE)
PARTITION BY HASH(sales_person)
PARTITIONS = 4
STORE IN ( sp1, sp2, sp3, sp4 );
```

Here the hash function will break the sales_data table into four partitions.

Composite Partitioning

A composite partition is one in which two different types of partitioning are used. For example, you can range partition by date, and within each region, you can use hash partitioning. This is good for extremely large tables where one partitioning method does not sufficiently reduce the amount of data that is accessed. An example of a composite partition is shown here:

```
CREATE TABLE sales_data
(region  VARCHAR2(10),
sales_person INT,
sales_amount NUMBER(10)
sales_date    DATE)
PARTITION BY RANGE(sales_date)
SUBPARTITION BY HASH(sales_person)
SUBPARTITIONS=4
(
PARTITION jan2001 VALUES LESS THAN(TO_DATE('02/01/2001','DD/MM/YYYY'))
(
    SUBPARTITION jan2001_a TABLESPACE ts1,
    SUBPARTITION jan2001_b TABLESPACE ts2,
    SUBPARTITION jan2001_c TABLESPACE ts3,
    SUBPARTITION jan2001_d TABLESPACE ts4
),
PARTITION feb2001 VALUES LESS THAN(TO_DATE('03/01/2001','DD/MM/YYYY'))
(
    SUBPARTITION feb2001_a TABLESPACE ts1,
    SUBPARTITION feb2001_b TABLESPACE ts2,
    SUBPARTITION feb2001_c TABLESPACE ts3,
    SUBPARTITION feb2001_d TABLESPACE ts4
),
    .
    .
    .
PARTITION dec2001 VALUES LESS THAN(TO_DATE('01/01/2002','DD/MM/YYYY'))
(
    SUBPARTITION dec2001_a TABLESPACE ts1,
    SUBPARTITION dec2001_b TABLESPACE ts2,
    SUBPARTITION dec2001_c TABLESPACE ts3,
    SUBPARTITION dec2001_d TABLESPACE ts4
),
PARTITION maxval VALUES LESS THAN(MAXVALUE)
);
```

This creates a partitioned table using a combination of range and hash partitioning. Depending on your data and how that data is accessed, the performance increase can be dramatic.

PARTITIONING BENEFITS

My first experience with Oracle partitioning was when range partitioning was first introduced. I was working for a computer company in a group that ran database benchmarks. When we first started running benchmarks with partitioning, we saw dramatic increases in performance. Some queries performed as much as 10 times faster.

You might not see this type of performance increase, but in those cases where partitioning does benefit you, the results are dramatic.

Benefits of Partitioning

Partitioning offers several benefits:

- The I/O operations and CPU usage can be reduced during large table scans that can be partitioned.

- You have the ability to load data at the partition level, rather than at the table level.

- You have the ability to prune data by dropping a partition, rather than having to perform large deletes using SELECT statements.

- Partitioning is completely transparent to the users and to the application.

- Data can be maintained at the partition level, rather than at the table level.

These benefits can increase performance dramatically in many situations; however, your data and your application must be suitable for partitioning.

Partitioning and Indexes

Several different options are available for Oracle indexes using partitioning. The indexes can be partitioned or not, depending on your preference. Indexes are partitioned in the same way that tables are partitioned. Some of the many different options for partitioning indexes include these:

- You can create a non-partitioned index on a partitioned table. This is called a global non-partitioned index.

- You can partition an index on a partitioned table or on a non-partitioned table. The partitioning key need not be the same as the partitioning key that was used on the table.

- You can create a partitioned index on a partitioned table using a different partitioning key. This is known as a global partitioned index.

- You can create a different index on each partition individually. This is called a local partitioned index.

As with the partitioned table, the idea of a partitioned index is to reduce the amount of data that is being retrieved. A common case would be to create an index on sales_person, yet partition by ranges of dates. For large tables, the partitioning reduces the size of the index that is traversed by the query. Of course, for this to work effectively, both keys must be referenced in the WHERE clause.

Plan Stability

Plan stability is a new feature in which execution plans that the Oracle optimizer has generated can be stored for future use. The idea of saving execution plans and even allowing them to be edited is a great idea. This will keep the system executing in a stable manner in the event that external factors change, such as statistics and even the version of the Oracle Optimizer.

Plan stability can be quite useful when system changes degrade query performance due to new plans. The optimizer is very good, though, and most decisions that the optimizer makes are for the best. Thus, plan stability might not provide the best performance in all cases.

Multithreaded Server

The user connection into the Oracle instance can occur either via a dedicated server process or a multithreaded server (MTS) process. In either case, to the end user they appear and act identically under most conditions. Because each dedicated server process takes a significant amount of memory and system resources, it is often necessary to use the Oracle MTS feature to multiplex those connections.

Sometimes it is necessary to connect via the dedicated server process, such as in the following cases:

- To start up and shut down
- To perform media recovery
- To run a batch job

Under these conditions, the system performs better by using a dedicated server process. The method for forcing a dedicated server process is described next.

Dedicated Server

When a SQL request from a user is sent to the RDBMS, it is not that process, but rather the server process, that executes that command. This mechanism protects Oracle from being directly manipulated by a user process, which increases the stability and robustness of the Oracle9 RDBMS. A diagram of the dedicated server process is shown in Figure 4.10.

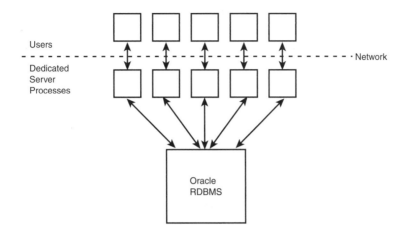

FIGURE 4.10
Dedicated server.

With a dedicated server process, a one-to-one correlation exists between the user process and the server process. Each server process is dedicated to one user process. To request a dedicated server process when the system is running with the multithreaded server enabled, include the parameter "SERVER=DEDICATED" in the connect string. This creates a dedicated server process for that user process.

Multithreaded Server

The multithreaded server allows many user processes to share a number of shared server processes. This is diagramed in Figure 4.11.

As you can see, all requests to the shared server processes must go through the dispatcher process, which in turn, queues the request in the large pool in the SGA. After the request has been processed, it is returned to the dispatcher through the large pool in the SGA.

CAUTION

Because the multithreaded server uses the shared pool for queueing requests and returning data, it is important that the large pool is large enough.

The main advantage of using the multithreaded server is the reduction of server processes, which can greatly reduce CPU usage as well as memory usage. As you might guess, however, the multithreaded server does add additional overhead to the system. This is why a dedicated server process is recommended for long-running batch jobs.

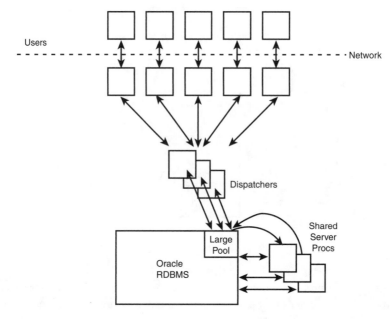

FIGURE 4.11
Multithreaded server.

Tuning the Multithreaded Server

To configure the multithreaded server for use and to tune it, you need to tune the following parameters in your parameter file. You should also monitor the large pool carefully to make sure that you are not running out of space.

Try monitoring the shared session memory with a small number of users. This can tell you how much memory they are using. You can then interpolate how much memory all of the sessions will take. This can be accomplished by using the following SQL statement:

```
SELECT SUM(value) || 'bytes' "Memory"
FROM v$sesstat, v$statname
WHERE name = 'session memory'
AND v$sesstat.statistic# = v$statname.statistic#;
```

This tells you how much memory you are using. By dividing out by the number of connections, you can determine the amount of memory per session. You can then tell from this how much memory you will need in the large pool for all the sessions that you will be supporting.

If you think that the large pool size might be too low, you can increase it by tuning the parameter "LARGE_POOL_SIZE." Remember, the large pool is also used for parallel query execution.

The number of dispatchers per protocol is determined by the initialization parameter "MTS_DISPATCHERS." By increasing this number, each session will potentially see greater performance because it will not have to wait on a dispatcher to become available. Following is an example of how you would set five dispatcher processes for the TCP/IP protocol:

```
MTS_DISPATCHERS = "TCP, 5"
```

Each network protocol is set separately. For protocols with fewer users, set the number lower. The more concurrent sessions per dispatcher, the greater the possibility that you will have to wait for a dispatcher when you need one.

Other parameters that are related to the multithreaded server include the following:

MTS_MAX_DISPATCHERS	The maximum number of dispatcher processes that can be created in the instance. This includes all protocols combined.
MTS_SERVERS	The initial number of shared server processes. If this value is set to 0, Oracle will not use shared server processes. The number of shared server processes will increase dynamically to meet the needs of the system.
MTS_MAX_SERVERS	This value specifies the maximum number of shared server processes.

The number of dispatcher processes and the minimum number of shared server processes can be changed dynamically with the ALTER SYSTEM parameter.

Summary

This chapter discussed many concepts and ideas that you can use to further enhance performance. This chapter looked at more specific topics that might or might not apply, depending on your configuration. In fact, some of the things described in this chapter can hurt performance if they are not handled correctly.

Clusters and indexes are useful when the application can take advantage of them. In update-intensive applications in which indexes are used, these indexes can degrade performance because the indexes must be updated along with the data. Similarly, clusters can be beneficial if the data-access patterns use the cluster; otherwise, they can be a burden.

The Oracle Parallel Query option and the Parallel Server option can offer significant performance benefits. The Parallel Query option provides a mechanism to improve system utilization by splitting queries into multiple processes. The Parallel Server option provides a robust scaleable clustering option that can increase performance and provide instantaneous failover capabilities. Your applications and needs will determine whether these options can benefit you.

When tuning a system, it is important to remember the risks you are taking. The previous chapter discussed different tuning topics such as shared pool size and database block buffer size. Increasing the size of the shared pool and block buffers can increase cache hits; it also has little risk of hurting performance. However, some of the topics addressed in this chapter might hurt performance if they are not configured correctly. You must assess the risks involved whenever you reconfigure, especially if this reconfiguration is going into production without intensive testing.

If you think about what you are changing and what those changes will affect and if you understand the data-access patterns of your applications, you will minimize the risks. Think about how the changes you are making will affect the system. Try to understand how your applications will react. By doing so, you will minimize risks and optimize results.

TUNING WORKLOADS

One method of improving the performance of a system is to tune the workloads. You can do this by modifying the attributes of the work that is being processed on your Oracle system to improve the performance of all work or specific work. You can accomplish workload tuning in several different ways, including the following:

- Using resource groups and resource management

- Using profiles to limit users

- Using distributed systems to distribute the workload

This is not an exclusive list; you might come up with innovative solutions of your own to manage workloads.

The method you use to manage workloads really depends on what your primary goal is. You might have several goals in performing this type of tuning:

- Optimizing performance for all applications and users

- Optimizing performance for a single user or a single set of users

- Optimizing performance for a certain task or type of task

- Your own goal for optimization

This chapter examines ways of tuning your system by managing the workload.

Parameters Used in This Chapter

This chapter includes the use of many Oracle initialization parameters. Chapter 2, "Using the Oracle Configuration Parameters," introduced you to these parameters and explained how to use them. This chapter covers the following initialization parameters:

- RESOURCE_LIMIT. RESOURCE_LIMIT determines whether resource limits are enforced in database profiles.

- RESOURCE_MANAGER_PLAN. RESOURCE_MANAGER_PLAN specifies the top-level resource plan to use for an instance. The resource manager loads this top-level plan along with all its descendants (sub plans, directives, and consumer groups).

Using Resource Consumer Groups

In Oracle, it is possible to use resource consumer groups to allocate resources based on the group to which you have been assigned. This allows you to give groups of users and subgroups various allocations of resources. In Oracle9i, the resource manager functionality has been vastly improved for performance, and it allows for much finer control of resource consumer groups.

Resource consumer groups provide a flexible, configurable system that provides features to tune your system with fine granularity. Using resource consumer groups provides some of the following abilities:

- Allocate minimal amounts of CPU time to certain processes or groups of processes.

- Limit the degree of parallelism based on who the user or group is.

- Regulate long-running processes so that they do not exceed preset limits.

Much flexibility is available to allow you to regulate work within the Oracle9i RDBMS. This section begins with an overview of resource consumer groups, followed by specifics on how to configure them, and concluding with examples of how they can be used.

Overview of Resource Consumer Groups

The basic principle of resource consumer groups is the ability to classify different types of users. These different types of users can then be given limits of resources that can be used. This differs from the ability to put resource limitations on individual jobs in that an entire class of jobs can be limited. This does not preclude you from placing limitations on individual jobs; in fact, both can be done.

With these limitations, certain tasks such as reporting functions, batch jobs, and other resource-intensive tasks can run concurrently with more latency-sensitive tasks, yet their impact can be limited. This can be used both to satisfy OLTP users as well as reporting users.

The way in which this can help you will be determined by your own needs and system configuration. Later in this section, you will see some examples of how resource consumer groups can help.

Configuring Resource Consumer Groups

DBMS_RESOURCE_MANAGER and DBMS_RESOURCE_MANAGER_PRIVS packages manage resource consumer groups. In addition, setting the initialization parameter RESOURCE_MANAGER_PLAN enables the resource manager plans. Together, they enable resource consumer groups.

The first step in enabling resource consumer groups is to create a resource manager plan, and then set the system to use that plan. The plans define the different groups and the resource limitations that those groups are allowed to use.

Each user or group of users is assigned to a group, and this group is then managed via the plan. An example of this is shown in Figure 5.1. This figure illustrates how the CPU resources can be allocated among four different groups, each of which is allocated a certain percentage of the CPU time.

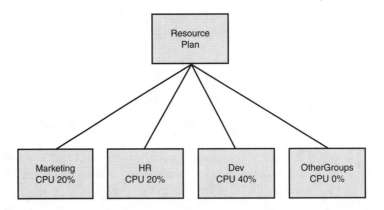

FIGURE 5.1
Resources divided among four groups.

Within each group, you can specify the following resources:

- Degree of parallelism

- Number of active sessions

- Percentage of CPU

- Maximum execution time

- Undo pool

The steps involved in configuring resource consumer groups are to create the plan, modify the plan, and assign users to the groups.

Creating the Plan

The first step in creating a plan involves creating a pending area. The pending area is like a scratch space Oracle uses to store and validate the plan before it's finally implemented. It is created with the following command:

```
EXEC DBMS_RESOURCE_MANAGER.CREATE_PENDING_AREA;
```

The plan is created with the CREATE_PLAN stored procedure within the DBMS_RESOURCE_MANAGER package as follows:

```
EXEC DBMS_RESOURCE_MANAGER.CREATE_PLAN(PLAN => 'sample_plan',
    COMMENT => 'Sample Plan');
```

This creates a plan with the name sample_plan. Before you can put this plan into effect, you must configure the rules and groups.

Allocating the Consumer Groups

The groups are created within the DBMS_RESOURCE_MANAGER package using the CREATE_GROUP stored procedure as follows:

```
EXEC DBMS_RESOURCE_MANAGER.CREATE_CONSUMER_GROUP (CONSUMER_GROUP => 'sales',
    COMMENT => 'sample sales group');
```

As before, this procedure simply creates the group. You must then populate the group before it can be used.

Setting the Directives

You then set directives to determine the rules for how the plan operates. You can include directives for CPU resources, degree of parallelism, maximum execution time, and so on. An example of setting directives is shown here:

```
EXEC DBMS_RESOURCE_MANAGER.CREATE_PLAN_DIRECTIVE (PLAN => 'sample_plan',
        GROUP_OR_SUBPLAN => 'sales', COMMENT => 'sample sales group',
        CPU_P1 => 40, PARALLEL_DEGREE_LIMIT_P1 => 4,
        MAX_EST_EXEC_TIME => 3600, UNDO_POOL => sales_undo);
```

Of course, having a directive for only one group doesn't make much sense; therefore, it is necessary to add other groups to the plan. In addition to adding groups to a plan, you can add a subplan as well. Simply use the same statement, but use the name of another plan instead of the group name.

To create a plan as shown in Figure 5.1, you can add the other groups, as shown here:

```
EXEC DBMS_RESOURCE_MANAGER.CREATE_PLAN_DIRECTIVE (PLAN => 'sample_plan',
        GROUP_OR_SUBPLAN => 'marketing', COMMENT => 'sample marketing group',
        CPU_P1 => 20, PARALLEL_DEGREE_LIMIT_P1 => 2,
        MAX_EST_EXEC_TIME => 1800, UNDO_POOL => marketing_undo);

EXEC DBMS_RESOURCE_MANAGER.CREATE_PLAN_DIRECTIVE (PLAN => 'sample_plan',
        GROUP_OR_SUBPLAN => 'hr', COMMENT => 'sample HR group',
        CPU_P1 => 20, PARALLEL_DEGREE_LIMIT_P1 => 2,
        MAX_EST_EXEC_TIME => 1800, UNDO_POOL => hr_undo);

EXEC DBMS_RESOURCE_MANAGER.CREATE_PLAN_DIRECTIVE (PLAN => 'sample_plan',
        GROUP_OR_SUBPLAN => 'OTHER_GROUPS', COMMENT => 'required group',
        CPU_P1 => 0, PARALLEL_DEGREE_LIMIT_P1 => 2,
        MAX_EST_EXEC_TIME => 1800, UNDO_POOL => other_undo);
```

This plan allows for four different groups with the allocation of resources shown in Figure 5.2.

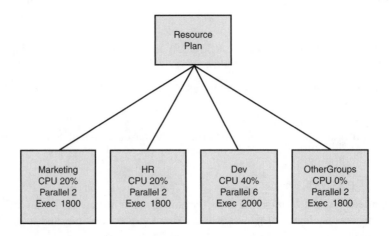

FIGURE 5.2
Resources divided among four groups with more details.

As mentioned earlier, the plan that you want to run is enabled in the Oracle initialization file. Because the initialization file is only read at startup time, you can initialize the resource plan immediately by issuing an ALTER SYSTEM statement. This immediately puts the resource plan into effect, as shown here:

```
ALTER SYSTEM SET RESOURCE _MANAGER_PLAN = sample_plan;
```

If you decide that you want to disable the resource manager all together, you can do this with the ALTER SYSTEM statement as well, by specifying a NULL plan name as shown here:

```
ALTER SYSTEM SET RESOURCE_MANAGER_PLAN = '';
```

This disables the resource manager and puts Oracle back to normal scheduling.

Subplans can be created and assigned to plans using the same statements that were shown earlier. A subplan is created in the same manner as a plan, but when allocating resources, allocate them to the plan instead of a group. Then the group is responsible for allocating its resources within the group. As you might imagine, resource plans can become quite complicated. An example of a plan with subplans is shown in Figure 5.3.

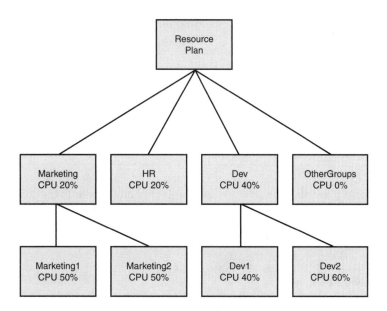

FIGURE 5.3
A resource plan with subplans.

The resource commerce groups can be quite useful under the right circumstances; however, as with any advanced feature, your mileage might vary. Beware of side effects as well.

Adding Users to the Plan

You can add a user to a consumer group by first granting him permission to set his default consumer group and then by setting it. By setting the initial consumer group, all new sessions that the user creates will go into that group. An example of setting the user named scott into the sales group is shown here:

```
EXEC DBMS_RESOURCE_MANAGER_PRIVS.GRANT_SWITCH_CONSUMER_GROUP -
        ('scott', 'sales', TRUE);
EXEC DBMS_RESOURCE_MANAGER.SET_INITIAL_CONSUMER_GROUP('scott', 'sales');
```

As an alternative, you can move an active session immediately by using the SWITCH_ CONSUMER_GROUP_FOR_SESS command. Here, you must provide the session ID (SID) and the session serial number for the session that you want to switch:

```
EXEC DBMS_RESOURCE_MANAGER.SWITCH_CONSUMER_GROUP_FOR_SESS -
('17', '12345', 'sales');
```

You can obtain the SID and session serial number from the v$session view.

After you have created the plans and the resources and added users to the groups, you are set to go.

Monitoring the Consumer Groups

You don't have to monitor much in terms of the resource groups; however, you can look at a few things to see that the plan has taken effect and observe how well it is distributing resources within the system. The most important performance view is V$RESOURCE_CONSUMER_ GROUP. By using the following query, you can see how the resources are being used within the plan:

```
SELECT name, active_sessions, consumed_cpu_time, queue_length
FROM v$rsrc_consumer_group;
NAME                        ACTIVE_SESSIONS CONSUMED_CPU_TIME QUEUE_LENGTH
--------------------------- --------------- ----------------- ------------
SYS_GROUP                                 1              1943            0
OTHER_GROUPS                              0              1083            0
LOW_GROUP                                 0                 0            0
```

If you see too much CPU going to OTHER_GROUP, you might want to go back and assign more users to groups.

Tuning User Resources

Tuning individual user's resource limits is another good way to tune the workload that is being run on your system. This is accomplished by creating a profile that is then assigned to each user in the system. Every user is assigned a profile; if one is not explicitly assigned, the DEFAULT profile is used, which is the default.

The profile creates classes of users. Permissions and resource limitations can be assigned to profiles, and then each user is assigned to a profile. When creating or modifying a profile, you can assign the following resources:

SESSIONS_PER_USER	This is the number of sessions that each user can spawn. When this limit is reached, the attempt to create a new session fails.
CPU_PER_SESSION	This limit specifies the length of time in 1/100 of a second that the session can use before being disconnected.

CPU_PER_CALL	This specifies the maximum amount of CPU time in 1/100 of a second that each call can use.
CONNECT_TIME	This specifies the total elapsed time in minutes before the user's session is disconnected.
IDLE_TIME	This specifies the maximum amount of contiguous time in minutes that a session can remain inactive before being disconnected.
LOGICAL_READS_PER_CALL	This resource limits the total number of logical reads allowed within one call.
LOGICAL_READS_PER_SESSION	This limit specifies the total number of logical reads allowed for the session.
COMPOSITE_LIMIT	This is a composite of several limits rolled into one. With the composite limit, you can determine the weight of each portion of the composite.

Many more parameters can be configured for a profile, but only the performance parameters used for resource limitations are listed here. An example of creating a profile is shown here:

```
CREATE PROFILE sales_user LIMIT
    SESSIONS_PER_USER            2
    CPU_PER_SESSION              UNLIMITED
    CPU_PER_CALL                 3000
    CONNECT_TIME                 45
    IDLE_TIME                    5
    LOGICAL_READS_PER_SESSION    DEFAULT
    LOGICAL_READS_PER_CALL       1000;
```

After this profile is created, users who work in the sales group can be assigned to this profile.

The reason for using profiles to limit the amount of resources used by particular sessions is to tune the workload on the system. This would be useful in several scenarios.

OLTP Systems

Typical OLTP systems consist of many online users accessing the system and performing many short-running operations that demand immediate response. Any long-running batch-type operations or large queries could adversely affect the performance of the system. By using profiles and limiting long-running operations, the overall performance of the system can be enhanced. These long-running jobs can be assigned to a user who can only run them during off hours, or on another system.

Response Time

The profile is used to create an environment in which only certain types of operations are allowed. Because the profile allows maximums to be set, you are essentially disallowing operations that exceed these maximums. You can improve response times of shorter operations by removing longer-running operations from the system. This might or might not improve the amount of work being done on the system, but response times should improve in most cases.

Relocating Functions to Different Systems

Another excellent way to tune the workload that is running on your system is by distributing functions to different systems. A system that runs both OLTP and long-running jobs can sometimes be inefficient due to the effect of the long-running queries on the OLTP functions. By distributing this kind of system in which the OLTP workload runs on one server and the reporting function runs on a subordinate server, you might be able to greatly improve the performance of both of these.

This can be accomplished in several ways depending on your system's workload as well as your individual needs. You will now see a few examples of how a system can be distributed.

Distributing Historical Reports

Historical reports that cover months or even years often do not require up-to-the-minute data. Often, these types of systems can be run on data that is a little stale. In these cases, it is possible to use several different methods to create a reporting server. You can create these types of reporting servers by using backups or by using Oracle Data Guard (formerly known as Standby Database).

Reporting Server Using Backups

For reporting systems that can live with data that is a day or two old, you can take nightly backups and apply them to the reporting server. During the day, the reports can be run against this data, knowing that every night the data will be refreshed. This is an excellent way to create reporting servers in an environment where the database is small enough to make a backup every night, and restore it to another server before the users begin working in the morning. This type of solution offers several advantages:

- The main OLTP server has little to no overhead. In many cases, these nightly backups would be done anyway.

- The reporting server can be dedicated to running reports and will not affect the OLTP server.

- This solution is elegant in its simplicity. Little can go wrong.

Backups do not work for all environments. The database must be small enough to be backed up each night without affecting the OLTP users. In addition, the reporting functions must be read-only because the database will be restored every night.

Reporting Server Using Data Guard

Along the same lines of the previous solution, the reporting servers can be kept more up-to-date by using Data Guard, or the Automated Standby-Database system. This involves keeping the reporting server constantly in restore mode, restoring archive log files as soon as they are created. The reporting server will be minutes or hours behind the OLTP server, but for many types of historical reports, this is acceptable. As with the backup method, this solution offers several advantages:

- The main OLTP server has little to no overhead. The archive log process occurs regardless of whether you are applying archived logs to another server.

- The reporting server can be dedicated to running reports and will not affect the OLTP server.

- This provides a built-in disaster survival plan because Data Guard is an excellent solution for that.

- This solution is a little more complicated than the previous example, but not to extremes.

Again, this will not work for all environments, but the database does not need to be backed up every night. In addition, the reporting functions must be read-only because the database will be restored every night. Both of these solutions would be good for historical reporting. For online reporting, a more complicated solution is required.

Distributing Online Reports

An online report consists of a report or long-running query being run while the user is waiting on the result (hence the term online reports). These reports take significantly longer than a normal OLTP transaction, but might require up-to-the-minute data. With these types of reports, your only option might be to use Oracle replication. By using replication, you can keep the reporting server fairly up-to-date with the OLTP system (within a few seconds).

This allows you to still offload work to the reporting system while keeping both systems in sync. In those rare occasions in which the reporting servers must be allowed to update data, you can use multi-master replication. This replication allows several systems to act as the master, thereby allowing updates to occur on both or all of them.

Application Support for Distributed Systems

To offload reports, you must modify the application to understand where the particular function is to be run. You can accomplish this at the application level by hard coding where the reports are to be run. Alternatively, you can create a lookup table to point to where the individual reports are to be run. By using a lookup table, you can redirect reports as more systems are added, or you can redirect all work to run on the main OLTP system if a subordinate system is not working. Using the lookup table provides for more flexibility. Of course, depending on how your application is written, you might have other options.

Summary

This chapter addressed a common tuning method: tuning the workload. It is not uncommon to use different methods to govern how much of each type of work is being run on your system. This chapter discussed several ways of accomplishing this:

- Using resource groups and resource management

- Using profiles to limit users

- Using distributed systems to distribute the workload

Of course, you can probably tune the workload in many other ways based on the particular application that you are using, but the goal is the same: reduce one type of load so that another type of load can run more efficiently. The next few chapters turn back to more traditional tuning methods by looking at the Oracle performance statistics.

THE ORACLE
PERFORMANCE VIEWS

One of the best features of Oracle is its ability to get statistics on just about everything. These statistics are stored in what is referred to as the *Oracle Dynamic Performance Views*. They are also sometimes known as the V$ views or the V$ tables. These objects are views to underlying tables that start with X$. The X$ tables contain the underlying data, but it is not recommended that you access the X$ tables directly; rather, you should access this data via the V$ views.

Although the V$ views and underlying structures appear to be based on normal tables, these statistics are actually in memory structures that are created when the instance is started and are lost whenever the instance is shut down. Thus, the V$ performance views are not maintained after the instance is shut down. All of this data is lost whenever the instance is stopped.

The Dynamic Performance Views are made up of counters that store data on various aspects of Oracle performance. By themselves, most of the performance counters are not very useful; however, the difference in the performance counters over time can be insightful. This is because these counters begin counting when the instance is started and keep counting until the instance has been shut down. By taking the difference between these counters over a period of time, you can learn about how the system has performed in that time period.

Analyzing the performance counters can be done either by hand, or via several utilities that are provided by Oracle. The Oracle software distribution includes some SQL scripts that are used to take differences in these counters. The scripts work by taking a snapshot of various counters into a table. Later, a second snapshot is taken and the differences are calculated. This can be done via the UTLBSTAT and UTLESTAT utilities or the Oracle Statspack utility. These utilities are described in Chapter 7, "Using UTLBSTAT and UTLESTAT."

In addition to the Oracle utilities for analyzing the dynamic performance views, many third-party applications access these views as well. Many excellent performance-monitoring tools are on the market today. These tools serve several purposes. First, they take the Oracle performance data and display it in a graphical format, which makes it easier to interpret. Second, these tools usually include thresholds that can be set and used to alert you if these thresholds are reached. They can even contain rules to perform certain tasks if specific conditions are reached.

Regardless of the type of tools that you use, they are accessing the same underlying Oracle performance data. These performance views contain a wealth of data that you can use to analyze the performance of your system, as you will learn in this chapter.

The V$ Views Versus the G$ Views

The V$ views are the primary way of finding performance information within the Oracle instance. However, if you are working in an Oracle9i Real Application Cluster (RAC) environment, a set of performance views also begins with the G$ prefix. The V$ and G$ views are similar, except that the G$ views are used for RAC performance information, whereas the V$ views are used for single instance performance data.

A G$ view exists for almost every V$ view. Within the G$ view is an additional field that stores the instance number. With this additional information, you can view performance data for a particular instance or all instances within the cluster.

Overview of the Dynamic Performance Views

The dynamic performance views cover a number of different areas. Although it is fairly boring, this chapter provides a brief overview of the different V$ views and how they can be used. This information is provided for reference purposes. Rather than listing and describing all 190+ performance views, only the most important views (as they relate to performance tuning) will be described here. Please view the Oracle documentation for more details on all of the dynamic performance views.

V$ACCESS	This view provides information on which sessions are accessing an object. Although this is not directly related to performance, it can certainly be useful for debugging performance problems by determining which sessions might be having contention issues and on what object.
V$BUFFER_POOL	This view contains information on the buffer pool. This information can be used to determine the performance characteristics of the buffer pool as well as information on how it is configured.
V$BUFFER_POOL_STATISTICS	This view contains more detailed information on the current state and performance characteristics of the buffer pool.
V$CACHE	This is a RAC view that is used to observe information about each block in the SGA of the current instance in the cluster. This information can be used to track down the number of blocks that specific objects use.
V$CACHE_LOCK	This is similar to the V$CACHE view, but it includes platform-specific lock manager information as well as specific block information.
V$CLASS_PING	This is a RAC counter that displays information on the number of pings based on the class of the block. This can be useful for determining which class of block is experiencing pinging.
V$DB_CACHE_ADVICE	This counter is used to estimate the cache efficiency of different size blocks. This can be useful for helping you to determine if changing the block size or adding a nonstandard block would be an advantage.
V$DB_OBJECT_CACHE	This view displays information on which objects are currently cached in the library cache. This allows you to determine the efficiency of the library cache as well as specific object caching.

V$DISPATCHER	The V$DISPATCHER view is used to monitor the multithreaded server (MTS) dispatcher processes. By looking at the busy time and idle time of the dispatchers, you can determine if more dispatchers are necessary.
V$DISPATCHER_RATE	This view can supplement the V$DISPATCHER view and provide more information on rate information for many activities that the dispatcher is performing.
V$DML_ALL_LOCKS	This view lists all of the locks known to the Oracle RAC lock manager. This can be useful for debugging lock problems in a RAC system.
V$DML_CONVERT_LOCAL	This view displays statistics on the elapsed time for local lock conversion.
V$DML_CONVERT_REMOTE	This view provides the elapsed time for remote lock conversion operations.
V$DML_LOCKS	This view provides information on all locks known to the lock manager that are being blocked or blocking others. This is a subset of V$DML_ALL_LOCKS.
V$ENQUEUE_LOCK	This view contains information on locks owned by enqueue state objects.
V$EVENT_NAME	This view contains information about wait events.
V$EXECUTION	This view provides information on parallel execution.
V$FALSE_PING	This view provides information on buffers that might be getting false pings. False pings are pings on locks that cover a number of blocks where the pinging is not directed at the same block on both nodes. This can be useful in RAC tuning.
V$FILE_PING	This view provides information on the number of blocks that is being pinged per data file. This can provide valuable information on PCM lock tuning.
V$GLOBAL_BLOCKED_LOCKS	This view provides information on all blocked locks in the system.
V$GLOBAL_TRANSACTION	This view displays information on all of the global transactions that are currently running in the system.
V$INSTANCE	This view provides information on the current instance.
V$LATCH	This important view provides information on latch usage and performance.
V$LATCH_CHILDREN	This view provides information on child latches. This is a subset of V$LATCH.
V$LATCH_MISSES	This view provides information on missed attempts to acquire a latch.

V$PARENT_LATCHES	This view provides information on parent latches. This is a subset of V$LATCH.
V$LIBRARY_CACHE	This important view provides information on the performance of the library cache. This view is used to help tune the shared pool.
V$LOCK	This view contains information on outstanding locks and requests for locks.
V$LOCKED_OBJECT	This view contains information on all of the objects that are locked in the system.
V$LOCKS_WITH_COLLISONS	This view contains information on locks that cover multiple blocks that have been force-read or force-written at least 10 times. This view could indicate locks that are experiencing false pings.
V$LOCK_ACTIVITY	This RAC view provides information on RAC locking in the current instance.
V$LOCK_ELEMENT	This RAC view provides information on the PCM locks that are used in the buffer cache.
V$MTS	This view provides information on the multithreaded server process. This can be useful in determining if additional servers are necessary.
V$PARAMETER	This view provides information on the parameters that are set for the session. It is important that you know how the parameters are set. Don't assume anything.
V$PARAMETER2	This is another way of viewing the information that is provided in the V$PARAMETER view.
V$PING	This is similar to V$CACHE, but it only displays the blocks that have been pinged at least once.
V$PQ_SESSTAT	This view provides parallel query session statistics, which can be useful for determining the effectiveness of parallel query.
V$PQ_SLAVE	This view provides information on the parallel execution servers in the instance.
V$PQ_SYSSTAT	This view provides system statistics for parallel queries.
V$PQ_TQSTAT	This view provides information on parallel execution processes.
V$PROCESS	This important performance view contains information on the currently active processes.
V$PX_PROCESS	This view provides information on the processes that are running parallel execution.
V$PX_PROCESS_SYSSTAT	This view provides global information on the sessions that are running parallel execution.

V$PX_SESSION	This view provides information on the sessions that are running parallel execution.
V$PX_SESSTAT	This view provides more detailed information on the sessions that are running parallel execution.
V$QUEUE	This view provides information on the multithreaded message queues.
V$REQDIST	This view provides a histogram of MTS dispatcher request times.
V$RESOURCE_LIMIT	This view provides information on resource limits and how close those limits are to being reached.
V$ROWCACHE	This important view provides information on data dictionary usage statistics.
V$ROWCACHE_PARENT	This view provides information on data dictionary statistics on parent objects.
V$ROWCACHE_SUBORDINATE	This view provides information on data dictionary statistics on subordinate objects.
V$RSRC_CONSUMER_GROUP	This view provides statistics on resource commerce group statistics, which is important for determining the performance of resource commerce groups.
V$SESSION	This important view provides session information on each current session.
V$SESSION_CURSOR_CACHE	This view displays information on cursor usage for the current session.
V$SESSION_EVENT	This view provides information on event waits on a per-process basis, which is useful for determining if waits are a problem.
V$SESSION_LONGOPS	This view provides information on operations that run longer than six seconds. This is an easy way to determine long-running operations.
V$SESSION_OBJECT_CACHE	This view provides information on object cache statistics for the current user session.
V$SESSION_WAIT	This view provides information on resources or events for which sessions are waiting. This is useful for determining where session performance problems might be occurring.
V$SESSTAT	This view provides valuable session statistics. This view is joined to V$STATNAME to provide session statistics.
V$SESS_IO	This view provides session I/O statistics for each user, which is valuable for debugging I/O problems.
V$SHARED_POOL_RESERVED	This view provides information on the reserved shared pool, which is important for tuning the shared pool reserved size.

V$SHARED_SERVER	This view provides information on the shared server processes that are used in MTS. This is important for tuning MTS.
V$SORT_SEGMENT	This view provides information on the sort segment that can be useful for tuning.
V$SORT_USAGE	This view provides information on sorts, which can be useful for tuning the temporary space.
V$SQL	This view provides statistics on the shared SQL area.
V$SQLAREA	This view provides information on the shared SQL area, with one line per SQL statement.
V$SQLTEXT	This view provides information on the SQL statements that belong to shared SQL cursors in the SGA.
V$SQL_MEMORY_USAGE	This view provides memory usage statistics. These statistics are used internally by Oracle for determining memory allocation.
V$SQL_PLAN	This view contains information on the execution plan for each child cursor that is loaded in the library cache.
V$STATNAME	This view provides information on statistics names that are used in V$SYSTAT and V$SESSTAT.
V$SYSSTAT	This view provides system statistics. This view is used in conjunction with V$STATNAME.
V$SYSTEM_EVENT	This view provides information on total waits on an event, which is useful for tracking down wait problems.
V$SYSTEM_PARAMETER	This view provides a listing of system parameters and their values used in this instance.
V$TEMPSTAT	This useful view provides information on file read/write statistics.
V$TEMP_EXTENT_POOL	This view provides information on the state of temporary space that is cached and used by a particular instance.
V$TEMP_PING	This RAC view provides statistics on the number of blocks pinged per data file. This can be very useful in determining access patterns to data files and in determining data lock design.
V$TRANSACTION	This view lists all of the active transactions in the system.
V$TRANSACTION_ENQUEUE	This view displays locks that are owned by transaction state objects.
V$UNDOSTAT	This view provides statistics on undo usage in the form of a histogram.
V$WAITSTAT	This view provides statistics on block contention. This view is only updated when timed statistics is enabled.

Using the Dynamic Performance Views

You can use the dynamic performance views in many ways. The same underlying data is used regardless of how these statistics are gathered and presented. The way to access this data can be as simple and straightforward as creating a SQL query against these views. More information can be gathered by using the Oracle-supplied utilities such as UTLBSTAT/UTLESTAT and Statspack. You can use this same data in more sophisticated Oracle and third-party programs that can graphically display Oracle statistics and even provide features such as alerting.

Using Queries to Access the Dynamic Performance Views

The most basic method of accessing the data in the dynamic performance views is via SQL queries. The V$ views can be accessed just like any other tables, and the data can be quite useful. When accessing data directly from the V$ views, you will not get trend data or information on what changes are happening in the system. You will only get instantaneous data.

The following sections provide examples of where the V$ views can be accessed directly.

Buffer Cache Hit Ratio

You can determine the buffer cache hit ratio by using the following query:

```
SELECT NAME, VALUE
FROM V$SYSSTAT
WHERE NAME IN ('DB BLOCK GETS', 'CONSISTENT GETS', 'PHYSICAL READS');
```

You can then take the output of this query and use the following equation:

```
Hit Ratio = 1 - (PHYSICAL READS / (DB BLOCK GETS + CONSISTENT GETS))
```

Another example of using queries to access the dynamic performance views relates to the shared pool.

Library Cache Hit Ratio

You can determine the library cache hit ratio by using a query against the V$LIBRARYCACHE view, as shown here:

```
SELECT (SUM(PINS - RELOADS)) / SUM(PINS) "LIB CACHE" FROM V$LIBRARYCACHE;
```

Data Dictionary Cache Hit Ratio

You can determine the data dictionary cache hit ratio by using a query against the V$ROWCACHE view, as shown here. The data dictionary cache is also known as the row cache:

```
SELECT (SUM(GETS - GETMISSES - USAGE - FIXED)) / SUM(GETS) "ROW CACHE"
FROM V$ROWCACHE;
```

Shared Pool Free Space

To find the free space in the shared pool, use the following query:

```
SELECT *
FROM V$SGASTAT
WHERE POOL = 'shared pool' and NAME = 'free memory';
```

You can use this query to determine if free space is available. If free space is low, this is an indication that problems might exist and that the shared pool might need to be increased.

Using UTLBSTAT/UTLESTAT and Statspack

The Oracle-supplied SQL script UTLBSTAT initiates a collection of V$ view values into a temporary table. The SQL script UTLESTAT takes another snapshot of this data, compares it to the previous data, and creates a difference in those values (where applicable). In addition, the UTLESTAT script cleans up by deleting the temporary table. The UTLBSTAT/UTLESTAT pair is covered in more detail in the next chapter.

Statspack is an Oracle-supplied package that gathers statistics in a similar method to the UTLBSTAT/UTLESTAT pair, but with a few differences. Statspack is an Oracle package that is called to initiate snapshots. These snapshots don't delete the previous snapshot, but simply add more snapshots. By running the report script, you can select which snapshots to compare. Thus, Statspack is more flexible, and the data is presented in a different way. Statspack is also covered in the next chapter.

Using Performance-Monitoring Tools

Many performance-monitoring tools are available to the Oracle DBA. Oracle provides numerous tools, and various third-party tools are available on the market as well.

Oracle Tools

Oracle provides the following tools with the Oracle Enterprise Edition RDBMS or as a part of Oracle Enterprise Manager:

Performance Manager	This application displays a number of Oracle performance statistics in a graphical form. Performance Manager can be used to invoke other tools such as Top Sessions.
Top Sessions	This straightforward tool lists in descending order the top resource-consuming sessions in the instance.
Capacity Planner	The Capacity Planner utility is used for long-term trend analysis.
Trace Data Viewer	This tool is used to analyze the output of Oracle Trace.
SQL Analyze	This tool is used to analyze SQL statements that are running in the instance.

Third-Party Tools

Many excellent third-party tools are available on the market. The Oracle tools give you a basic graphical display of performance data. Third-party tools include the same functionality, but most of them provide additional functionality such as analysis of data, alerting, and integration with other RDBMS products. Some of the advantages of third-party tools include the following:

- Integration with other RDBMS products. If you run more than just Oracle, it is advantageous to use a monitoring tool that can monitor all of the RDBMS products that you have, in an integrated manner.

- Alerting functionality. The alerting function of these products is the largest advantage. These products can be used to page you when a threshold is reached, send e-mails, or alert you in other ways.

- Data analysis. Many of these products can help you to analyze and fix problems, not just view instantaneous performance data.

- Trend analysis. These tools can be used to store long-term performance data for trend analysis.

- User extensions. Most of these tools allow you to extend them by adding your own monitoring objects. This can allow you to instrument your own application.

- Expandable nature. By using multiple tools from the third-party vendor, you can expand to add SQL analyzing tools to your alerting system.

Take a look at what is available on the market. You might find a tool that does exactly what you need to effectively monitor and manage your system.

Summary

This chapter provided a list of the most important V$ views that you might need to access. It showed ways to use combinations of V$ views to provide detailed information about the Oracle instance. It also introduced the Oracle Statspack and the UTLBSTAT/UTLESTAT scripts. The next chapter teaches you how to interpret the output of UTLBSTAT/UTLESTAT and Statspack.

USING UTLBSTAT AND UTLESTAT

Looking at the internal statistics of Oracle can open a new way of monitoring your database performance—if you understand and can interpret what is being measured and reported. Using Oracle's UTLBSTAT and UTLESTAT utilities, commonly known as BSTAT/ESTAT, provides you with an easier way to gather statistics about what is happening in your Oracle database. This chapter explores running UTLBSTAT and UTLESTAT, important Oracle statistics, and monitoring and detecting contention based on output from UTLBSTAT and UTLESTAT.

UTLBSTAT/UTLESTAT

One of the ways to gather statistics is via the Oracle utilities UTLBSTAT and UTLESTAT. In this section, you will learn how to run UTLBSTAT and UTLESTAT and how to interpret the data. Later in the chapter, you will learn how to use an Oracle8i/Oracle9i feature, Statspack.

Running UTLBSTAT/UTLESTAT

The SQL scripts for running the UTLBSTAT and UTLESTAT utilities are stored in the $ORACLE_HOME/rdbms/admin directory. UTLBSTAT.sql is run at the beginning of the reporting measurement interval. UTLBSTAT.sql creates the statistics tables that are used to store snapshots of certain dynamic performance statistics and collects beginning statistics. UTLESTAT.sql is run at the end of the reporting measurement interval. UTLESTAT.sql collects ending statistics, creates the output file, and drops the statistics tables that UTLBSTAT creates. The output file is always "report.txt," and it will be saved to the current directory unless you change it within the script code.

The following are tips to get an accurate picture of your database activity:

- Run UTLBSTAT.sql after your database has had time to warm up and is in a steady measurement interval.

- Make sure that your measurement interval contains the time during which the problem is occurring if you are trying to diagnose a problem in performance. The length of the measurement interval depends on how long you want to monitor your system, whether it be a few hours or a few days.

- Set TIMED_STATISTICS to TRUE to obtain timing statistics. TIMED_STATISTICS can be set in the Oracle initialization file before the database is opened. An ALTER SYSTEM statement can be used to set TIMED_STATISTICS to TRUE if the database has already been opened. The default value for TIMED_STATISTICS is FALSE.

TOO MUCH MONITORING

Having TIMED_STATISTICS set to TRUE and running BSTAT/ESTAT incurs system overhead, which can have a substantial impact on your database performance. When you have finished gathering statistics, set TIMED_STATISTICS to FALSE so that you do not have the increased overhead and reduced performance of gathering Oracle statistics. After setting TIMED_STATISTICS to FALSE, a database restart is required for this change to become effective.

The UTLBSTAT/UTLESTAT Output File

The UTLBSTAT/UTLESTAT output file, called report.txt, contains the overall statistics for the measurement interval. This report file can be found in the current directory if run from a SQL*Plus command or in the directory defined by the SQLPATH environment variable, which by default is the /ORACLE_HOME/dbs directory.

You must consider a couple of factors when looking at the UTLBSTAT/UTLESTAT output file.

- It's important to have a baseline report file, which has been run during a measurement interval with an acceptable level of performance. Looking at some of the numbers might not tell what's really happening without comparing those numbers to a baseline. The baseline report will also enable you to track the impact of changes you make to your database system.

- UTLESTAT.sql reports statistics that are usually not equal to zero or haven't changed since UTLBSTAT.sql was run. This is beneficial because it doesn't inundate the DBA with statistics that haven't impacted the database system during the measurement interval.

Interpreting BSTAT/ESTAT Statistics

Oracle statistics are separated into different categories in the BSTAT/ESTAT output file. These sections include Library Cache, Database Statistics, System-Wide Wait Events, Latches (Willing-to-Wait and Immediate-Gets), Buffer Busy Waits, Rollback Segments, INIT.ORA Parameters, Dictionary Cache, Tablespace I/O, File I/O, BSTAT/ESTAT Start and End Times, and Versions.

Library Cache

The library cache statistics are selected from the v$librarycache table. The following example shows the SQL code that is used to create the library cache section and its output that is generated for the report.txt file:

```
SVRMGR> Rem Select Library cache statistics.  The pin hit rate should be high.
SVRMGR> select namespace library,
     2>        gets,
     3>        round(decode(gethits,0,1,gethits)/decode(gets,0,1,gets),3)
     4>          gethitratio,
     5>        pins,
     6>        round(decode(pinhits,0,1,pinhits)/decode(pins,0,1,pins),3)
     7>          pinhitratio,
     8>        reloads, invalidations
     9>   from stats$lib;
```

LIBRARY	GETS	GETHITRATI	PINS	PINHITRATI	RELOADS	INVALIDATI
BODY	250	.988	250	.988	0	0
CLUSTER	47	.894	90	.867	0	0
INDEX	28	.857	28	.857	0	0
OBJECT	0	1	0	1	0	0
PIPE	0	1	0	1	0	0
SQL AREA	1850	.958	12138	.987	1	0
TABLE/PROCED	400	.925	1212	.915	0	0
TRIGGER	0	1	0	1	0	0

```
8 rows selected.
```

The namespace values are different types of library cache activity. The number of pins is the number of times that something in the library cache was executed. The number of reloads is the number of times that a user process tried to execute something that had already been flushed out of the library cache. The number of reloads should be less than 1% of the number of pins for each namespace. The number of invalidations is incremented when an object referenced in a SQL statement has changed. When this occurs, the SQL statement must be reparsed before it is executed again.

The overall library cache hit ratio can be calculated by the following:

Library cache hit ratio = (sum (pins – reloads) /
sum (pins)) * 100

The library cache hit ratio should be at least 99%. If it is less than 99%, try increasing the size of the SHARED_POOL initialization parameter.

Database Statistics

The database statistics section of report.txt contains a variety of Oracle statistics, listed in alphabetical order. For ease of reading, this chapter groups these statistics into the following categories: cache, enqueue, sorts, and redo. Each category contains the most important or common database statistics. A complete listing of statistic definitions can be found in the Oracle9i Reference Manual.

The database statistics are system wide. The following example shows the SQL code that is used to create the database statistics section and a partial listing of the output generated for the report.txt file.

```
SVRMGR>
SVRMGR> select n1.name "Statistic",
    2>         n1.change "Total",
    3>         round(n1.change/trans.change,2) "Per Transaction",
    4>         round(n1.change/((start_users + end_users)/2),2)  "Per Logon",
    5>         round(n1.change/(to_number(to_char(end_time,  'J'))*60*60*24 -
    6>                     to_number(to_char(start_time, 'J'))*60*60*24 +
    7>             to_number(to_char(end_time,  'SSSSS')) -
    8>             to_number(to_char(start_time, 'SSSSS')))
    9>               , 2) "Per Second"
   10>    from
   11>         stats$stats n1,
   12>         stats$stats trans,
   13>         stats$dates
   14>    where
   15>      trans.name='user commits'
   16>      and  n1.change != 0
   17>      order by n1.name;
```

Statistic	Total	Per Transact	Per Logon	Per Second
CR blocks created	2548	.01	424.67	2.53
DBWR buffers scanned	624032	1.89	104005.33	620.31
DBWR checkpoint buffers wri	1055	0	175.83	1.05

Cache

The Cache section of the statistics includes information about the usage of the database block buffers. This information can be useful in determining if the buffer cache is set high enough. The cache hit ratio is one of the first things that you will analyze when tuning an Oracle system.

- Consistent changes. The number of times that a user process has applied rollback entries to perform a consistent read on a block. A consistent change happens when one user process updates a block and another user requests current data from that block. This number should be relatively low when compared to consistent gets. If this number is too high, your queries might be taking too long to complete.

- Consistent gets. The number of times a data block was accessed for SELECT statements. Combined with db block gets, this number represents the total number of logical reads. It is an important component used to calculate the buffer cache hit ratio.

- Db block gets. The number of times a data block was accessed for INSERT, UPDATE, and DELETE statements. Combined with consistent gets, this number represents the total number of logical reads.

- Physical reads. The number of times a data block was read from disk to satisfy SELECT, INSERT, UPDATE, and DELETE statements.

- Dirty buffers inspected. The number of dirty buffers that a user process searching for a free buffer skips over. A large number of dirty buffers inspected indicates either that the buffer cache is too small or that DBWR is not keeping up with its workload. Check the buffer cache hit ratio to see if the buffer cache hit ratio is below 90%. If so, try increasing DB_CACHE_SIZE or DB_BLOCK_BUFFERS. Otherwise, you might try to increase the number of DBWRs.

- Free buffer inspected. The number of buffers that a user process searching for a free buffer skips over. This includes dirty buffers that are inspected plus any buffers that are currently busy, have been allocated to or requested by a user, or are currently being read or written.

- Hot buffers moved to head of LRU. The number of times a hot buffer has reached the tail of the replacement list, requiring that the hot buffer be moved to the head of the LRU list. Many hot buffers moved to the head of the LRU indicates that the buffer cache or the _DB_PERCENT_HOT_DEFAULT initialization parameter might be too small. The _DB_PERCENT_HOT_DEFAULT parameter specifies what percentage of the default buffer pool is considered to be hot.

Enqueue

The Enqueue section of the statistics addresses the performance and usage of the system enqueues. An *enqueue* can be thought of as a lock that has a queue associated with it. This queue is made up of the processes that want to acquire that lock.

- Enqueue deadlocks. The total number of deadlocks between table or row locks in different sessions. This number should be as close to zero as you can get. If enqueue deadlocks is high, evaluate your application(s) workload to determine if the workload can be changed or the SQL code modified to avoid deadlocks.

- Enqueue timeouts. The number of times that an enqueue lock was not available when requested. The number of enqueue timeouts should be zero. If it is not, the ENQUEUE_RESOURCES initialization parameter can be increased. By default, ENQUEUE_RESOURCES is derived from the SESSIONS initialization parameter. For a non-default ENQUEUE_RESOURCES value to be used, it must be greater than the value of DML_LOCKS plus 20.

Sorts

Oracle provides information on sort operation performance. This is useful because you can tune the amount of memory allocated to each user for sorts.

- Sorts (disk). The total number of sorts that could not fit into memory and required writing I/O to disk. This number should be close to zero because sorts to disk require much greater resources than sorts in memory. If the number for sorts (disk) is more than 5% of sorts (memory), try increasing the SORT_AREA_SIZE initialization parameter.

- Sorts (memory). The total number of sorts that were completed entirely in memory, without creating any extra disk I/O.

Redo

Many parameters are related to the performance of the redo log. The redo log and its performance are critical to the performance of the Oracle instance.

- Redo buffer allocation retries. The total number of times that a user process tried to allocate space in the redo buffer and it was unavailable. This number should be zero. If it is not zero, then either a log switch or checkpoint has occurred or the LGWR is not keeping up with its workload. Check the Oracle alert log to determine recent log switch and checkpoint activity. To increase the time between log switches or checkpoints, you can increase the size of redo log files, increase the LOG_CHECKPOINT_TIMEOUT (specified in seconds) initialization parameter, or increase the LOG_CHECKPOINT_ INTERVAL (specified in number of redo log file blocks) initialization parameter. To increase the efficiency of LGWR, you can either put the redo log files on a faster disk or try increasing the LOG_BUFFER initialization parameter.

- Redo size. The total number of bytes written to the redo buffer. This number divided by the length of the measurement interval provides the average log requirements per unit of time. This is helpful in determining the size of your redo log files.

System-Wide Wait Events

Report.txt contains two sections of system-wide wait events: non-background and background. The following example contains the SQL code used to create the non-background system-wide wait events statistics.

```
SVRMGR>
SVRMGR> Rem System-wide wait events for non-background processes (PMON,
SVRMGR> Rem SMON, and so on).  Times are in hundredths of seconds.  Each one of
SVRMGR> Rem these is a context switch that costs CPU time.  By looking at
SVRMGR> Rem the Total Time, you can often determine the bottleneck
SVRMGR> Rem that processes are waiting for.  This shows the total time spent
SVRMGR> Rem waiting for a specific event and the average time per wait on
```

```
SVRMGR> Rem that event.
SVRMGR> select      n1.event "Event Name",
    2>              n1.event_count "Count",
    3>       n1.time_waited "Total Time",
    4>        round(n1.time_waited/n1.event_count, 2) "Avg Time"
    5>       from stats$event n1
    6>       where n1.event_count > 0
    7>       order by n1.time_waited desc;
```

Event Name	Count	Total Time	Avg Time
SQL*Net message from client	429121	0	0
SQL*Net message to client	429121	0	0
control file parallel write	19	0	0
control file sequential read	77	0	0
db file sequential read	3841293	0	0
direct path read	115	0	0
direct path write	84	0	0
latch free	150813	0	0
enqueue	594	0	0
buffer busy waits	2702	0	0

Following is the SQL code that is used to create the background system-wide wait events statistics.

```
SVRMGR>
SVRMGR> Rem System-wide wait events for background processes (PMON, SMON, etc)
SVRMGR> select      n1.event "Event Name",
    2>              n1.event_count "Count",
    3>       n1.time_waited "Total Time",
    4>        round(n1.time_waited/n1.event_count, 2) "Avg Time"
    5>       from stats$bck_event n1
    6>       where n1.event_count > 0
    7>       order by n1.time_waited desc;
```

Event Name	Count	Total Time	Avg Time
LGWR wait for redo copy	32606	0	0
control file parallel write	337	0	0
control file sequential read	19	0	0
db file parallel write	1403	0	0
db file sequential read	9	0	0

The event name identifies the name of each system-wide wait event. The count column identifies how many times the event has occurred. The total time is the amount of time that the user processes had to wait for the event. The avg time is the total time divided by count. Both total time and avg time are listed in hundredths of a second. Note: If TIMED_STATISTICS is not set to TRUE, your total time and avg time will be zero.

When looking at system-wide wait events, it is important to look at the total and average wait times. If these times are large, then you need to research further to determine the cause of the wait. The following are some key wait events to monitor:

- Buffer busy waits. Oracle is waiting on a buffer to become available. This can happen if a session is waiting for a another session to read the buffer into the buffer cache or if another session is changing the buffer in the buffer cache. The normal wait time for buffer busy waits is one second. If it is higher than one second, it might indicate freelist contention. If this is the case, you can query the v$session_wait view and select the file, block, and ID for each buffer busy wait. You can then determine the object with freelist contention by querying the dba_extents table using the following SQL code:

```
SELECT segment_name, segment_type
FROM DBA_EXTENTS
WHERE file_id = <file>
AND <block> BETWEEN <ID> AND <ID> + <blocks>;
```

  To alleviate freelist contention, you can increase the INITRANS storage parameter for the object. You can also reduce the PCTFREE and PCTUSED values for the object, which requires less of the block to be filled before it is placed back on the freelist.

- Free buffer waits. These occur when a session tries to move dirty buffers to a dirty queue that has been filled or when no free buffer is found during inspection of free buffer inspected buffers. If the dirty queue has been filled, DBWR might not be keeping up with its workload. If no free buffer is found, Oracle will wait for one second and then try to obtain the buffer again.

Latches

Two types of latch statistics are reported by BSTAT/ESTAT: latches that are willing-to-wait and immediate-gets latches shown in the examples to follow. Both of these sections of statistics get their information from the v$latch and v$latchholder views.

```
SVRMGR>
SVRMGR> Rem Willing-to-wait latch statistics
SVRMGR> Rem Latch statistics. Latch contention will show up as a large value for
SVRMGR> Rem the 'latch free' event in the wait events.
SVRMGR> Rem Sleeps should be low.  The hit_ratio should be high.
SVRMGR> select name latch_name, gets, misses,
     2>      round((gets-misses)/decode(gets,0,1,gets),3)
     3>        hit_ratio,
```

```
    4>      sleeps,
    5>      round(sleeps/decode(misses,0,1,misses),3) "SLEEPS/MISS"
    6>    from stats$latches
    7>      where gets != 0
8>    order by name;
```

LATCH_NAME	GETS	MISSES	HIT_RATIO	SLEEPS	SLEEPS/MISS
cache buffer handl	353	0	1	0	0
cache buffers chai	155392131	46348	1	8521	.184
cache buffers lru	4541982	7304	.998	2314	.317

The willing-to-wait latch statistics represent requests that are willing to wait for a latch to become available. They are measured in gets, misses, hit_ratio, sleeps, and sleeps/miss. Gets is the total number of times that a latch was available when it was requested. Misses is the total number of times that a latch was requested but was not available. Hit_ratio is equal to (gets – misses) / gets. Sleeps is the total number of processes that have waited to receive a latch. Sleeps/miss is equal to sleeps / misses. The hit_ratio for these latches should be as close to one as possible. If this is not the case, you should investigate the latches with a low hit_ratio.

```
SVRMGR>
SVRMGR> Rem Immediate-gets latch statistics
SVRMGR> Rem Statistics on no_wait gets of latches.  A no_wait get does not
SVRMGR> Rem wait for the latch to become free. It immediately times out.
SVRMGR> select name latch_name,
    2>      immed_gets nowait_gets,
    3>      immed_miss nowait_misses,
    4>      round((immed_gets/(immed_gets+immed_miss)), 3)
    5>       nowait_hit_ratio
    6>    from stats$latches
    7>      where immed_gets + immed_miss != 0
8>    order by name;
```

LATCH_NAME	NOWAIT_GETS	NOWAIT_MISSES	NOWAIT_HIT_RATIO
redo allocation	0	0	0
redo copy	54	0	54
redo writing	0	0	0

The immediate-gets latch, or no-wait latch, statistics represent requests that are not willing to wait for a latch to become available. These latches will automatically rerequest a latch if one is not available when one is first requested. The immediate-gets latches are measured in nowait_gets, nowait_misses, and nowait_hit_ratio. Nowait_gets is the number of times that an immediate request for a latch is satisfied. Nowait_misses is the number of times that an immediate request for a latch is not satisfied. Nowait_hit_ratio is equal to (nowait_gets – nowait_misses) / nowait_gets. The nowait_hit_ratio should be as close to one as possible. If this is not the case, investigate the latches with a low nowait_hit_ratio.

To determine user processes and which latches they are holding, you can query the v$latch view using the following SQL code. This will help determine if specific user processes are continually holding latches.

```
SELECT h.pid, n.name
FROM v$latchholder h, v$latchname n, v$latch l
WHERE h.laddr = l.addr
AND l.latch# = n.latch#;
```

The following are some important types of latches to monitor:

- Cache buffers LRU chain. A hit ratio of less than .99 on a cache buffers LRU chain latch indicates LRU latch contention. The default number of LRU latches is one-half of the number of CPUs in your database system. If your system has only a single processor, Oracle will use only one LRU latch. If the hit ratio is less than .99 and you have a multi-processor system, you can increase the number of LRU latches by increasing the DB_BLOCK_LRU_LATCHES initialization parameter. When you modify DB_BLOCK_LRU_LATCHES, keep in mind that the maximum number of LRU latches you can allocate is the lower of (1) DB_CACHE_SIZE or DB_BLOCK_BUFFERS divided by 50, or (2) six times the number of CPUs in your system.

- Redo allocation. This allows access to write redo information to the redo log buffer. Each Oracle instance has only one redo allocation latch. After a user process has this latch, the process might write up to the number of bytes specified by the LOG_SMALL_ENTRY_MAX_SIZE initialization parameter. LOG_SMALL_ENTRY_MAX_SIZE should be small to minimize the number of waits for the redo allocation latch.

- Redo copy. If a user process needs to write more to the redo log buffer than allowable by LOG_SMALL_ENTRY_MAX_SIZE, then the user process must obtain a redo copy latch. A redo copy latch allows the user to finish writing redo information to the redo log buffer. The number of redo copy latches is defined by the LOG_SIMULTANEOUS_COPIES initialization parameter. Increasing LOG_SIMULTANEOUS_COPIES should increase a low redo copy hit ratio.

Buffer Busy Waits

The buffer busy waits statistics show the classes of buffers that are busy when requested by a user process. Data for this section is retrieved from the v$waitstat view. The following example contains the SQL code used to create the buffer busy waits statistics. Note that if you do not have TIMED_STATISTICS set to TRUE, the time column of these statistics will be zero.

```
SVRMGR>
SVRMGR> Rem Buffer busy waits statistics
SVRMGR> Rem Buffer busy waits statistics.  If the value for 'buffer busy waits'
in
SVRMGR> Rem the wait event statistics is high, then this table will identify
SVRMGR> Rem which class of blocks is having high contention.  If there are high
SVRMGR> Rem 'undo header' waits, then add more rollback segments.  If there are
SVRMGR> Rem high 'segment header' waits, then adding freelists might help.
Check
SVRMGR> Rem v$session_wait to get the addresses of the actual blocks having
SVRMGR> Rem contention.
SVRMGR> select * from stats$waitstat
     2>    where count != 0
     3>    order by count desc;
CLASS                      COUNT              TIME
----------------- ----------------- -----------------
data block                   647                 0
undo header                  373                 0
undo block                   281                 0
free list                     23                 0
```

The following are some key buffer classes to monitor:

- Data block. A high number of data block buffer busy waits indicates that your buffer cache might be too small. If this number is high, try increasing the DB_CACHE_SIZE or DB_BLOCK_BUFFERS initialization parameter.

- Undo header. A high number of undo header buffer busy waits indicates that you might not have enough rollback segments. If this number is high, try adding rollback segments.

- Free list. A high number of free list buffer busy waits indicates that you might have free-list contention. See the buffer busy waits statistic under the earlier "System-Wide Wait Events" section for information on identifying and alleviating freelist contention.

Rollback Segments

The rollback segments statistics section is retrieved from the v$rollstat view. The example that follows shows the SQL code that is used to create the rollback segment statistics.

```
SVRMGR>
SVRMGR> Rem High waits_for_trans_tbl implies you should add rollback segments.
SVRMGR> select * from stats$roll;
```

```
UNDO_SEGMENT          TRANS_TBL_GETS        TRANS_TBL_WAITS
UNDO_BYTES_WRITTEN    SEGMENT_SIZE_BYTES    XACTS                 SHRINKS               WRAPS
------------------    ------------------    ------------------    ------------------    ------------------
------------------    ------------------    ------------------    ------------------    ------------------
                 0                    10                     0
 0               407552                     0                     0                     0
                31                 14813                     0
 10091936            79872                     0                     0                   308
                32                 15004                     1
 10395378           120832                     0                     0                   309
                33                 14970                     0
 10022030           120832                    -1                     0                   302
                34                 15131                     0
 10143616            79872                     0                     0                   310
```

The undo segment identifies the rollback segment number. The trans tbl gets column specifies the total number of requests for a segment header in that rollback segment. The trans tbl waits column specifies the total number of requests that had to wait for a segment header. The undo bytes written is the total number of bytes written to the rollback segment. The segment size bytes is the size in bytes of the rollback segment. The xacts column contains the number of active transactions in the rollback segment. Shrinks is the number of times that the size of the rollback segment decreases because it was larger than the optimal size. Wraps is the number of times that the rollback segment has been wrapped.

The trans tbl waits should be relatively low. If trans tbl waits is more than 5% of trans tbl gets, increase the number of rollback segments in your database system. A large shrinks value might indicate that your rollback segments are too small and that you should increase the size of your rollback segments until the shrinks value is closer to zero.

INIT.ORA Parameters

The INIT.ORA parameters section lists all the non-default Oracle initialization parameters that were in effect when UTLESTAT.sql was run. This section is helpful in performance tuning with BSTAT/ESTAT because you have a written record of initialization parameters with each generated report.txt file. This section is retrieved using the following SQL code:

```
SELECT name, value FROM v$parameter where isdefault = 'FALSE' order by name;
```

To capture all Oracle initialization parameters—including parameters set to the default value—you can modify the SQL statement in UTLESTAT.SQL to be the following:

```
SELECT name, value FROM v$parameter order by name;
```

KNOW YOUR PARAMETERS

Several years ago, I helped a friend of mine who was going to give a presentation at a customer site. In preparing for the presentation, he wanted to point out some tuning tips that pertained directly to the customer, and as such acquired a UTLBSTAT/UTLESTAT report from the customer.

As I started at the top and started calculating statistics, I noticed a dramatically low cache hit ratio. As I finally reached the section in report.txt, I found that the customer had not set the DB_BLOCK_BUFFERS parameter and it was running with the default of 800. In addition, the customer had set the shared pool to 400MB.

I immediately pointed out this error. From then on, the first thing that I check is the initialization parameters. Then I check the statistics.

Dictionary Cache

The dictionary cache section of BSTAT/ESTAT contains information about the data dictionary and is retrieved from the v$rowcache view. The example that follows shows the SQL code that is used to create the dictionary cache statistics.

```
SVRMGR>
SVRMGR> Rem get_miss and scan_miss should be very low compared to the requests.
SVRMGR> Rem cur_usage is the number of entries in the cache that are being used.
SVRMGR> select * from stats$dc
    2>  where get_reqs != 0 or scan_reqs != 0 or mod_reqs != 0;
```

NAME	GET_REQS	GET_MISS	SCAN_REQ	SCAN_MIS	MOD_REQS	COUNT	CUR_USAG
dc_tablespaces	25908	3	0	0	0	15	5
dc_free_extents	276	20	18	0	72	100	77
dc_segments	170	70	0	0	18	313	305
dc_rollback_seg	262193	0	0	0	0	248	242

Name refers to the cache area in the data dictionary. Get_reqs is the total number of requests for information on a data object in the data dictionary cache. Get_miss is the total number of times information was requested on a data object and that object was not in the dictionary cache. Scan_req is the total number of times the dictionary cache was scanned for an object. Scan_miss is the number of times the dictionary cache was scanned for an object and the object was not found. Mod_reqs is the number of inserts, updates, and deletes made to the dictionary cache. Count is the total number of entries in the cache. Cur_usage is the total number of cache entries that contain valid data.

The cache hit ratio for the dictionary cache can be calculated using the following SQL code:

```
SELECT     SUM ( gets - getmisses ) as hits,
        SUM ( getmisses ) as misses,
        ROUND (( sum( gets - getmisses ) / sum( gets )) * 100 , 2) as hit_ratio
FROM    v$rowcache;
```

Oracle recommends a dictionary cache hit ratio of at least 85%. If the dictionary cache hit ratio is less than 85%, your shared pool might be too small. If this is the case, increase your SHARED_POOL initialization parameter.

Tablespace and File I/O

BSTAT/ESTAT makes monitoring disk I/O easier for the DBA. Rather than calculating I/O on your own to locate the hot spot of disk contention, BSTAT/ESTAT does the calculations for you and puts them into two types of I/O reports: I/O per tablespace and I/O per data file. The example that follows shows the SQL code that is used to generate the I/O per tablespace statistics. Once again, if you do not have TIMED_STATISTICS set to TRUE, the read and write times will be zero.

In the following example from utlestat.sql, the table stats$files is created and populated within utlestat.sql.

```
SVRMGR>
SVRMGR> Rem Sum IO operations over tablespaces.
SVRMGR> select
     2>   table_space||'                                                '
     3>      table_space,
     4>   sum(phys_reads) reads,  sum(phys_blks_rd) blks_read,
     5>   sum(phys_rd_time) read_time,  sum(phys_writes) writes,
     6>   sum(phys_blks_wr) blks_wrt,  sum(phys_wrt_tim) write_time,
     7>   sum(megabytes_size) megabytes
     8>  from stats$files
     9>  group by table_space
    10>  order by table_space;
TABLE_SPACE
➥READS      BLKS_READ  READ_TIME  WRITES     BLKS_WRT   WRITE_TIME MEGABYTES
------------------------------------------------------------------------------
➥---------- ---------- ---------- ---------- ---------- ---------- ----------
DATA
➥3840766    3840719           0    580235     580235          0     300790
ROLL_1
➥29         29         0          57         57         0          84
SYSTEM
➥330        330         0         258        258         0         735
```

The example that follows shows the SQL code that is used to generate the I/O per data file statistics.

```
SVRMGR> Rem I/O should be spread evenly across drives. A big difference between
SVRMGR> Rem phys_reads and phys_blks_rd implies table scans are going on.
SVRMGR> select table_space, file_name,
     2>          phys_reads reads, phys_blks_rd blks_read, phys_rd_time read_time,
     3>          phys_writes writes, phys_blks_wr blks_wrt, phys_wrt_tim
write_time,
     4>          megabytes_size megabytes,
     5>          round(decode(phys_blks_rd,0,0,phys_rd_time/phys_blks_rd),2)
avg_rt,
     6>          round(decode(phys_reads,0,0,phys_blks_rd/phys_reads),2)
"blocks/rd"
     7>   from stats$files order by table_space, file_name;
```

TABLE_SPACE		FILE_NAME				
READS	BLKS_READ	READ_TIME	WRITES	BLKS_WRT	WRITE_TIME	MEGABYTES
AVG_RT	blocks/rd					
DATA		\\.\DATA_1_1				
45483	45483	0	3592	3592	0	4297
0	1					
DATA		\\.\DATA_1_2				
88673	88673	0	20337	20337	0	4297
0	1					
DATA		\\.\DATA_1_3				
71664	71663	0	11087	11087	0	4297
0	1					
DATA		\\.\DATA_1_4				
44042	44042	0	2863	2863	0	4297
0	1					
DATA		\\.\DATA_1_5				
59236	59235	0	3239	3239	0	4297
0	1					

Table_space is the tablespace name. File_name is the name of the datafile. Phys_reads is the total number of physical reads that is requesting data from the data file. Phys_blks_rd is the total number of blocks read from disk to satisfy the physical reads. Phys_rd_time is the total amount of time it took to read the phys_blks_rd from disk and is listed in hundredths of a second. Phys_writes is the total number of physical writes to the data file. Phys_blks_wrt is the total number of blocks written to disk to satisfy the physical writes. Phys_wrt_time is the total amount of time it took to write phys_blks_wrt to disk and is listed in hundredths of a second. Megabytes_size is the size of the data file in megabytes.

Both the tablespace and data file I/O statistics enable you to take a more detailed look at your disk I/O. The data file I/O statistics provide a more granular level of detail than the tablespace I/O statistics. For an optimally tuned database, your disk I/O should be spread as evenly as possible across all of your drives. If the total I/O (phys_blks_rd + phys_blks_wrt) for each tablespace or data file is not evenly distributed, you might need to investigate how you can arrange your data within your tablespaces or data files, so that the I/O distribution is more even. You might also want to place tablespaces or data files with heavier I/O on faster drives. If you have a tablespace or a datafile that has particularly more I/O, you might want to add one or more data files to the tablespace and distribute those data files across multiple physical drives.

It is also important that you do not exceed the I/O recommendations of your hard drives. I/O recommendations are usually identified in I/Os per second. To get the number of I/Os per second per drive, you need to add all of the phys_reads and phys_writes for each data file residing on a single disk or disk array. If you are calculating I/O rates on a disk array, you will need to divide the sum of the I/O on that disk array by the number of drives in the disk array. If the number of I/Os per second per drive is larger than recommended, you can either add more hard drives or move some of the I/O to another disk or disk array.

The ratio of phys_blks_rd to phys_reads shows the average number of blocks per physical read. A high ratio might indicate that table scans are being done. If this ratio is high, you might want to look at your database applications and make sure they are correctly using indexes.

BSTAT/ESTAT Start and End Times

This section of the BSTAT/ESTAT report lists the start and end times of your measurement interval. This information is useful for documentation purposes when you compare BSTAT/ESTAT output files. You can also use the elapsed time to determine space requirements such as how much log space was used over a period of time.

KNOW YOUR TIME ───────────────────────────

It is important to know when and for how long the statistics were run. This allows you to calculate rates and to know if you are actually averaging rates in slow times as well as peak times. It is convenient that Oracle has provided this for you.

Versions

This section of the BSTAT/ESTAT report lists the Oracle products and versions that are running in your database system.

Statspack

Oracle9i Statspack is a new and different way to take snapshots of Oracle statistics. The Oracle9i Statspack is a package that is loaded into the shared pool just like any other package, and is then run whenever you want to take a snapshot. Statspack collects more data than UTLBSTAT/UTLESTAT did, and does not delete the snapshot tables after it has finished running. The process involves taking snapshots whenever you want and then processing differences between the selected snapshots. In this section, you will learn how to install, run, and interpret Statspack statistics. Remember: Whether you are using UTLBSTAT/UTLESTAT or Statspack, the data is coming from the same place: the dynamic performance views.

Installing Statpack

Statpack is installed by running a SQL script that creates the Staspack package. This script is called spcreate.sql and is in the rdbms/admin directory in the ORACLE_HOME directory structure. To run this script, connect into the instance using an administrative account as SYSDBA using the command:

```
SQL> CONNECT name/password AS SYSDBA
```

Then run the spcreate script using the following command for Unix:

```
SQL> @?/rdbms/admin/spcreate
```

For NT, use the following command:

```
SQL>  @%ORACLE_HOME%\rdbms\admin\spcreate
```

This creates the Statspack package and the perfstat user.

Running Statspack

Statspack is run by connecting into the instance under the perfstat username and running the statspack.snap stored procedure. This creates a snapshot of the dynamic performance data. An example of this is shown here:

```
SQL>  CONNECT perfstat/perfstat
SQL>  EXECUTE statspack.snap;
```

After you have taken enough snapshots, you then must create the results file. The first step in creating the results file is to determine which set of snapshots to use as the beginning and ending points. Then choose these points and the report file will be created for you. The SQL script spreport displays the available snapshots and creates the report as shown here.

```
SQL> @spreport

Current Instance
~~~~~~~~~~~~~~~~

    DB Id    DB Name     Inst Num Instance
 ----------- ----------- -------- ------------
  716551076 ORAC               1 ORAC



Instances in this Statspack schema
~~~~~~~~~~~~~~~~~~~~~~~~~~~~~~~~~~~

    DB Id    Inst Num DB Name     Instance     Host
 ----------- -------- ----------- ------------ ------------
  716551076         1 ORAC        ORAC         ptc6

Using  716551076 for database Id
Using           1 for instance number

Completed Snapshots

                              Snap                  Snap
Instance     DB Name          Id   Snap Started     Level Comment
------------ ------------ ----- ---------------- ----- ---------------------
ORAC         ORAC             1 21 Dec 2001 09:08     5
                              2 21 Dec 2001 09:12     5
                              3 21 Dec 2001 09:13     5



Specify the Begin and End Snapshot Ids
~~~~~~~~~~~~~~~~~~~~~~~~~~~~~~~~~~~~~~~~
Enter value for begin_snap: 1
Begin Snapshot Id specified: 1

Enter value for end_snap: 3
End   Snapshot Id specified: 3



Specify the Report Name
~~~~~~~~~~~~~~~~~~~~~~~~~
```

```
The default report file name is sp_1_3.  To use this name,
press <return> to continue, otherwise enter an alternative.
Enter value for report_name:
```

After you choose the report name and press Return, the screen is filled with the Statspack output. This output is also written to the results file that was specified.

Administering Statspack

Occasionally, you might want to truncate the Statspack tables. You can do this by calling the SQL statement sptrunc.sql. This truncates all the Statspack data and warns you before it continues. Sptrunc.sql is located in the rdbms/admin directory.

Statspack Results

The Statspack results file contains much of the same information as the UTLBSTAT/UTLESTAT results file, and more. This section walks you through the main pieces of data that are shown in the results file. This data is interpreted in the same manner as UTLBSTAT/UTLESTAT.

General Information

The information starts out with the information on the system configuration and the duration of the statistics gathering, as shown here.

```
STATSPACK report for

DB Name         DB Id      Instance      Inst Num Release      Cluster Host
-----------     ---------- ------------  -------- -----------  ------- -----------
ORAC            714359326 orac                  1 9.0.1.1.1    NO      PTC5


                Snap Id    Snap Time         Sessions Curs/Sess Comment
                -------    ----------------- -------- --------- ------------------
Begin Snap:      1 05-Dec-01 06:24:02             7       5.3
  End Snap:      2 05-Dec-01 06:25:30             8       5.1
  Elapsed:                 1.47 (mins)


Cache Sizes (end)
~~~~~~~~~~~~~~~~~
              Buffer Cache:        32M    Std Block Size:        4K
         Shared Pool Size:        44M        Log Buffer:       512K
```

System Load

This gives you an overview of the load that was put on the system during the statistics collection period. Depending on your system, this might be very high or relatively low.

```
Load Profile
~~~~~~~~~~~~                          Per Second        Per Transaction
                                      ---------------    ---------------
                 Redo size:            4,279.14            188,282.00
             Logical reads:               30.05              1,322.00
             Block changes:               11.89                523.00
            Physical reads:                0.20                  9.00
           Physical writes:                0.00                  0.00
                User calls:                0.51                 22.50
                   Parses:                 1.31                 57.50
               Hard parses:                0.20                  9.00
                    Sorts:                 1.31                 57.50
                   Logons:                 0.01                  0.50
                 Executes:                 2.22                 97.50
             Transactions:                 0.02


  % Blocks changed per Read:  39.56    Recursive Call %:   97.78
  Rollback per transaction %:  0.00    Rows per Sort:      64.75
```

Cache

These statistics show the efficiency of the various caches in the SGA.

```
Instance Efficiency Percentages (Target 100%)
~~~~~~~~~~~~~~~~~~~~~~~~~~~~~~~~~~~~~~~~~~~~~~~~~
              Buffer Nowait %:  100.00      Redo NoWait %:  100.00
              Buffer  Hit   %:   99.32    In-memory Sort %:  100.00
              Library Hit   %:   85.53       Soft Parse %:   84.35
          Execute to Parse %:   41.03       Latch Hit %:   100.00
  Parse CPU to Parse Elapsed %:  41.67    % Non-Parse CPU:   99.91


  Shared Pool Statistics      Begin    End
                              ------   ------
              Memory Usage %:  45.40    46.84
        % SQL with executions>1:  43.56    49.06
     % Memory for SQL w/exec>1:  49.92    70.38
```

Wait Events

These statistics are useful for finding where the RDBMS waits on resources.

```
Top 5 Wait Events
~~~~~~~~~~~~~~~~~~                                    Wait     % Total
Event                               Waits   Time (s)  Wt Time
.................................. ........ .......... ........
control file parallel write            28        0     30.24
control file sequential read           42        0     28.29
db file sequential read                18        0     16.35
log file parallel write                 6        0     15.01
log file sync                           2        0     10.11
          -------------------------------------------------------------
Wait Events for DB: ORAC  Instance: orac  Snaps: 1 -2
-> s  - second
-> cs - centisecond -    100th of a second
-> ms - millisecond -   1000th of a second
-> us - microsecond - 1000000th of a second
-> ordered by wait time desc, waits desc (idle events last)


                                                      Avg
                                        Total Wait    wait     Waits
Event                    Waits   Timeouts  Time (s)    (ms)     /txn
.......................  ......  ........ .......... ...... ........
control file parallel write     28        0          0        13     14.0
control file sequential read    42        0          0         8     21.0
db file sequential read         18        0          0        11      9.0
log file parallel write          6        5          0        29      3.0
log file sync                    2        0          0        59      1.0
SQL*Net message from client     37        0        111      3003     18.5
virtual circuit status           2        2         60     30003      1.0
SQL*Net message to client       38        0          0         0     19.0
          -------------------------------------------------------------
Background Wait Events for DB: ORAC  Instance: orac  Snaps: 1 -2
-> ordered by wait time desc, waits desc (idle events last)


                                                      Avg
                                        Total Wait    wait     Waits
Event                    Waits   Timeouts  Time (s)    (ms)     /txn
.......................  ......  ........ .......... ...... ........
control file parallel write     28        0          0        13     14.0
log file parallel write          6        5          0        29      3.0
```

```
control file sequential read          6          0          0     16     3.0
rdbms ipc message                     95         92        261   2750    47.5
pmon timer                            33         33         87   2642    16.5
          -------------------------------------------------------------------
```

Top-Running SQL

These statistics show the top-running SQL statements ordered by DB gets. In other words, these are the statements that read the most pages. The statistics have been truncated.

```
SQL ordered by Gets for DB: ORAC  Instance: orac  Snaps: 1 -2
-> End Buffer Gets Threshold:   10000
-> Note that resources reported for PL/SQL include the resources used by
   all SQL statements called within the PL/SQL code.  As individual SQL
   statements are also reported, it is possible and valid for the summed
   total % to exceed 100

                                                    CPU     Elapsed
  Buffer Gets    Executions  Gets per Exec  %Total Time (s)  Time (s) Hash Value
- - - - - - - - - - -  - - - - - - - - - -  - - - - - - - - - -  - - - - - -  - - - - - - - -  - - - - - - - - -  - - - - - - - - - -
          728           105            6.9   27.5    0.02      0.10 1536916657
select con#,type#,condlength,intcols,robj#,rcon#,match#,refact,n
vl(enabled,0),rowid,cols,nvl(defer,0),mtime,nvl(spare1,0) from c
def$ where obj#=:1


...


            6             2            3.0    0.2    0.00      0.01  931956286
select grantee#,privilege#,nvl(col#,0),max(mod(nvl(option$,0),2)
)from objauth$ where obj#=:1 group by grantee#,privilege#,nvl(co
l#,0) order by grantee#


            4             2            2.0    0.2    0.00      0.01 1453445442
select col#, grantee#, privilege#,max(mod(nvl(option$,0),2)) fro
m objauth$ where obj#=:1 and col# is not null group by privilege
#, col#, grantee# order by col#, grantee#
```

Top-Running SQL by Reads

These statistics show the top-running SQL statements ordered by DB reads. In other words, these are the statements that read the most pages from disk. The statistics have been truncated.

```
SQL ordered by Reads for DB: ORAC  Instance: orac  Snaps: 1 -2
-> End Disk Reads Threshold:     1000


                                                 CPU     Elapsed
Physical Reads  Executions  Reads per Exec %Total Time (s)  Time (s) Hash Value
--------------- ------------ --------------- ------ -------- --------- ----------
            19         102            0.2  105.6     0.05      0.47 199702406
select i.obj#,i.ts#,i.file#,i.block#,i.intcols,i.type#,i.flags,
i.property,i.pctfree$,i.initrans,i.maxtrans,i.blevel,i.leafcnt,i
.distkey, i.lblkkey,i.dblkkey,i.clufac,i.cols,i.analyzetime,i.sa
mplesize,i.dataobj#, nvl(i.degree,1),nvl(i.instances,1),i.rowcnt
,mod(i.pctthres$,256),i.indmethod#,i.trunccnt,nvl(c.unicols,0),n


             5         105            0.0   27.8     0.02      0.10 1536916657
select con#,type#,condlength,intcols,robj#,rcon#,match#,refact,n
vl(enabled,0),rowid,cols,nvl(defer,0),mtime,nvl(spare1,0) from c
def$ where obj#=:1


...

             2           2            1.0    0.00     0.00 189272129
select o.owner#,o.name,o.namespace,o.remoteowner,o.linkname,o.su
bname,o.dataobj#,o.flags from obj$ o where o.obj#=:1


             2           2            1.0    0.00     0.01 931956286
select grantee#,privilege#,nvl(col#,0),max(mod(nvl(option$,0),2)
)from objauth$ where obj#=:1 group by grantee#,privilege#,nvl(co
l#,0) order by grantee#
```

Top-Running SQL by Executions

These statistics show the top-running SQL statements ordered by DB executions. In other words, these are the statements that have executed the most commands. The statistics have been truncated.

```
SQL ordered by Executions for DB: ORAC  Instance: orac  Snaps: 1 -2
-> End Executions Threshold:     100


                                          CPU per  Elap per
Executions  Rows Processed  Rows per Exec  Exec (s)  Exec (s) Hash Value
----------- --------------- --------------- ---------- ---------- ----------
          2               0            0.0     0.00      0.01 1453445442
select col#, grantee#, privilege#,max(mod(nvl(option$,0),2)) fro
m objauth$ where obj#=:1 and col# is not null group by privilege
```

```
#, col#, grantee# order by col#, grantee#


            2               2            1.0      0.00        0.00 1930240031
select pos#,intcol#,col#,spare1,bo#,spare2 from icol$ where obj#
=:1


...


            2               2     0.02 1930240031
select pos#,intcol#,col#,spare1,bo#,spare2 from icol$ where obj#
=:1


            2               7     0.02 2085632044
select intcol#,nvl(pos#,0),col# from ccol$ where con#=:1


            1               2     0.01  931956286
```

Top-Running SQL by Parse Calls

These statistics show the top-running SQL statements ordered by parse calls. In other words, these are the statements that have caused the most parses to be done. These statistics have been truncated.

```
SQL ordered by Parse Calls for DB: ORAC  Instance: orac  Snaps: 1 -2
-> End Parse Calls Threshold:       1000


                           % Total
Parse Calls Executions    Parses  Hash Value
----------- ------------ -------- ----------
select grantee#,privilege#,nvl(col#,0),max(mod(nvl(option$,0),2)
)from objauth$ where obj#=:1 group by grantee#,privilege#,nvl(co
l#,0) order by grantee#


            1               2     0.01 1453445442
select col#, grantee#, privilege#,max(mod(nvl(option$,0),2)) fro
m objauth$ where obj#=:1 and col# is not null group by privilege
#, col#, grantee# order by col#, grantee#


...


            0               0     0.00  641766606
insert into col$(obj#,name,intcol#,segcol#,type#,length,precisio
n#,scale,null$,offset,fixedstorage,segcollength,deflength,defaul
```

```
t$,col#,property,charsetid,charsetform,spare1,spare2,spare3)valu
es(:1,:2,:3,:4,:5,:6,decode(:7,0,null,:7),decode(:5,2,decode(:8,
-127/*MAXSB1MINAL*/,null,:8),178,:8,179,:8,180,:8,181,:8,182,:8,


          0          0    0.00   787265282
BEGIN        /* NOP UNLESS A TABLE OBJECT */       IF dictionary_
obj_type = 'TABLE' THEN          sys.dbms_cdc_publish.change_tabl


SQL ordered by Parse Calls for DB: ORAC  Instance: orac  Snaps: 1 -2
-> End Parse Calls Threshold:     1000


                       % Total
 Parse Calls  Executions  Parses  Hash Value
 ----------- ----------- -------- ----------
```

Instance Activity

This portion of the output is the information gathered from V$SYSTAT and represents the activity that has been going on in the instance.

```
Instance Activity Stats for DB: ORAC  Instance: orac  Snaps: 1 -2
```

Statistic	Total	per Second	per Trans
CPU used by this session	175	2.0	87.5
CPU used when call started	175	2.0	87.5
CR blocks created	1	0.0	0.5
SQL*Net roundtrips to/from client	36	0.4	18.0
background timeouts	85	1.0	42.5
buffer is not pinned count	333	3.8	166.5
buffer is pinned count	254	2.9	127.0
bytes received via SQL*Net from c	4,446	50.5	2,223.0
bytes sent via SQL*Net to client	8,425	95.7	4,212.5
calls to get snapshot scn: kcmgss	242	2.8	121.0
calls to kcmgas	22	0.3	11.0
calls to kcmgcs	61	0.7	30.5
change write time	0	0.0	0.0
cleanouts only - consistent read	1	0.0	0.5
cluster key scan block gets	57	0.7	28.5
cluster key scans	41	0.5	20.5
commit cleanout failures: callbac	4	0.1	2.0
commit cleanouts	94	1.1	47.0
commit cleanouts successfully com	90	1.0	45.0

consistent changes	1	0.0	0.5
consistent gets	1,617	18.4	808.5
consistent gets - examination	240	2.7	120.0
current blocks converted for CR	0	0.0	0.0
cursor authentications	1	0.0	0.5
data blocks consistent reads - un	1	0.0	0.5
db block changes	1,046	11.9	523.0
db block gets	1,027	11.7	513.5
deferred (CURRENT) block cleanout	17	0.2	8.5
enqueue releases	131	1.5	65.5
enqueue requests	131	1.5	65.5
execute count	195	2.2	97.5
free buffer requested	118	1.3	59.0
immediate (CR) block cleanout app	1	0.0	0.5
immediate (CURRENT) block cleanou	39	0.4	19.5
leaf node splits	16	0.2	8.0
logons cumulative	1	0.0	0.5
messages received	5	0.1	2.5
messages sent	5	0.1	2.5
no buffer to keep pinned count	1,010	11.5	505.0
no work - consistent read gets	237	2.7	118.5
opened cursors cumulative	114	1.3	57.0
parse count (failures)	0	0.0	0.0
parse count (hard)	18	0.2	9.0
parse count (total)	115	1.3	57.5
parse time cpu	15	0.2	7.5
parse time elapsed	36	0.4	18.0
physical reads	18	0.2	9.0
physical reads direct	0	0.0	0.0
physical writes	0	0.0	0.0
physical writes direct	0	0.0	0.0
physical writes non checkpoint	0	0.0	0.0
prefetched blocks	0	0.0	0.0
process last non-idle time	1,007,555,058	11,449,489.3	############
recursive calls	1,984	22.6	992.0
recursive cpu usage	79	0.9	39.5
redo blocks written	689	7.8	344.5

Instance Activity Stats for DB: ORAC Instance: orac Snaps: 1 -2

Statistic	Total	per Second	per Trans
redo entries	567	6.4	283.5
redo size	376,564	4,279.1	188,282.0

```
redo synch time                           12            0.1          6.0
redo synch writes                          2            0.0          1.0
redo wastage                           1,496           17.0        748.0
redo write time                           23            0.3         11.5
redo writes                                6            0.1          3.0
rollback changes - undo records a          0            0.0          0.0
rollbacks only - consistent read           1            0.0          0.5
rows fetched via callback                  8            0.1          4.0
session connect time           1,007,555,058   11,449,489.3 ############
session logical reads                  2,644           30.1      1,322.0
session pga memory                   173,900        1,976.1     86,950.0
session pga memory max               173,900        1,976.1     86,950.0
session uga memory                    63,668          723.5     31,834.0
session uga memory max                91,080        1,035.0     45,540.0
shared hash latch upgrades - no w      1,075           12.2        537.5
sorts (memory)                           115            1.3         57.5
sorts (rows)                           7,446           84.6      3,723.0
switch current to new buffer               1            0.0          0.5
table fetch by rowid                     219            2.5        109.5
table fetch continued row                  0            0.0          0.0
table scan blocks gotten                  10            0.1          5.0
table scan rows gotten                    27            0.3         13.5
table scans (long tables)                  0            0.0          0.0
table scans (short tables)                11            0.1          5.5
user calls                                45            0.5         22.5
user commits                               2            0.0          1.0
```

I/O Statistics

This section gives I/O statistics by both tablespace and data file.

```
Tablespace IO Stats for DB: ORAC  Instance: orac  Snaps: 1 -2
->ordered by IOs (Reads + Writes) desc
```

```
Tablespace
------------------------------

               Av      Av     Av                    Av     Buffer Av Buf
       Reads Reads/s Rd(ms) Blks/Rd     Writes Writes/s    Waits Wt(ms)
------------- ------- ------ ------- ------------ -------- ---------- ------
SYSTEM
          18       0   11.1     1.0            0        0         0    0.0
          --------------------------------------------------------------
```

```
File IO Stats for DB: ORAC  Instance: orac  Snaps: 1 -2
->ordered by Tablespace, File
```

Tablespace				Filename					
		Av	Av	Av			Av	Buffer	Av Buf
	Reads	Reads/s	Rd(ms)	Blks/Rd		Writes	Writes/s	Waits	Wt(ms)
SYSTEM				C:\ORACLE\ORADATA\ORAC\SYSTEM01.DBF					
	18	0	11.1	1.0		0	0	0	

Buffer Pool Statistics

The buffer pool statistics give you an easy way to determine your cache hit ratio. The Statspack output does this for you rather than making you calculate the values yourself by hand.

```
Buffer Pool Statistics for DB: ORAC  Instance: orac  Snaps: 1 -2
-> Standard block size Pools  D: default,  K: keep,  R: recycle
-> Default Pools for other block sizes: 2k, 4k, 8k, 16k, 32k
```

P	Number of Buffers	Cache Hit %	Buffer Gets	Physical Reads	Physical Writes	Free Buffer Waits	Write Complete Waits	Buffer Busy Waits
D	7,864	99.3	2,489	18	0	0	0	0

Instance Recovery Statistics

These statistics provide information on how many redo blocks and estimated I/O operations are necessary were the instance required to recover. This can be useful for planning recovery operations without actually having to crash your system.

```
Instance Recovery Stats for DB: ORAC  Instance: orac  Snaps: 1 -2
-> B: Begin snapshot,  E: End snapshot
```

	Targt MTTR (s)	Estd MTTR (s)	Recovery Estd IOs	Actual Redo Blks	Target Redo Blks	Log File Size Redo Blks	Log Ckpt Timeout Redo Blks	Log Ckpt Interval Redo Blks
B	83	67	7864	13725	40233	184320	40233	#########

```
E    83    67       7864       14338        40922        184320       40922 ##########
     ------------------------------------------------------------------
```

PGA Memory Statistics

The PGA memory statistics provide information on the Program Global Area (PGA). The *PGA memory* is the memory used to store the data and control information for a server process. This memory is created by each server process on behalf of a user and is private to that user. These statistics are used to determine how much PGA memory is being used.

```
PGA Memory Stats for DB: ORAC   Instance: orac   Snaps: 1 -2
-> WorkArea (W/A) memory is used for: sort, bitmap merge, and hash join ops
```

Statistic	Begin (M)	End (M)	% Diff
maximum PGA allocated	8.411	8.608	2.35
total PGA allocated	8.411	8.608	2.35

Rollback Segment Statistics

Here you can determine the effectiveness of the rollback segments and whether more rollback segments are needed. Ignore these statistics if you are using Automatic Undo with Undo tablespaces.

```
Rollback Segment Stats for DB: ORAC   Instance: orac   Snaps: 1 -2
->A high value for "Pct Waits" suggests more rollback segments may be required
->RBS stats may not be accurate between begin and end snaps when using Auto Undo
  management, as RBS may be dynamically created and dropped as needed
```

RBS No	Trans Table Gets	Pct Waits	Undo Bytes Written	Wraps	Shrinks	Extends
0	1.0	0.00	0	0	0	0
1	5.0	0.00	0	0	0	0
2	3.0	0.00	0	0	0	0
3	8.0	0.00	0	0	0	0
4	5.0	0.00	0	0	0	0
5	79.0	0.00	112,582	0	0	0
6	3.0	0.00	122	0	0	0
7	4.0	0.00	1,704	0	0	0
8	7.0	0.00	0	0	0	0
9	9.0	0.00	0	0	0	0
10	1.0	0.00	0	0	0	0

```
        ------------------------------------------------------------
Rollback Segment Storage for DB: ORAC  Instance: orac  Snaps: 1 -2
->Optimal Size should be larger than Avg Active

RBS No    Segment Size     Avg Active     Optimal Size     Maximum Size
------    ------------     ----------     ------------     ------------
    0         425,984              0                            425,984
    1       4,321,280        104,857                          4,321,280
    2       8,515,584        104,857                          8,515,584
    3       7,335,936        104,857                          7,335,936
    4       4,321,280              0                          4,321,280
    5       2,224,128              0                          2,224,128
    6       2,224,128              0                          2,224,128
    7       7,467,008              0                          7,467,008
    8       7,598,080              0                          7,598,080
    9       3,338,240              0                          3,338,240
   10       5,369,856              0                          5,369,856
```

Latch Activity Statistics

These statistics help you determine if you are experiencing excessive waits on latches.

```
Latch Activity for DB: ORAC  Instance: orac  Snaps: 1 -2
->"Get Requests", "Pct Get Miss" and "Avg Slps/Miss" are statistics for
  willing-to-wait latch get requests
->"NoWait Requests", "Pct NoWait Miss" are for no-wait latch get requests
->"Pct Misses" for both should be very close to 0.0
-> ordered by Wait Time desc, Avg Slps/Miss, Pct NoWait Miss desc
```

| | | Pct | Avg | Wait | | Pct |
| | Get | Get | Slps | Time | NoWait | NoWait |
Latch	Requests	Miss	/Miss	(s)	Requests	Miss
cache buffers chains	6,921	0.0		0	115	0.0
process allocation	1	0.0		0	1	0.0
redo copy	0			0	561	0.0
FOB s.o list latch	1	0.0		0	0	
SQL memory manager worka	67	0.0		0	0	
channel handle pool latc	1	0.0		0	0	
checkpoint queue latch	545	0.0		0	0	
dml lock allocation	54	0.0		0	0	
enqueues	400	0.0		0	0	
file number translation	17	0.0		0	0	

library cache load lock	96	0.0	0	0
sequence cache	6	0.0	0	0
row cache objects	582	0.0	0	0
redo writing	125	0.0	0	0
redo allocation	595	0.0	0	0
process group creation	1	0.0	0	0
post/wait queue latch	4	0.0	0	0
ncodef allocation latch	2	0.0	0	0
messages	193	0.0	0	0
list of block allocation	44	0.0	0	0
user lock	2	0.0	0	0
undo global data	196	0.0	0	0
transaction branch alloc	2	0.0	0	0
transaction allocation	60	0.0	0	0
sort extent pool	2	0.0	0	0
shared pool	1,272	0.0	0	0
session timer	33	0.0	0	0
session switching	2	0.0	0	0
session idle bit	103	0.0	0	0
session allocation	25	0.0	0	0
library cache	7,763	0.0	0	0
event group latch	1	0.0	0	0
enqueue hash chains	240	0.0	0	0
child cursor hash table	191	0.0	0	0
channel operations paren	30	0.0	0	0
cache buffers lru chain	119	0.0	0	0
active checkpoint queue	28	0.0	0	0

```
          -------------------------------------------------------------
```

Data Dictionary Cache Statistics

These statistics show the data dictionary cache hit rates. The percent misses should be low; however, in the following example, the sample size is so small that this is not the case.

```
Dictionary Cache Stats for DB: ORAC  Instance: orac  Snaps: 1 -2
->"Pct Misses"  should be very low (< 2% in most cases)
->"Cache Usage" is the number of cache entries being used
->"Pct SGA"     is the ratio of usage to allocated size for that cache
```

Cache	Get Requests	Pct Miss	Scan Reqs	Pct Miss	Mod Reqs	Final Usage	Pct SGA
dc_object_ids	50	4.0	0		0	341	98
dc_objects	105	9.5	0		0	1,214	99

```
dc_profiles                         1    0.0     0              0          1   6
dc_segments                        66    9.1     0              0        149  89
dc_user_grants                      6   50.0     0              0         19  95
dc_usernames                       35    2.9     0              0         12  57
dc_users                           31    3.2     0              0         27  90
         ----------------------------------------------------------------
```

Library Cache Statistics

These statistics show the library cache hit rates. The percent misses should be low; however, in this example, the sample size is so small that this is not the case.

```
Library Cache Activity for DB: ORAC  Instance: orac  Snaps: 1 -2
->"Pct Misses"  should be very low
```

Namespace	Get Requests	Pct Miss	Pin Requests	Pct Miss	Reloads	Invali- dations
BODY	2	0.0	2	0.0	0	0
CLUSTER	2	0.0	2	0.0	0	0
SQL AREA	121	4.1	570	9.5	0	0
TABLE/PROCEDURE	240	4.2	380	22.1	0	0

SGA Memory Summary

This section summarizes how the SGA is divided and what space is being used. This is a useful reference that you should look at early in your analysis of the data.

```
SGA Memory Summary for DB: ORAC  Instance: orac  Snaps: 1 -2
```

SGA regions	Size in Bytes
Database Buffers	33,554,432
Fixed Size	282,576
Redo Buffers	532,480
Variable Size	83,886,080
	----------------
sum	118,255,568

```
SGA breakdown difference for DB: ORAC  Instance: orac  Snaps: 1 -2
```

Pool	Name	Begin value	End value	% Diff
java	free memory	27,934,720	27,934,720	0.00
java	memory in use	5,619,712	5,619,712	0.00
shared	1M buffer	1,049,088	1,049,088	0.00
shared	Checkpoint queue	141,152	141,152	0.00
shared	DML lock	100,408	100,408	0.00
shared	FileIdentificatonBlock	323,292	323,292	0.00
shared	FileOpenBlock	695,504	695,504	0.00
shared	KGK heap	3,756	3,756	0.00
shared	KGLS heap	1,287,864	1,330,116	3.28
shared	KSXR pending messages que	226,636	226,636	0.00
shared	KSXR receive buffers	1,060,000	1,060,000	0.00
shared	PL/SQL DIANA	2,869,468	2,869,468	0.00
shared	PL/SQL MPCODE	248,656	248,656	0.00
shared	PLS non-lib hp	2,068	2,068	0.00
shared	VIRTUAL CIRCUITS	266,120	266,120	0.00
shared	character set object	315,704	315,704	0.00
shared	db_handles	93,000	93,000	0.00
shared	dictionary cache	912,928	925,052	1.33
shared	enqueue	171,860	171,860	0.00
shared	errors	55,208	55,208	0.00
shared	event statistics per sess	1,356,600	1,356,600	0.00
shared	fixed allocation callback	60	60	0.00
shared	free memory	25,191,232	24,525,628	-2.64
shared	joxlod: in ehe	318,400	318,400	0.00
shared	joxlod: in phe	114,316	114,316	0.00
shared	joxs heap init	4,220	4,220	0.00
shared	ksm_file2sga region	148,652	148,652	0.00
shared	library cache	3,527,568	3,614,696	2.47
shared	message pool freequeue	772,672	772,672	0.00
shared	miscellaneous	2,333,672	2,350,200	0.71
shared	parameters	9,396	9,396	0.00
shared	processes	127,800	127,800	0.00
shared	sessions	395,760	395,760	0.00
shared	simulator trace entries	98,304	98,304	0.00
shared	sql area	1,728,272	2,234,972	29.32
shared	table definiti	840	1,680	100.00
shared	transaction	182,376	182,376	0.00
shared	trigger defini	2,324	2,324	0.00
shared	trigger inform	1,108	1,140	2.89
shared	trigger source	1,060	1,060	0.00

```
db_cache_size or                      33,554,432       33,554,432     0.00
db_block_buffers
fixed_sga                                282,576          282,576     0.00
log_buffer                               524,288          524,288     0.00
    ----------------------------------------------------------------
```

Init.ora Parameters

The summary of the parameters is important. This should be one of the first things that you look at to determine if something is out of order (see the sidebar earlier in this chapter titled "Know Your Parameters").

```
init.ora Parameters for DB: ORAC  Instance: orac  Snaps: 1 -2
```

```
                                                          End value
Parameter Name               Begin value                 (if different)
-------------------------    -----------------------      --------------
background_dump_dest         C:\oracle\admin\ORAC\bdump
compatible                   9.0.0
control_files                C:\oracle\oradata\ORAC\CONTROL01.
core_dump_dest               C:\oracle\admin\ORAC\cdump
db_block_size                4096
db_cache_size                33554432
db_domain
db_name                      ORAC
dispatchers                  (PROTOCOL=TCP)(SER=MODOSE), (PROT
fast_start_mttr_target       300
ifile                        C:\oracle\admin\ORAC\pfile\init.o
instance_name                ORAC
java_pool_size               33554432
large_pool_size              1048576
open_cursors                 300
processes                    150
remote_login_passwordfile    EXCLUSIVE
shared_pool_size             46137344
sort_area_size               524288
timed_statistics             TRUE
undo_management              AUTO
undo_tablespace              UNDOTBS
user_dump_dest               C:\oracle\admin\ORAC\udump
    ----------------------------------------------------------------
```

```
End of Report
```

Summary

Although Oracle's BSTAT/ESTAT utilities still require DBAs to know a lot about Oracle statistics to tune their database systems, these utilities also provide an easier way to gather statistics. Further information on Oracle's BSTAT/ESTAT utilities can be found in the Oracle9i Reference Manual and the Oracle9i Tuning Guide.

In addition to BSTAT/ESTAT, the Oracle Statspack package provides a different view of the same statistics. Those of you who are already familiar with BSTAT/ESTAT might prefer to stick with what you know; however, you might find some benefit from migrating to Statspack. Its presentation and ease of use are certainly beneficial.

PART II

Oracle Hardware Topics

IN THIS PART

8 Oracle and System Hardware

9 I/O Concepts

10 Oracle and I/O

ORACLE AND SYSTEM HARDWARE

Oracle depends on the system hardware to function, and the way in which the hardware interacts with Oracle determines the system performance. In this chapter, you will learn how Oracle9i works and how it uses the system hardware. By understanding how the hardware is used, you can more easily determine which hardware components might be limiting Oracle performance and how either the hardware or Oracle can be tuned to perform better.

The chapter begins with an overview of the Oracle instance. This is followed by a survey of different hardware components and their performance characteristics. From there, the chapter compares different types of hardware. Finally, an introduction to clustering is covered at the end of the chapter.

Parameters Used in This Chapter

This chapter includes the use of many Oracle initialization parameters. Chapter 2, "Using the Oracle Configuration Parameters," introduced you to these parameters and explained how to use them. In this chapter, the following initialization parameters are covered:

- DB_CACHE_SIZE. This parameter specifies the amount of memory that is used for the Oracle buffer cache. This parameter can be specified in K, M, or G for Kilobytes, Megabytes, or Gigabytes.

- DB_2K_CACHE_SIZE, DB_4K_CACHE_SIZE, DB_8K_CACHE_SIZE, DB_16K_CACHE_SIZE, DB_32K_CACHE_SIZE, DB_64K_CACHE_SIZE. These parameters set the nonstandard block size cache sizes.

- DB_BLOCK_SIZE. DB_BLOCK_SIZE sets the size of the standard block.

- DBWR_PROCESSES. This sets the number of database writer processes. For systems in which database writing is heavy, this might improve performance.

- DBWR_IO_SLAVES. This is used in systems with one DBWR process. By setting a number of IO slaves, asynchronous I/O can be simulated. This is useful on systems in which asynchronous I/O is not available.

- DISK_ASYNCH_IO. This specifies whether asynchronous I/O operations can be performed.

Overview of the Oracle Instance

The Oracle Relational Database Management System (RDBMS) is a product that is designed to allow simultaneous access into large amounts of stored information. The RDBMS consists of the database (the information) and the instance (the embodiment of the system). The database consists of both the physical files that reside on the system and the logical pieces such as the database schema. These database files take various forms, as described in the following section. The instance is the method that is used to access the data and consists of processes and system memory.

The Oracle instance consists of the Oracle processes and shared memory that is necessary to access information in the database. The instance is made up of the user processes, the Oracle background processes, and the shared memory that is used by these processes (see Figure 8.1).

The Oracle Instance

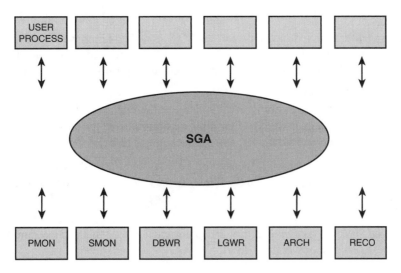

FIGURE 8.1
The Oracle instance.

It's a good time to look at the various pieces that make up the Oracle instance, starting with the shared memory, and then look at the various Oracle processes.

The Oracle Memory Structure

Oracle uses shared memory for several purposes, including caching of data and indexes as well as storing shared program code. This shared memory is used for several functions, and it is broken into various pieces, or memory structures. The basic memory structures that are associated with Oracle are the System Global Area (SGA) and the Program Global Area (PGA).

SGA

The SGA is a shared memory region that Oracle uses to store data and control information for one Oracle instance. The SGA is allocated when the Oracle instance starts; it is deallocated when the Oracle instance shuts down. Each Oracle instance that starts has its own SGA. The information in the SGA is made up of the database buffers, the redo log buffer, and the shared pool; each has a fixed size and is created at instance startup.

- Database buffer cache. The buffer cache stores the most recently used data blocks. These blocks can contain modified data that has not yet been written to disk (sometimes known as *dirty blocks*), blocks that have not been modified, or blocks that have been written to disk since modification (sometimes known as *clean blocks*). Because the buffer cache keeps blocks based on a most recently used algorithm, the most active buffers stay in memory to reduce I/O and improve performance. With Oracle9i, you can have multiple buffer caches as well as buffer caches with different block sizes.

- Redo log buffer. The redo log buffer of the SGA stores redo entries or a log of changes made to the database. The redo log buffers are written to the redo log as quickly and efficiently as possible. Remember that the redo log is used for instance recovery in the event of a system failure.

- The large pool. The large pool is an optionally configurable area that serves many different purposes. The large pool can be used for session memory for multithreaded server processes, for I/O server processes, and for backup and recovery operations.

- Shared pool. The shared pool is the area of the SGA that stores shared memory structures such as shared SQL areas in the library cache, and internal information in the data dictionary.

Each area of the SGA has its own purpose, and sizing each one correctly can optimize performance. The next sections look at these areas.

The Buffer Cache

The buffer cache stores the most recently used data blocks so that they can be accessed more quickly. These blocks contain both unmodified data that has been read into the cache as well as data that has been modified (dirty blocks). These blocks are stored as part of a least recently used list, where the blocks that have not been accessed recently will be reused first. When a block in cache is accessed, it is again moved to the most recently used part of the list.

In earlier versions of Oracle, the block size in the buffer cache was the same block size that was used for the creation of the database. With Oracle9i, it is possible to have multiple block sizes both on disk and in the buffer cache. When the database is created, it is created with a default block size. Tablespaces can now be created with nondefault block sizes.

The DB_CACHE_SIZE parameter determines the amount of memory that is allocated for the buffer cache. The DB_BLOCK_SIZE parameter sets the standard block size, and DB_2K_CACH_SIZE (among others) sets nonstandard cache sizes.

Using multiple block sizes can be an advantage in an environment where mixed workloads are present. This might include OLTP, which benefits from a smaller block size, and data warehousing applications that benefit from a larger block size.

The Log Buffer

The redo log buffer is a cache where redo log entries are placed before they are written to the redo log. The server processes write to the redo log buffer. The log writer reads the redo log buffer and then writes those entries to the redo log files.

The Large Pool

The large pool is an area in the SGA that is used for session memory for the multithreaded server processes as well as for backup and restore operations. The large pool is optional.

The Shared Pool

The shared pool is important because an insufficient amount of memory allocated to the shared pool can cause performance degradation. The shared pool is made up of both the library cache and the data dictionary cache.

The Library Cache

The library cache is used to store shared SQL. Here is the cached parse tree and the execution plan for every unique SQL statement. If multiple applications issue the same SQL statement, each of them can access the shared SQL area to reduce the amount of memory that is needed and to reduce the processing time that is used for parsing and execution planning.

Data Dictionary Cache

The data dictionary contains a set of tables and views Oracle uses as a reference to the database. Oracle stores information here about both the logical and physical structure of the database. The data dictionary contains information such as the following:

- User information such as user privileges

- Integrity constraints defined for tables in the database

- Names and data types of all columns in database tables

- Information on space allocated and used for schema objects

Oracle frequently accesses the data dictionary for the parsing of SQL statements. This access is essential to the operation of Oracle; performance bottlenecks in the data dictionary affect all Oracle users. By making sure that you have allocated a sufficient amount of memory to the shared pool, you should see no performance problems.

PGA

The PGA is a memory area that contains data and control information for the Oracle server processes. The amount and content of the PGA depends on the Oracle server options that you have installed. This area is made up of the following components:

- Stack space. This is the memory that holds the session's variables, arrays, and so on.

- Session information. If you are not running the multithreaded server, the session information is stored in the PGA. If you are running the multithreaded server, the session information is stored in the SGA.

- Private SQL area. This is an area in the PGA where information such as binding variables and runtime buffers are kept.

Processes

The term *process* is used in this book to describe a thread of execution, or a mechanism that can execute a set of code. In many operating systems, traditional "processes" have been replaced with "threads" or "lightweight processes." In this book, the term process refers to the mechanism of execution and can refer to either a traditional process or a thread.

The Oracle RDBMS uses two types of processes: the user processes and the Oracle processes (also known as *background processes*). In some operating systems, such as Windows NT, these processes are actually threads, but for consistency, they will be called processes here.

User Processes

User, or client, processes are the user's connections into the RDBMS system. The user process manipulates the user's input and communicates with the Oracle server process through the Oracle program interface. The user process is also used to display the information that the user requests and, if necessary, it can process this information into a more useful form.

Oracle Processes

The Oracle processes perform functions for the users. The Oracle processes can be split into two groups: server processes (which perform functions for the invoking process) and background processes (which perform functions on behalf of the entire RDBMS).

Server Processes (Shadow Processes)

The server processes, also known as *shadow processes*, communicate with the user and interact with Oracle to carry out the user's requests. For example, if the user process requests a piece of data that is not already in the SGA, the shadow process is responsible for reading the data blocks from the data files into the SGA. A one-to-one correlation can exist between the user processes and the shadow processes (as in a dedicated server configuration). Although one shadow process can connect to multiple user processes (as in a multithreaded server configuration), doing so reduces the utilization of system resources.

Background Processes

Background processes are the Oracle processes that are used to perform various tasks within the RDBMS system. These tasks vary from communicating with other Oracle instances, performing system maintenance and cleanup, to writing dirty blocks to disk. Following are brief descriptions of the nine Oracle background processes:

DBWR	(Database Writer). DBWR is responsible for writing dirty data blocks from the database block buffers to disk. When a transaction changes data in a data block, it is not necessary for that data block to be immediately written to disk. Because of this, the DBWR can write this data out to disk in a manner that is more efficient than writing when each transaction completes. Usually, the DBWR writes only when the database block buffers are needed for data to be read in. When data is written out, it is done in a least recently used fashion. For systems in which asynchronous I/O (AIO) is available, only one DBWR process should exist. For systems in which the amount of log activity is high and asynchronous I/O is not available, you can enhance performance by increasing the number of DBWR processes or increasing the number of DBWR slaves.
LGWR	The Log Writer Process. The LGWR process is responsible for writing data from the log buffer to the redo log.
CKPT	The Checkpoint Process. The CKPT process is responsible for signaling the DBWR process to perform a checkpoint and to update all the data and control files for the database to indicate the most recent checkpoint. A *checkpoint* is an event in which the DBWR writes all modified database buffers to the data files. The CKPT process is optional. If the CKPT process is not present, the LGWR assumes these responsibilities.
PMON	The Process Monitor Process. PMON is responsible for keeping track of database processes and cleaning up if a process prematurely dies (PMON cleans up the cache and frees resources that might still be allocated). PMON is also responsible for restarting any dispatcher processes that might have failed.
SMON	The System Monitor Process. SMON performs instance recovery at instance startup. This includes cleaning up temporary segments and recovering transactions that have died because of a system crash. SMON also defragments the database by coalescing free extents within the database.
RECO	The Recovery Process. RECO is used to clean up transactions that were pending in a distributed database. RECO is responsible for committing or rolling back the local portion of the disputed transactions.

ARCH	The Archiver Process. ARCH is responsible for copying the online redo log files to archival storage when they become full. ARCH is active only when the RDBMS is operated in ARCHIVELOG mode. When a system is not operated in ARCHIVELOG mode, it might not be possible to recover after a system failure.
LCKn	The Parallel Server Lock Processes. Up to 10 LCK processes are used for inter-instance locking when the Oracle Parallel Server option is used.
Dnnn	The Dispatcher Processes. When the multithreaded server option is used, at least one Dispatcher process is used for every communications protocol in use. The Dispatcher process is responsible for routing requests from the user processes to available shared server processes and back.

System Architecture Overview

Your computer system is made up of thousands of individual components that are all working in harmony to process data. Each of these components has its own job to perform, and each has its own performance characteristics.

The brain of the system is the central processing unit (CPU), which actually processes all the calculations and instructions that run on the computer. The job of the rest of the system is to keep the CPU busy with instructions to process. It is better to be bound by the performance of the CPUs rather than by the performance of other subsystems. However, because you will most likely want to have some capacity left over for peak processing times, it is unwise to constantly run the CPU(s) at 100%.

How does the system keep the CPUs busy? In general, the system is made up of different layers, or tiers, of progressively slower components. Because the faster components are typically the most expensive, you must perform a balancing act between speed and cost efficiency.

The following sections look at the performance tiers.

CPUs and Caches

The CPU and the CPU cache are the fastest components of the system. The cache is high-speed memory that is used to store recently used data and instructions so that it can provide quick access if this data is used again in a short time. Most CPU hardware designs actually have a cache built into the CPU core. This internal cache is known as a Level 1 (or L1) cache. Typically, an L1 cache is small, on the order of 8–16 kilobytes (KB) in size.

When a certain piece of data is wanted, the hardware first looks in the L1 cache. If the data is there, the hardware processes that data immediately. If the data is not available in the L1 cache, the hardware looks in the L2 cache, which is external to the CPU core but resides on the chip because speed is important. The L2 cache is connected to the CPU chip(s) on the same side of the memory bus as the CPU. To get to main memory, you need to use the memory bus, which affects the speed of the memory access.

Although the L2 cache is twice as slow as the L1 cache, it is usually much larger. Its larger size provides a better chance of getting a cache hit. Typical L2 caches range from 128KB to 4MB in size.

Slower yet is the speed of the system memory. It is probably five times slower than the L2 cache. The size of system memory can range from 64MB for a small desktop PC up to 4 or 8 gigabytes (GB) for large server machines. Some supercomputers have even more system memory than that.

Figure 8.2 demonstrates the relative latencies of the various components that make up a computer system.

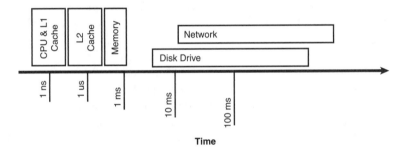

FIGURE 8.2
Component speed comparison.

As you can see from the timeline, an enormous difference exists between retrieving data from the L1 cache and retrieving data from the disk. This is why it's beneficial to spend time trying to take advantage of the SGA in memory. This is also why hardware vendors spend so much time designing CPU caches and fast memory busses.

Now look at some of these components and at the different types of computers and architectures.

CPU Design

The CPU is the brain of the computer. This is where most of the instruction processing happens. Although some intelligent devices such as disk controllers can process some instructions, the instructions that these devices can handle are limited to the control of data moving to and from the devices.

The CPU works off of the system clock and executes instructions based on clock signals. The clock rate and type of CPU determine how fast these instructions are executed.

The CPU usually falls into one of two groups of processors: Complex Instruction Set Computer (CISC) or Reduced Instruction Set Computer (RISC), as described following.

CISC Processors

CISC processors (such as the type of processors that Intel builds) are by far the most popular processors sold today. CISC processors are more traditional and offer a large instruction set to the program developer. Some of these instructions can be quite complicated; most instructions require several clock cycles to complete.

CISC processors are complex and difficult to build. Because these CPU chips contain millions of internal components, the components are extremely close together. The physical closeness causes problems because no room for error exists. Each year, technology allows more complex and faster chips to be built, but eventually physics limit what can be done.

CISC processors carry out a wide range of tasks and can sometimes perform two or more instructions at the same time. CISC processors perform most tasks such as RDBMS processing very well.

RISC Processors

RISC processors are based on the principle that if you can reduce the number of instructions the CPU processes, the CPU can be simpler to build and can run faster. By putting fewer internal components inside the chip, the speed of the chip can be turned up. One of the most popular RISC chips on the market today is the DEC Alpha.

Remember that the system compiler determines which instructions are executed on the CPU chips. When the number of instructions was reduced, compilers were written to take advantage of this fact and compensate for the missing instructions.

By reducing the instruction set, RISC manufacturers have been able to push the clock speed up many times that of CISC chips. Although the faster clock speed is beneficial in some cases, it offers little improvement in other cases. One result of a faster CPU is that the surrounding components such as L2 cache and memory must also run faster at an increase in cost.

Another goal of some RISC manufacturers is to design the chip so that the majority of instructions complete within one clock cycle. Some RISC chips today can already do this. But because some operations that are a single instruction for a CISC chip might be many instructions for a RISC chip, a speed-to-speed comparison cannot be made.

CISC VERSUS RISC

Both types of processors have their advantages and disadvantages. It is up to you to decide whether a RISC processor or a CISC processor will do the best job in your implementation.

When comparing the two types of processors, be sure that you look at performance data and not just at clock speed. Although the RISC chips have a much faster clock speed, they actually do less work per instruction. The performance of the system cannot be determined by clock speed alone.

Multiprocessors

Multiprocessor systems can provide significant performance with good value. With a multiprocessor system, you can start out with one or two processors and add additional processors as your business needs grow. Multiprocessors fall into several categories; two of the main types of multiprocessor systems are the Symmetric Multiprocessor (SMP) systems and the Massively Parallel Processing (MPP) systems.

Oracle typically scales well with additional CPUs. By adding additional CPUs, you can see significant performance improvement with little additional cost. Some factors that determine how much improvement you will get by adding more processors are the CPU cache and memory bus bandwidth.

SMP Systems

SMP systems usually consist of a standard computer architecture with two or more CPUs that share the system memory, I/O bus, and disks. The CPUs are called symmetric because each processor is identical to any other processor in terms of function. Because the processors share system memory, each processor looks at the same data and the same operating system. In fact, the SMP architecture is sometimes called a tightly coupled architecture because the CPUs can even share the operating system.

In the typical SMP system, only one copy of the operating system runs. Each processor works independently by taking the next available job that is ready to run. Because the Oracle architecture is based on many processes each working independently, you can see great improvement by adding additional processors.

The SMP system has these advantages: It is cost effective, high performing, and easily upgradeable. Upgrades consist simply of adding an additional CPU to the system to instantly and significantly increase performance. A typical SMP system supports from four to eight CPUs. Because the SMP system shares the system bus and memory, only a certain amount of activity can take place before the bandwidth of the bus is saturated. To add more processors, you must go to an MPP architecture.

MPP Systems

MPP architecture systems are based on many independent units. Each processor in an MPP system typically has its own resources such as its own local memory and I/O system. Each processor in an MPP system runs an independent copy of the operating system and its own independent copy of Oracle. An MPP system is sometimes referred to as a *loosely coupled architecture*.

You can think of an MPP system as large clusters of independent units that communicate through a high-speed interconnect. As with SMP systems, as you add processors, you will eventually hit the bandwidth limitations of the interconnect. However, the number of processors with which you hit this limit is typically much larger than with SMP systems.

If you can divide the application among the nodes in the cluster, MPP systems can achieve quite high scalability. Although MPP systems can achieve much higher performance than SMP systems, they are less economical: MPP systems typically are much higher in cost than SMP systems.

Regardless of whether you use a single-processor system, an SMP system, or an MPP system, the basic architecture of the CPUs is similar. In fact, you can find the same Intel processors in both SMP and MPP systems.

CPU Cache

As you learned earlier in this chapter, the system cache is important to the system. The job of the cache is to allow quick access to recently used instructions or data. A cache stores and retrieves data more quickly than the next level of storage (the L1 cache is faster than the L2 cache; the L2 cache is faster than main memory; and so on).

By caching frequently used instructions and data, you increase the likelihood of a cache hit, which can save precious clock cycles that otherwise would have been spent retrieving data from memory or disk.

A large CPU cache allows more data and executable code to be stored on the local processor than in memory, which reduces the number of times that the CPU must access main memory. Whenever the CPU accesses memory, a slowdown occurs while the CPU is waiting for that data or code to be retrieved. It is especially bad when the memory bus is busy and the CPU waits even longer until the bus becomes free.

32-Bit Versus 64-Bit Processors

64-bit processors have been available for several years, but they are not mainstream because far more 32-bit systems are sold than 64-bit systems. They tend to be included in more high-end workstations and servers rather than desktop personal computers. 64-bit processors have several advantages over 32-bit processors, including the ability to address more memory and the wider bus.

64-Bit Addressing

Probably the biggest benefit of 64-bit processors is the ability to address more memory than 32-bit processors. 32-bit processors are limited to addressing 4GB of RAM. With 64-bit systems you can access up to 16 terabytes (TB) of RAM. This can be a great advantage for larger databases. Although it is unlikely that anyone will use 16TB of RAM in the near future, it is quite likely that systems will find hundreds of gigabytes of RAM quite useful.

Bus Width

The 64-bit bus is twice as large as the 32-bit bus, thus allowing more data to be transferred from I/O to CPU, CPU to memory at a time. This is useful, especially when performing 64-bit mathematical calculations.

64-Bit Math

64-bit systems can now use a 64-bit wide integer and floating point number, making calculations of larger numbers possible. In addition, the accuracy of these calculations is also increased.

System Memory Architecture

The system memory is basically a set of memory chips, either protected or unprotected, that stores data and instructions that are used by the system. System memory can be protected by parity or a more sophisticated advanced ECC correction method. The system memory can range in size from 4MB on a small PC to 4GB on a large 32-bit SMP server and up to 16TB on a 64-bit processor.

Earlier in this chapter, you read an overview of how the system hardware operates. It is clear that any operation that has to access slower components, such as disk or network, slows down processing operations. Thus, it is important to have a sufficient amount of memory in your system.

This system memory is allocated to Oracle and used for database caching, user memory, and the shared pool, which is used for both the data dictionary and the library cache. It is important that you have enough memory for the shared pool because an insufficient shared pool can hurt performance. After the shared pool is satisfied, the more database buffers you can allocate to the DBMS the better. Be careful, though, not to starve out the PGA memory that is needed by your processes, and at all costs, avoid paging. You can never have too much memory in your system. Anything that can be cached reduces system I/O and improves performance.

The CPUs access system memory through a high-speed bus that allows large amounts of data and instructions to be moved from the CPU to L2 cache quickly. Typically, data and instructions are read from memory in large chunks and put into the cache, anticipating that the next instruction or data in that chunk is likely to be accessed next. This process is known as *prefetching*.

Depending on the specific implementation of an SMP system, the memory bus might be shared by all system processors. Alternatively, each processor might have a private bus to memory.

The amount of memory that is available to processes might be limited by the physical memory in the system or it might be more if you are using a virtual memory system.

Virtual Memory System

In a virtual memory system, the OS and hardware allow programs and users to use more memory than is actually available in the system hardware. This memory is known as *virtual memory*, a large amount of memory that can be mapped to physical memory. Virtual memory must be in physical memory to be used; it is copied out to disk if it is not being used and the space in physical memory is needed. The process of mapping virtual memory onto physical memory by copying the memory to and from disk is called *paging*, or *swapping* (depending on the OS architecture).

Paging and swapping serve the same purpose, but they operate slightly differently. In a swapping system, an entire process is *swapped out* (moved from memory to disk) or *swapped in* (moved from disk to memory). In a paging system, the movement of data to and from the secondary storage is done on a memory page basis; when more memory is needed, one or more pages are *paged out* (moved from memory to disk) to make room. If data is requested from virtual memory and is not in physical memory, the data is *paged in* (moved from disk to memory) as needed. The rest of this section uses the term *paging* to describe both paging and swapping.

Suppose that you have a computer system with 16M of physical memory. If you have a program that needs to access 20M of data, it is obvious that the process won't fit in physical memory. In a virtual memory system, the data is read in until little memory is left (the OS reserves some for itself); then the OS copies some of the data pages to disk with the paging mechanism. Usually, this is done using a least recently used algorithm in which the oldest data is moved out. When some memory has been freed, the program can read more data into memory. As far as the program is concerned, all the data is still in memory. In fact, it is in virtual memory. As the program begins to reread some of the data and manipulate it, different pieces might be paged in (from disk to physical memory) and paged out (from physical memory to disk).

As you can imagine, the process of paging in or paging out can be quite time consuming and uses substantial system resources. This is why you have been warned several times in this book not to use so much memory that you cause paging or swapping. Access to disk is approximately 50 times slower than access to memory.

Bus Design

So many bus designs are in use today that this book cannot go into much detail. A *bus* is a connection path that the system uses to move data from one place to another. Although this description sounds simple at first, when you look at it from a performance perspective, you encounter things like the capacity, or bandwidth, of the bus.

The term *bandwidth* is used to describe the amount of data that can be transmitted across the bus in a certain time. Bandwidth was originally used to describe the electronic characteristics of a circuit. Over the years, this term has been adopted by computer designers and is often used to describe the capacity of the bus in megabytes per second (or some other metric).

Several bus designs have been introduced in the past few years, all with the same goal: increased capacity. As processors, network hardware, disk controllers, and disks become increasingly fast, it is necessary for the bus to support the load that these faster devices generate.

You really don't have to worry about the bus under most circumstances. As computers increase in performance, computer designers are taking that performance into account; the system bus should not be a bottleneck in your system.

Having reviewed how the actual computer system works, it is now possible to understand how the hardware and the software affect system performance. This section will now look specifically at the areas that affect Oracle performance.

I/O Bus

The I/O bus is typically not a problem because the system is usually limited by the performance of the disk drives and I/O subsystem rather than the bus. It is unlikely that the speed of the I/O bus can become a bottleneck.

Network

The network is often a performance bottleneck when it is not properly designed. Aside from upgrading outdated hubs with higher-performing switches, you can't do much to tune the network. Designing a network with sufficient capacity is the best thing to do.

To Cluster or Not to Cluster

Oracle Real Application Clusters (RACs) can be another way to improve hardware capacity and provide a higher level of fault tolerance in your system. RACs are covered later in Chapter 16, "Oracle 9i Real Application Clusters."

Summary

In this chapter, you learned what makes a computer tick, and in doing so, you learned what Oracle has to work with. By understanding these components, you should better be able to live within the boundaries that you are given by these components. As you will see in Chapter 9, "I/O Concepts," living within the performance capacity of your components is important.

I/O CONCEPTS

Some of the most common Oracle performance problems involve the I/O subsystem. Because Oracle's main function is to manipulate data, and that data resides either in memory or on the I/O subsystem, any I/O performance problems result in Oracle performance problems. Much of the design of the Oracle RDBMS is intended to make accessing the I/O subsystem as efficient as possible.

In this chapter, the fundamental concepts and tuning of I/O subsystems are explored in great detail. By understanding the limitations of the I/O subsystem, you will be able to design and properly size it so that performance can be optimized. This chapter begins by describing the basics of how a disk drive works and what its limitations are. Next, the chapter describes RAID subsystems and explains how to properly configure and optimize them. Finally, the chapter covers advanced I/O subsystems, such as SAN and NAS storage.

In the next chapter, you will learn how Oracle interacts with the I/O subsystem. After you understand how the two interact, you can better configure your I/O subsystem for Oracle. A properly configured I/O subsystem allows Oracle to perform optimally. A poorly configured I/O subsystem can easily become a bottleneck and can severely affect performance.

The Disk Drive

The basic component of the I/O subsystem is the disk drive, also commonly known as the hard disk drive or hard disk. Anyone who has anything to do with computers knows what a disk drive is. This section presents a brief overview of how the disk drive operates and what the limiting factors are.

Later in this chapter, you will see how disk drives are used to create RAID arrays and how the disk drive performance limits interact with the RAID controller performance characteristics. By understanding these limitations, you can determine if you have a properly sized and configured I/O subsystem and solve any problems that you might have.

Overview

The disk drive is one of the few mechanical components in your computer's system. Being a mechanical component presents several challenges. Because the disk drive is made up of several motors and servos, some of which are running at high speeds, the disk drive can and does generate a great deal of heat. Because of this and frictional forces, the disk drive is one of the most likely components to fail in your system. In fact, most disk drive specifications tell you the average time between failures.

Because the disk drive is a mechanical component, certain laws of physics involved in its operation cannot be broken. This means that certain performance limitations cannot be altered.

Disk drives are made up of one or more disks, which are referred to as *platters*. A platter is a round disk that actually holds the data magnetically. Data is written around the platter in tracks just like a CD or record. A data track is in turn made up of individual chunks of data called *sectors*. A typical sector is 512 bytes. A platter is shown in Figure 9.1.

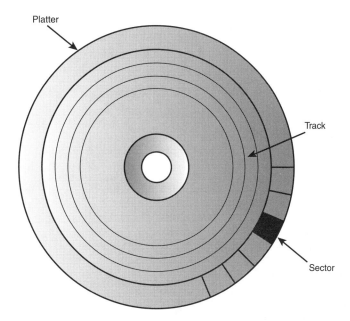

Platter

Track

Sector

FIGURE 9.1
A disk platter.

A disk armature rides above the disk drive and has a component on the end of it called the *head*. The head is used to read data from the sectors. This armature can only move in and out of the platter. The disk drive relies on the rotation of the platter to move the requested data under the disk head. The movement of the armature and head in and out over the platter is referred to as *disk seeks*. The movement of the sectors under the head is referred to as *rotation*.

For a requested sector to be read, the armature must first seek to the proper track. After it is at the correct track, the disk must wait for the requested sector to rotate under the head. The time it takes for the drive to seek is called the *seek time*. The time it takes for the data to rotate under the head is known as *rotational latency*. Seek time and rotational latency are shown in Figure 9.2. Later in this section, both of these concepts are covered in greater detail.

A typical disk drive is made up of more than one platter, and both sides of the platter are used. These platters are stacked on top of each other and have multiple heads connected to a single armature. Because all of the heads are stacked on top of each other and can read or write simultaneously, it is more efficient to do this. Thus, a disk drive reads or writes multiple sectors simultaneously.

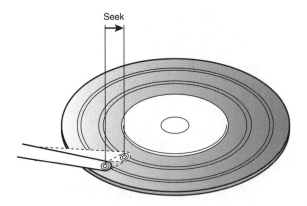

FIGURE 9.2
Seek time and rotational latency.

The stack of tracks that is used to store data is called a *cylinder*. Disk cylinders are shown in Figure 9.3.

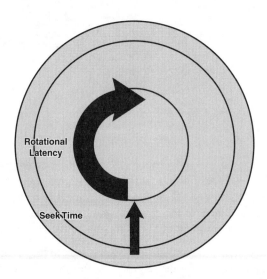

FIGURE 9.3
Disk cylinders.

To understand the performance of a disk drive, you must understand the performance of seeks and rotational latency.

Seek Time

Seeks can be divided into three different types: full disk seeks, track-to-track seeks, and random seeks. Although functionally the same, they are categorized separately due to the different performance characteristics.

Full disk seeks occur when the armature must move from the outermost track to the innermost track or vice-versa. *Track-to-track* seeks involve the armature moving from one track to an adjacent track (hence the name track-to-track seek) and incur little overhead. *Random seeks* are somewhere between the other two, and the overhead is relatively significant. This chapter will concentrate primarily on random seeks. Full disk seeks rarely, if ever, occur.

The full disk seek time of a high-performance SCSI (small computer system interface) disk drive is approximately 7.5 milliseconds (ms) for reads and 8ms for writes. Although full disk seeks rarely occur, the full disk seek time is provided to give you a worst-case scenario.

The random seek time for a high-performance SCSI disk drive is approximately 3.9ms for reads and 4.5ms for writes. This type of seek is likely to cause performance problems.

The track-to-track seek time for this same SCSI disk drive is 0.5ms for reads and 0.7ms for writes. You can see that the track-to-track seek time is considerably less than the random seek times.

Rotational Latency

After the armature has completed a seek to the track where the data resides, the disk must wait for the platter to spin underneath it to where the data resides. The rotation primarily depends on how fast the disk drive is spinning. Thus a 15,000-rpm disk drive has a smaller rotational latency than a 10,000-rpm disk drive.

The average rotational latency is approximately half of the maximum rotational latency. The maximum rotational latency can be derived from the rotational velocity. For a 15,000-rpm disk drive, the maximum rotational latency is as follows:

Maximum Rotational Latency = (1 / 15,000-rpm)*(1 min / 60 sec) = 1.11 microseconds

As you can see, even the maximum rotational latency is minute compared to the random, or even the track-to-track seek time. In fact, in the entire I/O subsystem, nothing comes close to the random seek time in terms of latencies. If the average rotation is estimated as half of the maximum rotational latency, the result is about 0.55 microsecond.

Disk Drive Performance

The time it takes to read data from a disk drive is made up of the accumulation of several different functions. These functions are as follows:

- The seek time
- The rotational latency
- The transfer time

In addition to the disk drive latencies, the data must be transferred across the I/O bus to the controller, and controller latency will be incurred as well. The latencies that are external to the disk drive are covered later in this chapter in the section titled "RAID Disk Subsystems."

So that you can get a more accurate estimate of the performance of disk drives, some calculations will be performed. After you know the specification of a disk drive and a little about the type of I/Os being done, you can get a pretty good idea of the performance of the disk drive.

Reading the Disk Spec Sheet

The first step in determining the performance of a particular disk drive is to look at the disk drive specification sheet. This specification provides the information that you need to calculate the maximum and optimal performance of the disk drive. The specific performance depends on the types of I/Os that are being performed.

A typical disk drive specification sheet contains the following information and looks something like Table 9.1.

Table 9.1   Disk Drive Specification

Description	Value
Model Number	Acme Disk (fictitious)
Model Name	Big Disk
Formatted Capacity	18GB
Interface Type	Ultra SCSI 160
Buffer Cache Size	4096KB
Rotational Speed	15K RPM
Number of Disks (Physical)	5
Number of Heads (Physical)	10
Total Cylinders	10,377
Total Tracks	103,770
Bytes Per Sector	512
Sectors Per Track	345
MTBF (Mean Time Between Failures)	1,200,000 hours
Internal Transfer Rate (Minimum)	385 Megabits per second (Mbps)

Table 9.1   Continued

Description	Value
Internal Transfer Rate (Maximum)	508Mbps
External (I/O) Transfer Rate (Maximum)	160MBps
Average Seek Time, Read	3.9ms
Average Seek Time, Write	4.5ms
Track-to-Track Seek, Read	0.5ms
Track-to-Track Seek, Write	0.7ms
Full Disc Seek, Read	7.5ms
Full Disc Seek, Write	8ms

In addition, a wealth of information exists about operating conditions, such as minimum and maximum temperature, humidity, and power requirements. This example is not intended as a complete disk drive specification, only a sample.

From the information that is available about this disk drive, you can make some calculations on I/O rates and maximum and optimal performance. This will be divided into performance for both random and sequential I/Os.

DISK I/O CAPACITY

As a database performance consultant, I see a number of different types of performance problems. One of the most common problems is insufficient I/O capacity. It is quite common for the number and size of disk drives to be chosen purely by the amount of space needed. This is a common mistake.

As you can see from this chapter, a physical disk drive can only perform a certain number of I/Os before it becomes overloaded and latencies begin to increase. Increased latencies can be the root cause of excessive resource contentions and slow response times.

In most cases, configuring your system with 4–9GB disk drives rather than 1–36GB disk drives provides better overall performance. In rare cases, however, the I/O subsystem is simply not a problem, regardless of the number of disk drives. By sizing your system for both performance and space, you can achieve optimal performance.

Sequential I/O Performance

When accessing data sequentially, seek time is not as much of an issue as when you are accessing data randomly. You can determine the time it takes to do a sequential I/O by using the following formula:

Seconds per I/O = (Track-to-Track Seek Time) + (Average Rotational Latency) + (Transfer Time) = (0.6ms) + (0.5 microsec) + (approx. 10ns) = 0.6ms (approx.)

Here, it is assumed that a track-to-track seek exists between each I/O. Because the specification sheet explains that, on average, 345 sectors exist per track, a track-to-track seek is unlikely if you are doing truly sequential I/O. However, when depending on the Oracle block size and multiblock I/O, the effects of this are unknown.

Assuming that the calculation is correct and it takes approximately 0.6ms to perform one sequential I/O, the maximum number of sequential I/Os that can be performed on this disk drive is calculated by the following formula:

I/Os per second (IOPS) = 1 / (seconds per I/O) = 1 / (0.6ms / 1,000ms per sec) = 1,666 IOPS

This number is approximate; you don't really know how many I/Os require the track-to-track seek. You can say that at least 1,666 IOPS per second can be performed sequentially.

Random I/O Performance

The calculation for random I/Os is a little more exact because you know that random seeks occur during random I/O for each I/O operation. As with the sequential I/O, the time that it takes for a random I/O to occur is determined by the same formula:

Seconds per I/O = (Random Seek Time)+(Average Rotational Latency)+(Transfer Time) = (4.3ms)+
(0.5 microsec)+(approx. 10ns) = 4.3ms (approx.)

Here, it is assumed that a random seek exists between each I/O. In addition, a mixture of reads and writes is assumed; thus 4.3ms is used rather than 3.9ms for reads and 4.5ms for writes.

Assuming that the calculation is correct and it takes approximately 4.3ms to perform one random I/O, the maximum number of random I/Os that can be performed on this disk drive is calculated by the following formula:

I/Os per second (IOPS) = 1 / (seconds per I/O) = 1 / (4.3ms / 1,000ms per sec) = 232 IOPS

This doesn't provide the entire story, however. If you have ever taken queuing theory, you will remember that as you get close to reaching the bandwidth limit of a device, the chances of queuing increase. This means that as you get closer to the limit of 232 IOPS per second, the chance for queuing is greater; thus, the I/Os will begin to take longer.

This queuing is illustrated in Figure 9.4.

You can see that the closer you get to the maximum theoretical performance, the longer the disk latencies get. Because Oracle performance is sensitive to I/O latencies, it is important that you not overdrive the I/Os.

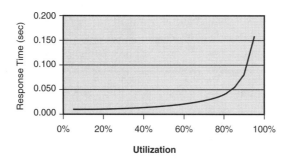

FIGURE 9.4.
I/O queuing.

FIRST COME, FIRST SERVED

A disk drive handles only one I/O at a time. If the disk drive is busy handling an I/O when a request for another I/O comes into the controller, this request is queued until the first I/O is completed. Thus, it is possible and common to experience queuing even at low I/O rates.

To avoid overdriving, you would optimally want to run the disk drives at the point on the chart known as the *knee of the curve*. This is the point where the slope of the curve starts to move sharply upward and occurs at about 75% of capacity. Thus, random I/Os should optimally not exceed 174 I/Os per second in this example.

Additional Considerations

In the previous two sections, you have seen that, theoretically, a disk drive can access data at the following rates:

Sequential I/Os: 1,666 IOPS

Random I/Os: 174 IOPS

In addition to the latencies incurred by the disk drive, the I/O controller and the operating system device driver can incur an additional latency. This additional latency can be small or large depending on how busy the device is. Because this additional latency is dependent on specifics of the I/O subsystem, it will not be covered here. Regardless, you should be aware of it.

RAID Disk Subsystems

You can use several different types of I/O subsystems with your computer systems. For database servers, RAID subsystems are probably the most popular. RAID systems come in a variety of different types and configurations, as you will see in this section.

The acronym RAID stands for Redundant Array of Inexpensive Disks. RAID I/O subsystems serve two main purposes. The first purpose is to provide a fault-tolerant I/O subsystem. A fault-tolerant I/O subsystem is one that can survive the failure of a component in the system (usually a disk drive) without incurring the loss of data. The second purpose of a RAID subsystem is to allow multiple individual disk drives to be configured into a larger virtual disk drive. This is done for both the ease of administration and performance reasons.

The RAID subsystem can combine two or more disk drives into one larger logical disk drive by using disk striping. *Disk striping* takes the logical disk layout and, using different algorithms, places that data on two or more disk drives. Disk striping does not make a logical disk drive fault-tolerant, but disk striping can be combined with fault-tolerant features of the controller.

Most RAID controllers offer a number of different options for configuring logical disk volumes using different striping options and different fault-tolerant RAID types. The different RAID configurations, commonly known as *RAID levels,* define how the data is striped across the different disks in the I/O subsystem. These RAID levels offer different levels of fault-tolerance, performance characteristics, and cost. Some RAID levels involve disk striping and some RAID levels do not.

Hardware Versus Software RAID

A RAID I/O subsystem can be formed either by purchasing a hardware RAID subsystem or by using software RAID. Both of these options have advantages and disadvantages.

The hardware RAID subsystem offers greater performance because other processes running on the system CPU do not affect it. In addition, hardware RAID subsystems can support features that software RAID subsystems might not be able to, such as hot-swappable disk drives and pre-failure alerting. However, a hardware RAID subsystem can only be configured to stripe the drives that are attached to that controller, so the number of drives in a logical disk volume is limited to the number of drives that the controller can support.

Software RAID subsystems have the advantage of price because it is not necessary to purchase additional hardware. In addition, a software RAID subsystem can be configured to stripe across all of the disk drives in the system and is not limited by controllers. Thus, you can create a software RAID volume across disk drives that are attached to many I/O controllers.

It is also possible to use software striping to stripe hardware disk volumes that are logical RAID volumes on a hardware RAID controller. Thus, the two can be combined to create massive logical disk volumes, but it's not recommended because of the overhead involved in software RAID.

This book is performance focused and will assume a hardware RAID device.

Striping

Striping involves spreading data across multiple disk drives to create a logical disk drive that is larger than any individual disk drive in the system. Disk striping involves dividing the logical disk drive into pieces that are referred to as either *stripes* or *chunks*. Typically, these stripes are distributed to the individual disk drives in a round-robin fashion as shown in Figure 9.5.

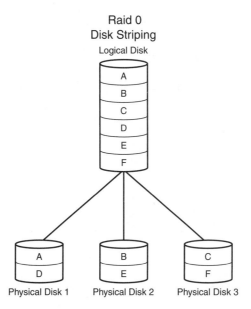

FIGURE 9.5
Disk striping.

As mentioned previously, the logical RAID volume appears as one large disk drive to the OS and to the users. If you are using a hardware RAID controller, the OS does not even know the difference. Striping is used in several of the different RAID levels that are supported by most RAID subsystems. This section examines the different RAID levels and how they operate.

RAID 0

RAID 0 is actually a misnomer. RAID 0 is disk striping with no fault tolerance. Thus, RAID 0 is not redundant. With a RAID 0 configuration, you can stripe data across multiple disk drives to create a large logical disk volume. However, a failure of any of the disk drives in the volume results in loss of the entire logical volume.

RAID 0 is disk striping only and typically works in a round-robin fashion as shown in Figure 9.5. RAID 0 is the most economical of the RAID levels and provides the highest performance, as you will see later in this section. You will see that, as in most things, trade-offs are involved. RAID 0 provides high performance and value as the expense of no fault tolerance.

RAID 1

RAID 1 is also known as *disk mirroring*. In RAID 1, all the data stored on a disk drive is duplicated on another disk in the array, as shown in Figure 9.6. Each time a write occurs to the logical disk, the data must be written to *both* physical disks before the logical write is considered completed. With disk mirroring, a single disk is mirrored to another disk; these disks can also be striped with other disks to form a larger logical volume. This combination of disk striping and mirroring is known as *RAID 10*.

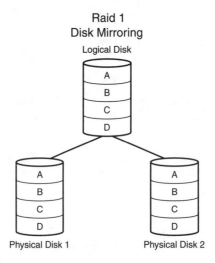

FIGURE 9.6
A RAID 1 configuration.

Because the mirroring is on a one-to-one basis, half of the disk drives in the system could actually fail (depending on which disks they are) and the system would still be operational. With most disk array controllers, you can split the mirror across SCSI busses. This arrangement allows for the failure of an entire SCSI bus (for example, a cabinet failure) without affecting operation.

With disk mirroring, you can use only half the disks in the system (the other half are used for the mirrors). In other words, if you use disk mirroring with two 18GB disk drives, you can use only 18GB of space. When writing, you get the benefit of only one disk in terms of performance because a logical write invokes two physical writes.

You might see a benefit from reading from a mirrored drive. Some disk array controllers support split seeks, in which reads can occur simultaneously on different mirrored drives to different data. The disk with the heads closest to the requested data retrieves the data. Depending on the data access methods, this feature might or might not provide benefits.

If you can afford the cost of disk mirroring, RAID 1 is the best choice when fault tolerance is required. With disk mirroring, you achieve the highest level of protection as well as the fastest disk access possible for a fault-tolerant volume.

RAID 10

RAID 10 is a combination of RAID 0 and RAID 1. With a RAID 10 volume, each disk drive has its contents mirrored onto another disk drive. At the same time, these mirrored disks participate as part of a stripe set, as shown in Figure 9.7.

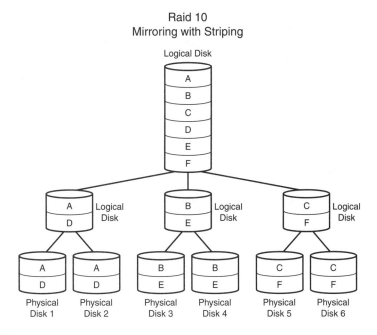

FIGURE 9.7
A RAID 10 configuration.

The advantage of a RAID 10 volume is that you can achieve the administrative and performance advantages of a RAID 0 volume while achieving the fault-tolerance of a RAID 1 volume. The down side is that RAID 10 volumes are the most expensive because half of the usable space is lost to the mirror.

For database operations, RAID 10 is the most preferable.

RAID 2

RAID 2 is a parallel access RAID level where an error correction scheme called Hamming Code is used to correct errors. With RAID 2, because all disk drives are used for all I/O operations, high throughput can be provided at the speed of one disk drive. RAID 2 is shown in Figure 9.8.

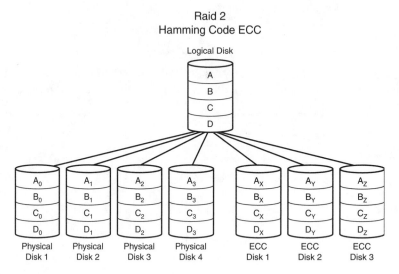

FIGURE 9.8
A RAID 2 configuration.

Although RAID 2 can provide for a great deal of throughput, it takes three disk drives to provide the fault tolerance.

RAID 3

RAID 3 is a parallel access fault-tolerant method, similar to RAID 2. The difference is that RAID 3 requires only one disk drive for fault tolerance. This is because RAID 3 uses a bit-wise parity rather than error-correcting code. RAID 3 is shown in Figure 9.9.

RAID 3 can achieve a high transfer rate, but as with RAID 2, only one I/O can be processed at a time. For small random I/Os, this can be a liability. RAID 2 and RAID 3 are both good for large sequential transfers, such as streaming video feeds.

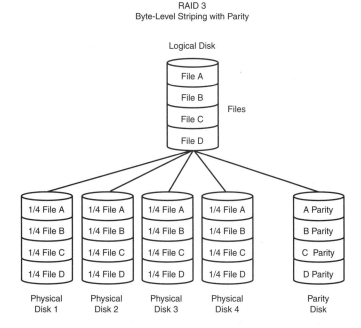

RAID 3
Byte-Level Striping with Parity

FIGURE 9.9
A RAID 3 configuration.

RAID 4

RAID 4 is known as *drive parity*, or *data guarding*. In RAID 4, one of the drives in the volume is used for data parity, as shown in Figure 9.10. If any one of the disks fails, the other disks continue running by reconstructing the missing data from the parity drive. The space available in a RAID 4 incurs the loss of one disk drive's worth of space.

Unlike RAID 2 and RAID 3, RAID 4 uses an independent access technique where multiple disk drives can be accessed simultaneously. This is good for random I/Os because they can be accessed in parallel. Thus, the number of I/Os per second can reach the sum of the individual disk drive limits.

When you write to a RAID 4 volume, extra I/Os are incurred to keep the parity up-to-date. In fact, because the parity must be kept up-to-date whenever data is added, the following process occurs:

1. Both the old data and the old parity stripes are read.

2. Perform an XOR on old data and old parity.

3. Take value and XOR with new data to get new parity.

4. Both the new data and new parity drives are written out.

Thus, for a single RAID 4 write, four physical I/Os are incurred. For a RAID 4 read, no additional I/O overhead is incurred.

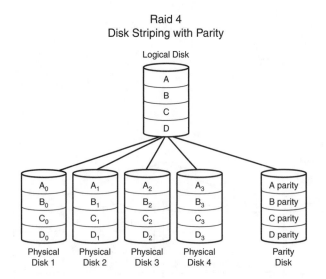

FIGURE 9.10
A RAID 4 configuration.

The greatest disadvantage in RAID 4 is the dedicated parity disk. Because the parity drive is involved in every write operation, only one write to the volume can be performed at a time. Other writes will begin to queue up under heavy write activity, and reads that depend on those writes will also begin to queue. Add this to the expense of the additional physical operations for each logical write, and you quickly build to a huge performance bottleneck on one disk.

RAID 5

RAID 5 is also known as *distributed data guarding*. RAID 5 is similar to RAID 4 except that the parity is not isolated to one disk drive. Rather, the parity is distributed across all of the disk drives in the system, as shown in Figure 9.11.

As with RAID 4, RAID 5 writes have a penalty associated with them. For each write to disk, two reads take place, a calculation of the parity is done, and then two writes are done. Although a read generates only one I/O, a write generates four I/Os. This is done to maintain the parity.

RAID 5 does not suffer from the same write contention to a single disk that RAID 4 does. Because the parity is distributed among all drives in the volume, more than one write operation can be in progress at a time. Potentially, half as many writes can occur as there are disks in the volume.

RAID 4 and RAID 5 are both economical because you only lose one disk drive's worth of space to provide fault-tolerance; however, both levels pay the price in terms of performance when a lot of write activity exists.

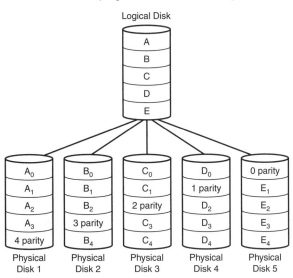

Raid 5
Disk Striping with Distributed Parity

FIGURE 9.11
A RAID 5 configuration.

Parity Overview

RAID 3, RAID 4, and RAID 5 use a parity to maintain fault tolerance. A *parity* is a binary method where the sum of the individual pieces add up to either an even or an odd value. The bits are added using binary arithmetic, and either a 0 or a 1 is added as a parity bit. The value of this parity bit depends on what is needed to maintain the proper parity of the sum of all of the bits.

Parity Example

Now look at an example using three different bits and one parity bit. This example will use even parity; thus, the sum of all of the bits must add up to an even number. The following three values

A=1

B=0

C=1

add up to 2; thus, the sum of A+B+C+Parity equals an even number (2) if the value of the parity bit is 0.

Another example will take the following values:

A=1

B=1

C=1

For the sum of these values A+B+C+Parity to equal an even number (2), the value of the parity bit must be 1. An example of parity on a set of nine-bit words is shown in Figure 9.12.

```
214 = 11010110          214 = 11010110
XOR        XOR          XOR        XOR
 75 = 01001011           75 = 01001011
XOR        XOR          XOR        XOR
174 = 10101110            6 = 00000110
XOR        XOR          XOR        XOR
 53 = 00110101           53 = 00110101
equals    equals        equals    equals
  6 = 00000110          174 = 10101110
```

FIGURE 9.12
Parity.

In this manner, parity is created on every disk drive in the RAID controller byte by byte and bit by bit.

Creating Parity

To create a RAID 3, RAID 4, or RAID 5 volume, each data stripe must be read off of each disk drive and the parity calculated. This is sometimes known as *data scrubbing*. If you have created one of these RAID volumes, you might have noticed it taking a long time to create. This is because every disk in the volume must be read, the parity created, and the parity written out. This can be quite time consuming depending on the size of the disk drives and the number of disk drives in the array.

Maintaining Parity

After the volume has been created, you don't need to recalculate the parity each time. Because the parity has already been calculated, it is possible to modify the parity based on the changes made by the insertion or modification of data. For example, if a data bit does not change, the parity bit does not need to change. If the data bit changes, then so must the parity bit. This is done using a bit-wise exclusive "OR" operation (or XOR) on both the data and the parity bits.

Thus, to modify parity data, you must follow these steps:

1. Read data and parity stripes.

2. XOR old data and parity.

3. Calculate a new parity using an XOR operation and new data.

4. Write out both new data and new parity.

Thus, for a parity write, four physical I/Os and two XORs are incurred. Not only are the additional I/Os important due to disk drive limitations, but for the order as well. Because two I/Os, two calculations, and two additional I/Os exist, the latency is at minimum twice the latency of a non-parity I/O (assuming infinitely fast parity calculation). This is important considering how sensitive Oracle is to I/O latency.

RAID Performance Overview

Now that you have seen the different RAID levels, it's time to look at how they perform. This section until the end of the chapter looks at the most common RAID levels: RAID 0, RAID 1, RAID 10, and RAID 5. Although you might encounter other RAID levels, it is rare.

You must first review a few facts:

- I/Os occur at the speed of one disk drive. No matter how many disk drives are in the RAID volume, the I/O is going to one of them, so you cannot exceed that speed.

- If you do exceed the physical performance limitations of the disk drive, queuing occurs and latencies increase.

- The optimal performance rate for random I/Os is 175 IOPS (in these examples). Exceeding this rate might cause increased latencies.

- Almost all I/O operations are random in nature. Even if you are doing a sequential table scan, if someone else is accessing the same disk, the I/Os will become random.

Now you will learn about the performance of some of the common RAID levels.

RAID 0

RAID 0 is the most straightforward RAID level to calculate performance characteristics. Assuming access to the RAID 0 volume is random, and assuming 175 IOPS per disk drive, the optimal number of IOPS to the volume is calculated by the following formula:

(# of reads) + (# of writes) = (175 * n)

where n = number of disk drives in the array. Thus, a 10-disk drive array could handle 1,750 reads and writes per second.

RAID 1 and RAID 10

RAID 1 and RAID 10 volumes incur the write penalty of two physical writes for each write to the logical volume. This is because all of the data on a disk drive must be duplicated on its mirror. Thus, the optimal number of reads and writes on a RAID 10 and RAID 1 volume is calculated using the following formula:

(# of reads) + (# of writes * 2) = (175 * n)

where n = number of disk drives in the array. For a RAID 1 array, n = 2.

RAID 5

RAID 5 volumes incur a penalty of four physical I/Os for every logical write. The old data and parity must be read, two XOR operations must be performed, and the new data and parity must be written. The optimal number of reads and writes on a RAID 5 volume can be calculated using the following formula:

(# of reads) + (# of writes * 4) = (175 * n)

where n = number of disk drives in the array.

RAID Level Performance Comparison

Compare the different RAID levels:

- RAID 0 is the highest-performing RAID level because of the absence of fault tolerance overhead; unfortunately, however, there is no fault tolerance.

- RAID 1 and RAID 10 incur a 2x penalty on writes. They have the best level of fault tolerance, but they are also the most expensive.

- RAID 5 has the worst write penalty, incurring four physical I/Os for each write operation. RAID 5 provides fault tolerance, but can only tolerate the loss of one disk drive in the volume. However, RAID 5 is the most economical of the RAID levels.

None of these RAID levels incur a penalty for reads. A comparison of the economics versus performance versus fault tolerance is shown in Figure 9.13.

RAID Level Comparison

RAID Level	Performance	Fault Tolerance	Economics
0	Best	Worst	Best
1	Good	Best	Worst
5	Worst	Good	Good

FIGURE 9.13
RAID comparison.

As you can see, you should consider several factors when selecting a RAID level. In the next chapter, you will see how Oracle I/O considerations should also be taken into account when selecting a RAID level.

RAID PERFORMANCE

As you have seen from this section, different performance characteristics are available for different RAID levels. RAID 5 is popular because of the economics; you only lose one disk drive's worth of space while achieving some level of fault tolerance. However, in most cases, RAID 5 is not appropriate for use with Oracle.

My rule of thumb is not to use RAID 5 unless the read/write ratio is 90/10. In other words, unless 90% of the I/O operations are reads, RAID 5 is inappropriate. Of course, your mileage might vary, and if the I/O rate is sufficiently low, then this is not an issue.

When calculating how many IOPS per disk drive are being done at the physical level, remember to multiply the RAID 5 writes by 4. This can drastically change your resulting data. For fault tolerance and performance, I prefer RAID 10.

RAID Controller Performance Features

To improve I/O performance RAID controllers, several features have been added to many of the most popular controllers. Depending on your needs and concerns, some of these features might be useful in your configuration.

Elevator Sorting

Imagine an elevator that went from floor to floor in a building in the order of which buttons were pushed. The elevator would bypass floors where people wanted to get off only to go back to those floors later. Although some riders would get to their destination more quickly, most of the riders would have a much longer ride.

Similar to how elevators work, disk controllers can sort I/O requests such that the disk armatures move in the same direction for longer periods of time. Any single I/O might take slightly longer, but in general, most I/O response times are faster. Elevator sorting is shown in Figure 9.14.

Elevator sorting can provide for faster overall I/O performance, but it is only useful when more than one I/O is to be done. Several I/Os must be in the queue for sorting to occur. In fact, many controllers have a threshold that must be exceeded before sorting is enabled.

For a RAID controller, sorting is done on an individual disk drive basis. Thus, I/Os are submitted into the controller, a determination is made as to which disk drive they are assigned, and then the I/Os are queued up for that disk drive. A large logical volume that spans many disks has many individual queues.

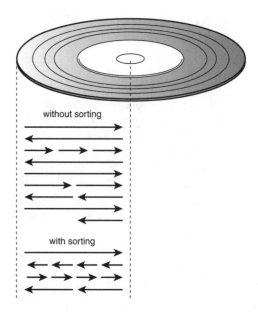

FIGURE 9.14
Elevator sorting.

Controller Caches

Another common feature is the controller cache. The controller cache can exist in several different forms, but it is essentially memory that is used for caching data. Controller caches can be used for both read caching and write caching. Typically, write caches and read caches are configured on a per-volume basis.

Read Cache

Read caches are primarily used for read-ahead. When large sequential reads are issued, the controller detects this and automatically begins to retrieve the next data in sequence on the logical disk volume. This is done in anticipation of additional sequential requests. If those requests are made, they are satisfied from cache. If those anticipated requests are not made, the data eventually ages out of cache.

Read cache can also take advantage of reading data from the write cache instead of reading directly from disk. Some controllers will only enable read cache (different from read-ahead cache) if write caching is enabled.

Write Cache

Write caches are used to speed write operations. When the write is written to the cache, the controller returns an EOI (End of IO) signal to the OS, signifying that the I/O is complete. In reality, the I/O has yet to be written out to disk. This is done at a later time.

Because the I/O has not been written to disk, data loss is possible. Most controllers that support write cache include a battery backup and mirrored memory. This provides a better assurance that data will not be lost in the event of a power failure or system failure.

Because data loss is a possibility, it is sometimes not recommended that certain data be stored on volumes with write caching enabled. This is covered in more detail in the next chapter.

Hardware XOR Engines

RAID 5 uses an XOR operation to update the parity when data is modified. To improve the performance of RAID 5 writes, hardware XOR engines are often used. Because the XOR calculation is done within a piece of hardware, the performance of this operation is greatly improved. In addition, the main RAID controller CPU is relieved of the task of calculating XORs, an expensive operation for a general-purpose processor. In most cases, any operation that can be done in hardware is much faster than the same operation performed in software. This additional hardware is only useful when using RAID 5 volumes.

Stripe Size

Some controllers allow you to specify the stripe size when you create the RAID volume, and some controllers use a fixed stripe size. Depending on the type of operations being performed on your system and the Oracle block size, some stripe sizes might provide better performance than others. Typically, RAID controllers are tuned for a particular stripe size. Making the stripe size larger or smaller should be carefully considered first, and it should be based on the Oracle block size and data access profile.

Internal Versus External RAID Systems

RAID controllers are either internal or external. The internal RAID controller is typically one that resides in the expansion bus inside the computer system. On some newer systems, RAID controllers are even embedded on the motherboard. The external RAID controller is one that resides in a storage system that resides external to the computer system.

Internal RAID Systems

The internal RAID controller typically uses a SCSI bus to connect to a number of disk drives that either reside inside the computer system or that reside external to the system. With the internal RAID system, all of the intelligence is local to the computer system, as shown in Figure 9.15. Any external storage contains a bus only.

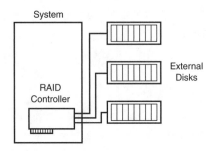

FIGURE 9.15
Internal RAID system.

Typically, internal RAID systems are less costly than external RAID subsystems.

External RAID Systems

An external RAID system is one in which the computer system contains only a simple I/O device and the RAID logic resides in an external storage cabinet. The I/O device in the computer system is usually a host bus adapter (HBA) that just passes I/Os to the external RAID system. The external RAID system is responsible for all of the caching and RAID processing. An external RAID system is shown in Figure 9.16.

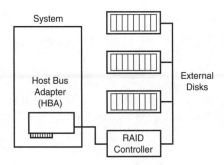

FIGURE 9.16
External RAID system.

Most external RAID systems use a fibre channel interface between the host system and the RAID storage system. The fibre channel architecture allows for both copper and fiber-optic interfaces. External RAID subsystems are the basic building blocks of the storage area network (SAN) architecture.

When using a fibre channel system, it is important to note that a fibre channel bus has a bandwidth of 100MBps. If more bandwidth than this is required, you must configure several fibre channel busses.

SAN Systems

A SAN system is an external storage system that allows multiple computer systems to access the same storage. The RAID controller inside the external storage system is able to take requests for different logical volumes within the storage system from different HBAs. This allows for several different features. An example of this is shown in Figure 9.17.

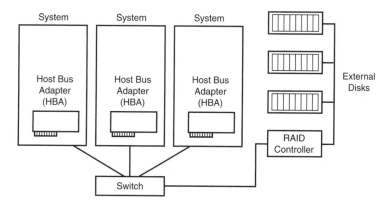

FIGURE 9.17
A SAN system.

Because multiple HBAs can access the external storage system, it is possible to configure two HBAs within the computer system for one to act as a failover controller. If the primary controller fails, the secondary controller takes over, as shown in Figure 9.18. This requires additional system software to be configured in this manner.

In addition to using SANs for failover, they can also be used for storage consolidation. Because multiple computer systems can access the same RAID system (but not the same volumes), it is possible to consolidate all of your storage into the same storage subsystem and allocate individual volumes to the different systems. Using a SAN in this manner is shown in Figure 9.19.

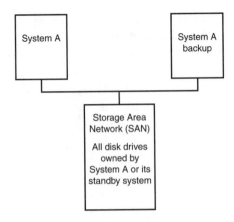

FIGURE 9.18
A SAN system used for failover.

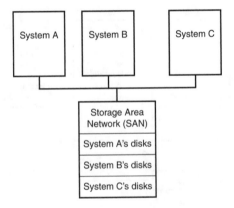

FIGURE 9.19
A SAN system used for storage consolidation.

Yet another use for a SAN system is for clustering. Failover clusters and shared disk clusters are the two types of clusters. These different clusters use the SAN in slightly different ways and have different requirements.

Failover clusters use a shared disk subsystem that allows one of two systems to access the same storage. Even though both systems can access the storage, only one will be used at a time. In a failover cluster, if one server fails, the second server can resume operation by taking control of the storage and the Oracle database that resides on that shared storage. Oracle Fail Safe for Windows NT is a failover cluster that Oracle uses. An Oracle Fail Safe cluster is shown in Figure 9.20.

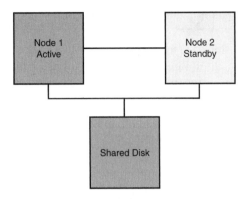

FIGURE 9.20
An Oracle Fail Safe cluster.

Oracle Parallel Server (OPS) and Oracle9i Real Application Clusters (RAC) both require a shared disk subsystem. Typically, a SAN is used for this shared disk subsystem. With OPS and RAC, the same disk subsystem must be accessible simultaneously from multiple servers, as shown in Figure 9.21.

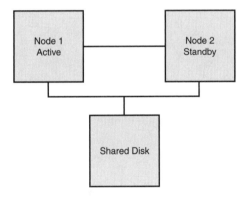

FIGURE 9.21
An Oracle9i Real Application cluster.

OPS and RAC systems are used for both failover and for performance. Because multiple systems can access the same database, you can achieve more performance than a single system. RAC is covered more thoroughly in Chapter 15, "Using Hints."

Network Attached Storage (NAS) Systems

Network attached storage is similar to the SAN system in that the brains of the storage are external to the computer system. However, unlike the SAN system where the storage is connected via a fibre channel connection, a NAS system is accessed via the network. This is illustrated in Figure 9.22.

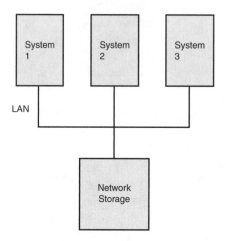

FIGURE 9.22
A NAS system.

Although the NAS system is supported under Oracle, the NAS system usually cannot support the performance required by Oracle unless you use a sufficiently fast network interface. The speed of the NAS is usually limited by the speed of the network interface.

Summary

This chapter introduced you to the basics of I/O subsystem tuning. Tuning an I/O subsystem involves two steps: proper configuration and proper sizing. Proper configuration involves setting up the subsystem correctly, such as choosing a stripe size and sizing controller caches. Proper sizing involves configuring enough disk drives to keep I/O usage within the proper limits.

This chapter provided the fundamental information that you need to set up the I/O subsystem optimally. In the next chapter, you will learn some Oracle-specific I/O issues and how to set up the I/O subsystem for Oracle.

ORACLE AND I/O

The Oracle RDBMS is extremely dependent on the OS and the I/O subsystem. The OS sometimes gets in Oracle's way. Oracle is almost like its own operating system. You must utilize the OS for several key functions, including the memory management system, the process scheduler, and of course, the I/O subsystem. Of these areas of the operating system, the I/O subsystem and its performance are critical to the performance of the Oracle RDBMS. The main function of Oracle is to maintain and serve data to the user community; the location of that data (when it is not in the buffer cache) is within the I/O subsystem. As you will learn in this chapter, the performance of Oracle is directly tied to the performance of the I/O subsystem.

Parameters Used in This Chapter

This chapter includes the use of many Oracle initialization parameters. Chapter 2 introduced you to these parameters and explained how to use them. In this chapter, the following initialization parameters are covered:

- DB_CACHE_SIZE. This parameter specifies the amount of memory that is used for the Oracle buffer cache. This parameter can be specified in K, M, or G for kilobytes, megabytes or gigabytes.

- DB_2K_CACHE_SIZE, DB_4K_CACHE_SIZE, DB_8K_CACHE_SIZE, DB_16K_CACHE_SIZE, DB_32K_CACHE_SIZE, DB_64K_CACHE_SIZE. These parameters set the non-standard block size cache sizes.

- DBWR_IO_SLAVES. DBWR_IO_SLAVES is relevant only on systems with one database writer process (DBW0). It specifies the number of I/O server processes that the DBW0 process uses.

- DB_BLOCK_SIZE. DB_BLOCK_SIZE specifies the size (in bytes) of Oracle database blocks. Typical values are 2048 and 4096. The value for DB_BLOCK_SIZE in effect at the time you create the database determines the size of the blocks. The value must remain set to its initial value.

- DB_BLOCK_CHECKING. DB_BLOCK_CHECKING controls whether Oracle performs block checking for data blocks. When this parameter is set to true, Oracle performs block checking for all data blocks.

- DB_BLOCK_CHECKSUM. DB_BLOCK_CHECKSUM determines whether DBWn and the direct loader calculate a checksum (a number calculated from all the bytes stored in the block) and store it in the cache header of every data block when writing it to disk. Checksums are verified when a block is read-only if this parameter is true and the last write of the block stored a checksum. Enabling this option can incur significant overhead.

- DB_FILE_MULTIBLOCK_READ_COUNT. DB_FILE_MULTIBLOCK_READ_ COUNT is one of the parameters you can use to minimize I/O during table scans. It specifies the maximum number of blocks that are read in one I/O operation during a sequential scan.

- DB_WRITER_PROCESSES. DB_WRITER_PROCESSES is useful for systems that modify data heavily. It specifies the initial number of database writer processes for an instance.

- DISK_ASYNC_IO. DISK_ASYNCH_IO controls whether I/O to data files, control files, and log files is asynchronous (that is, whether parallel server processes can overlap I/O requests with CPU processing during table scans). If your platform supports asynchronous I/O to disk, Oracle Corporation recommends that you leave this parameter set to its default value.

Oracle's Dependency on I/O

The main job of the Oracle RDBMS is to maintain data. Data within the Oracle RDBMS resides in one of two places: memory and disk. The data that is in memory either came from disk or will most likely end up on disk. The Oracle RDBMS is quite dependent on the I/O subsystem.

Just as the Oracle RDBMS is dependent on the I/O subsystem, the Oracle RDBMS's performance is dependent on the performance of the I/O subsystem. In fact, the performance of Oracle is dependent on the performance of the I/O subsystem. Most operations that the RDBMS performs involve some I/O, and many involve a great deal of I/O.

To fully appreciate the performance implications of poor I/O performance, you need to see a few examples. First, you need to quickly review some of the key concepts from the previous chapter.

Disk drives have certain performance limitations due mainly to the seek time and the rotational latency. Because of this, it takes about 6.3 milliseconds (msec) for a random I/O request to be satisfied by the I/O subsystem. This is known as *read latency*. Writing to the disk drive incurs a similar amount of time known as *write latency*.

Why Read Latency Is Important

Oracle is sensitive to read latency because a read request for data is done on behalf of a user request. The user might be waiting for this data, so the longer it takes for the data to be read, the longer the user will wait.

You might ask yourself why anyone would care about a read time that only took 6msec. The answer is, nobody would, if it only took 6msec. The problem is that one read doesn't satisfy your request.

Read Latency Example

The following simple query shows why the read latency, although small, could add up to a big problem:

```
SELECT id FROM employees WHERE lname="Bush";
```

If you are lucky, the lname column is indexed. Depending on the size of the employees table and the size of the index, this might take anywhere from 10 requests up. Because the index is traversed in a tree structure, the first node must be read and analyzed before Oracle knows which index node to read next. You need to add a little time—perhaps 5msec—between nodes for processing. After you read the 10 index blocks and find where the data is, an additional read is required to retrieve that data. The following calculates how long it takes to retrieve the data:

```
Index reads = 10 * 6 msec = 60 msec
Processing time = 10 * 5 msec = 50 msec
Data retrieval time = 1 * 6 msec = 6 msec
Total = 116 msec
```

This is a long time in computer terms—and it's only to select one piece of data. Take this a step further. Typically, you don't just select a simple piece of data from the database. Your normal queries are much more complicated and involve joins and aggregates.

Joining two tables often involves reading many records of data, and sometimes the entire table. Take this 116msec and multiply it by 10,000 reads, or 1,000,000 reads. Get the picture?

If the query needed to read 10,000 rows of data, you could estimate that it would take 1160 seconds, or 19 minutes. Fortunately, when a block of data is read into the buffer cache, it contains many rows of data that the RDBMS might need. If you are lucky, the block that you need is already in cache.

Read latency is still an issue. An inefficient I/O subsystem could cause large queries to take hours instead of minutes. However, in most systems, the I/O subsystem is constantly being used; in many cases, the I/O latencies can be quite high. This is always an indication that Oracle performance might be suffering due to I/O performance.

Read Latency Rule-of-Thumb

In Chapter 9, "I/O Concepts," you learned that a random I/O takes about 6msec. This time assumes that queuing is not taking place because you are running optimally. Unfortunately, it is likely that queuing *is* taking place. By monitoring the I/O latency via your system's performance monitor, you can get a better idea of what performance you are experiencing.

In general, read latencies are in the range of 10–20msec due to queuing on the system and the random nature of the I/Os. These values are fairly reasonable, although 20msec is on the higher end of what is preferable.

How bad can it get? It is common to see 50–100msec latencies in overdriven I/O subsystems. This is most likely causing performance problems within Oracle. It is possible to see read latencies in the hundreds of milliseconds. Read latencies can even reach values as high as 250msec and higher. In these systems, I/O performance is bad. Because processes that are waiting on these I/Os are most likely holding locks, the performance problem compounds itself. As you can see, read latency is important.

Write Latency

The dependency of Oracle on write latency is mixed. Whereas user processes frequently wait on reads to complete to obtain the desired data, this is not the case for writes. As you saw in the review of the Oracle architecture in Chapter 8, "Oracle and System Hardware," the user processes make changes to data only in the buffer cache. Only the DBWR process is allowed to make changes to the data files on disk.

Because the DBWR process makes these changes in the background, the performance of these writes is not as critical as the performance of reads. This is true of all user data files. Why do you specify user data files? An exception to this rule is the undo tablespace or the rollback tablespace, depending on which method you choose to use. In addition, the redo log files are sensitive to write performance.

Write Latency and the Redo Log Files

The redo log files are used to maintain recoverability in the Oracle RDBMS. Because of this, a transaction cannot be considered committed until the redo log record has been written out. Redo log records are written to the redo log buffer where the Log Writer Process (LGWR) writes them out to the redo log files.

As long as the log writer process is able to keep up, transactions flow smoothly. If the log buffer were to fill up, transactions would be forced to wait until the log writer were able to clear out the log buffer. In addition, the slower the log writes are, the longer that commits will take to process, and the longer that locks will be held. Thus, write performance of redo log drives is extremely important.

Write Latency and the Undo Tablespace Files

In addition to the redo log disk drives, the undo tablespace drives are also somewhat sensitive to write performance. When your system changes frequently, the undo tablespace can be quite heavily used. Because the undo tablespace is accessed in a write-intensive manner, it is likely that there are many writes to the data files. Because of this, writes are somewhat sensitive to latencies because of the extent of the I/Os.

Write Latency and the Data Files

Write latency on the data files is not usually an issue. Writes are differed and occur in the background by the Database Writer (DBWR) process. As long as the DBWR process is able to keep up and checkpoint processes don't take too long, then write latencies are not a problem.

If the DBWR is not able to keep up, this could cause some problems. If no free buffers are available and the DBWR process is not able to clean them out as fast as they are requested, then processing could halt. This is an unlikely occurrence, however.

Fault Tolerance

In addition to performance considerations such as read and write latency, Oracle depends on the I/O subsystem to keep the data safe. If the data is corrupted on disk, the database is useless. It is because of this that some sort of fault tolerance should be used on your Oracle data files. Later in this chapter, you will learn how to best utilize fault tolerance on your Oracle system.

Configuring the I/O Subsystem for Oracle

Because I/O performance is so important to Oracle, it is important that you carefully configure your system to achieve optimal I/O performance. Many factors contribute to this because each system and its requirements are different. You must take into consideration fault tolerance as well as performance and economics. In this section, you will get a bit of review from the previous chapter and then explore some ideas on how to set up your I/O subsystem for Oracle.

Performance Versus Fault Tolerance Versus Cost

As you learned in the previous chapter, performance versus fault tolerance trade-off is an issue, as are cost versus fault tolerance. A review of those trade-offs is shown in Table 10.1.

Table 10.1   Performance Versus Fault Tolerance Versus Cost

Raid Level	Performance	Fault Tolerance	Cost
RAID 0	Good	None	Best
RAID 1 or 10	Good Read/OK Write	Best	Most Expensive
RAID 5	Good Read/Bad Write	OK	Least Expensive

RAID 1 or 10 offers the best performing fault-tolerant RAID level with good performance, but at the highest cost. RAID 5 offers fault tolerance at a lower cost, but write performance is poor.

For a thorough explanation of the RAID levels mentioned in Table 10.1, refer to Chapter 9, "I/O Concepts."

Protecting Your Investment

In most cases, cost is no object when it comes to protecting your data. In other cases, you might have to stay within a certain budget. In any case, because the disk drives are the most likely component to fail in your system, you should use some sort of fault tolerance. Here are a few ideas on how to maximize your performance and minimize your cost.

Best Solution (Most Expensive)

The best solution for fault tolerance is to maximize the use of RAID 1 and RAID 10. Set up your system using these guidelines. Of course, your needs are dependent on your workload and application.

OS and Oracle binaries	Use RAID 1. The OS and Oracle binaries are difficult to reinstall and reconfigure, so protect these files.
Redo log files	Each redo log file is on its own RAID 1 volume. This allows for optimal performance, even after a log switch where the previous redo log file is being archived.
Archive log files	If you are archiving locally, this should be a RAID 10 volume for both protection and performance.
Data files	Data files should be on their own RAID 10 volume. Use as many disk drives as necessary to keep IOPS per disk less than 125.

This represents a best-case scenario where you can afford to use all RAID 1 and RAID 10 volumes. This provides the highest level of fault tolerance and performance.

Good Solution

The good solution for fault tolerance is to mix RAID 10 and RAID 5. Set up your system using these guidelines. Of course, your needs are dependent on your workload and application.

OS and Oracle binaries	Use RAID 1. The OS and Oracle binaries are difficult to reinstall and reconfigure, so protect these files.
Redo log files	The redo log files can share a RAID 1 or RAID 10 volume (depending on how much space is needed). Some degradation will occur during archiving, but this will finish quickly.
Archive log files	If you are archiving locally, this should be a RAID 10 or RAID 5 volume for both protection and performance.
Data files	Data files should be on their own RAID 10 volume. Use as many disk drives as necessary to keep IOPS per disk below 125.

This represents a good scenario where both RAID 10 and RAID 5 volumes are mixed. This provides the highest level of fault tolerance and performance.

Budget Solution

The budget solution for fault tolerance is to use RAID 1 and RAID 5. Set up your system using these guidelines. Of course, your needs are dependent on your workload and application.

OS and Oracle binaries	Use RAID 1. The OS and Oracle binaries are difficult to reinstall and reconfigure, so protect these files.
Redo log files	Each redo log file is on its own RAID 1 volume. This allows for optimal performance even after a log switch where the previous redo log file is being archived.
Archive log files	If you are archiving locally, this should be a RAID 10 or RAID 5 volume for both protection and performance.
Data files	Data files can be placed on RAID 5 or RAID 0 volumes. You might need to use RAID 0 to provide the necessary performance. Use as many disk drives as necessary to keep IOPS per disk below 125.

This represents a budget scenario when you cannot afford to use all RAID 1 and RAID 10 volumes. Performance will be less than the other proposed solutions, and fault-tolerance might not be used (requiring a restore in the event of a failure), but this is a cheaper solution.

Notes and Exceptions

The following is a list of exceptions and notes to the sample configurations given previously:

- If no fault-tolerance is used, the database must be restored in the event of a disk failure. This might be an acceptable solution for your system.

- Fault-tolerant disk volumes are not an excuse not to do backups. Backups are still necessary and critical.

- Your system might vary. These are generalized guidelines. Of course, if you are not updating or inserting into the database, the performance of the redo log files is not an issue.

- It's all about sizing. Getting a sufficient number of disk drives is what it is all about.

These suggestions should help you design and implement an optimal Oracle system.

Tuning I/O

I/O is probably one of the most common problems facing Oracle users. In many cases, the performance of the system is entirely limited by disk I/O. In some cases, the system actually becomes idle waiting for disk requests to complete. These systems are said to be *I/O bound* or *disk bound*.

As you saw in the previous chapter, disks have certain inherent limitations that cannot be overcome. Therefore, the way to deal with disk I/O issues is to understand the limitations of the disks and design your system with these limitations in mind. Knowing the performance characteristics of your disks can help you in the design stage.

Optimizing your system for I/O should happen during the design stage. This I/O design is highly dependent on the type of system that you are implementing; different types of systems have different I/O patterns and require different I/O designs. After the system is built, you should first tune for memory and then tune for disk I/O. The reason you tune in this order is to make sure that you are not dealing with excessive cache misses, which cause additional I/Os.

The strategy for tuning disk I/O is to keep all drives within their physical limits. Doing so reduces queuing time and increases performance. In your system, you might find that some disks process many more IOPS than other disks. These disks are called *hot spots*. Try to reduce hot spots whenever possible. Hot spots occur whenever contention is large on a single disk or set of disks.

Understanding Disk Contention

Disk contention occurs whenever the physical limitations of a disk drive are reached and other processes have to wait. Disk drives are mechanical and have a physical limitation on both disk seeks per second and throughput. If you exceed these limitations, you have no choice but to wait.

You can find out if you are exceeding these limits both through Oracle's file I/O statistics and through operating system statistics. This chapter looks at the Oracle statistics; however, these OS statistics can also be quite useful.

Although the Oracle statistics give you an accurate picture of how many I/Os have taken place for a particular data file, they might not accurately represent the entire disk because other activity outside of Oracle might be incurring disk I/Os. Remember that you must correlate the Oracle data file to the physical disk on which it resides.

Information about disk accesses is kept in the dynamic performance table V$FILESTAT. Important information in this table is listed in the following columns:

PHYRDS	The number of physical reads done to the data file
PHYWRTS	The number of physical writes done to the data file

The information in V$FILESTAT is referenced by file number. The dynamic performance table V$DATAFILE contains a reference to this number as well as other useful information:

NAME   The name of the data file

STATUS   The type of file and its current status

BYTES   The size of the data file

Together, the V$FILESTAT and V$DATAFILE tables can give you an idea of the I/O usage of your data files. Use the following query to get this information:

```
SQL> SELECT substr(name,1,40), phyrds, phywrts, status, bytes
  2  FROM v$datafile df, v$filestat fs
  3  WHERE df.file# = fs.file#;
```

SUBSTR(NAME,1,40)	PHYRDS	PHYWRTS	STATUS	BYTES
C:\UTIL\ORAWIN\DBS\wdbsys.ora	221	7	SYSTEM	10485760
C:\UTIL\ORAWIN\DBS\wdbuser.ora	0	0	ONLINE	3145728
C:\UTIL\ORAWIN\DBS\wdbrbs.ora	2	0	ONLINE	3145728
C:\UTIL\ORAWIN\DBS\wdbtemp.ora	0	0	ONLINE	2097152

The total I/O for each data file is the sum of the physical reads and physical writes. It is important to make sure that these I/Os don't exceed the physical limitations of any one disk. I/O throughput problems to one disk might slow down the entire system depending on what data is on that disk. It is particularly important to make sure that I/O rates are not exceeded on the disk drives.

Identifying Disk Contention Problems

To identify disk contention problems, you must analyze the I/O rates and latencies of each disk drive in the system. If you are using individual disks or disk arrays, the analysis process is slightly different.

For individual disk drives, simply invoke your operating system or third-party tools and check the number of IOPS on an individual disk basis. This process gives you an accurate representation of the I/O rates on each drive. As you saw in the previous chapter, a general rule of thumb is not to exceed 125 IOPS per drive with random access, or 300 IOPS per drive with sequential access. If you are experiencing a disk I/O problem, you might see excessive idle CPU cycles and poor response times.

In addition to checking the number of IOPS per disk drive, it is extremely important that you check the latencies. This can usually be accomplished via the OS monitoring tools or via the utilization statistics (if TIMED_STATISTICS) if turned on. The OS statistics are probably more accurate than the Oracle statistics. Look for latencies that are greater than 10msec. 10–20msec latencies are acceptable; anything over 20msec is in the range of I/O problems.

For a disk array, also invoke your operating system or third-party tools and check the same items—specifically the number of IOPS per disk. The entire disk array appears as one disk. For most popular disk arrays on the market today, it is accurate to simply divide the I/O rate by the number of disks to get the IOPS per disk rate. However, the latencies being reported for the entire array are correct and no calculations need to be done.

THE KNOWN VERSUS THE UNKNOWN

Although the Oracle dynamic performance tables can be quite useful in telling you how many physical I/Os are generated for each individual data file, they cannot accurately report I/O rates. Oracle only reports the number of I/Os, not the rate at which they occur. Oracle also does not report disk activity outside of the Oracle instance.

The next step in identifying a disk contention problem is to determine the I/O profile for your disk. It is sufficient to split this up into two major categories: sequential and random I/O. Here is what to look for:

Sequential I/O	In sequential I/O, data is written or read from the disk in order, so little head movement occurs. Access to the redo log files is always sequential.
Random I/O	Random I/O occurs when data is accessed in different places on the disk, causing head movement. Access to data files is almost always random. For database loads, access is sequential; in most other cases (especially OLTP), the access patterns are almost always random.

With sequential I/O, the disk can operate at a much higher rate than it can with random I/O. If *any* random I/O is being done on a disk, the disk is considered to be accessed in a random fashion. Even if you have two separate processes that access data in a sequential manner, the I/O pattern is random.

With random I/O, you not only have access to the disk, but a large amount of head movement is involved, which reduces the performance of the disks. This was covered in detail in Chapter 9.

Finally, check these rates against the recommended I/O rates for your disk drives. Here are some good guidelines:

Sequential I/O	A typical ULTRA-SCSI-160 disk drive can support approximately 300 sequential IOPS.
Random I/O	A typical ULTRA-SCSI-160 disk drive can support approximately 125 random IOPS.

Solving Disk Contention Problems

There are a few rules-of-thumb you should follow in solving disk contention problems:

- Isolate sequential I/Os. Because sequential I/Os can occur at a much higher rate, isolating them allows you to run these drives much faster.

- Spread out random I/Os as much as possible. You can do this by striping table data through Oracle striping, OS striping, or hardware striping.

- Separate data and indexes. By separating a heavily used table from its index, you allow a query to a table to access data and indexes on separate disks simultaneously.

- Eliminate non-Oracle disk I/O from disks that contain database files. Any other disk I/Os slow down Oracle access to these disks.

STRIPING

Striping is the act of transparently dividing the contents of a large data source into smaller sources. Striping can be done through Oracle, the OS, or through hardware disk arrays.

The following sections look at each of these solutions and determine how they can be accomplished.

Isolate Sequential I/Os

Isolating sequential I/Os allows you to drive sequentially accessed disks at a much higher rate than randomly accessed disks. Isolating sequential I/Os can be accomplished by simply putting the Oracle redo log files on separate disks.

Be sure to put each redo log file on its own disk—especially the mirrored log file (if you are mirroring within Oracle). If you are mirroring with OS or hardware mirroring, the redo log files will already be on separate volumes. Although each log file is written sequentially, having the mirror on the same disk causes the disk to seek between the two log files between writes, thus degrading performance.

WHEN SEQUENTIAL BECOMES RANDOM

A common mistake is to put multiple redo log files on the same disk. Although each redo log file is written sequentially, after a log switch occurs and the next log in the sequence is being written to, the ARCH processes start archiving the previous log. This causes two sequential processes to access data sequentially to the same disk, thus randomizing the access.

It is important to protect redo log files against system failures by mirroring them. You can do this through Oracle, or by using OS or hardware fault tolerance features.

Spread Out Random I/Os

By the very nature of random I/Os, accesses are to vastly different places in the Oracle data files. This pattern makes it easy for random I/O problems to be alleviated by simply adding more disks to the system and spreading the Oracle tables across these disks. You can do this by striping the data across multiple drives or (depending on your configuration) by simply putting tables on different drives.

Oracle Striping

Oracle striping involves dividing a table's data into small pieces and further dividing these pieces among different data files. Oracle striping is done at the tablespace level with the CREATE TABLESPACE command. To create a striped tablespace, use a command similar to this one:

```
SQL> CREATE TABLESPACE mytablespace
  2  DATAFILE 'file1.dbf' SIZE 500K,
  3            'file2.dbf' SIZE 500K,
  4            'file3.dbf' SIZE 500K,
  5            'file4.dbf' SIZE 500K;

Tablespace created.
```

To complete this task, you must then create a table within this tablespace with four extents. This creates the table across all four data files, which (hopefully) are each on their own disk. Create the table with a command like this one:

```
SQL> CREATE TABLE mytable
  2    ( name varchar(40),
  3      title varchar(20),
  4      office_number number(4) )
  5    TABLESPACE mytablespace
  6    STORAGE ( INITIAL 495K NEXT 495K
  7    MINEXTENTS 4 PCTINCREASE 0 );

Table created.
```

In this example, each data file has a size of 500K. This is called the *stripe size*. If the table is large, the stripes are also large (unless you add many stripes). Large stripes can be an advantage when you have large pieces of data within the table, such as BLOBs. In most OLTP applications, it is more advantageous to have a smaller striping factor to distribute the I/Os more evenly.

The size of the data files depends on the size of your tables. Because it is difficult to manage hundreds of data files, it is common to have one data file per disk volume per tablespace. If your database is 10GB in size and you have 10 disk volumes, your data file size will be 1GB.

By adding more data files of a smaller size, your I/Os will be distributed more evenly, but they will be harder to manage because of the additional files.

Oracle striping can be used in conjunction with OS or hardware striping.

OS Striping

Depending on the operating system, striping can be done at the OS level either through an operating system facility or through a third-party application. OS striping is done at OS installation time.

OS disk striping is done by taking two or more physical disks and creating one large logical disk. A *logical disk* is the storage space that the OS and applications will see after the striping is performed, rather than two individual physical disks. In sequence, the stripes appear on the first disk, then the second disk, and so on. The size of each stripe depends on the OS and the striping software you are running.

To figure out which disk has the desired piece of data, the OS must keep track of where the data is. To do this, a certain amount of CPU time must be spent maintaining this information. If fault tolerance is used, even more CPU resources are required.

THE HIDDEN COSTS OF SOFTWARE STRIPING

Under certain operating systems, the overhead involved in using software striping can be extreme. In one case that I worked on recently, the I/O latencies were in the upper teens, averaging about 18msec. Upon further investigation, it was determined that the I/O rate per disk was fairly low and that approximately half of that 18msec was caused by the addition of software striping. Beware of the overhead that is involved in your I/O subsystem.

Depending on the software you are using to stripe the disks, the OS monitoring facilities might display disk I/O rates on a per-disk basis or on a per-logical-disk basis. Regardless of how the information is shown, you can easily determine the I/O rate per disk.

Hardware Striping

Hardware striping has a similar effect to OS striping. Hardware fault tolerance is obtained by replacing your disk controller with a disk array. A *disk array* is a controller that uses many disks to make one logical disk. The system takes a small slice of data from each of the disks in sequence to make up the larger logical disk, as was covered in detail in the previous chapter.

Whether you use OS or hardware striping, the effect is the same. The main difference between the two is where the actual overhead of maintaining the disk array is maintained.

Hardware fault tolerance has the advantage of not taking additional CPU or memory resources on the server. All the logic to do the striping is done at the controller level. As with OS striping, hardware striping can also take advantage of RAID technology for fault tolerance.

Review of Striping Options

Whether you use Oracle striping, OS striping, or hardware striping, the goal is the same: Distribute the random I/Os across as many disks as possible. In this way, you can keep the number of IOPS requested within the bounds of the physical disks.

If you use Oracle striping or OS striping, you can usually monitor the performance of each disk individually to see how hard they are being driven. If you use hardware striping, remember that the OS monitoring facilities typically see the disk volume as one logical disk. You can easily determine how hard the disks are being driven by dividing the I/O rate by the number of drives.

With hardware and OS striping, the stripes are small enough that the I/Os are usually divided among the drives fairly evenly. Be sure to monitor the drives periodically to verify that you are not up against I/O limits.

Use this formula to calculate the I/O rate per drive:

```
I/Os per disk = ( Number of IOPS per volume ) / (Number of drives in the volume)
```

Suppose that you have a disk array with four drives generating 120 IOPS. The number of IOPS per disk is calculated as follows:

```
I/Os per disk = 120 / 4 = 30 IOPS per disk
```

For data volumes that are accessed randomly, don't push the disks past 125 IOPS per disk. To estimate how many disks you need for data volumes, use this formula:

```
Number of disks = IOPS needed / 125 IOPS per disk
```

If your application requires a certain data file to supply 500 IOPS (based on analysis and calculations), you can estimate the number of disk drives needed as follows:

```
Number of disks = 500 IOPS / 125 IOPS per disk = 4 disks
```

This calculation gives you a good approximation for how many drives to use to build the data volumes with no fault tolerance. The previous chapter looked at various RAID levels and additional I/Os that are incurred by adding disk fault tolerance. In addition to this, you also might want to consider adding drives to the volumes for future growth needs.

Separate Data and Indexes

Another way to reduce disk contention is to separate the data files from their associated indexes. Remember that disk contention is caused by multiple processes trying to obtain the same resources. For a particularly "hot" table with data that many processes try to access, the indexes associated with that data are "hot" also.

Placing the data files and index files on different disks reduces the contention on particularly hot tables. Distributing the files also allows more concurrency by allowing simultaneous accesses to the data files and the indexes. Look at the Oracle dynamic performance tables to determine which tables and indexes are the most active.

Eliminate Non-Oracle Disk I/Os

Although it is not necessary to eliminate all non-Oracle I/Os, reducing significant I/Os will help performance. Most systems are tuned to handle a specific throughput requirement or response time requirement. Any additional I/Os that slow down Oracle can affect both of these requirements.

Another reason to reduce non-Oracle I/Os is to increase the accuracy of the Oracle dynamic performance table, V$FILESTAT. If only Oracle files are on the disks you are monitoring, the statistics in this table should be accurate.

Reducing Unnecessary I/O Overhead

Reducing unnecessary I/O overhead can increase the throughput available for user tasks. Unnecessary overhead such as chaining and migrating of rows hurts performance.

Migrating and chaining occur when an UPDATE statement increases the size of a row so that it no longer fits in the data block. When this happens, Oracle tries to find space for this new row. If a block is available with enough room, Oracle moves the entire row to that new block. This is called *migrating*. If no data block is available with enough space, Oracle splits the row into multiple pieces and stores the pieces in several data blocks. This is called *chaining*.

Migrated and Chained Rows

Migrated rows cause overhead in the system because Oracle must spend the CPU time to find space for the row and then copy the row to the new data block. This takes both CPU time and I/Os. Therefore, any UPDATE statement that causes a migration incurs a performance penalty.

Chained rows cause overhead in the system not only when they are created, but also each time they are accessed. A chained row requires more than one I/O to read the row. Remember that Oracle reads from the disk data blocks; each time the row is accessed, multiple blocks must be read into the SGA.

You can check for chained rows with the LIST CHAINED ROWS option of the ANALYZE command. You can use these SQL statements to check for chained or migrated rows:

```
SQL> Rem
SQL> CREATE TABLE chained_rows (
  2   owner_name    varchar2(30),
  3   table_name    varchar2(30),
```

```
  4   cluster_name  varchar2(30),
  5   head_rowid    rowid,
  6   timestamp     date);

Table created.

SQL> Rem
SQL> Rem Analyze the Table in Question
SQL> Rem
SQL> ANALYZE
  2    TABLE scott.emp LIST CHAINED ROWS;

Table analyzed.

SQL> Rem
SQL> Rem Check the Results
SQL> Rem
SQL> SELECT * from chained_rows;

no rows selected
```

If any rows are selected, you have either chained or migrated rows. To solve this problem, copy the rows in question to a temporary table, delete the rows from the initial table, and reinsert the rows into the original table from the temporary table.

Run the chained-row command again to show only chained rows. An abundance of chained rows is an indication that the Oracle database block size is too small. You might want to export the data and rebuild the database with a larger block size.

You might not be able to avoid having chained rows, especially if your table has a LONG column or long CHAR or VARCHAR2 columns. If you are aware of large columns, it can be advantageous to adjust the database block size before implementing the database.

A properly sized block ensures that the blocks are used efficiently and that I/Os are kept to a minimum. Don't over build the blocks or you might end up wasting space. The block size is determined by the Oracle parameter DB_BLOCK_SIZE. Remember that the amount of memory used for db block buffers is calculated as follows:

```
Memory used = DB_BLOCK_BUFFERS (number) * DB_BLOCK_SIZE (bytes)
```

Be careful to avoid paging or swapping caused by an SGA that doesn't fit into RAM.

Dynamic Extensions

Additional I/O is generated by the extension of segments. Remember that segments are allocated for data in the database at creation time. As the table grows, extents are added to accommodate this growth.

Dynamic extension not only causes additional I/Os, but it also causes additional SQL statements to be executed. These additional calls, known as *recursive calls*, as well as the additional I/Os can impact performance.

You can check the number of recursive calls through the dynamic performance table, V$SYSSTAT. Use the following command:

```
SQL> SELECT name, value
  2  FROM v$SYSSTAT
  3  WHERE name = 'recursive calls';


NAME                                                             VALUE
------------------------------------------------------------ ----------
recursive calls                                                   5440
```

Check for recursive calls after your application has started running and then 15 to 20 minutes later. This information will tell you approximately how many recursive calls the application is causing. The following also cause recursive calls:

- Execution of Data Definition Language statements
- Execution of SQL statements within stored procedures, functions, packages, and anonymous PL/SQL blocks
- Enforcement of referential integrity constraints
- The firing of database triggers
- Misses on the data dictionary cache

As you can see, many other conditions can also cause recursive calls. One way to check whether you are creating extents dynamically is to check the table DBA_EXTENTS. If you see that many extents have been created, it might be time to export your data, rebuild the tablespace, and reload the data.

Sizing a segment large enough to fit your data properly benefits you in two ways:

- Blocks in a single extent are contiguous and allow multiblock reads to be more effective, thus reducing I/O.
- Large extents are less likely to be dynamically extended.

Try to size your segments so that dynamic extension is generally avoided and space for growth is adequate.

PCTFREE and PCTUSED Command Options

Another way to improve performance and decrease overhead is to use the PCTFREE and PCTUSED options of the STORAGE clause in the CREATE CLUSTER, CREATE TABLE, CREATE INDEX, and CREATE SNAPSHOT commands. By using PCTFREE and PCTUSED, you have more exact control over the use of the data blocks. In many cases, knowing your application and your data can help you improve overall system performance.

You use PCTFREE and PCTUSED for several purposes. Both options are of a performance nature and are space related. PCTFREE and PCTUSED can effectively speed up access to data blocks, but at the price of wasting space if you're not careful. Another important effect of PCTFREE and PCTUSED is to reduce chaining.

THE GLASS SHOULD BE HALF EMPTY

Every now and then, there's always that one annoying waiter at a restaurant who always hovers around the table, refilling your water glass every time you take even the tiniest sip. He can help demonstrate PCTFREE and PCTUSED.

I instruct this waiter not to refill my glass until I drink at least 50% of my water. I also tell him not to fill it more that 7/8 full when he does get to refill it, just to prevent him from pouring too much and spilling water everywhere. What I've done is set a low water mark of 50% and a high water mark of roughly 88%.

Think of PCTFREE as a high water mark and PCTUSED as a low water mark. We don't want to fill our data blocks if our percentage of free space in each block is less than PCTFREE. We also don't want to add more data to a block unless the percentage of used space in the block is less than PCTUSED. Free space in a block can occur if the block is a new block or if data has been deleted or moved to other blocks. If free space exists below PCTUSED, we can add more data to that block again until we reach our high water mark, PCTFREE.

The sum of PCTFREE and PCTUSED cannot exceed 100. Because PCTFREE actually represents a high water mark of 100 PCTFREE, if the sum of the two exceeds 100, an inconsistency exists in the formula and PCTFREE is less than PCTUSED.

AN EXAMPLE

Assume that you have the following values for PCTFREE and PCTUSED:

```
PCTFREE = 20
PCTUSED = 40
```

In this example, you can add new rows to the data block until the data block becomes 80% full (100%, 20% free). When this occurs, no more rows can be added to this data block; the space is reserved for growth of the existing rows.

You can add new rows to the data block only when the percentage of available space in the block has been reduced to 40% (used). This effectively saves space in the data blocks for growth of rows and avoids chaining.

The defaults for PCTFREE and PCTUSED are as follows:

```
PCTFREE = 10
PCTUSED = 40
```

PCTFREE

PCTFREE has the effect of reserving space in the data block for growth of existing rows. New rows can be added to the data block until the amount of space remaining in the data block is less than PCTFREE percent.

A high PCTFREE value has the following effects:

- A large amount of space is available for growth of existing rows.

- Performance is improved because blocks don't have to be organized as frequently and because chaining is reduced.

- More space is usually required because blocks are not used as efficiently. A moderate amount of empty space will always be in the data blocks.

A lower PCTFREE value has the opposite effects:

- Less space for growth of existing rows is available.

- Performance is reduced because reorganization might become more frequent and because rows might have to be chained more often, increasing CPU use as well as causing additional I/Os.

- Space is used more effectively. Blocks are filled more completely, thus reducing wastage.

Using PCTFREE can help if you have an application that frequently inserts new data into rows. Because the PCTFREE option is used in the CREATE CLUSTER, CREATE TABLE, CREATE INDEX, and CREATE SNAPSHOT commands, it is worth the effort to look at each of your tables, clusters, and indexes individually and decide on an effective PCTFREE value for each.

PCTUSED

When PCTFREE is reached, no new rows can be inserted into the data block until the space in the block has fallen below PCTUSED. Another feature of PCTUSED is that Oracle tries to keep a data block at least PCTUSED full before using new blocks.

A high PCTUSED value has the following effects:

- It decreases performance because you usually have more migrating and chained rows.

- It reduces space wastage by filling the data block more completely.

A lower value for PCTUSED has the following effects:

- Performance is improved because of the drop in the number of migrated and chained rows.

- Less efficient space usage is available because of more unused space in the data blocks.

Just as with PCTFREE, it is worth the effort to look at each table individually and determine a value for PCTUSED that more accurately fits your application. Doing so can improve your system's performance.

A Review of the PCTFREE and PCTUSED Options

As with most tuning efforts, a trade-off is available between space usage and performance. Following are a few things to keep in mind when you are adjusting the values for PCTFREE and PCTUSED:

- Because PCTFREE and PCTUSED are used as high water and low water marks, the sum of the two cannot exceed 100. On the other hand, the sum does not have to equal 100.

- The closer the sum of the two values gets to 100, or the closer that PCTFREE is to PCTUSED, the more overhead is incurred and the more efficient space usage is.

- If the sum of PCTFREE and PCTUSED equals 100, Oracle attempts to keep exactly PCTFREE free space, increasing CPU usage.

- Fixed block overhead is not included in the calculation of PCTFREE and PCTUSED.

- A good compromise of performance and space is to keep approximately one row difference between PCTFREE and PCTUSED. For example, with a 100-byte row in a 2048-byte data block with 100 bytes of overhead, use the following formula:

```
Space = 2048 - 100 = 1948
Average Row = 100 or 5 % of the data block
( 100 - PCTFREE ) - PCTUSED = 5
```

A large difference between PCTFREE and PCTUSED means more empty space. Leaving one row difference is usually sufficient.

Following are a few guidelines to follow when adjusting PCTFREE and PCTUSED:

- Update Activity, High Row Growth. If your application frequently uses updates that affect the size of rows, set PCTFREE fairly high and set PCTUSED fairly low. This arrangement allows for a large amount of space in the data blocks for row size growth. For example:

```
PCTFREE = 20-25
PCTUSED = 35-40
( 100 - PCTFREE _) - PCTUSED = 35 to 45
```

- Insert Activity, Small Row Growth. If most inserts are new rows and there is very little update with row growth, set PCTFREE low with a moderate value for PCTUSED to avoid chaining of new rows. This arrangement allows new rows to be inserted into the data block until the point at which more insertions are likely to cause migration or chaining. When this point is reached, no more insertions occur there until a fair amount of space is left in the block; then inserting can resume.

```
PCTFREE = 5-10
PCTUSED = 50-60
( 100 - PCTFREE _) - PCTUSED = 30 to 45
```

- Performance Primary, Space Abundant. If performance is critical and you have plenty of space available, you can ensure that migration and chaining never occur by setting PCTFREE very high and PCTUSED extremely low. Although this can waste quite a bit of space, all chaining and migration should be avoided.

```
PCTFREE = 30
PCTUSED = 30
( 100 - PCTFREE _) - PCTUSED = 40
```

- Space Critical, Performance Secondary. If you have large tables or if you have moderate-sized tables and disk space is at a premium, set PCTFREE low and PCTUSED high. This arrangement ensures that you take maximum advantage of the available space. Note that you will see some performance loss caused by increased chaining and migration.

```
PCTFREE = 5
PCTUSED = 90
( 100 - PCTFREE _) - PCTUSED = 5
```

A Review of I/O Reduction Techniques

Reduction of I/O is important for performance because I/O is one of the slowest operations in the computer system. Caching data is many times faster than an access from disk. In fact, a read from memory can occur more than 100,000 times faster than a read from disk.

You have seen that you can speed up I/O by separating the sequential and the random I/Os and separating data from indexes to get maximum concurrency. You have also seen how to speed up I/Os by avoiding them altogether, such as by reducing dynamic extensions and by avoiding migrated and chained rows.

As you will see in later chapters, the speed of I/O from disk is a fixed value that you can work around only by caching, reducing contention, and avoiding I/Os if possible.

Block Size

Typically, the default block size is sufficient for all applications. In a few cases, however, increasing the size of the database buffers is beneficial. Depending on your operating system, different limitations on the value of DB_BLOCK_SIZE exist.

If you have a large system with many disks, think about increasing the database block size. These large systems typically use a block size of 4K or larger. The larger block size might benefit the overall performance of the system.

The size of the database block has several effects of which you should be aware. If the block size is too small for the data stored in the database, you suffer the following effects:

- Unnecessary I/O. This is caused by the additional chaining and migration of rows that do not fit in the block.

- Unnecessary latch operations. This is caused by redo information not fitting in the redo log buffer.

- Wasted space. This is caused because the smaller blocks are less likely to be entirely filled.

All these problems result in unnecessary overhead in space, CPU, and I/Os. By increasing the block size, many of these problems can be eliminated.

Be careful. A block size that is too large can cause the following effects on your system:

- More I/Os. Because the block size is larger, fewer database block buffers are available in memory for the same size SGA. This situation results in more I/Os because buffers must be written out to make room for new ones.

- Larger I/Os. The larger the I/O, the longer it takes to copy data into memory. If the large amount of data is needed, one long I/O is much better than two shorter I/Os.

- Longer disk queuing. Because of the longer I/Os, disk queuing takes longer, which is also worthwhile if the data you retrieved is useful.

Other effects of a larger block size include a reduction in the depth of the B*-Tree index and less disk-seek overhead to retrieve data blocks. Another effect of a larger block size is an increase in the size of cluster buckets.

Following are a few guidelines to help you decide whether changing the size of DB_BLOCK_SIZE can benefit you:

- OLTP systems benefit from smaller blocks. If your application is OLTP in nature, you will not benefit from larger blocks. OLTP data typically fits well in the default block size; larger blocks unnecessarily eject blocks from the SGA.

- DSS systems benefit from larger blocks. In the DSS system where table scans are common, retrieving more data at a time results in a performance increase.

- Larger databases benefit from larger blocks. Larger databases see a space benefit because less wastage exists per block.

- Databases with large rows benefit from larger blocks. If your rows are extremely large (such as images or text) and don't fit in the default block, you will see a definite benefit from a larger block size.

When changing the block size, be careful to set DB_BLOCK_SIZE only to a multiple of the OS block size. Doing so guarantees that you are not reading OS blocks and only using part of the block. For example, if you are using 1KB Oracle blocks and 2KB OS blocks, the OS will read 2KB from the disk every time you request a 1KB block.

You should change the database block size only after careful consideration. If you see excessive chained rows or wasted space, consider a larger block size. If you are running a DSS system, you might also want to consider a larger block size. Larger block sizes can be beneficial, but they can also be detrimental if you change them unnecessarily.

Using Multiple Block Sizes

One of the most exciting new features of Oracle9i is the ability to mix multiple block sizes in the same database. This allows you to take advantage of both the DSS advantages of a large block size and the OLTP advantages of a small block size. This can be quite useful, but it is dependent on you knowing your system and your data.

To use multiple block sizes, you must do two different things. First, you must set up the Oracle buffer cache to be divided into different parts based on block size. Then you must create tablespaces using the non-standard block sizes.

A PIECE OF ADVICE ————————————————————

By setting the parameter DB_CACHE_ADVICE to ON, statistics relating to the performance benefits of multiple block sizes are gathered and are available in the table V$DB_CACHE_ADVICE performance view.

Setting Up the Oracle Buffer Cache for Non-Standard Block Sizes

As mentioned in Chapter 8, "Oracle and System Hardware," the DB_CACHE_SIZE parameter determines the amount of memory that is allocated for the default buffer cache. The DB_BLOCK_SIZE parameter sets the standard block size, and DB_2K_CACHE_SIZE, DB_4K_CACHE_SIZE, and so on set the non-standard cache sizes.

Set the parameter DB_CACHE_SIZE to be the amount of memory that you want to allocate to the default block size. Set DB_2K_CACHE_SIZE, DB_4K_CACHE_SIZE, and so on to the amount of memory to which you want each of those block sizes to have access. Please note that multiple buffer caches using the KEEP, RECYCLE, and DEFAULT cache settings only apply to the default block size.

Creating Tablespaces with Non-Standard Block Sizes

To create a tablespace with a non-standard block size, you must use the BLOCKSIZE keyword when creating the tablespace. This keyword is followed by the block size that you are setting for this tablespace. An example of this is shown here:

```
CREATE TABLESPACE oltp_ts
DATAFILE '/u/oracle/data/oltp1.dat' SIZE 100M,
'/u/oracle/data/oldp2.dat' SIZE 100M
BLOCKSIZE 2K
```

This example creates a 2K tablespace. Other size tablespaces can also be created.

Fragmentation

Fragmentation occurs when pieces of the database are no longer contiguous. Fragmentation can consist of disk fragmentation or tablespace fragmentation. Both types of fragmentation usually affect performance.

Disk fragmentation usually causes multiple I/Os to occur where one I/O should have been sufficient (such as with chained or migrated rows). Disk fragmentation can also be caused when the extents that make up the database segments are noncontiguous, as happens when excessive dynamic growth occurs (see Figure 10.1).

The dropping and creation of segments, which can cause large free areas between segments, cause *Tablespace fragmentation*. The free areas result in the inefficient use of space and cause excessive disk seeks over the empty areas (see Figure 10.2). Tablespace fragmentation can also prevent Oracle from taking advantage of multiblock reads.

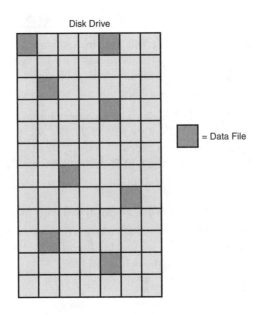

FIGURE 10.1
Disk fragmentation.

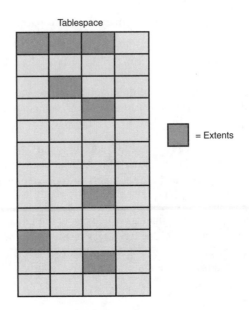

FIGURE 10.2
Tablespace fragmentation.

Tablespace fragmentation can be detected by looking in the Oracle table DBA_EXTENTS with a query such as this one:

```
SQL> SELECT SUBSTR(tablespace_name,1,25) "Tablespace Name",
  2         block_id "Block",
  3         blocks "Number of Blocks",
  4         SUBSTR(segment_name,1,25) "Segment Name"
  5  FROM dba_extents
  6  WHERE tablespace_name = 'SYSTEM'
  7  ORDER BY block_id;
```

Tablespace Name	Block	Number of Blocks	Segment Name
SYSTEM	2	25	SYSTEM
SYSTEM	27	25	SYSTEM
SYSTEM	52	60	C_OBJ#
SYSTEM	112	5	I_OBJ#
SYSTEM	117	5	C_TS#
SYSTEM	122	5	I_TS#
SYSTEM	127	10	C_FILE#_BLOCK#
SYSTEM	137	5	I_FILE#_BLOCK#
SYSTEM	142	5	C_USER#
SYSTEM	147	5	I_USER#
SYSTEM	152	5	UNDO$
SYSTEM	157	5	FILE$
SYSTEM	162	5	OBJ$
SYSTEM	167	5	CON$
SYSTEM	172	25	C_COBJ#
SYSTEM	197	5	I_COBJ#
SYSTEM	202	5	I_TAB1
SYSTEM	207	5	I_UNDO1
SYSTEM	212	5	I_OBJ1
SYSTEM	217	5	I_OBJ2
SYSTEM	222	5	I_IND1

By examining the blocks, you can determine whether any segments are missing, a process that is quite time consuming and tedious. Another way to detect fragmentation is by using one of many third-party monitoring and defragmentation tools.

One way to eliminate fragmentation is to export the table or tablespace data, remove and re-create the table or tablespace, and import the data. Although this process fixes the problem at hand, it might not solve the problem that caused the fragmentation to occur in the first place.

You can prevent fragmentation by properly sizing segment storage parameters so that your tables don't span excessive numbers of extents. Grouping segments with similar growth characteristics in the same tablespaces also helps. In addition, it is beneficial to avoid unnecessary table or index drops, which cause fragmentation. Probably of most importance is to separate temporary segments into their own tablespaces.

By eliminating fragmentation, you can reduce excessive I/O and CPU usage, streamlining data accesses. When you reduce overhead and unnecessary I/O, you improve system performance.

Summary

In the previous chapter, you learned how the I/O subsystem and RAID worked. In this chapter, you built on that knowledge and related it to how Oracle works and to what is important to Oracle for performance. This knowledge will be used to help you understand why the number of IOPS per disk is limited, which will relate to how you lay out Oracle on the I/O subsystem. In addition, you learned other techniques and guidelines for optimizing the Oracle I/O subsystem for optimal performance.

PART III

Application and SQL Tuning

IN THIS PART

11 Using EXPLAIN PLAN and SQL Trace

12 Index Tuning

13 The Oracle Optimizer

14 Tuning SQL

15 Using Hints

USING EXPLAIN PLAN
AND SQL TRACE

Probably the best way to determine whether your SQL statements are properly optimized is by using the Oracle SQL Trace facility and the EXPLAIN PLAN command. The SQL Trace facility is used to determine what operations are being done in your system by monitoring the entire instance or one or more sessions. The SQL Trace facility is used to gather these statistics, and the Oracle program TKPROF is used to translate trace files.

You use SQL Trace to gather information into a trace file; the Oracle program TKPROF formats the trace information into useful, understandable data. Without TKPROF, this information would be in an unreadable form.

The EXPLAIN PLAN command is used to display the execution plan that is chosen by the Oracle optimizer for SELECT, UPDATE, INSERT, and DELETE statements. By analyzing the execution plan the Oracle optimizer has chosen and knowing your data and application, you should be able to determine whether the optimizer has chosen the correct execution plan for your application. EXPLAIN PLAN is run on a specific SQL statement that you pass to the EXPLAIN PLAN command.

EXPLAIN PLAN can be used to try different variations on your SQL statements or in conjunction with schema modifications such as the addition of indexes. By analyzing the output, you might be able to provide hints that the Oracle optimizer can use to better take advantage of your data knowledge. By using hints, you might be able to better take advantage of features such as the Oracle Parallel Query option.

By the end of this chapter, you should be able to monitor your system using SQL Trace and analyze execution plans using EXPLAIN PLAN. You should also understand the value of registering applications for later use when tracking performance problems. These Oracle options can greatly improve the stability and performance of your system.

SQL Trace

The SQL Trace facility and the Oracle program TKPROF are designed to give performance information about activity in your system. This information can be used to determine hot spots and problem areas that should be optimized.

You can enable SQL Trace for a session or for an entire instance. Of course, because this facility gathers an abundance of information about SQL statement functionality and performance, SQL Trace has an effect on the performance of the system. If you use SQL Trace on a single session, the effect is fairly minimal, but if you use SQL Trace on an entire instance, you will see a substantial effect on the performance of the system. Avoid running SQL Trace on an entire instance for this reason.

SQL Trace Initialization

Before you run SQL Trace, make sure that certain Oracle initialization parameters are set:

Parameter	Description
TIMED_STATISTICS	Setting TIMED_STATISTICS=TRUE enables SQL Trace and some of the dynamic performance tables to collect timed statistics such as CPU and elapsed times. Enabling timed statistics incurs significant overhead because most Oracle operations are now being timed and should be avoided except when necessary.
MAX_DUMP_FILE_SIZE	This specifies the maximum size of trace file dumps in OS blocks. Set this to the amount of space that you are willing to use for your trace files. The default is 500. If the SQL Trace output files are being truncated, increase this value.
USER_DUMP_DEST	This parameter specifies the destination for the trace file. The default destination is the same as for system dumps on your OS.

Controlling SQL Trace

You can enable the SQL Trace facility on a per-session basis or for the entire instance. The following sections explain how to enable and disable SQL Trace for both of these cases.

Enable SQL Trace for a Session

To enable SQL Trace for your own session, use this Oracle command:

```
ALTER SESSION
SET SQL_TRACE = TRUE;
```

Alternatively, you can use the Oracle procedure RDBMS_SESSION.SET_SQL_TRACE.

To enable SQL Trace for a session other than your own, you can use the Oracle procedure RDBMS_SYSTEM.SET_SQL_TRACE_IN_SESSION with the arguments SID, Serial#, and TRUE. To determine the values for SID and Serial#, use the following SQL statements:

```
SQL> SELECT sid, serial#, osuser
  2    FROM v$session
  3   WHERE osuser = 'Ed Whalen';

    SID    SERIAL# OSUSER
--------- --------- ---------------
      7          4 Ed Whalen
```

To turn SQL Trace on for that session, use the Oracle stored procedure as follows:

```
SQL> EXECUTE RDBMS_system.set_sql_trace_in_session(7,4,TRUE);
PL/SQL procedure successfully completed.
```

Disable SQL Trace for a Session

To disable SQL Trace for a session, use this Oracle command:

```
ALTER SESSION
SET SQL_TRACE = FALSE;
```

The SQL Trace facility is also disabled when your session disconnects from Oracle.

To disable SQL Trace for a session other than your own, use the Oracle procedure RDBMS_SYSTEM.SET_SQL_TRACE_IN_SESSION with the arguments SID, Serial#, and FALSE as shown here:

```
SQL> EXECUTE RDBMS_system.set_sql_trace_in_session(7,4,FALSE);
PL/SQL procedure successfully completed.
```

Enable SQL Trace for an Instance

To enable SQL Trace for your instance, set the Oracle initialization parameter SQL_TRACE to TRUE. Doing so enables SQL Trace for all users of this instance for the duration of the instance.

Disable SQL Trace for an Instance

The SQL Trace facility cannot be disabled for the entire instance without shutting down the Oracle instance and setting the Oracle initialization parameter SQL_TRACE to FALSE. Alternatively, you can remove the parameter because its default value is FALSE.

When SQL Trace is enabled for the entire instance, it is still possible to disable it on a per-session basis. You can disable SQL Trace on a per-session basis with the SQL shown in the previous section.

SQL Trace Functionality

After SQL Trace is enabled, it gathers the following information:

- Parse, execute, and fetch counts. These counts can give you vital information about the efficiency of the SQL statements.

- CPU and elapsed times. This information can tell you which statements take the most time to execute.

- Physical and logical reads. This information can help you determine the effectiveness of the database buffer pool.

- Number of rows processed. This information can be used as an indication that more rows are being processed than you expected, thus indicating a problem.

- Library cache misses. This information can show you the effectiveness of the shared SQL area and how well you are reusing already parsed SQL statements.

SQL Trace puts this information into a trace file in an unreadable form. You then use the Oracle program TKPROF to format the trace information into useful, understandable data.

TKPROF Functionality

You use the Oracle program TKPROF to convert the SQL Trace information into data that is formatted for human understanding. By specifying certain options, you can customize the output of TKPROF to some degree. TKPROF is invoked with the following syntax:

```
TKPROF inputfile outputfile [ Optional Parameters ]
```

where *inputfile* is the data file generated by SQL Trace and *outputfile* is the name of the file where you desire the output of TKPROF to be written.

The optional parameters to TKPROF are as follows:

Parameter	Description
EXPLAIN = *username/password*	This option automatically runs the EXPLAIN PLAN command and adds the execution plan to the output of SQL Trace.
TABLE = *schema.table*	This option specifies the schema and table name of the temporary table that TKPROF uses when processing the SQL Trace data. If this option is not specified, TKPROF will create, use, and then delete a temporary table.
INSERT = *scriptfile*	This option creates a file named *scriptfile* that contains the SQL statements that TKPROF uses for storing trace file statistics.
SYS = [*YES/NO*]	This option determines whether SQL statements that are generated by user SYS or recursive SQL statements are listed.
PRINT = *number*	This option generates the output of only the first *number* sorted SQL statements.
RECORD = *recordfile*	This option creates a file named *recordfile* that contains all recursive SQL statements.

Parameter	Description
SORT = *sort_option*	This option sorts the output of SQL Trace in descending order based on the *sort_option* specified. The *sort_option* variable can be any of the following values:

PRSCNT	Sorted by parse count
PRSCPU	Sorted by CPU time spent parsing
PRSELA	Sorted by elapsed time spent parsing
PRSDSK	Sorted by number of physical reads from disk during parse
PRSQRY	Sorted by number of consistent mode block reads during parse
PRSCU	Sorted by number of current mode block reads during parse
EXECNT	Sorted by number of executes
EXECPU	Sorted by CPU time spent executing
EXEELA	Sorted by elapsed time spent executing
EXEDSK	Sorted by number of physical reads during execute
EXEQRY	Sorted by number of consistent mode block reads during execute
EXECU	Sorted by number of current mode block reads during execute
EXEROW	Sorted by number of rows processed during execute
EXEMIS	Sorted by number of library cache misses during execute
FCHCNT	Sorted by number of fetches
FCHCPU	Sorted by CPU time spent fetching
FCHELA	Sorted by elapsed time spent fetching
FCHDSK	Sorted by number of physical reads from disk during fetch
FCHQRY	Sorted by number of consistent mode block reads during fetch
FCHCU	Sorted by number of current mode block reads during fetch
FCHROW	Sorted by number of rows fetched

With these options, SQL Trace can provide an abundance of data that can help you analyze your SQL statements. The following section examines some of the data that SQL Trace provides.

Interpreting SQL Trace

This section looks at some of the statistics available from SQL Trace and how to interpret them. For each SQL statement executed, SQL Trace provides the following information:

Parameter	Description
count	Number of times the OCI procedure was executed. (The OCI interface is the standard set of calls used to access the Oracle database.)
CPU	CPU time in seconds executing. This value is the amount of time that Oracle used to process the statement.
elapsed	Elapsed time in seconds executing. This value is equivalent to the user's response time.
disk	Number of physical reads of buffers from disk. This value tells you how many reads actually missed the buffer cache and had to go to physical disk.
query	Number of buffers gotten for consistent read. This value represents the number of buffers retrieved in consistent mode. Consistent mode guarantees consistent reads throughout the transaction; it is used for most queries.
current	Number of buffers gotten in current mode (usually for update). In current mode, the data blocks gotten reflect the value at that instant in time.
rows	Number of rows processed by the fetch or execute call. This value gives you an idea of how many instructions have been executed.

By looking at each of these parameters, you can get an idea of how your SQL statements are being processed and which statements are taking the most time. By analyzing which statements are taking the longest, you might be able to find some inefficiencies that you can correct.

You will now see an example that demonstrates the use of SQL Trace.

The SQL Trace facility was enabled in a session by using this Oracle command:

```
EXECUTE RDBMS_system.set_sql_trace_in_session(7,3,TRUE);.
```

In another session (with SID = 7, Serial# = 3), the following SQL statement was executed:

```
SELECT * FROM emp, dept
WHERE emp.deptno = dept.deptno
ORDER BY empno;
```

The SQL Trace facility was later disabled using this Oracle command from the first session:

```
EXECUTE RDBMS_system.set_sql_trace_in_session(7,3,FALSE);
```

Following the execution of the SQL statements, the trace file was translated by running TKPROF as follows:

```
tkprof orclshad.trc trace.out sys=no explain=scott/tiger
```

where

orclshad.trc	This is the trace file that is generated by SQL Trace.
trace.out	This is where I want the output to go.
sys=no	This indicates that no SYS or recursive SQL statements should be printed.
explain=scott/tiger	This generates EXPLAIN PLAN output.

TKPROF generated the output file shown in Listing 11.1.

Listing 11.1   The TKPROF Output File for a Sample Trace

```
TKPROF: Release 7.2.2.3.0 - Beta on Sun Nov 26 13:03:20 1995


Copyright (c) Oracle Corporation 1979, 1994.  All rights reserved.


Trace file: orclshad.trc
Sort options: default


*************************************************************************
count    = number of times OCI procedure was executed
cpu      = cpu time in seconds executing
elapsed  = elapsed time in seconds executing
disk     = number of physical reads of buffers from disk
query    = number of buffers gotten for consistent read
current  = number of buffers gotten in current mode (usually for update)
rows     = number of rows processed by the fetch or execute call
*************************************************************************

SELECT
    SUBSTR(dogname,1,20) "Dog Name",
    SUBSTR(breed_name,1,20) "Breed",
    SUBSTR(owner,1,20) "Owner"
FROM
    dogs, breeds
WHERE
    dogs.breed = breeds.breed
ORDER BY
    dogs.breed
```

Listing 11.1   Continued

call	count	cpu	elapsed	disk	query	current	rows
Parse	1	0.00	0.57	2	0	4	0
Execute	1	0.00	0.00	0	0	0	0
Fetch	2	0.00	0.08	2	2	6	25
total	4	0.00	0.65	4	2	10	25

```
Misses in library cache during parse: 1
Optimizer hint: CHOOSE
Parsing user id: 10  (ED)


Rows      Execution Plan
-------   -------------------------------------------------
     0   SELECT STATEMENT   HINT: CHOOSE
    60    MERGE JOIN
     0      SORT (JOIN)
     0       TABLE ACCESS (FULL) OF 'BREEDS'
     0      SORT (JOIN)
     0       TABLE ACCESS (FULL) OF 'DOGS'
```

```
********************************************************************************
```

OVERALL TOTALS FOR ALL NON-RECURSIVE STATEMENTS

call	count	cpu	elapsed	disk	query	current	rows
Parse	1	0.00	0.57	2	0	4	0
Execute	1	0.00	0.00	0	0	0	0
Fetch	2	0.00	0.08	2	2	6	25
total	4	0.00	0.65	4	2	10	25

```
Misses in library cache during parse: 1

    1  user  SQL statements in session.
    8  internal SQL statements in session.
    9  SQL statements in session.
    1  statement EXPLAINed in this session.
```

Listing 11.1 Continued
```
********************************************************************************
Trace file: orclshad.trc
Trace file compatibility: 7.02.01
Sort options: default

      1   session in tracefile.
      1   user  SQL statements in trace file.
      8   internal SQL statements in trace file.
      9   SQL statements in trace file.
      6   unique SQL statements in trace file.
      1   SQL statements EXPLAINed using schema:
            ED.prof$plan_table
              Default table was used.
              Table was created.
              Table was dropped.
    109 lines in trace file.
```

Notice that three user SQL statements are defined in the output from SQL Trace (Listing 11.1), but only one SQL statement is shown. This is because the Oracle commands used by the other session to enable SQL Trace are included in the output. For now, focus on the output related to the following SQL statements (the output follows the SQL statements):

```
SELECT
    SUBSTR(dogname,1,20) "Dog Name",
    SUBSTR(breed_name,1,20) "Breed",
    SUBSTR(owner,1,20) "Owner"
FROM
    dogs, breeds
WHERE
    dogs.breed = breeds.breed
ORDER BY
    dogs.breed
```

call	count	cpu	elapsed	disk	query	current	rows
Parse	1	0.00	0.57	2	0	4	0
Execute	1	0.00	0.00	0	0	0	0
Fetch	2	0.00	0.08	2	2	6	25
total	4	0.00	0.65	4	2	10	25

```
Misses in library cache during parse: 1
Optimizer hint: CHOOSE
Parsing user id: 10  (ED)
```

From this output, you can see that the majority of the elapsed time was spent in the parse phase. The CPU time to execute this statement was less than 0.01 seconds, which is the resolution of timed statistics. The following chart describes these statistics in a little more detail.

Parameter	Value and Meaning
count	The count value is 1, 1, and 2 (Parse, Execute, and Fetch), indicating that the SQL statement executed an OCI call once during the parse, again in the execute phases, and twice during the fetch.
CPU	The CPU time spent in each of the phases was 0.0, 0.0, and 0.0 seconds (Parse, Execute, and Fetch). These minuscule times are the result of the tiny size of the database tables and the query. Your SQL statements will probably use much more CPU time.
elapsed	This is the elapsed time. By far, the majority of the time executing this SQL statement is in the parse phase. However, this is not true for more complex statements and larger tables.
disk	Notice that it is only during the parse and fetch phases that disk activity occurs.
query	Because this SQL statement is a query, the fetches are done in consistent mode rather than current mode.
current	The reads for the parsing phase and some of the reads for the fetching phase were done in current mode. Reads are done in current mode whenever possible.
rows	The fetch phase processed 25 rows. Because this is a query operation, this value indicates how many rows were returned. In an UPDATE, INSERT, or DELETE operation, the rows parameter in the fetch phase would indicate how many rows were processed in each of these statements.

This information can give you valuable insight into how your queries are running. Although the output for the EXPLAIN PLAN command was also given here, it is described later in this chapter.

In addition to the preceding information about the SQL statements statistics, SQL Trace also provides the following information about library cache statistics and optimizer hints:

```
Misses in library cache during parse: 1
Optimizer hint: CHOOSE
Parsing user id: 10  (ED)
```

With this particular SQL statement, one library cache was missed, which is quite high, considering that only one SQL statement was executed. The Optimizer hint: The CHOOSE line indicates that the optimization method was left to Oracle to decide.

Also of importance are any recursive SQL statements that Oracle must execute on behalf of the user's SQL statement. In this example, TKPROF was used with the parameter SYS=NO to prevent the reporting of recursive statements. This was done to manually turn SQL Trace on and off without showing a lot of irrelevant output. It was understood that the sample SQL statement would not generate recursive calls.

Do *not* set SYS=NO unless you are in a similar situation. It is useful to obtain an indication of recursive calls being executed. Later in this chapter, you use EXPLAIN PLAN to get an idea of how the SQL statement has been executed.

REVIEW OF SQL TRACE

The first part of this chapter looked at SQL Trace, a powerful facility provided by Oracle for debugging SQL performance problems. SQL Trace can provide valuable information that you can use to debug many different types of performance problems.

SQL Trace provides valuable information on such things as these:

- Parse, execute, and fetch counts
- CPU and elapsed times
- Physical and logical reads
- Number of rows processed
- Library cache misses

The EXPLAIN PLAN Command

The EXPLAIN PLAN command shows you the execution plan that the Oracle optimizer has chosen for your SQL statements. With this information, you can determine whether the Oracle optimizer has chosen the correct execution plan based on your knowledge of the data and the application. You can also use EXPLAIN PLAN to determine whether additional optimization should be done to your database (for example, the addition of an index or the use of a cluster).

The EXPLAIN PLAN command displays the execution plan chosen by the Oracle optimizer for SELECT, UPDATE, INSERT, and DELETE statements. After using EXPLAIN PLAN, you can rewrite your SQL statements and see whether the new SQL statement is better optimized than the original statement. By analyzing the output, you might be able to provide hints that the Oracle optimizer can use to better take advantage of the data. (Hints are described in Chapter 15, "Using Hints"). By using hints, you can take better advantage of features such as the Oracle Parallel Query option.

EXPLAIN PLAN Initialization

When you run SQL statements with the EXPLAIN PLAN command, the output of EXPLAIN PLAN is put into a table with the default name plan_table. You must create this table before you can run EXPLAIN PLAN. You can create the table in one of two ways:

- Using the UTLXPLAN.SQL script that Oracle provides

- Creating the plan_table table by hand

The plan_table table is defined as follows:

```
SQL> describe plan_table
Name                              Null?    Type
--------------------------------- -------- ---------------------------
STATEMENT_ID                               VARCHAR2(30)
TIMESTAMP                                  DATE
REMARKS                                    VARCHAR2(80)
OPERATION                                  VARCHAR2(30)
OPTIONS                                    VARCHAR2(255)
OBJECT_NODE                                VARCHAR2(128)
OBJECT_OWNER                               VARCHAR2(30)
OBJECT_NAME                                VARCHAR2(30)
OBJECT_INSTANCE                            NUMBER(38)
OBJECT_TYPE                                VARCHAR2(30)
OPTIMIZER                                  VARCHAR2(255)
SEARCH_COLUMNS                             NUMBER
ID                                         NUMBER(38)
PARENT_ID                                  NUMBER(38)
POSITION                                   NUMBER(38)
COST                                       NUMBER(38)
CARDINALITY                                NUMBER(38)
BYTES                                      NUMBER(38)
OTHER_TAG                                  VARCHAR2(255)
PARTITION_START                            VARCHAR2(255)
PARTITION_STOP                             VARCHAR2(255)
PARTITION_ID                               NUMBER(38)
OTHER                                      LONG
DISTRIBUTION                               VARCHAR2(30)
CPU_COST                                   NUMBER(38)
IO_COST                                    NUMBER(38)
TEMP_SPACE                                 NUMBER(38)
```

You do not have to name the table plan_table. You can direct EXPLAIN PLAN to use a table of another name if you want.

Invoking EXPLAIN PLAN

Invoke the EXPLAIN PLAN command with the following Oracle command sequence:

```
EXPLAIN PLAN
    SET STATEMENT_ID = 'Testing EXPLAIN PLAN'
    INTO plan_table
    FOR
        SQL Statement;
```

STATEMENT_ID should reflect the statement's function so that you can recognize it at a later time. The plan_table parameter is the name of the table you created as described in the preceding section. If the INTO clause is omitted, the command defaults to the name plan_table.

Following is an example of a completed command:

```
SQL> EXPLAIN PLAN
  2   SET STATEMENT_ID = 'Testing EXPLAIN PLAN'
  3   INTO plan_table
  4   FOR
  5   SELECT * FROM emp, dept
  6   WHERE emp.deptno = dept.deptno
  7   ORDER BY empno;

Explained.
```

The results of the EXPLAIN PLAN are written into the table plan_table. The following section explains how to retrieve the information in that table.

Extracting EXPLAIN PLAN Results

The output of EXPLAIN PLAN is written to the table that is specified in the EXPLAIN PLAN command (by default, to the table named plan_table). You must extract this information to look at the results of EXPLAIN PLAN. The results can be displayed with a query such as this:

```
SELECT SUBSTR(LPAD(' ',2*(LEVEL-1))||operation,1,30)
||' '||SUBSTR(options,1,15)
||' '||SUBSTR(object_name,1,15)
||' '||SUBSTR(DECODE(id, 0, 'Cost = '||position),1,12)
"Statement Execution Plan",
SUBSTR(optimizer, 1, 10) "Optimizer"
```

```
FROM
    plan_table
START WITH
    id = 0 AND statement_id = 'Testing EXPLAIN PLAN'
CONNECT BY PRIOR
    id = parent_id
AND
    statement_id = 'Testing EXPLAIN PLAN';
```

This query results in the following output:

```
Statement Execution Plan                                Optimizer
--------------------------------------------------      ---------
SELECT STATEMENT   Cost           CHOOSE               NESTED LOOPS
    TABLE ACCESS BY INDEX ROWID EMP
      INDEX FULL SCAN PK_EMP
    TABLE ACCESS BY INDEX ROWID DEPT
      INDEX UNIQUE SCAN PK_DEPT

6 rows selected.
```

If the optimizer had chosen a cost-based approach, the cost of the query would have been reflected in the first line of the optimization plan. Any features such as parallel query are also reflected here.

Oracle provides several scripts for you. The script utlxpls.sql explains serial plans and the script utlxplp.sql explains parallel plans. Both of these scripts reside in the rdbms/admin directory under ORACLE_HOME.

With this information, you can tell whether your SQL statements take advantage of indexes, clusters, or hash clusters. If you use EXPLAIN PLAN, you can see precisely how your SQL statement is being executed and what effect any changes you make to the SQL statements have on the execution plan. Changing your SQL statements to take advantage of an index or a cluster, for example, will show an immediate improvement. EXPLAIN PLAN output is ideal for pointing out your execution plan and might indicate that where you thought that you were taking advantage of an index, you actually were not.

Registering Applications

When you register an application, the name and the actions that are performed by that application are stored in the database to assist with debugging and performance tuning efforts. When an application is registered, its name and actions are recorded in the V$SESSION and V$SQLAREA views. This information can be used later in tracking problems.

To register an application, use the following procedures, available in the DBMS_APPLICA-TION_INFO package:

Procedure	Description
SET_MODULE	Sets up the name of the module that is currently being run
SET_ACTION	Sets up the name of a certain action that is currently being performed
SET_CLIENT_INFO	Sets up information for the client information field
READ_MODULE	Reads the current values of the module and action fields for the current session
READ_CLIENT_INFO	Reads the current client information field for the currently running session

By registering the application, you can track many different parameters. Some of the values available through V$SQLAREA are given here:

- Memory used

- Number of sorts

- Number of executions

- Number of loads

- Number of parse calls

- Number of disk reads

- Number of buffer gets

- Number of rows processed

These parameters can provide valuable information when you are trying to debug various modules within your application. The information is enhanced by the addition of actions, which can further identify sections of your application.

Summary

Determining whether your SQL statements are properly optimized can be as important as anything you can do to tune your system. An improperly tuned SQL statement can nullify any work you have done to optimize the database system. A well-tuned server system that is handling hundreds or thousands of unnecessary SQL statements can be perceived to have poor performance when, in reality, an abundance of excess work is being done.

The Oracle SQL Trace facility and the EXPLAIN PLAN command can be valuable tools in debugging inefficient SQL code. The SQL Trace facility and its companion program TKPROF can give valuable information into such areas as these:

- Parse, execute, and fetch counts

- CPU and elapsed times

- Physical and logical reads

- Number of rows processed

- Library cache misses

The EXPLAIN PLAN command is used to display the execution plan that is chosen by the Oracle optimizer for SELECT, UPDATE, INSERT, and DELETE statements. By analyzing the execution plan that the Oracle optimizer has chosen and by knowing your data and application, you should be able to determine whether the optimizer has chosen the correct execution plan for your application. If you do not agree with the execution plan that has been chosen, you can change it by modifying your SQL statements or by using hints.

EXPLAIN PLAN can help you rewrite your SQL statements to take better advantage of such things as indexes and hash keys. By analyzing the output, you might be able to provide hints that the Oracle optimizer can use to take better advantage of your knowledge of your data. By using hints, you might be able to take better advantage of features such as the Oracle Parallel Query option.

Together, SQL Trace, EXPLAIN PLAN, and application registration can assist in optimizing your SQL statements and your application. By using these features, you can enhance the performance of your system.

INDEX TUNING

One of the most important performance tuning tools that is available within an RDBMS is the index. An index is an auxiliary structure that is used to improve the performance of queries by reducing the amount of processing and I/Os that are required to find the desired data. Just like the index in this book, an Oracle index is logically and physically independent of the data in the associated table or cluster. You can use the index to speed access to the data, or you can retrieve the data independently from the index by searching the tables for it. When optimally configured and used, indexes can significantly reduce I/O to the data files and greatly improve performance.

The presence of an index is transparent to the user or application and requires no application changes. However, if you are aware of an index, you might be able to take advantage of it when forming SQL statements. The only indication of an index might be an improved access time to data.

After an index has been created for a table, Oracle automatically maintains that index. Inserts, updates, and deletions of rows in the table automatically update the related indexes.

A table can have any number of indexes, but for each index in the table, additional overhead is incurred during table updates, inserts, and deletions. This overhead is incurred because all associated indexes must be updated whenever table data is altered or deleted.

WORKING IN PARALLEL

You can create an index with the Parallel Index Creation feature of the Parallel Query option. Using this feature greatly reduces index-creation time, but it can in some cases increase page fragmentation and space utilization.

One of the primary uses of indexes is to reduce the amount of data processed. I/O operations are expensive, both in CPU usage and in time waiting on the I/O to complete. By reducing I/Os, performance and the capacity of the system improve. Without the use of indexes, all of the data in the table would have to be read to find the data that is requested.

For example, look at the following query:

```
SELECT *
FROM emp
WHERE employee_id = 10290
```

Without the use of an index, the entire emp table would have to be scanned and each row examined for the value of employee_id. If the emp table is large, this could mean significant I/O operations and processing time.

If an index were placed on the emp column, the index would be traversed and a ROWID found for the row in question. After the ROWID were known, one additional I/O would be used to retrieve the data.

The best case is where one row of data is retrieved. Something like the employee_id is probably a unique value. This will return only one row and will be quite efficient.

Sometimes the index must return a large amount of data, as in the following example:

```
SELECT *
FROM customers
WHERE region = 'North'
```

This will most likely return a large amount of data. Because the index operations will return a large number of ROWIDs and these ROWIDs must be accessed independently, it might be more efficient not to use an index in this case. A table scan might be more efficient. The better solution largely depends on the number of rows and the organization of the data in the table.

Parameters Used in This Chapter

This chapter includes the use of many Oracle initialization parameters. Chapter 1, "Tuning," introduced you to these parameters and explained how to use them. In this chapter, the following initialization parameters are covered:

- OPTIMZER_INDEX_CACHING: OPTIMIZER_INDEX_CACHING allows you to adjust the behavior of cost-based optimization to favor nested loops joins and IN-list iterators.

- OPTIMIZER_INDEX_COST_ADJ: OPTIMIZER_INDEX_COST_ADJ allows you to tune optimizer behavior for access path selection to be more or less index friendly—that is, to make the optimizer more or less prone to selecting an index access path over a full table scan.

Index Types

Indexes are of several different types. An index can be limited to one column value or can consist of several columns. An index can be either unique or nonunique.

A *unique index* is an index value that has the additional constraint that the index value cannot be duplicated. Although this constraint might be specified, it is usually better to associate this constraint with the table rather than with the index. Oracle enforces UNIQUE integrity constraints by automatically defining a unique index on the unique key.

A *nonunique index* does not impose the constraint that the index value be unique. Such an index can be quite useful when quick access is desired on a nonunique value.

Another type of index is a *composite index*, which indexes several columns in a table. These column values can be in any order, and the columns do not have to be adjacent in the table.

A composite index is useful when SELECT statements have WHERE clauses that reference several values in the table. Because the index is accessed based on the order of the columns used in the definition, it is wise to base this order on the frequency of use. The most-referenced column should be defined first.

The index should be created based on the values that are accessed in the application; the application should be developed to take advantage of these indexes. Having knowledge of and influence over these indexes can be useful to the application developer.

A subcategory of the B*-Tree index is the Index Organized Table (IOT). An IOT allows slightly faster access to the data within the index in certain situations, as you will see later in this chapter.

The second major category of index that is available with Oracle is the bitmap index. A bitmap index is completely different from the B*-Tree index. Rather than traversing the tree as the B*-Tree does, the bitmap index creates a bitmap of ROWIDS for each unique value that the index covers. Whereas a B*-Tree index is appropriate for columns with good selectivity (many unique values), a bitmap index is appropriate on columns with few unique values. In this chapter, you will learn when a bitmap index is appropriate and how to use it.

In addition to B*-Tree indexes and bitmap indexes, Oracle also has function-based indexes. These indexes allow you to create an index on a function, which speeds up access to the desired data, provided that the function is supplied in the WHERE clause. Function-based indexes are also covered in this chapter.

Using the B*-Tree Index

When an index is created, an index segment is automatically allocated. This index segment contains information that speeds access to data by determining the location of indexed data with as few I/Os as possible. Oracle indexes data by using an index structure known as a *B*-Tree index*.

A B*-Tree index is designed to balance the access time to any row. A B*-Tree index is a tree of descending comparison values (see Figure 12.1). As you traverse down the index, you compare the desired value with the values in the upper-level index blocks, called *branch blocks*. Based on the outcome of the comparison with the branch blocks, you compare the desired value with more branch blocks until you reach the lowest-level index blocks. The index blocks on the lowest level, called *leaf blocks*, contain every indexed data value and the associated ROWID of that data.

With a unique index, one ROWID exists per data value in the leaf block (see Figure 12.2). With a nonunique index, several values might be associated with the data value. In the case of the nonunique index, the data values are sorted first by the index key and then by the ROWID.

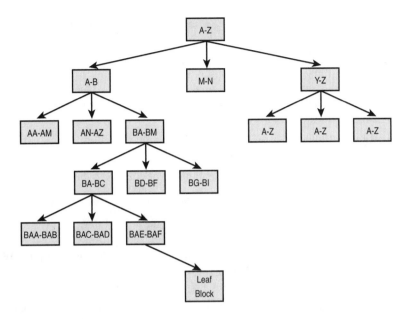

FIGURE 12.1
The B*-Tree index structure.

The index block structure

Index Key Value	ROWID
Babcock	ROWID
Baker	ROWID
Barry	ROWID

FIGURE 12.2
The index block structure.

With a B*-Tree index, all the leaf blocks are at the same level. Access of index data takes approximately the same time regardless of the value of the data. B*-Tree indexes provide quick access to data whether it is an exact match or a range query. In addition, B*-Tree indexes provides good performance regardless of the size of the table. Performance does not degrade as the table grows.

What Should Be Indexed

An index is effective only when it is used. The use of the index is primarily determined by the column values that are indexed. Remember that the more indexes you have on a table, the more overhead that is incurred during updates, inserts, and deletes. Therefore, it is important to index selectively.

Use the following guidelines for deciding which tables to index:

- Index tables when queries select only a small number of rows. Queries that select a large number of rows defeat the purpose of the index. Use indexes when queries access less than 5% of the rows in the table.

- Don't index columns in tables that are frequently updated. Updates, inserts, and deletes incur extra overhead when indexed. Base your decision to index on the number of updates, inserts, and deletes relative to the number of queries to the table.

- Index tables that don't have duplicate values on the columns that are usually selected in WHERE clauses. Tables in which the selection is based on TRUE or FALSE values are not good candidates for indexing.

- Index tables that are queried with relatively simple WHERE clauses. Complex WHERE clauses might not take advantage of indexes.

If you decide to use an index, it is important to decide the columns on which you put the index. Depending on the table, you might choose to index one or more columns.

Use the following guidelines for deciding which columns to index:

- Choose columns that are most frequently specified in WHERE clauses. Frequently accessed columns can most benefit from indexes.

- Don't index columns that do not have many unique values. Columns in which a good percentage of rows are duplicates cannot take advantage of indexing.

- Columns that have unique values are excellent candidates for indexing. Oracle automatically indexes columns that are unique or primary keys that are defined with constraints. These columns are most effectively optimized by indexes.

- Columns that are commonly used to join tables are good candidates for indexing.

In certain situations, the use of composite indexes might be more effective than individual indexes. Here are some examples of where composite indexes can be quite useful:

- When two columns are not unique individually but are unique together, composite indexes might work well. For example, although columns A and B have few unique values, rows with a particular combination of columns A AND B are mostly unique. Look for WHERE clauses with AND operators.

- If all values of a SELECT statement are in a composite index, Oracle does not query the table; the result is returned from the index.

- If several different queries select the same rows with different WHERE clauses based on different columns, consider creating a composite index with all the columns used in the WHERE statements.

Composite indexes can be quite useful when they are carefully designed. As with single-column indexes, they are most effective if applications are written with the indexes in mind.

After you have created the index, you should periodically use the SQL Trace facility to determine whether your queries are taking advantage of the indexes. It might be worth the effort to try the query with and without indexes and then compare the results to see whether the index is worth the space it uses.

Maintaining the Index

Oracle automatically maintains indexes. Whenever an UPDATE, INSERT, or DELETE statement changes data in a column that has an index on it, the index is automatically updated to reflect the changes to the data. This is both good and bad. Because the index is updated automatically, no additional programming is required and everything just seems to work. However, because the indexes must reflect changes in the data, the overhead can be high. This is especially true of cases in which multiple indexes are on a table.

When performing an UPDATE, INSERT, or DELETE statement, the COMMIT of the change will not be complete until all of the associated indexes are modified as well as the data. This might not only cause more overhead, but also increased time to commit.

YOU CAN HAVE TOO MUCH OF A GOOD THING

Several years ago, I was brought in to help a company with its new application and database. This application was performing wonderfully on SELECT queries, but INSERTS and UPDATES were slow. Upon examining the Oracle statistics, I noticed that the number of recursive calls was quite high, so I started looking at the schema.

It turned out that each table had as many as 25 or more indexes on it. In addition, each index covered every field in the table, just in a different order. The company had done this without realizing the overhead of index maintenance.

To make matters worse, whenever a field was to be updated, the application read each field of the old data, modified the field that was in question, and then did an update that updated every field. Even if only one field had changed, an UPDATE statement was issued that updated every field.

By explaining the overhead due to index maintenance and how it worked, the client was able to go back and rewrite the application and modify the database schema such that SELECT statements as well as UPDATE, INSERT, and DELETE statements all performed optimally.

An excellent new feature in Oracle9i is the ability to monitor indexes and see how frequently they are accessed. This allows you to reduce the number of indexes by removing unused or infrequently used indexes.

In addition to the overhead that is involved in maintaining the indexes, indexes have a tendency to become fragmented over time. Rather than having to go through the trouble of dropping and re-creating indexes, an easy way to defragment indexes as well as change their storage characteristics is by using the ALTER INDEX .. REBUILD statement. This statement re-creates an index without having to drop it and rebuild it. An example of the rebuild index statement is shown here:

```
ALTER INDEX eds_idx REBUILD
```

This takes the index named eds_idx and rebuilds it.

Indexes can also be compacted and rebuilt. The command ALTER INDEX .. COALESCE takes an existing index and coalesces or compacts leaf blocks to reduce index space requirements.

The Index Organized Table (IOT)

An IOT is similar to a B*-Tree index in general structure; however, instead of storing a ROWID in the leaf block of the index, the remaining data columns are stored there instead. This means that if the data is accessed via the index, the additional I/O to retrieve the data via the ROWID is not necessary. This can be an advantage when the data is always accessed via the index.

The disadvantage of the IOT is that the index is much larger because the leaf blocks must accommodate the data. This might force the index to have more levels from the root block to the leaf block, thus increasing I/Os. In addition, if the IOT is accessed via a method where the index is not used, it is less efficient than a normal table scan.

Use an IOT when you know that the data will be accessed via the index almost exclusively and when the chance of table scan activity is minimal. Tables in which the index column is frequently updated or in which the table is frequently inserted might not be good candidates for IOTs.

The Bitmap Index

Unlike a B*-Tree index in which it is most effective when selectivity is high, the bitmap index is effective when selectivity is low. A bitmap index works by creating a bitmap for each unique value in the index column. Each of these bitmaps contains a bitmap of the ROWIDs where these values exist. An example of a simple bitmap is shown in Figure 12.3.

Because data is stored in a bitmap for each value that is indexed, it can easily be determined which ROWIDs contain that data. However, because it was mentioned previously that the bitmap index is used for low cardinality values, you can see that a number of ROWIDs will be returned.

The Bitmap Index

Value = TRUE	Value = FALSE	Value = UNKNOWN
ROWID 0	ROWID 1	ROWID 0
ROWID 1	ROWID 0	ROWID 0
ROWID 0	ROWID 0	ROWID 1
ROWID 1	ROWID 0	ROWID 0
ROWID 1	ROWID 0	ROWID 0
ROWID 0	ROWID 1	ROWID 0

FIGURE 12.3
The bitmap index.

Because many ROWIDs will be returned in a bitmap index, it is not extremely useful on its own. However, because a bitmap is used, it can easily be combined with other bitmaps to reduce the amount of data returned quickly. This bitmap combining makes the bitmap index most useful. An example of this bitmap combining is shown in Figure 12.4.

Using multiple bitmaps for data reduction

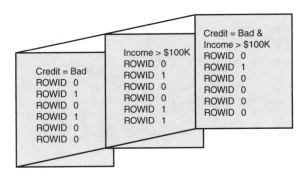

FIGURE 12.4
Using multiple bitmaps for data reduction.

As you can see, the bitmap index can be quite powerful when it is used correctly. In the next section, you will see more examples of how to best use the bitmap index.

When to Use a Bitmap Index

Bitmap indexes are used when individual column values do not have good selectivity, but when combinations of those column values do have good selectivity. Bitmap indexes are also good on those column values when selectivity is poor on some values, but good on others, such as bad credit. In this section, you will be presented with a few examples of how bitmap indexes should be used and what type of data is good for bitmap indexes.

The bitmap index is most effective when you have multiple low cardinality values that can be combined in a query to result in a high cardinality value. For example, suppose that your customer table contains columns in which credit is good or bad and another column in which the account is active or inactive. Both of these columns might return a large number of rows; however, if you are trying to find out only the active accounts that have bad credit, you might only be returned a small number of rows. The bitmap index will quickly find this intersection of values. An example of this is shown in Figure 12.4.

Function-Based Indexes

A function-based index is one in which the system designer or DBA creates a specific function that is used to index the data. The function can either be an arithmetic function or a PL/SQL function. A function-based index is useful only when the function on which the index is based is used within a WHERE clause of a SELECT statement.

Perhaps Company A wants to send out a letter of appreciation to all customers whose purchases have increased in the last year. A query to determine which customer IDs to select might look something like this:

```
SELECT c_id
FROM customers
WHERE this_years_sales - last_years_sales > 0
```

A function-based query can be created on the c_id column that looks like the function shown here:

```
CREATE INDEX idx ON customers (this_years_sales - last_years_sales)
```

Having this index both reduces load on the system and improves performance of this query.

Using Hints

Even though the optimizer has been finely tuned and works well, it might not know as much about your data as you do. In those cases, you can use a hint to suggest the use of a better index. By specifying the use of an index other than what the optimizer has chosen, queries might perform better.

For example, perhaps you have indexed a column that specifies good or bad credit. This index will most likely have poor selectivity because of few possible values. If you are selecting the customers that have good credit, many customer IDs will probably be returned, and a table scan would probably be most effective. However, if you are selecting the customers with bad credit, you might only be selecting a few customer IDs, and an index lookup might be more efficient than a table scan. As you can see, by knowing the data, you will be able to specify a better access method than the optimizer might.

Monitoring and Analyzing Indexes

As mentioned earlier in this chapter, having too many indexes is inefficient and causes excess overhead on the system. By monitoring the indexes that are used on your system and determining how often and how frequently the indexes are used, you can reduce the overhead on the system by removing unnecessary indexes. A great new feature of Oracle9i is the ability to monitor indexes using the index-monitoring feature.

ALTER INDEX MONITORING USAGE

Indexes are monitored by enabling index monitoring and then analyzing the index usage by selecting the index monitoring statistics from the dynamic performance views. Use ALTER INDEX *index*_name MONITORING USAGE to track index usage. Look in the system tables ALL_INDEXES, USER_INDEXES, and DBA_INDEXES to determine how often indexes are accessed.

Summary

Indexes can significantly improve performance in your system if they are used properly. You must first decide whether an index is appropriate for the data and access patterns in your particular system. After you decide to use an index, you must decide which columns to index.

Indexing an inappropriate column or table can actually reduce performance. Indexing appropriately can greatly improve performance by reducing I/Os and speeding access times.

Careful planning and periodic testing with the SQL Trace feature can lead to an effective use of indexes, with optimal performance as the outcome.

THE ORACLE OPTIMIZER

The Oracle optimizer is used to generate the execution plans that SQL statements use when they are run against the Oracle database. Using statistics that Oracle has gathered on the objects in the database, the Oracle optimizer generates an access plan (what objects are used) and an execution plan (what type of operations are used) from these statements. This chapter explains the fundamentals of the Oracle optimizer and tells you how you can alter the execution plan for your own benefit.

This chapter includes the use of many Oracle initialization parameters. Chapter 2, "Tuning," introduced you to these parameters and explained how to use them. In this chapter, the following initialization parameters are covered:

- OPTIMIZER_FEATURES_ENABLE. OPTIMIZER_FEATURES_ENABLE allows you to change the behavior of the Oracle optimizer based on a release number.

- OPTIMIZER_INDEX_CACHING. OPTIMIZER_INDEX_CACHING allows you to adjust the behavior of cost-based optimization to favor nested loops joins and IN-list iterators.

- OPTIMIZER_INDEX_COST_ADJ. OPTIMIZER_INDEX_COST_ADJ allows you to tune optimizer behavior for access path selection to be more or less index friendly—that is, to make the optimizer more or less prone to selecting an index access path over a full table scan.

- OPTIMIZER_MAX_PERMUTATIONS. OPTIMIZER_MAX_PERMUTATIONS restricts the number of permutations of the tables that the optimizer will consider in queries with joins. Such a restriction ensures that the parse time for the query stays within acceptable limits. However, a slight risk exists that the optimizer will overlook a good plan it would have found otherwise.

- OPTIMIZER_MODE. OPTIMIZER_MODE establishes the default behavior for choosing an optimization approach for the instance. The choices are rule, choose, first_rows, and all_rows.

Understanding the Optimizer

During the execution of SQL statements, Oracle chooses an execution plan by which these statements are executed. The Oracle optimizer determines the execution plan by using the optimization approach that is specified in the initialization parameters. The optimization approach can be overridden by the use of hints.

The effectiveness of the execution plan depends mainly on the optimization method chosen. This optimization method can consist of either a rule-based or a cost-based approach. The approach you take depends on both your application and your data.

How the Optimizer Works

To understand how the optimizer optimizes your SQL statements, it is useful to first look at how the optimizer works. When a SQL statement is parsed and passed off to the optimizer, the following occurs:

1. The optimizer analyzes and evaluates the SQL statement. In this first stage, the optimizer checks the SQL statement.

2. The optimizer modifies the SQL statement. If the statement is complex, the optimizer might change the statement to be more effectively processed, if necessary.

3. The optimizer performs view merging. If the statement is accessing a view, the Oracle optimizer sometimes merges the query in the statement with a query in the view before optimization.

4. The optimizer chooses between a cost-based or rule-based optimization approach based on the amount of analysis data that is available for the object and also on any hints.

5. The optimizer chooses one or more access paths to each table that is referenced in the SQL statement.

6. The optimizer chooses the join order. If more than one join is performed in the SQL statement, Oracle chooses the most appropriate order in which the joins will occur.

7. The optimizer chooses the most appropriate operations to use to perform the joins.

As you can see, the process through which the optimizer chooses the most optimal execution plan for the SQL statement is quite complex, but it is in this fashion that the best execution plan is usually chosen. At the basic level, the optimizer breaks the statements into their constituent components and determines their individual costs.

Optimizer Initialization Parameters

Many Oracle initialization parameters can be set to modify the behavior of the optimizer. These parameters can be used to configure the optimizer mode, to set the amount of time that is spent in the optimizer, and to set other optimizer defaults.

The optimization modes (cost-based or rule-based) can be chosen using either of the following methods:

- The OPTIMIZATION_MODE initialization parameter

- The OPTIMIZER_GOAL parameter of the ALTER SESSION command

When specifying the optimization method with either the initialization file or the ALTER SESSION command, you can specify the following options:

Option	Description
CHOOSE	This option allows the Oracle optimizer to choose an optimization mode based on the availability of statistics on a particular table, cluster, or index. If statistics are available for any of the tables that are accessed in the SQL statement, the cost-based approach is used with the goal of best throughput. If none of the tables has statistics available, the rule-based approach is used; the rule-based approach is also the default if no optimization approach is specified.
RULE	This option causes the Oracle optimizer to always use the rule-based optimization approach, regardless of statistics that might have been gathered for the tables being accessed.
ALL_ROWS	This option causes the optimizer to use the cost-based approach on all SQL statements, even if no statistics are available for the tables that are being accessed. This approach has the goal of best throughput, with the least amount of system resources being used.
FIRST_ROWS	This option causes the optimizer to use the cost-based approach on all SQL statements, even if no statistics are available for the tables being accessed. This approach has the goal of best response time.

If the cost-based optimization approach is used and no internal statistics are available for a table that is being accessed, other information such as the number of data blocks in the table is used to estimate the cost of various operations.

Other optimizer parameters that can be set include the following:

Option	Description
OPTIMIZER_FEATURES_ENABLED	This parameter can be set to 8.0.0, 8.0.3, 8.0.4, 8.0.5, 8.0.6, 8.1.0, 8.1.3, 8.1.4, 8.1.5, 8.1.6, 8.1.7, or 9.0.0. The effect of setting this parameter is to set other initialization parameters. Depending on the value of this parameter, many different parameters exist. All of the subordinate parameters can be set independently as well.
OPTIMIZER_INDEX_COST_ADJ	OPTIMIZER_INDEX_COST_ADJ allows you to tune optimizer behavior for access path selection to be more or less to select an index access path over a full table scan. The default value of 100 indicates normal operation. A value of 50 makes the index path seem half as expensive as normal, and the optimizer will more likely choose an index path.

Option	Description
OPTIMZER_INDEX_CACHING	OPTIMIZER_INDEX_CACHING allows you to adjust the behavior of cost-based optimization to favor nested loops joins and IN-list iterators. This value can be set between 0 and 100. This indicates to the optimizer the percentage of index blocks that you feel is in cache. The higher the value, the more likely that nested loops joins and IN-list operators will be used.
OPTIMIZER_MAX_PERMUTATIONS	This specifies the maximum number of tables in the FROM clause for which all possible join permutations are considered. By setting this low, the optimizer will spend less time considering different possibilities. If the FROM clause has many tables, the optimizer time can be significant.

By configuring the optimizer for your particular needs, you will achieve better results.

Optimization Methods

In general, the cost-based approach is the recommended approach. In most cases, the cost-based approach determines an execution plan that is as good as or better than the rule-based approach. However, if you have manually tuned your SQL statements, you might get better performance with rule-based optimization than with cost-based optimization.

The rule-based approach can be useful if you are moving a highly tuned application from an older version of Oracle that has been using the rule-based approach. This and a lack of statistics might cause rule-based optimization to be more efficient than the cost-based approach. However, as you gather statistics on your database, you might want to migrate to cost-based optimization.

The following sections examine both approaches. Hints can also be useful in optimizing the execution of your SQL statements.

Rule-Based Approach

The rule-based approach to Oracle optimization is the simpler of the two methods. In the rule-based approach, the execution plan is derived by examining the available paths and comparing them against a table of the rank of these paths. The table of costs is shown in Table 13.1.

Table 13.1   Cost of Access Paths for Rule-Based Optimization

Rank	Access Path
1	Single row by ROWID
2	Single row by cluster join
3	Single row by hash cluster key with unique or primary key
4	Single row by unique or primary key
5	Cluster join
6	Hash cluster key
7	Indexed cluster key
8	Composite key
9	Single-column indexes
10	Bounded range search on indexed columns
11	Unbounded range search on indexed columns
12	Sort-merge join
13	MAX or MIN of indexed column
14	ORDER BY on indexed columns
15	Full table scan

Because the rule-based approach is based simply on the SQL statements, statistics about the database tables are unnecessary. The rule-based approach follows these steps to determine the execution plan:

1. Determine the possible execution plans.

2. Rank the different plans according to Table 13.1.

3. Choose the approach with the lowest ranking.

In this way, the rule-based optimization approach is efficient and works well. However, if statistics are available for your tables, clusters, or indexes, the cost-based approach can be efficient.

Cost-Based Approach

The cost-based approach to optimization uses information about the structure and contents of your database to choose the most efficient execution plan. During the normal operation of the RDBMS or by executing the ANALYZE command or the DBMS_STATS package, statistics are gathered on the data distribution and storage characteristics or your database tables, clusters, and indexes. The cost-based optimizer uses this information to determine the most optimal execution plan.

This approach is accomplished in three steps:

1. The optimizer generates a set of possible execution plans, just as the rule-based optimization approach does.

2. The cost of each plan is determined based on statistics that are gathered about the database. This cost is based on CPU time, I/O, and memory necessary to execute the plan.

3. The optimizer compares the costs and chooses the execution plan with the smallest cost based on your specifications.

The initialization parameter OPTIMIZER_MAX_PERMUTATIONS can set the number of tables in the FROM clause that the optimizer uses to determine the best join permutation, as described next.

The default goal of the cost-based optimizer is to generate an execution plan that gives the best throughput. You can specify other optimization goals, including the following:

Optimization Goal	Description
Minimal Resources	This goal causes the optimizer to choose the execution plan that uses the least amount of system resources.
Best Response Time	This goal causes the optimizer to choose the execution plan that has the best response time.

By choosing the optimization approach that best suits your particular installation and application, the performance of your SQL statements can be tuned to specifically meet your needs.

Using the DBMS_STATS Package

Although the use of the ANALYZE command is still supported for the use of gathering statistics, it will soon be made obsolete. Instead of using ANALYZE, it is recommended that you use the DBMS_STATS package for statistics gathering. However, ANALYZE is still used for getting chained row statistics. Data integrity can now be checked by using the ANALYZE or the DBVERIFY utility.

The DBMS_STATS package can not only be used to update statistics, but it can also be used to create new statistics, save old statistics, and restore statistics (if necessary). This package is much more flexible than the traditional ANALYZE command. To create statistics, first create a stats table and then gather statistics as follows.

Creating a Statistics Table

In most cases, it is not necessary to create a statistics table; however, if you want to save the current statistics before gathering new statistics, it is necessary to create a statistics table. You can create a statistics table via the CREATE_STAT_TABLE function of the DBMS_STATS package. This function creates a table (that you specify) in the user's schema. This table will be used to hold statistics data that you might save when gathering new statistics. The following parameters are taken by this function:

ownname	The ownname variable specifies the schema where the statistics table will be created.
stattab	The stattab variable specifies the name of the statistics table to be created. This value should be used as the stattab parameter to other DBMS_STATS procedures.
tblspace	The tblspace variable is the name of the tablespace where the statistics table is created. By default, this is in the user's tablespace.

The following is an example of how to use the CREATE_STAT_TABLE function of the DBMS_STATS package.

```
DBMS_STATS.CREATE_STAT_TABLE ('scott', 'mystats');
```

This creates a stats table in the scott schema with the name "mystats". This table name will be used in further functions when it is populated with statistics data.

Gathering Table Stats

Gathering statistics is done via the GATHER_TABLE_STATS function of the DBMS_STATS package. This function populates a statistics table that you have created with the CREATE_STAT_TABLE function. This function gathers table, column, and index statistics. The following parameters are taken by this function:

ownname	The ownname variable specifies the schema of the table to analyze.
tabname	The tabname variable specifies the name of the table to analyze.
partname	This is the name of the partition of the table to analyze.
estimate_percent	The estimate_percent parameter specifies the percentage of rows to be used for estimating statistics.
block_sample	The block_sample parameter allows you to use random block sampling rather than random row sampling.
method_opt	This specifies the options that are used for statistics gathering.
degree	This is the degree of parallelism that is used when gathering statistics.

granularity	The granularity parameter specifies the level of granularity that is used when gathering partition statistics.
cascade	The cascade parameter specifies whether to gather index statistics.
stattab	This parameter specifies the name of a table to store the current statistics. Using this parameter, you can back up the current statistics. This is normally the name provided for the stattab parameter of the CREATE_STAT_TABLE function.
statid	This is an identifier that is used to identify these specific statistics.
statown	This is the schema that is used for these statistics (if other than the owner's schema). This is normally the ownname parameter of the CREATE_STAT_TABLE function.

The following is an example of how to use the GATHER_TABLE_STATS function of the DBMS_STATS package:

```
DBMS_STATS.GATHER_TABLE_STATS ('scott', 'emp', 1, stattab => 'scott.mystats');
```

This function is used to gather table stats on the "emp" table in the "scott" schema. The current statistics are saved to a stats table called "mystats".

Statistics created in a statistics table using the DBMS_STATS package can only be read using other DBMS_STATS package functions or by querying certain data dictionary views. The stats tables, queried directly, will make little sense.

Deleting Statistics

You can delete a statistics table via the DELETE_TABLE_STATS function of the DBMS_STATS package. This function is used to delete table stats as specified in the parameters. The following parameters are taken by this function:

ownname	The ownname variable specifies the owner/schema of the analyzed table.
tabname	The tabname variable specifies the name of the analyzed table.
partname	This specifies the partition of the analyzed table.
stattab	This specifies the name of the statistics table.
statid	This is the identifier of the statistics.
cascade_parts	This specifies that statistics for all of the partitions in this table are deleted as well.
cascade_columns	This parameter specifies that DELETE_COLUMN_STATS should be run to delete the column statistics under this table.
cascade_indexes	This parameter specifies that DELETE_INDEX_STATS should be run to delete the index statistics under this table.
statown	This variable is the name of the schema where the statistics are kept.

The following is an example of how to use the DELETE_TABLE_STATS function of the DBMS_STATS package:

```
DBMS_STATS.DELETE_TABLE_STATS ('scott', 'emp');
```

This example deletes statistics on the "emp" table in the "scott" schema.

Restoring Statistics

You might need to use several miscellaneous statistics functions. One of the most important functions is the IMPORT_TABLE_STATS function. In the previous section, you saw how to delete table stats. In the section before that, you saw how to save the current statistics while gathering the new statistics. The IMPORT_TABLE_STATS function is used for this. The parameters used in the IMPORT_TABLE_STATS function are as follows:

ownname	The ownname variable specifies the owner/schema of the analyzed table.
tabname	The tabname variable specifies the name of the analyzed table.
partname	This specifies the partition of the analyzed table.
stattab	This specifies where to get the statistics.
statid	This is the identifier of the statistics.
cascade	This specifies whether all of the subordinate statistics are restored as well.
statown	This variable is the name of the owner/schema where the statistics are kept.

An example of restoring statistics is shown here:

```
DBMS_STATS.IMPORT_TABLE_STATS ('scott', 'emp', 5, stattab => 'mystats');
```

This restores the statistics called "mystats" that was shown in the earlier examples.

Other DBMS_STATS Package Functions

In addition to gathering table statistics as shown earlier, you can also gather statistics on indexes, schema, or even at a system level. These different functions allow flexibility in the gathering of statistics. These functions are used for the following:

Index statistics	The index statistics functions are used to gather statistics on a particular index. They include SET_INDEX_STATS, GET_INDEX_STATS, DELETE_INDEX_STATS, EXPORT_INDEX_STATS, IMPORT_INDEX_STATS, and GATHER_INDEX_STATS.
Table statistics	The table statistics functions are used for table, index, and column statistics. They include the following statistics functions: SET_TABLE_STATS, GET_TABLE_STATS, DELETE_TABLE_STATS, EXPORT_TABLE_STATS, IMPORT_TABLE_STATS, and GATHER_TABLE_STATS.

System statistics	The system statistics functions are used to collect system activity statistics. They include the following statistics functions: SET_SYSTEM_STATS, GET_SYS-TEM_STATS, DELETE_SYSTEM_STATS, EXPORT_SYSTEM_STATS, IMPORT_SYS-TEM_STATS, and GATHER_SYSTEM_STATS.
Schema statistics	These statistics operate on a schema level and include the following functions: DELETE_SCHEMA_STATS, EXPORT_SCHEMA_STATS, IMPORT_SCHEMA_STATS, and GATHER_SCHEMA_STATS.
Database statistics	These statistics are used for database statistics and include the following functions: DELETE_DATABASE_STATS, EXPORT_DATABASE_STATS, IMPORT_DATABASE_STATS, and GATHER_DATABASE_STATS.

The DBMS_STATS package is flexible and allows many different statistics functions.

Working with Statistics

One of the great features of storing statistics in this manner is that you can create different statistics for different time periods and then use the statistics that are most appropriate. For example, at the end of the month, you might save statistics when you are doing your end-of-the-month reporting. These statistics can be used whenever you are doing these reports. During the rest of the month, you can use normal statistics. By using the import feature, you can easily switch between the appropriate statistics.

Using the ANALYZE Command

You can still use the ANALYZE command to gather statistics about your system for the cost-based optimizer, although ANALYZE will be retired soon. This command can be used not only for statistics gathering but for other purposes as well. The ANALYZE command can be used to do the following:

Function	Description
Gather statistics	The ANALYZE command can be used to gather statistics about tables, clusters, and indexes to assist the cost-based optimizer in choosing the best execution plan for your system. Although this is still supported in Oracle9i, it is not recommended that you use ANALYZE.
Check data integrity	The ANALYZE command can be used to validate the integrity of the structure of a table, index, or cluster.
Chained-row statistics	The ANALYZE command can be used to gather statistics about the number of chained rows in a table or cluster.

The statistics that the ANALYZE command gathers can help the optimizer make the correct choice in determining an execution plan.

How to Run the ANALYZE Command

The way that you run the ANALYZE command is determined by the type of statistics or analysis you want to perform. You can use the ANALYZE command in several different modes. The mode you choose depends on the data you want to gather as well as on the configuration of your system.

Using ANALYZE to Gather Statistics

You can use the ANALYZE command to gather statistics in one of two modes. The first mode scans the entire table, cluster, or index and calculates statistics exactly, based on your data. Although this is the most accurate method, it requires enough temporary space to hold and sort all the rows of the table or cluster. (No space is required for an index.) Computing the statistics also uses a great deal of system resources.

The second mode of the ANALYZE command estimates statistics. This method performs a sampling of the table, cluster, or index to estimate statistics. In this method, the entire table or cluster is not scanned; a portion of the data is used to determine the statistics. You can specify the amount of data when you invoke the ANALYZE command.

Using ANALYZE to Compute Exact Statistics

To use the ANALYZE command to compute exact statistics, invoke it with one of the following syntaxes:

For Tables:

```
ANALYZE TABLE table_name
    COMPUTE STATISTICS;
```

For Clusters:

```
ANALYZE CLUSTER cluster_name
    COMPUTE STATISTICS;
```

For Indexes:

```
ANALYZE INDEX index_name
    COMPUTE STATISTICS;
```

Using ANALYZE with the COMPUTE STATISTICS option scans the entire table, cluster, or index and computes exact statistics. When you compute the exact statistics, the resultant data is more accurate than that achieved by estimating the statistics; however, you use much more system resources to get this information. When you compute statistics for tables and clusters, you must have enough temporary space to load and sort the entire table or cluster. You do not need this temporary space for indexes.

Using ANALYZE to Estimate Statistics

When you use the ANALYZE command to estimate statistics, Oracle does much less work and uses much less temporary space. To run the ANALYZE command to estimate statistics, use one of the following syntaxes:

For Tables:

```
ANALYZE TABLE table_name
    ESTIMATE STATISTICS;
```

For Clusters:

```
ANALYZE CLUSTER cluster_name
    ESTIMATE STATISTICS;
```

For Indexes:

```
ANALYZE INDEX index_name
    ESTIMATE STATISTICS;
```

When you use ANALYZE with the ESTIMATE STATISTICS option, Oracle scans a portion of the table, cluster, or index and computes estimated statistics. You can specify the amount of data scanned and used for statistics by including one or both of these additional parameters:

```
SAMPLE xxxx ROWS;
SAMPLE yy PERCENT;
```

Place the SAMPLE xxxx ROWS parameter at the end of the ANALYZE command, as follows:

```
ANALYZE TABLE table_name
    ESTIMATE STATISTICS
    SAMPLE 10000 ROWS;
```

Place the SAMPLE yy PERCENT parameter at the end of the ANALYZE command, as follows:

```
ANALYZE TABLE table_name
    ESTIMATE STATISTICS
    SAMPLE 40 PERCENT;
```

Although estimating statistics does not give you as accurate a representation as computing statistics does, the lesser amount of resources that is consumed usually makes estimating statistics a better choice. By making the percentage of data scanned as large as possible for your system, you can increase the effectiveness of the statistics you gather.

Using ANALYZE to Check Structural Integrity

In addition to gathering statistics, you can use the ANALYZE command to validate the structure of a table, cluster, or index. Run this command only if you believe that a problem exists with the structure of these objects. These problems can occur as the result of a hardware or software problem where data corruption might have occurred. By analyzing the structure of the schema objects, problems can be found immediately, thus avoiding a system crash.

When you analyze the integrity of the structure of tables, clusters, or indexes, the command returns any structural problems. If the structure of these objects is faulty, you should drop the object, re-create it, and reload the data.

Using ANALYZE to Determine Chained Rows

You can also use the ANALYZE command to determine the extent and existence of chained or migrated rows in your table or cluster. The existence of chained or migrated rows can cause severe performance degradation and should be corrected.

SUMMARY OF THE ANALYZE COMMAND

As you have seen, the ANALYZE command can be quite useful for gathering statistics as well as for analyzing the structural integrity of tables, clusters, and indexes. You can also use the ANALYZE command to determine the existence and extent of chained and migrated rows. By using the ANALYZE command to gather statistics, the effectiveness of the cost-based optimizer can be increased; therefore, performance can be increased.

Data Dictionary Statistics

When you use the DBMS_STATS package and the ANALYZE command to create statistics for the cost-based optimizer to use, these statistics are inserted into some internal Oracle performance tables. These tables can be queried through several views. Although these views provide essentially the same information depending on the particular view you choose, the scope of the information changes slightly. The following views are prefixed with the characters:

View	Description
USER_	This view contains information about the objects that the user owns.
ALL_	This view contains information about the objects that are accessible by the user. These are objects owned by the user as well as objects with PUBLIC access.
DBA_	This view contains information on all objects in the system.

These views provide information about different parts of the system, such as tables, clusters, indexes, and columns. Following is a brief list of the views that are available that contain performance information:

- Table views. USER_TABLES, ALL_TABLES, DBA_TABLES

- Cluster views. USER_CLUSTERS, ALL_CLUSTERS, DBA_CLUSTERS

- Index views. USER_INDEXES, ALL_INDEXES, DBA_INDEXES

- Column views. USER_TAB_COLUMNS, ALL_TAB_COLUMNS, DBA_TAB_COLUMNS

The optimizer uses the information that is contained in the internal tables that are referenced by these views to make decisions about which execution plan to take. The decision about which execution plan to take is also based on information about the size of the object and the data that is contained in the object. Some of the information that is contained in these tables is presented in Tables 13.2, 13.3, 13.4, and 13.5.

Table 13.2   Data for Tables in USER_TABLES, ALL_TABLES, DBA_TABLES

Column	Description of Contents
AVG_SPACE	The average amount of free space in the table
AVG_ROW_LEN	The average length of a row
BLOCKS	The number of blocks in the table
CHAIN_CNT	The number of chained rows
EMPTY_BLOCKS	The number of blocks that have never been used
NUM_ROWS	The number of rows in the table

Table 13.3   Data for Clusters in USER_CLUSTERS, ALL_CLUSTERS, DBA_CLUSTERS

Column	Description of Contents
AVG_BLOCKS_PER_KEY	The average number of blocks that have rows that use the same key
CLUSTER_TYPE	The type of cluster: whether it is an index cluster or a hash cluster
HASHKEYS	The number of hash keys if it is a hash cluster

Table 13.4   Data for Indexes in USER_INDEXES, ALL_INDEXES, DBA_INDEXES

Column	Description of Contents
AVG_LEAF_BLOCKS_PER_KEY	The average number of leaf blocks per key
AVG_DATA_BLOCKS_PER_KEY	The average number of data blocks per key
BLEVEL	The level of the B-tree
CLUSTERING_FACTOR	The amount of order or disorder in the table that the index is referencing
DISTINCT_KEYS	The number of distinct keys in the index
LEAF_BLOCKS	The number of leaf blocks (lowest level index blocks) in the index
UNIQUENESS	A statement of whether the index is UNIQUE or NONUNIQUE

III: APPLICATION AND SQL TUNING

Table 13.5   Column Data in USER_TAB_COLUMNS, ALL_TAB_COLUMNS, DBA_TAB_COLUMNS

Column Heading	Description of Contents
DENSITY	The density of the column (rows per data block)
HIGH_VALUE	The second-highest value in this column of the table
LOW_VALUE	The second-lowest value in this column of the table
NUM_DISTINCT	The number of distinct values in this column of the table

With this information, the optimizer can more precisely determine the optimal execution path based on data about your specific system. When you run the ANALYZE command with the ESTIMATE STATISTICS option, many of these values are estimates rather than actual computed results.

Transaction Processing

Transaction processing is the heart of any RDBMS. In fact, without transaction processing, no reason would exist for having an RDBMS. According to the ANSI/ISO SQL standard, a transaction is one or more SQL statements that are executed by a single user. The transaction starts with the execution of the first SQL statement and ends when it is explicitly committed or rolled back. In many cases, the commit or rollback statement is specifically executed; in others, the application such as SQL*Plus does the commit on behalf of the user automatically.

In a typical transaction, the following steps are executed.

A. Application Connection

1. The application processes the user input and creates a connection to the server through Net8.

2. The server picks up the connection request and creates a server process on behalf of the user or passes the request to a shared server process via the dispatcher.

   The application-connection process occurs only when the application is signing on. The application does not have to connect each time a statement is processed.

B. Application Processing

1. The user executes a SQL statement and commits the transaction; for example, the user changes the value of a row in a table.

2. The server process takes this SQL statement and checks the shared pool to see whether a shared SQL area has this identical SQL statement. If it finds an identical shared SQL area, the server process checks to see whether the user has access privileges to the data and uses the shared SQL area to process the request. If a

shared SQL area is not found, a new shared SQL area is allocated, the statement is parsed, and it is finally executed.

3. The server process retrieves the data from the SGA (if present) or retrieves it from the data file into the SGA.

4. The server process modifies the data in the SGA. Remember that the server processes can only read from the data files.

5. The LGWR process writes out the redo information. Not until this redo information has been written to the log is the statement considered committed. At some later time, the DBWR process writes the modified blocks to permanent storage.

6. If the transaction is successful, a completion code is returned across the network to the client process. If a failure occurs, an error message is returned.

7. Return to phase B, "Application Processing," and submit more transactions until you are finished and want to exit the application.

   The application processing phase is repeated indefinitely until the user is finished with this particular application and exits the application.

COMMITTED IS ONLY COMPLETED WHEN...

A transaction is not considered committed until the write to the redo log file has been completed. This arrangement ensures that a committed transaction is recoverable in the event of a system failure. When a transaction has been committed and the redo entry has been written, the transaction is considered finished.

C. Application Termination

1. The application logs off the RDBMS. This event signals to Oracle that all the associated resources can be deallocated.

2. The Oracle PMON process makes sure that the server process has been terminated.

3. All resources are released. Any memory resources that the application has allocated are released.

While this process is occurring, the Oracle background processes are doing their jobs keeping the system running smoothly. Keep in mind that while your application is being processed, hundreds of other users might be doing similar tasks. It is Oracle's job to keep the system in a consistent state, managing contention and locking and performing at the necessary rate.

Even though your application might have modified some data in the database, that data might not yet be written to the data files. It might be some time later that the DBWR process writes those changes out to permanent storage.

With this overview of how the application is processed, you are ready to focus on what happens in step 2 of phase B: how the SQL statement is parsed and the execution plan is formed.

SQL Statement Processing

By understanding how Oracle processes SQL statements, you can have a better understanding of how to optimize these statements. The following sections look at the SQL statement parsing process and how an execution plan is formed. For each SQL statement that is executed, Oracle performs several steps:

1. A cursor is created.

2. The statement is parsed, if it is not already in the shared pool.

3. Any query in the statement is processed.

4. Variables are bound.

5. The statement is executed.

6. If possible, the statement is parallelized.

7. Rows to be returned are fetched.

Cursor Creation

Each time a SQL statement is executed, a cursor is automatically created on behalf of the statement. If you want, you can declare the cursor manually. Remember that a cursor is a handle to a specific private SQL area. You can think of a cursor as a pointer to, or the name of, a particular area of memory associated with a SQL statement.

Statement Parsing

After the cursor is created, Oracle determines whether the SQL statement is already present in the shared SQL area in the shared pool. If the SQL statement has already been parsed and is in the shared pool, parsing can cease and the execution of the SQL statement can continue. By using stored procedures or carefully crafting SQL statements to be identical, it's likely that those statements will be in the shared SQL area that is already parsed.

For a SQL statement to take advantage of SQL or PL/SQL statements that might have already been parsed, the following criteria must be met:

- The text of the SQL statement must be identical to the SQL statement that has already been parsed. This includes any whitespace.

- Reference to schema objects in the SQL statements must resolve to the same object.

- Bind variables must match the same name and data type.

- The SQL statements must be optimized using the same approach; in the case of the cost-based approach, the same optimization goal must be used.

You might think that these conditions make it difficult to take advantage of the shared SQL areas. In fact, users who share the same application code meet these criteria quite easily. It is to the advantage of the application developer to use the same SQL statements to access the same data, ensuring that SQL statements within the application can also take advantage of the shared SQL areas.

REUSE AND RECYCLE

Using stored procedures whenever possible guarantees that the same shared PL/SQL area is reused. Another advantage is that stored procedures are stored in a parsed form, eliminating runtime parsing altogether.

Standardizing on naming conventions for bind variables and spacing conventions for SQL and PL/SQL statements also increases the likelihood of reusing shared SQL statements.

The V$LIBRARYCACHE table contains statistics on how well you are using the library cache. The important columns to view in this table are PINS and RELOADS. The PINS column contains the number of times that the item in the library cache was executed. The RELOADS column contains the number of times that the library cache missed and the library object was reloaded. A few reloads relative to the number of executions indicates a high cache-hit rate for shared SQL statements.

If the already parsed SQL statement is not in the shared pool, Oracle performs the following steps to parse the SQL statement:

1. The statement is validated. The SQL statement must be verified as a valid statement.

2. The data is validated. The data dictionary lookups are performed to verify that the table and column definitions are correct.

3. Locks are allocated. Parse locks must be acquired to make sure that object definitions don't change during the execution of the parsing.

4. Privileges are verified. Oracle validates that the user has permission to use the schema objects that are being accessed.

5. The execution plan is determined. The optimal execution plan is determined based on several factors, including optimization plans, hints, and database analysis.

6. The statement is loaded into the shared SQL area. After the execution plan has been determined, the statement is loaded into the shared SQL area.

7. The distributed statement is routed. If the statement is used as a distributed transaction, all or part of the statement is routed to the other nodes that are involved in this statement.

As you can see from the number of steps that must be executed, keeping the SQL statements in the shared pool to avoid the parsing phase of the execution process is important.

Query Processing

Queries are handled differently from other SQL statements because queries return data as the result of the statement. Other SQL statements need only return a return code that indicates success or failure. In addition to the other steps that must be executed, queries might require the following additional functions:

- Read consistency. Because you might be executing several statements that take considerable time, it is important that the data remain consistent through the lifetime of the query.

- Use of temporary segments. Because queries might perform additional functions such as joins, order bys, sorts, and so on, it might be necessary to use temporary segments.

- Description of the results (optional). This phase is necessary if the characteristics of the query's results are not known. (For example, with an interactive query, you must determine the data types of the results before the results can be returned.)

- Output definition (optional). If the output location, size, and variable data types are defined, it might be necessary for Oracle to perform data conversions.

Only for queries are the preceding functions necessary in addition to the other SQL statement processing.

Bind Variables

You must define variables if you want a statement to be processed. The program must specify to Oracle the address of the variable before Oracle can *bind* that variable. Because the binding is done by reference, you do not have to rebind a variable before re-executing the statement; simply changing its value is sufficient.

You must supply the data type and length of each variable you bind to Oracle unless these data types or lengths are implied or defaulted.

Statement Execution

After the statement has been parsed and the variables have been defined, the statement is executed. In array processing, the execution step might happen many times. Any necessary locks are applied before the statement is executed.

Parallelization

If the Oracle Parallel Query option is used and the statement being executed is parallelizable, the following steps take place:

1. The query coordinator determines which operations can be performed in parallel.

2. The query coordinator determines how many query servers to enlist.

3. The query coordinator enlists query servers that perform the query.

4. The query coordinator reassembles the resulting data and passes it back to the user.

The degree of parallelism is determined using the following order of precedence:

1. Query hints. User-defined hints included in the SQL statement have the highest precedence.

2. Table definition. The default degree of parallelism that is defined for the table is second in the order of precedence.

3. Initialization parameters. The Oracle initialization parameters are used to determine parallelism.

The processes that execute the query are taken from the set of query servers that is available in the query server pool. The Oracle initialization parameter PARALLEL_MAX_SERVERS specifies this number.

Fetch Rows to Be Returned

If the statement is a query, the final step in the processing of the SQL statement involves fetching the returned data in a loop until all the requested data has been returned to the user process.

REVIEW OF SQL STATEMENT PROCESSING

By understanding the process that takes place when a SQL statement is executed, you can see the value in avoiding some of these steps.

Taking advantage of SQL statements that have already been parsed is one way to limit the amount of overhead that is associated with the processing of the statement.

This chapter explored ways to produce a well-tuned application. The key to having an optimized application is at the heart of the application: the SQL statements. Optimizing your SQL statements and reducing unnecessary overhead will result in an optimized application.

An optimized application together with the tuned and optimized RDBMS server will provide a well-balanced, highly tuned system. Because users are primarily interested in response times, having both a well-tuned application and an optimized server is essential. To get an optimized application, you must start with an optimized SQL statement.

The following list provides some of the characteristics of a well-tuned SQL statement:

- Makes efficient use of RDBMS features. The well-tuned SQL statement uses indexes or hashing as available. If possible, the application should also take advantage of features such as array processing and discrete transactions.

- Uses PL/SQL to improve performance. PL/SQL allows blocks of statements to be sent to the Oracle server at one time. If you don't use PL/SQL, you must send each statement individually.

- Uses stored procedures. By using stored procedures, you reduce the amount of data that must be sent across the network and increase the chance that the statement might already be parsed in the shared SQL area.

- Uses packages. Packages increase performance because the entire package is loaded when the package is called for the first time.

- Uses cached sequences to generate primary key values. This improves the performance of key generation and makes it unnecessary to generate the key in the application.

- Makes efficient use of space. The SQL statement uses the VARCHAR2 data type instead of CHAR, when possible, to avoid unnecessary blank padding.

- Uses hints where necessary. A well-tuned SQL statement uses hints where appropriate to allow the programmer's understanding of the SQL statement and the database design to override Oracle's choice of optimization method.

These attributes in conjunction with your own specific attributes make a well-tuned SQL statement in your configuration. The properly tuned SQL statement avoids unnecessary functions and executes with the minimum amount of resources necessary to perform its function.

Analyzing SQL Statements

Badly tuned SQL statements tend to access the database in an inefficient way, causing unnecessary amounts of data to be scanned and transferred across the network. Badly tuned statements can cause a well-tuned server to expend large amounts of unnecessary processing power and I/O resources.

You can identify badly tuned SQL statements with the Oracle EXPLAIN PLAN command and SQL*Trace facility. Some of the attributes of a badly tuned SQL statement are listed here:

- Indexes are not used. If a query is not properly formed, you might bypass an index that could be used to reduce I/O and CPU processing.

- Hashing is bypassed. If a hashed cluster is improperly accessed, performance could be severely degraded.

- Unnecessary table scans are performed. If the SQL statement is improperly formed, you might be doing unnecessary table scans.

- Range partitions are not used. If the SQL statement does not contain the partitioning key column in the WHERE clause, range partitioning will be bypassed.

- Unnecessary amounts of data are returned. This is an undue burden not only on the network but also on the application.

These attributes should alert you to the fact that the SQL statements are not optimally tuned for the task being done. If your SQL statement exhibits any of these characteristics, you should make some correction to the statement.

In addition to looking at the SQL statement, you should look at the effect of the SQL statements. In many cases, some detail that is unimportant by itself can become a problem when the application and SQL statements are run by hundreds or thousands of users at the same time. The effect of this can be a bottleneck on a specific table or even a specific row. The following list provides some things to look for when analyzing the effect of the SQL statements:

- Is the SQL statement updating a specific row? If you update a specific row as a counter, it might cause a bottleneck.

- Where is the majority of the table activity? Is a specific table being heavily accessed? This could indicate an I/O bottleneck.

- Is there significant INSERT activity? Is it all to one table? This might indicate a contention problem on a certain table.

- How much activity is there? Can the system handle it? You might find that the SQL statements overload your particular system.

These are just a few of the things to consider when you are looking at the effects of the application on the system. Sometimes an application, fully tested in the lab, moves into production and fails because it was tested with only one or two users. It is important to take into account the effect of hundreds or thousands of users simultaneously accessing the application.

You can analyze the SQL statements with the Oracle tools SQL Trace and EXPLAIN PLAN. These are independent tools, but SQL Trace can be run in such a manner as to automatically run EXPLAIN PLAN.

Designing New SQL Statements

Although this part of the chapter is directed at tuning SQL statements that are associated with new applications, it might be appropriate for you to make these changes to existing applications if you have the flexibility to do so. The reason these guidelines are separate is because many of them involve not only tuning the SQL statements and applications, but also changing the database schema.

In the design stage, it is important to plan the application and the database design together. By properly designing the application to take advantage of the design and features of the database, you can take optimal advantage of both of them. At the same time, the database should be designed to function properly with the application that uses it. The design of the database should reflect the purpose of the application. The following sections look at some of the optimizations that are possible.

Packages, Procedures, and Functions

Another way to improve performance of your SQL statements is by using packages, procedures, and functions. Packages can help improve performance by storing together procedures and functions that are often used together. By storing these elements together, you can reduce the I/O that is required to bring them into memory from disk. Because these elements are often used together, you can also load them from disk together.

By using stored procedures, you benefit in several ways. Stored procedures allow you to reduce the amount of data that is sent across the network. The stored procedure requires fewer instructions to be sent to the server; in many cases, less data must be sent back to the client from the server.

A second benefit of a stored procedure is the increased chance that other processes can use the SQL statement. Because many processes define and use the SQL statement, chances are good that the SQL statement will already be parsed in the shared SQL area and available to other users.

Using Hints

The Oracle optimizer is efficient and works quite well to produce the best execution plan for your SQL statements based on the information with which it has to work. The optimizer does not, however, have the amount of information about your database and your data that you do. This is why Oracle allows you to use hints to tell the optimizer what kind of operations will be more efficient based on knowledge you have about your database and your data. Hints are covered in detail in Chapter 15, "Using Hints."

By using hints, you can tell the optimizer such things as these:

- The best optimization approach for a particular SQL statement
- The goal of the cost-based approach for a SQL statement
- The access path for a statement
- When table scans are more efficient than indexes
- The join order for a statement
- A join operation in a join statement
- The degree of parallelism in a parallel query statement

By using hints, you can use specific information that you know about your data and database to further enhance the performance on certain SQL statements. With hints, you can enhance specific operations that might otherwise be inefficient. Following are some examples of conditions in which hints might significantly improve performance:

- Indexed columns with a large number of duplicate values. Telling the optimizer to bypass the index when the value is one that you know has a large number of duplicates is more efficient than allowing the optimizer to use the index.
- Table access that performs a large table scan. By specifying a larger number of parallel query servers, you can improve performance.
- Table access that performs a small table scan. If you know that the amount of data to be scanned is small, you might want to disable the parallel query option for this particular operation.

These are just a few of the exceptional conditions in which the default optimization might not be efficient. The information you know about your data and application can be used to make more efficient optimization choices.

Because you know more about your data and your application than the Oracle optimizer does, you can make significant improvements to the execution plan of the SQL statements. The Oracle optimizer is efficient and works quite well to produce the best execution plan for your SQL statements based on the information that it has to work with; however, anything you can do to give the optimizer additional information about the execution process will help performance.

Summary

When SQL statements are executed, the Oracle optimizer determines the execution plan based on the available data. The Oracle optimizer uses the optimization approach that is specified in the initialization parameters to determine the execution plan, as you have seen in this chapter.

The effectiveness of the execution plan depends on the optimization method that you chose and the availability of good statistics for your database. When you are using the cost-based optimization approach, including more and better database performance statistics can enhance the effectiveness of the optimization. This chapter described the various optimization approaches, methods of displaying the execution plan, and ways to improve SQL performance. By taking advantage of features in Oracle such as the Parallel Query Option, indexes, and range partitioning, you can greatly enhance your performance. Implementing these features will only work if your SQL statements are coordinated with the features to take advantage of them.

TUNING SQL

Tuning SQL statements is not an exact process. It involves either taking an existing statement and modifying it to be more efficient, or designing a new SQL statement that is optimal. This might be a simple operation or it might be quite difficult. Tuning SQL might involve removing columns from the result set. It might involve the use of temporary tables, or it might involve changing the join type. Tuning SQL statements might also involve the use of hints. In this chapter, hints will be covered from the perspective of using them to modify SQL execution plans. Hints are covered in more detail in Chapter 15, "Using Hints."

Optimal SQL Statements

The goal of tuning SQL statements is to end with SQL statements that retrieve the desired data with a minimal amount of resources used. An optimized application together with the tuned and optimized RDBMS server will provide a well-balanced, highly tuned system. Because users are primarily interested in response times, having both a well-tuned application and an optimized server is essential. To get an optimized application, you must start with an optimized SQL statement.

The following recaps some of the goals of optimizing SQL statements from Chapter 13:

- Makes efficient use of RDBMS features
- Uses a minimal amount of resources
- Uses PL/SQL to improve performance
- Uses stored procedures
- Uses packages
- Uses cached sequences to generate primary key values
- Makes efficient use of space
- Uses hints where necessary

How to Identify Poorly Tuned SQL Statements

Poorly tuned SQL statements tend to access the database in an inefficient way, causing unnecessary amounts of data to be scanned and transferred across the network. Poorly tuned statements can cause a well-tuned server to expend large amounts of unnecessary processing power and I/O resources.

You can identify poorly tuned SQL statements with the Oracle EXPLAIN PLAN command and SQL Trace facility, as described in Chapter 11, "Using EXPLAIN PLAN and SQL Trace." Some of the attributes of a poorly tuned SQL statement are recapped here:

- Indexes are not used.

- Appropriate bitmap indexes are not used.

- Hashing is bypassed.

- Unnecessary table scans are performed.

- Unnecessary amounts of data are returned.

These attributes should alert you to the fact that the SQL statements are not optimally tuned for the task being done. If your SQL statement exhibits any of these characteristics, you should make some correction to the statement.

Join Types

As part of tuning SQL statements, you might want to modify the join type that the Oracle optimizer selects. Three different types of joins exist: nested loops join, merge join, and hash join. Each of these join types has its own attributes and performance. As with most things in life, using joins involves trade-offs. These attributes and performance characteristics make each join type appropriate for some types of operations and inappropriate for others.

Nested Loops Join

In a nested loops join, the outer table is read. For each of the rows to be joined with the inner table, the inner table is read to find a match. This nested loops join operation is CPU efficient, but typically I/O intensive. An illustration of a nested loops join is shown in Figure 14.1.

A Nested Loops Join

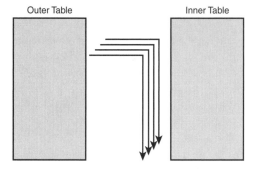

FIGURE 14.1
A nested loops join.

As you can see from this example, the outer table is read repeatedly. If the table is large, the data might have to be read from disk. If the table is small, the data will be read from memory. This makes it more efficient, but it still consumes much memory bandwidth and bus bandwidth. Reading large amounts of data from memory can also be CPU intensive.

Merge Join

In a merge or sort-merge join, both tables are read and sorted. After the sort has taken place, the tables are processed from the top. The first table is read and compared with the top of the second table. Because the data is sorted, if you pass the current value, you know that the value is not in the second table; thus, the next value in the first table is processed. For example, the value in the first table might be "a". After you hit "b" in the second table, you know that you don't have to read more values to find "a". This sort-merge join operation is CPU efficient, but typically I/O intensive. An illustration of a sort-merge join is shown in Figure 14.2.

A Sort-Merge Join

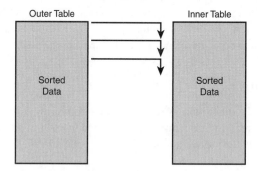

FIGURE 14.2
A sort-merge join.

As you can see from this example, the number of I/O operations is limited to those necessary to read both tables, sort them, and read them again. Thus, the amount of data that is read is less than that in a nested loops join. However, the CPU that is used in this type of join is higher than with a nested-loops join.

Hash Join

In a hash join, the two tables are read and a hashing function is created. This hashing function is used to join the two tables together. Because of the nature of the hash join, the operation can typically be parallelized well. The hash join uses a minimal amount of I/Os because each table needs to be read only once, but it is CPU and memory intensive. An illustration of a hash join is shown in Figure 14.3.

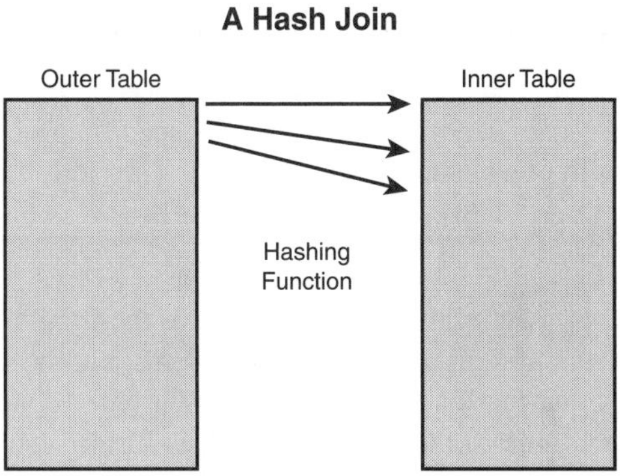

A Hash Join

Outer Table   Inner Table

Hashing
Function

FIGURE 14.3
A hash join.

As you can see from this example, the number of I/O operations is limited to those necessary to read both tables. Thus, the amount of data read is less than that in a sort-merge join. However, the CPU used in this type of join is higher than with a sort-merge join. In fact, the hash join uses more CPU than any of the other join types, but less I/Os.

Tuning SQL Statements

Tuning your SQL statements might be one of the most important tasks you can do to improve the performance of your Oracle system. By tuning your SQL statements to be as efficient as possible, you use your system to its full potential. Some of the things you can do to improve the efficiency of your SQL statements might involve as little effort as rewriting the SQL to take advantage of some property of your database or perhaps even changing the structure of the database.

Tuning SQL really falls into two separate categories:

- Tuning an existing application. This approach involves less flexibility in terms of changing the structure of the application and the database, but might provide performance improvements anyway.

- Designing a new application. With a new application, you have the flexibility to design both the application and perhaps even the database. With this approach, you can take advantage of indexes, clustering, and hashing.

This chapter looks at both of these categories. The amount of changes you can do and the flexibility you have in changing the design of the application and database depends on your particular situation. The more flexibility you have in designing the database along with the application, the better your overall results will be.

Tuning an Existing Application

Tuning an existing application can be easier in some respects and harder in others. It is easier in terms of determining the data access patterns and the specific problem areas because the application is already running and can be profiled easily with SQL Trace and EXPLAIN PLAN. However, fixing the problems can be a challenge because you might not have the flexibility to do so.

With an existing application, you might or might not have the flexibility to fix the problem. For example, you might have system performance problems, but the system is still stable enough and performs well enough for the users to get their work done. It is hard to justify the downtime involved in reconfiguring the system when it is still in a somewhat functional state.

In this type of situation, it is important to plan far in advance and take advantage of scheduled downtime to implement system enhancements to fix any current problems and anticipated additional growth in user activity. You can do this by changing Oracle or OS parameters or by adding disk drives, memory, and so on. If you can afford to build in an additional 20–30% growth, you might save yourself some reconfiguration time down the road.

People tend to take advantage of additional capacity much faster than they anticipate and plan for. It used to be inconceivable that anyone would ever need more than 64MB of memory or even think of needing a gigabyte of disk space on a desktop PC. Today, high-end PC servers support more than a gigabyte of RAM and are getting close to supporting a terabyte of disk space.

Problem Analysis

To tackle the problem of tuning an existing Oracle application, you can use some kind of methodology. Following are the steps to lead you to the problem's resolution:

1. Analyze the system. Decide if a problem exists; if it does, what is it?

2. Determine the problem. What do you think is causing the problem? Why?

3. Determine a solution and set goals. Decide what you want to try and what you think will result from your changes. What is it that you want to accomplish? Do you want more throughput? Faster response times?

4. Test the solution. Try it. See what happens.

5. Analyze the results. Did the solution meet the goals? If not, you might want to repeat these steps.

By following a plan of this sort, you will find it much easier to determine if a problem exists and to resolve it. You could spend a lot of time trying to solve a performance problem that might not even exist.

By looking at the performance of the system as it is and carefully examining its characteristics, you might be able to determine whether an action is necessary to fix the problem and how much effort is involved. As mentioned in Chapter 4, "Performance-Enhancing Features," performance problems can be put into one of three categories:

- It's broken. Performance is severely handicapped because of a configuration error or an incorrect parameter in the OS or RDBMS. Problems that fall into this category cause a performance swing of 50% or more. Problems that fall into this category are usually oversights during the system build, such as incorrectly building an index or forgetting to enable asynchronous I/O. This category of problem might indicate a more serious problem such as insufficient disk drives or memory.

- It's not optimized. Performance is slightly degraded because of a small miscalculation in parameters or because system capacity is slightly exceeded. Fine-tuning the configurations usually solves these types of problems easily.

- It's not a problem. Don't forget that sometimes no problem exists; you are just at the capacity of the system. Upgrading or adding more capacity easily solves this "nonproblem." Not all problems can be solved with tuning.

In the case of the system being broken, you might have to perform some drastic fix that probably involves rebuilding the database in some fashion. The solution might be as drastic as having to rebuild from scratch to add more disk drives, or as simple as adding an additional index.

In case of the system not being optimized, you might be able to tune the system with an OS or database configuration parameter. This is usually easy to do and does not involve much risk. However, this solution does not usually result in a huge increase in performance.

The final case of a "nonproblem" might involve adding an additional CPU (if you have an SMP or MPP machine) or upgrading to new hardware. Perhaps you will find that a problem doesn't exist after all and that everyone is happy with the performance of the system. One thing to remember: You rarely see the end users if everything is going fine. It's only when the users experience performance problems that you hear from them.

Tuning the Application

When analyzing the SQL statement, you should look for two things:

- The SQL statement. What does it do?

- The effect of the SQL statement. What is it doing it to? How does it fit into the big picture?

By looking at the SQL statement from these different angles, you might find a problem that you wouldn't find by just looking at it from one viewpoint.

For example, consider an application that does not use cached sequences to generate a primary key value. By itself, this approach is fine and the application is probably efficient. But add a thousand users executing the same application and the problem is quite apparent: You have contention getting the value for the primary key value.

The SQL Statement

The best way to go about tuning the SQL statements of an existing application is to follow these few steps:

1. Familiarize yourself with the application. You should be familiar not only with the specific SQL statements, but also with the purpose of the application and what it does.

2. Use the SQL Trace facility to analyze what the particular SQL statements are doing, what features of the RDBMS are being used, and how well those features are being used.

3. Use EXPLAIN PLAN within SQL Trace to analyze how the optimizer is executing those SQL statements.

The next section looks at some specifics of these steps.

Familiarize Yourself with the Application

Look not only at the SQL statements, but also at the effect of those statements. Make a chart of the different SQL statements and determine the number of accesses that each SQL statement makes to each table in the database. This chart can give you an effective visual idea of which tables are being accessed most frequently.

This chart is a good quick reference for which SQL statements are affecting which tables. You can take this a step further and split the chart into different types of statements such as SELECTs, INSERTs, UPDATEs, DELETEs, and so on. Depending on your system, whether your application is shrink-wrapped or developed in house, this might be or might not be practical.

Use SQL Trace to Analyze the SQL Statements

By running SQL Trace on the SQL statements, you can gather much valuable information about the specific operation of each of the SQL statements. SQL Trace provides such valuable information as the following:

- Parse, execute, and fetch counts

- CPU and elapsed times

- Physical and logical reads

- Number of rows processed

- Library cache misses

You can use this information to determine which SQL statements are efficient and which ones are not. Look for the following indications of inefficient statements:

SQL Trace Output	Comments
CPU and elapsed time	If the CPU or elapsed times are high, this SQL statement is a good candidate for tuning. It doesn't make much sense to spend time tuning statements that don't use many resources.
Executes	Focus on SQL statements that are frequently executed. Don't spend time on SQL statements that are infrequently used.
Rows Processed	A SQL statement with a high number of rows processed might not be using an index effectively.
Library Cache	Many library cache misses might indicate a need to tune the shared pool or to change the SQL statement to take advantage of the shared SQL area.

These clues might point you in the direction of the SQL statements that need to be tuned. You might have to alter these SQL statements to improve their efficiency. By using EXPLAIN PLAN, you might find additional areas to improve. For more information about SQL Trace, refer to Chapter 11.

Use EXPLAIN PLAN to Analyze Statement Execution

By running EXPLAIN PLAN as part of the SQL Trace report, you can get a better idea of how Oracle is executing the SQL statement. This information (and the information that is supplied by SQL Trace) helps you judge the efficiency of the SQL statement. The following list provides some of the things to look for:

- Are the table's indexes being used when they should be? If not, the statement might not be supplying the correct parameters in the WHERE clause.

- Are indexes being used when they should not be? In cases when you are selecting too much data, you might want to use the FULL hint to bypass the index.

- What is the cost of the SQL statement? This value is given in the *position* column of the first row of the table that EXPLAIN PLAN returns.

- How much overhead is incurred from SELECT/UPDATE operations? Too many read or write operations can cause memory thrashing or high CPU utilization.

- Is the statement being parallelized? You might have to provide a hint to effectively take advantage of the Parallel Query option.

You should ask these questions and your own specific questions as you review the EXPLAIN PLAN output. By knowing what your application is supposed to do, you might find important information about the efficiency of your statements by looking at this information. For more about the use of EXPLAIN PLAN, refer to Chapter 11.

The Effect of the SQL Statement

In addition to looking at the SQL statement, you should look at the effect of the SQL statements. In many cases, some detail that is unimportant on its own can become a problem when the application and SQL statements are run by hundreds or thousands of users at the same time. The effect of this can be a bottleneck on a specific table or even a specific row. Following is a list of some things to look for when analyzing the effect of the SQL statements:

- Is the SQL statement updating a specific row? If you update a specific row as a counter, it might cause a bottleneck.

- Where is the majority of the table activity? Is a specific table being heavily accessed? This could indicate an I/O bottleneck.

- Is there significant INSERT activity? Is it all to one table? This might indicate a contention problem on a certain table.

- How much activity is present? Can the system handle it? You might find that the SQL statements overload your particular system.

These are just a few of the things to consider when you are looking at the effects of the application on the system. Sometimes, an application that is fully tested in the lab moves into production and fails because it was tested with only one or two users. It is important to take into account the effect of hundreds or thousands of users simultaneously accessing the application.

REVIEW OF HOW TO TUNE AN EXISTING APPLICATION

Tuning an existing application can be quite a challenge. Determining whether the system is in need of optimization and figuring out how to do it is not always easy. The task might be easier if you take a methodical approach like this one:

1. Analyze the situation. It might be that your system is not in need of adjustment. Don't make changes to a stable system unless you have to.

2. Familiarize yourself with the application. Look at the SQL statements as well as the overall application. Understand the purpose of the application.

3. Make an analysis chart. Look at the table accesses that the application generates.

4. Run SQL Trace with EXPLAIN PLAN. See what the SQL statements are really doing. Choose the statements to focus on based on how often they are used and how many resources they use.

5. Understand how these SQL statements affect the server system. Look at Oracle and the OS. Determine which disks might be overused and where contention could occur when many users run the application.

With an existing application, you might or might not have the flexibility to fix the problem. Don't make changes to an existing application or a functioning system unless some specific performance problems are affecting users or limiting the capacity of the system.

Of course, if you have the flexibility to make changes and changes are needed, any of the design and application changes that are described in the following section, "Designing a New Application," also apply to an existing application.

Designing a New Application

Although this part of the chapter is directed at tuning SQL statements that are associated with new applications, it might be appropriate for you to make these changes to existing applications if you have the flexibility to do so. The reason these guidelines are separate is because many of them involve not only tuning the SQL statements and applications, but changing the database schema as well.

In the design stage, it is important to plan the application and the database design together. By properly designing the application to take advantage of the design and features of the database, you can take optimal advantage of both of them. At the same time, the database should be designed to function properly with the application that uses it. The design of the database should reflect the purpose of the application. The following sections look at some of the optimizations that are possible.

Indexes

An index is an optional structure that is designed to help you achieve faster access to your data. Just like the index in this book, an Oracle index is logically and physically independent of the data in the associated table or cluster. You can use the index to speed access to the data, or you can retrieve the data independently from the index by searching the tables for it. When optimally configured and used, indexes can significantly reduce I/O to the data files and greatly improve performance.

The presence of an index is transparent to the user or application and requires no application changes. However, if you know of the existence of the index and design the application to take advantage of the index, you can greatly reduce the I/Os that are necessary to retrieve the desired data. The only indication of an index might be improved time to access the data.

After you have created an index on a table, Oracle automatically performs the maintenance of that index. Inserts, updates, and deletions of rows are automatically updated in the related indexes.

A table can have any number of indexes, but the more indexes that exist, the more overhead that is incurred during table updates, inserts, and deletions. This overhead is incurred because all associated indexes must be updated whenever table data is altered.

WORKING IN PARALLEL

If you use the Oracle Parallel Query option, you can create the index in parallel, thus reducing the time it takes to create the index. This option does use more extents because each parallel process creates initial and next extents.

Index Types

Indexes come in several types:

Index Type	Description
Unique index	A unique index is an index value that has the additional constraint that it cannot be duplicated. Although this constraint might be specified, it is usually better to associate this constraint with the table than with the index. Oracle enforces UNIQUE integrity constraints by automatically defining a unique index on the unique key.
Nonunique index	A nonunique index does not impose the constraint that the index value be unique. Such an index is useful if you need quick access to a nonunique value.
Cluster index	A cluster index is an index that is created on the cluster key in an Oracle cluster. It is required that a cluster key be indexed.
Composite index	A composite index is an index on several columns in a table. The column values can be in any order and the columns do not have to be adjacent in the table.

A composite index is useful when SELECT statements have WHERE clauses that reference several values in the table. Because the index is accessed based on the order of the columns that are used in the definition, it is wise to base the index order on the frequency of use. The most referenced column should be defined first, and so on.

You should create the index based on the values that are accessed in the application; develop the application to take advantage of the indexes. Having knowledge of and influence over these indexes can be useful to the application developer.

What to Index

The index is usually determined by the column values that are indexed. Remember that the more indexes that are on a table, the more overhead that is incurred during updates, inserts, and deletes. Index selectively.

What Tables Should Be Indexed?

Use the following guidelines to decide which tables to index:

- Index tables when queries select only a small number of rows. Queries that select a large number of rows defeat the purpose of the index. Index the table when queries access less than 5% of the rows in the table.

- Don't index tables that are frequently updated. Updates, inserts, and deletes on indexed tables incur extra overhead. Base your decision about whether to index a table on the number of updates, inserts, and deletes relative to the total number of queries to the table.

- Index tables that don't have duplicate values on the columns that are usually selected in WHERE clauses. Tables for which the selection is based on TRUE/FALSE values are not good candidates for an index.

- Index tables that are queried with relatively simple WHERE clauses. Complex WHERE clauses might not be able to take advantage of indexes. This can be solved by creating a complex index, by simplifying the SQL statement, or by using a hint.

After you decide to use an index, you must then decide the columns on which to put the index. You might index one or more columns, depending on the table.

Which Columns Should Be Indexed?

Use the following guidelines to decide which columns to index:

- Choose columns that are frequently specified in WHERE clauses. Frequently accessed columns can most benefit from indexes.

- Don't index columns that do not have many unique values. Columns in which a good percentage of rows are duplicates cannot take advantage of indexing.

- Columns that have unique values are excellent candidates for indexing. Oracle automatically indexes columns that are unique or that are primary keys defined with constraints. These columns are most effectively optimized by indexes.

- Index columns that are foreign keys of referential integrity constraints in cases where many concurrent INSERT, UPDATE, and DELETE statements access both the parent and child tables. Such an index allows the child table to be updated without having to lock the parent table.

- Columns that are commonly used to join tables are good candidates for indexing.

- Frequently modified columns probably should not be index columns because of the overhead involved in updating the index.

DON'T PENALIZE YOURSELF

Remember that a penalty is associated with performing INSERT, UPDATE, and DELETE statements on columns that are indexed. If you have a high number of those statements, an index might hurt more than help. Use SQL Trace on the SQL statements that access that table both with and without an index. Compare the results.

Composite Indexes

Composite indexes might be more effective than individual indexes in situations such as the following:

- When two columns are not unique individually but are unique together, composite indexes might work very well. For example, columns A and B have few unique values, but rows with a particular A AND B are mostly unique. Look for WHERE clauses with AND operators.

- If all values of a SELECT statement are in a composite index, the table is not queried; the result is returned from the index.

- If several different queries select the same rows by using different WHERE clauses based on different columns, consider creating a composite index with *all* those columns used in the WHERE statements.

If composite indexes are carefully designed, they can be quite useful. As with single-column indexes, they are most effective if applications are written with the indexes in mind.

After you create the index, periodically use SQL Trace to determine whether your queries are taking advantage of the index. It might be worth the effort to try the query with and without indexes and compare the results to see whether the index is worth the space it is using.

How to Avoid an Index

If you have an application that can take advantage of an index but that contains a few SQL statements that result in poor performance when they use an index, you can tell the optimizer to bypass the index. You can do this in several ways:

- Write the SQL statement to avoid using a SELECT statement on an indexed column. By not selecting the column or set of columns that are indexed, you avoid the index.

- Use hints. When you use hints in your SQL statements, you can tell the optimizer not to use the index for this particular SQL statement. Hints are detailed in the next chapter.

In this manner, you can design your database to effectively use indexes and have the flexibility to avoid the index when it is not optimal to do so.

Summary

Poorly formed SQL statements can nullify optimizations you have made to the client or the server. If the SQL statements require unnecessary table scans or unnecessary processing, an optimized server can be brought to a standstill. To have the most optimal system possible, the clients, the SQL statements, the network, and the server should be tuned to take maximum advantage of available resources. The best way to improve performance is to reduce unnecessary processing and I/O.

You can do this by designing your SQL statements to take advantage of such features as the shared pool (where the library cache contains the shared SQL area). By designing your application so that it uses the same SQL statements to access the same data, you stand a good chance of your statements being in the library cache.

If you have long-running queries that perform table scans, take advantage of the Parallel Query option. By using this feature, you can cut down on the time it takes to perform the query.

The use of other Oracle features such as stored procedures and packages can also maximize the effectiveness of your SQL statement processing and provide for more efficient coding. All these things can help improve the overall performance of your system.

Of all the areas of the system that can be tuned, SQL statements offer the most potential. This is true not because SQL statements can be more effectively optimized, but because a poorly tuned SQL statement can degrade performance drastically. As you will see, having well-tuned SQL statements at the heart of your application is essential.

Tuning your SQL statements is one of the most important tasks you can do to improve performance. In fact, you should tune your SQL statements before tuning your RDBMS server. By tuning your SQL statements to be as efficient as possible, you can use your system to its full potential. Some of the things you can do to improve the efficiency of your SQL statements might involve as little effort as rewriting the SQL to take advantage of a property of your database or as much effort as changing the structure of the database.

As you have seen, tuning SQL falls into two categories:

- Tuning an existing application
- Designing a new application

By designing your system with the goals of optimization and performance, you can take advantage of numerous Oracle features. By far, the best-tuned systems are those tuned from the design stage. This chapter described many ways you can tune the new application; if you have enough flexibility, you can make these changes to an existing application as well.

USING HINTS

The Oracle optimizer is efficient and works quite well to produce the best execution plan for your SQL statements based on the information with which it has to work. The optimizer might not, however, have the amount of information about your database and your data that you do. This is why Oracle allows you to use hints to tell the optimizer what kind of operations will be more efficient based on knowledge you have about your database and your data.

By using hints, you can tell the optimizer such things as these:

- The best optimization approach for a particular SQL statement

- The goal of the cost-based approach for a SQL statement

- The access path for a statement

- The circumstances when table scans are more efficient than indexes

- The join order for a statement

- A join operation in a join statement

- The degree of parallelism in a parallel query statement

By using hints, you can use specific information that you know about your data and database to further enhance the performance of certain SQL statements. With hints, you can enhance specific operations that might otherwise be inefficient. Following are some examples of conditions in which hints can significantly improve performance:

- Indexed columns with a large number of duplicate values. Telling the optimizer to bypass the index when the value is one you know has a large number of duplicates is more efficient than letting the optimizer use the index.

- The use of bitmap indexes. If you have both B*-Tree indexes and bitmap indexes, you can specify the use of the bitmap index when the optimizer might choose the B*-Tree index.

- Table access that performs a large table scan. By specifying a larger number of parallel query servers, you can improve performance.

- Table access that performs a small table scan. If you know that the amount of data to be scanned is small, you might want to disable the parallel query option for this particular operation.

These are just a few of the exceptional conditions in which the default optimization might be inefficient. The information you know about your data and application can be used to make more efficient optimization choices.

This chapter looks at the different optimization hints available and when you can use them to improve the optimization of your SQL statements. This chapter first explains how hints are implemented within your SQL statements and then describes the hints categorized by function.

Implementing Hints

Hints are implemented by enclosing them within a comment to the SQL statement and adding the + sign immediately after opening the comment. A SQL statement can have only one comment containing hints, and these hints can follow only the SELECT, UPDATE, or DELETE keyword. Each hint applies only to the statement block in which the hint appears.

Hint Syntax

If you have a compound query in which several SELECTs are combined with the UNION operator, each query must contain its own hint. The hint applied to one of the SELECT statements does not carry over to any other SELECT. Oracle comments can have two forms:

/* comment */	The /* indicates the beginning of the comment; the */ indicates the end of the comment. The comment can be multiple lines long.
/*+ hint */	The /*+ indicates the beginning of the hint; the */ indicates the end of the hint. The hint can be multiple lines long.
-- comment	The comment consists of the remainder of the line following the -- characters.
--+ hint	The hint consists of the remainder of the line following the --+ characters.

Adding the + character following the beginning of the comment indicates to the parser that the following text is a hint to the optimizer so that it is parsed as such. An example of this is shown in the next section.

Hint Errors

If a hint is incorrectly specified, Oracle ignores it and does not return an error. The following conditions cause hints to be ignored:

- Comment does not follow a SELECT, UPDATE, or DELETE statement. If the comment containing the hint does not follow one of these statements, the hint is ignored.

- Syntax errors. A hint that contains syntax errors is ignored. Other hints within the same comment are evaluated individually.

- Conflicting hints. Conflicting hints (that is, FULL and INDEX) are ignored, but other non-conflicting hints within the same comment are evaluated individually.

Following is an example of how a hint in a SQL statement looks:

```
SELECT /*+ FULL(bank_account) */ account_no, name, balance
FROM bank_account WHERE account_no = '12631';
```

This hint specifies that the optimizer should perform a full table scan on the bank_account table, rather than using an index that the optimizer might choose.

Following is another example of a hint. (Notice that the statement is the same. To use the -- form of the comment, the comment and hint must be at the end of the line.)

```
SELECT --+ FULL(bank_account)
    account_no, name, balance
FROM
    bank_account
WHERE
    account_no = '12631';
```

Both of these methods for indicating hints are equivalent to the parser and optimizer.

Using Multiple Hints

Except in the case of conflicting hints, you can merge multiple hints. In some cases, merging hints can be useful and possibly essential.

In many Parallel Query hints, it is not uncommon for the FULL (full table scan) hint to be used in conjunction with the PARALLEL (parallel query) hint. By using these two hints together, you ensure that a full table scan is executed and that the parallel table scan feature of the parallel query option will be used.

To use multiple hints together, simply add hints within the same comment, as in this example that combines the FULL and PARALLEL hints:

```
SELECT /* FULL( dogs ) PARALLEL ( dogs, 5 ) */
    dogname, age, owner
FROM
    dogs
WHERE
    age < 5;
```

The following section describes some of the hints you can use and their functions.

Hints

The following sections describe the hints that are available to the Oracle optimizer. The hints are grouped into several categories based on function.

Optimization Approaches

The following hints allow you to indicate to Oracle to use a certain optimization approach, regardless of what optimization approach has been specified in the Oracle initialization file. The indicated approach takes precedence over any other specification of the optimization approach.

ALL_ROWS

The ALL_ROWS hint specifies that the cost-based optimizer should be used with the goal of best throughput. This method creates an execution plan with the least amount of total resource consumption and the best throughput. The cost-based optimization approach is used, regardless of the presence or absence of statistics.

The syntax of this hint is as follows:

```
/*+ ALL_ROWS */
```

If you include hints for access paths or join operations with the ALL_ROWS hint, the optimizer gives precedence to the access paths and join hints.

If no statistics are available for the tables involved and a hint forces the use of the cost-based optimizer, the optimizer uses default statistics to determine the most optimal execution plan. These default statistics include allocated storage and number of data blocks used. These statistics are not very good, but they are better than no statistics at all. If you intend to use the cost-based optimizer, use the DBMS_STATS package or run the ANALYZE command on the tables, indexes, and clusters to be accessed to get better statistics. This is covered in more detail in Chapter 13, "The Oracle Optimizer."

CHOOSE

The CHOOSE hint causes the optimizer to choose the rules-based or cost-based optimization approach based on the presence of statistics available on the tables that the SQL statements are accessing. If statistics are available for the tables being accessed, the optimizer chooses the cost-based approach, with the goal of best throughput. If no statistics exist for the tables that are being accessed, the rules-based optimizer is used.

The syntax of this hint is as follows:

```
/*+ CHOOSE */
```

FIRST_ROWS

The FIRST_ROWS hint specifies that the cost-based optimizer should be used with the goal of best response time for the first n rows. This method creates an execution plan with the least amount of resource consumption to return the first n rows. The cost-based optimization approach is used, regardless of the presence or absence of statistics.

The syntax of this hint is as follows:

```
/*+ FIRST_ROWS (n) */
```

When you use the FIRST_ROWS hint, the optimizer also makes the following choices:

- If an index scan is available, it might be chosen over a full table scan.

- If an index scan is available, the optimizer might choose a nested-loops join over a sort-merge join whenever the associated table is the potential inner table of the nested loops.

- If an index scan is available through an ORDER BY clause, the optimizer might choose it to avoid a sort operation.

The FIRST_ROWS hint is ignored in DELETE and UPDATE statements that contain the following keywords:

- Set operators (UNION, INTERSECT, MINUS, UNION ALL)

- GROUP BY clauses

- FOR UPDATE clauses

- Group or aggregate functions such as AVG, MIN, MAX, COUNT, SUM, STDDEV, and VARIANCE

- DISTINCT operator

These statements cannot be optimized for best response time by retrieving the first row because the operation involved requires that all rows be retrieved before returning the first row. If you use the FIRST_ROWS hint in any of these statements, the cost-based optimizer is still used, regardless of the presence of statistics on the tables involved.

If you include hints for access paths or join operations with the FIRST_ROWS hint, the optimizer gives precedence to the access paths and join hints.

If no statistics are available for the tables involved and a hint forces the cost-based optimizer, the optimizer uses default statistics to determine the most optimal execution plan. These default statistics include allocated storage and number of data blocks used. These statistics are not very good, but they are better than no statistics at all. If you intend to use the cost-based optimizer, run the ANALYZE command on the tables, indexes, and clusters to be accessed to get better statistics.

RULE

The RULE hint specifies that the rules-based optimization approach be used. This hint also causes the optimizer to ignore any other hints that might be specified in this statement block.

The syntax of this hint is as follows:

```
/*+ RULE */
```

Because the rules-based approach is based simply on the SQL statements, you must have statistics about the database tables. The rules-based approach uses the following steps to determine the execution plan:

1. Determine possible execution plans.

2. Rank the different plans according to a specific ranking (see Table 13.1 in Chapter 13).

3. Choose the approach with the lowest ranking.

In this way, the rules-based optimization approach is efficient and works well. However, if statistics are available for your tables, clusters, or indexes, the cost-based approach can be efficient.

Access Methods

The following hints provide the optimizer with the specific access method that you think is more appropriate based on information you know about your data and your application. These hints are valid only if the referenced index or cluster is available and the syntax of the SQL statement is correct. If the syntax is incorrect or the referenced index or cluster is not available, the hint is ignored.

When specifying an access path for a SQL statement, the table to be accessed must be specified exactly. If the table is accessed with an alias, you must specify the alias.

AND_EQUAL

The AND_EQUAL hint specifies an execution plan that uses an access path that merges the scans of several single-column indexes.

The syntax of this hint is as follows:

```
/*+ AND_EQUAL( table index index [ index .... index ] ) */
```

CLUSTER

The CLUSTER hint specifies that the optimizer should choose a cluster scan to access the specified table.

The syntax of this hint is as follows:

```
/*+ CLUSTER( table ) */
```

FULL

The FULL hint specifies that the optimizer should choose a full table scan to access the specified table.

The syntax of this hint is as follows:

```
/*+ FULL( table ) */
```

This hint specifies the use of a full table scan, even though an index might be present on this table and the index key is specified in the WHERE clause.

WHEN TO BYPASS

If you have an indexed table and you know that a certain value in your SELECT statement has a large number of duplicates (which is inefficient for indexes), you may want to use the FULL hint to bypass the index.

HASH

The HASH hint specifies that the optimizer should choose a hash scan to access the specified table.

The syntax of this hint is as follows:

```
/*+ HASH( table ) */
```

INDEX

The INDEX hint specifies that the optimizer should choose an index scan to access the specified table.

The syntax of this hint is as follows:

```
/*+ INDEX( table index [ index .. index ] ) */
```

This hint might contain one or more indexes. The optimizer can make the following choices:

- If no index is specified in the hint, the optimizer determines the cost of each index that can be used to access the specified table. After this determination is made, the index with the lowest cost is chosen for the index scan. The optimizer might choose to scan multiple indexes and merge the result if this path has the lowest cost. A full table scan is not considered.

- If one index is specified in the hint, this index is used for the index scan. The optimizer does not consider a full table scan or any other index scans.

- If multiple indexes are specified in the hint, the optimizer determines the cost of each index in the list that could be used to access the specified table. After this determination is made, the index with the lowest cost is chosen for the index scan. The optimizer might choose to scan multiple indexes in the list and merge the result if this path has the lowest cost. A full table scan is not considered.

The INDEX hint specifies the use of an index scan, even though the optimizer might not choose an index scan because of a low number of distinct values. If you know that the value in the WHERE clause is somewhat unique, you can improve performance by using this hint.

INDEX_ASC

The INDEX_ASC hint specifies that the optimizer should choose an index scan to access the specified table.

The syntax of this hint is as follows:

```
/*+ INDEX_ASC( table index [ index .. index ] ) */
```

This hint can contain one or more indexes. The INDEX_ASC hint is similar to the INDEX hint except that if the statement specifies an index range scan, the entries are scanned in ascending order of their indexed values.

This method is currently the default behavior for a range scan. However, because Oracle does not guarantee that this method will always be the default behavior, this hint is provided.

INDEX_COMBINE

The INDEX_COMBINE hint specifies that the optimizer should choose a bitmap index or set of bitmap indexes to access the specified table.

The syntax of this hint is as follows:

```
/*+ INDEX_COMBINE( table index [ index .. index ] ) */
```

The INDEX_COMBINE hint might contain one or more indexes.

INDEX_DESC

The INDEX_DESC hint specifies that the optimizer should choose an index scan to access the specified table.

The syntax of this hint is as follows:

```
/*+ INDEX_DESC( table index [ index .. index ] ) */
```

The INDEX_DESC hint might contain one or more indexes. This hint is similar to the INDEX hint except that if the statement specifies an index range scan, the entries are scanned in descending order of their indexed values.

INDEX_JOIN

The INDEX_JOIN hint specifies that the optimizer should choose an index join for the access path.

The syntax of this hint is as follows:

```
/*+ INDEX_JOIN( table index [ index .. index ] ) */
```

The INDEX_JOIN hint might contain one or more indexes, and these indexes must be appropriate to participate in the join operation.

INDEX_FFS

The INDEX_FFS hint specifies that the optimizer should choose an index fast full scan to access the specified table.

The syntax of this hint is as follows:

```
/*+ INDEX_FFS( table index [ index .. index ] ) */
```

The INDEX_FFS hint might contain one or more indexes.

NO_INDEX

The NO_INDEX hint specifies that the optimizer should access a path that avoids the use of the set of specified indexes.

The syntax of this hint is as follows:

```
/*+ NO_INDEX( table index [ index .. index ] ) */
```

The NO_INDEX hint might contain one or more indexes. The optimizer will not consider indexes that are included in the list. Indexes that are absent from the list of indexes in the hint are candidates for use.

ROWID

The ROWID hint specifies that the optimizer should choose a table scan by row ID to access the specified table.

The syntax of this hint is as follows:

```
/*+ ROWID( table ) */
```

This hint specifies the use of a table scan by ROWID, even though an index might be present for this table and the index key is specified in the WHERE clause.

USE_CONCAT

The USE_CONCAT hint forces combined OR conditions in the WHERE clause of a query to be transformed into a compound query using the UNION ALL set operator. Typically, this transformation is done only if the cost is cheaper with concatenation than without it.

The syntax of this hint is as follows:

```
/*+ USE_CONCAT */
```

Join Orders

The following hints are used to specify join orders and how to take advantage of information you know about your data to improve the performance of the joins.

ORDERED

The ORDERED hint causes the execution plan to join tables in the order that they are specified in the FROM clause.

The syntax of this hint is as follows:

```
/*+ ORDERED */
```

Because you know your data better than the Oracle optimizer, you might be able to specify the order of the join to make better choices for the inner and outer tables than the optimizer can.

STAR

The STAR hint can be used in conjunction with the ORDERED hint. The STAR hint forces a star query plan, if possible.

The syntax of this hint is as follows:

```
/*+ STAR */
```

If you know your data would benefit from a star query plan, this hint can help the optimizer choose the right plan.

Join Operations

The following hints are used to specify join operations and to take advantage of information you know about your data to improve the performance of the joins. When specifying a join operation for a SQL statement, it's imperative to specify exactly the table to be joined. If the table is accessed with an alias, you must specify the alias. The USE_MERGE and USE_NL hints must be used with the ORDERED hint.

USE_MERGE

The USE_MERGE hint causes the execution plan to join each specified table with another row source using a sort-merge join.

The syntax of this hint is as follows:

```
/*+ USE_MERGE ( table, table ) */
```

It should also be used with the ORDERED hint:

```
/*+ ORDERED USE_MERGE ( table [, table ] ) */
```

In this syntax, *table* refers to a table to be joined to the row source that results from joining other tables in the join order using a sort-merge join.

USE_NL

The USE_NL hint causes the execution plan to join each specified table with another row source using a nested-loops join. The specified table is used as the inner table.

The syntax of this hint is as follows:

```
/*+ USE_NL ( table [, table ] ) */
```

In this syntax, *table* refers to the table to be used as the inner table of the nested-loops join.

USE_HASH

The USE_HASH hint causes the execution plan to join each specified table with another row source using a hash join. The specified table is used as the inner table.

The syntax of this hint is as follows:

```
/*+ USE_HASH ( table [, table ] ) */
```

In this syntax, *table* refers to the table to be used as the inner table of the nested-loops join.

DRIVING_SITE

The DRIVING_SITE hint causes the execution of the query to be performed at a different site from the one that Oracle chose.

The syntax of this hint is as follows:

```
/*+ DRIVING_SITE ( table ) */
```

An example of this is shown here:

```
SELECT /*+DRIVING_SITE(dept)*/ *
FROM emp, dept@rsite
WHERE emp.deptno = dept.deptno;
```

In this example, the execution will be performed at rsite.

LEADING

The LEADING hint specifies that the named table will be the first table in the join operation.

The syntax of this hint is as follows:

```
/*+ LEADING ( table ) */
```

HASH_AJ, MERGE_AJ, and NL_AJ

This hint is used in the SELECT clause of a NOT IN subquery. It specifies a hash anti-join, merge anti-join, or nested loops anti-join.

The syntax of this hint is as follows:

```
/*+ HASH_AJ / or /*+ MERGE_AJ / or /+ NL_AJ */
```

HASH_SJ, MERGE_SJ, and NL_SJ

This hint is used in the SELECT clause of an EXISTS subquery. It specifies a hash semi-join, merge semi-join, or nested loops semi-join.

The syntax of this hint is as follows:

```
/*+ HASH_SJ / or /*+ MERGE_SJ / or /+ NL_SJ */
```

Parallel Query Hints

The following hints are related to the Oracle Parallel Query option. With the Parallel Query option, you can achieve great results.

PARALLEL

The PARALLEL hint specifies the desired number of query servers to be used for this specific operation.

The syntax of this hint is as follows:

```
/*+ PARALLEL ( table [ , degree ] [ , split ] ) */
```

Alternatively, you can use the PARALLEL hint with the FULL hint:

```
/*+ FULL( table ) PARALLEL ( table [ , degree ] [ , split ] ) */
```

Typically, the *table* and *degree* parameters are specified.

This hint takes two comma-separated values after the table definition. The first value specifies the degree of parallelism; the second value specifies the split among instances in a parallel server environment. If *degree* is not specified, the query coordinator chooses a value.

NOPARALLEL

The NOPARALLEL hint can be used to override the default parallel query operations, even though the default table parameters allow for parallel query processing.

The syntax of this hint is as follows:

```
/*+ NOPARALLEL ( table ) */
```

The NOPARALLEL hint can be useful for certain conditions in which you must reduce the load on the system or reduce I/O contention. This hint essentially disables parallel query processing for this SQL statement.

PQ_DISTRIBUTE

The PQ_DISTRIBUTE hint is used to specify how parallel operations are performed. With this hint, you can specify how the rows of the joined tables are split among the processes.

The syntax of the hint is as follows:

```
/*+ PQ_DISTRIBUTE ( table, outer distribution, inner distribution ) */
```

This hint is unusual in that the values for outer and inner distribution are fixed. Only certain combinations are allowed in this hint. These combinations are as follows:

Hash, hash	This combination uses a hash function on each of the tables in the join. This is good when both tables are roughly equivalent in size. It is used with hash and merge joins.
Broadcast, none	All rows of the outer table are broadcast to the query servers, and the inner table rows are randomly partitioned. This is recommended when the outer table is small compared to the inner table.
None, broadcast	All rows of the inner table are broadcast to the query servers, and the outer table rows are randomly partitioned. This is recommended when the inner table is small compared to the outer table.

Partition, none	This combination maps the outer table to the inner table based on the partitioning of the inner table. The inner table must be partitioned on the join key. This is recommended when the number of partitions is roughly equivalent to the number of query servers.
None, partition	This combination maps the rows of the inner table using the partitioning of the outer table. The outer table must be partitioned on the join key. Again, this is recommended when the number of partitions is roughly equivalent to the number of query servers.
None, none	With this hint, the query servers join each table on a partition-by-partition basis. It is required that each table is equally partitioned on the join key.

Many restrictions are involved in this hint based on the partitioning as well as on the number of query servers. This hint should only be used after some research and some thorough testing.

PARALLEL_INDEX

The PARALLEL_INDEX hint specifies the desired number of query servers to be used for parallel index range scans.

The syntax of this hint is as follows:

```
/*+ PARALLEL_INDEX ( table, index [ , degree ] [ , rac ] */
```

This hint takes the table name, the index that you are hinting, the degree of parallelism, and the number of instances in a RAC configuration to use. If you do not specify the degree of parallelism, the query coordinator chooses a value.

NOPARALLEL_INDEX

The NOPARALLEL_INDEX hint specifies that parallel index range scans are avoided.

The syntax of this hint is as follows:

```
/*+ NOPARALLEL_INDEX ( table [ , index ] ) */
```

Query Transformation

The following hints are used to actually modify how the query is transformed. A query can exist in several forms and still serve the same purpose and return the same result set. These hints allow the queries to be transformed internally.

STAR_TRANSFORMATION

The STAR_TRANSFORMATION hint specifies that a star transformation should be used on the query. In conjunction with this hint, the FACT and NO_FACT hints can be used.

The syntax of this hint is as follows:

```
/*+ STAR_TRANSFORMATION */
```

FACT

The FACT hint is used in conjunction with the STAR_TRANSFORMATION hint. The table given in the hint is assumed to be the fact table in the star schema.

The syntax of this hint is as follows:

```
/*+ FACT ( table ) */
```

NO_FACT

The NO_FACT hint is used in conjunction with the STAR_TRANSFORMATION hint. The table given in the hint is assumed not to be the fact table in the star schema.

The syntax of this hint is as follows:

```
/*+ NO_FACT ( table ) */
```

USE_CONCAT

The USE_CONCAT hint forces combined conditions in OR clauses to be transformed into a complex query using a UNION ALL operator. The USE_CONCAT hint also turns off IN list processing.

The syntax of this hint is as follows:

```
/*+ USE_CONCAT */
```

MERGE

The MERGE hint is used to enable view merging on a per-table basis. The table given in the hint is assumed not to be the fact table in the star schema.

The syntax of this hint is as follows:

```
/*+ MERGE ( table ) */
```

NO_MERGE

The NO_MERGE hint specifies that mergible views are not merged. This gives you more control over how the view is processed.

The syntax of this hint is as follows:

```
/*+ NOMERGE */
```

NO_EXPAND

The NO_EXPAND hint prohibits OR expansion in queries.

The syntax of this hint is as follows:

```
/*+ NO_EXPAND */
```

REWRITE

The REWRITE hint forces the optimizer to rewrite the query taking into account materialized views, when possible, without factoring the cost of that operation.

The syntax of this hint is as follows:

```
/*+ REWRITE ( view [, view …] )  */
```

NOREWRITE

The NOREWRITE hint disables query rewriting. This overrides the setting of the QUERY_REWRITE_ENABLED parameter setting. With this parameter set, queries will not be rewritten.

The syntax of this hint is as follows:

```
/*+ NOREWRITE */
```

Miscellaneous Hints

This section consists of hints that don't fit into the other categories.

CACHE

The CACHE hint specifies that the blocks retrieved for the table in the hint are placed at the most recently used end of the least recently used (LRU) list in the buffer cache when a full table scan is performed. When a full table scan occurs, the entries are usually put on the end of the LRU to age more quickly. This is done because most of the data read in a full table scan is usually discarded. The CACHE hint can be useful if most of the data in a full table scan is used.

The syntax of this hint is as follows:

```
/*+ CACHE ( table ) */
```

Alternatively, you can use the CACHE hint with the FULL hint:

```
/*+ FULL( table ) CACHE ( table ) */
```

NOCACHE

The NOCACHE hint specifies that the blocks retrieved for the table in the hint are placed at the least recently used end of the LRU list in the buffer cache when a full table scan is performed. This is the default behavior in a table scan. The buffer entries are put on the end of the LRU to age more quickly. This is done because most of the data read in a full table scan is usually discarded. The NOCACHE hint can be useful if little of the data in a full table scan is used.

The syntax of this hint is as follows:

```
/*+ NOCACHE ( table ) */
```

Alternatively, you can use the NOCACHE hint with the FULL hint:

```
/*+ FULL( table ) NOCACHE ( table ) */
```

The NOCACHE hint can be useful if you think you will be reading large amounts of data that will unnecessarily be held in the buffer cache.

PUSH_SUBQ

The PUSH_SUBQ hint causes nonmerged subqueries to be evaluated at the earliest possible place in the execution plan. Normally, subqueries that are not merged are executed as the last step in the execution plan. If the subquery is inexpensive and reduces the number of rows significantly, you can improve performance by executing it earlier.

The syntax of this hint is as follows:

```
/*+ PUSH_SUBQ */
```

APPEND

The APPEND hint specifies that in an INSERT operation, data is simply appended to a table. This avoids the use of free space within existing tables, and data is appended to the end of the table. This can be useful for cases when INSERT performance is critical.

The syntax of this hint is as follows:

```
/*+ APPEND */
```

NOAPPEND

The NOAPPEND hint overrides APPEND mode.

The syntax of this hint is as follows:

```
/*+ NOAPPEND */
```

UNNEST

The UNNEST hint enables subquery unnesting. This merges the body of a subquery into the body of the statement that contains it.

The syntax of this hint is as follows:

```
/*+ UNNEST */
```

NO_UNNEST

The NO_UNNEST hint disables subquery unnesting for the particular query.

The syntax of this hint is as follows:

```
/*+ NO_UNNEST */
```

PUSH_PRED

The PUSH_PRED hint forces pushing of a join predicate into the view used in the query.

The syntax of this hint is as follows:

```
/*+ PUSH_PRED ( table ) */
```

NO_PUSH_PRED

The NO_PUSH_PRED hint prevents pushing of a join predicate into the view used in the query.

The syntax of this hint is as follows:

```
/*+ NO_PUSH_PRED ( table ) */
```

ORDERED_PREDICATES

The ORDERED_PREDICATES hint forces the optimizer to preserve the order of predicate evaluation. This hint is used in the WHERE clause of SELECT statements.

The syntax of this hint is as follows:

```
/*+ ORDERED_PREDICATES */
```

CURSOR_SHARING_EXACT

The CURSOR_SHARING_EXACT hint forces the optimizer to execute the SQL statement without attempting to replace literals with bind variables.

The syntax of this hint is as follows:

```
/*+ CURSOR_SHARING_EXACT */
```

Summary

Because you know more about your data and your application than the Oracle optimizer does, you can make significant improvements to the execution plan of the SQL statements. The Oracle optimizer is efficient and works quite well to produce the best execution plan for your SQL statements based on the information with which it has to work; however, anything you can do to give the optimizer additional information about the execution process will help performance.

By using hints, specific information that you know about your data and database can be used to further enhance the performance on certain SQL statements. By using hints, you can enhance specific operations that might otherwise be inefficient. The best way you can significantly improve the performance of your system is by knowing it. Understand the data access patterns. Determine what the users are most likely to access and how they will access it.

By knowing your application and data, you can significantly improve the performance of your server and your application. Hints can help you transfer your knowledge of your data and application to the Oracle optimizer.

PART IV

Advanced Topics

IN THIS PART

16 Oracle9i Real Application Clusters

17 Tuning Backup and Recovery

18 Creating a High-Performance Disaster Survival System

19 Oracle Networking Performance

ORACLE9I REAL APPLICATION CLUSTERS

Oracle9i Real Application Clusters (RAC) is the latest version of Oracle Parallel Server (OPS) and has been vastly improved. The Oracle9i RAC system is composed of many computer systems that allow multiple Oracle instances to access the same database. Using RAC not only improves performance, but it also makes a great failover system; any node in the cluster can take over for a failed node in the event of a system failure. In this chapter, you will learn about what RAC is, how to tune it, and when it might be of use for you.

Overview of RAC

The Oracle9i RAC system is an option to the Oracle9i server; it enables you to link several computers to form a cluster. A *cluster* is a group of computers that work together to provide a unified service. In the case of the Oracle Parallel Server cluster, these systems are linked together to form one large RDBMS system.

Primary among the reasons that many people choose RAC is fault tolerance, but many also use the Parallel Server for increased performance. However, an Oracle RAC system can only achieve good performance scalability if you properly design and configure the system.

The Oracle RAC system is made up of several *nodes*, or cluster members, each of which runs an Oracle instance. Each of these instances accesses the same database through a shared disk system. Because the redo log files and rollback segments also reside on the shared disk system, it is possible for a node to perform instance recovery on another cluster member in the event of a failure. If a node fails, the other nodes in the cluster are unaffected.

The Oracle9i RAC system is a true cluster in that it is made up of two or more systems that actually allow you to access the same data in the same database. Many systems today claim to be clusters, but a difference exists between a cluster that is used only for failover, and a system cluster that truly allows multiple systems to act as one. With a failover system, only one instance of the database or application can be used at a time, and the other computer system is used in a standby mode. In some instances, the standby system is used for some other function, or even another database instance, but this is still a failover system. RAC allows multiple computer systems and multiple Oracle instances to access the same database.

The Oracle9i RAC system is a cluster whereby several computer systems access the same database. Any node in the cluster can access any data in the database. Oracle9i RAC uses multiple instances (one on each node), but each instance accesses the same database. A sophisticated locking mechanism that allows each node to lock the data that it is using maintains data consistency. These locks are called Parallel Cache Management (PCM) locks. The PCM locks are exchanged between the different nodes in the system so that no two nodes can modify the same block at the same time. Although multiple nodes can read the same data at the same time, only one node can modify a block at a time.

In OPS, the previous generation of RAC, when a request was made from a node for data that was locked on another node, that data had to be written out to disk before the lock could be relinquished. The process has been referred to as a *ping*. With Oracle9i RAC, the requested data is now transmitted between nodes on a high-speed data interconnect as this data is needed. This is much faster than having to flush the data out to disk before transferring it between nodes. This new feature of transferring blocks over the interconnect is known as *cache fusion*.

Oracle9i RAC is primarily a software solution, but it does require some specialized hardware. Without this hardware, the RAC system would not be possible. The following list looks at the hardware that is required for an Oracle9i RAC.

Computer systems	To build a cluster, you must have two or more computer systems. These systems can be any server type system and do not have any particular requirements except that they must be capable of running Oracle9i.
Shared disk subsystem	It is necessary that a disk subsystem exists that supports concurrent access to the disk volumes from all systems that are participating in the cluster. This will most likely be some type of storage area network (SAN) subsystem.
Server interconnect	The server interconnect is a connection between the nodes in the cluster that is used for communication. This can be as simple as an Ethernet network or something much more complex, such as a memory channel interconnect or high-speed network.

Computer Systems

Without the computer systems to make up a cluster, a cluster cannot exist. To have a cluster, you must have at least two computer systems. These systems are not strictly required to be equivalently equipped, but it is certainly recommended. If the systems are not similar in terms of memory and CPU type, speed, and number of CPUs, it might be more difficult to balance the load across the systems in the cluster. By configuring the systems with the same number and type of CPUs and the same amount of memory, you can more easily balance the load across these systems.

Depending on the OS that you are running, you might not need an individual disk drive on each cluster node to boot the system and to store the Oracle program files. Some operating systems enable you to add multiple systems without having local storage. This is known as a *single image cluster*.

Shared Disk Subsystem

The shared disk subsystem is a critical component of the cluster. The shared disk subsystem is an I/O subsystem that can be accessed from all of the systems in the cluster. This I/O subsystem should be able to handle the I/O load that will be generated by the sum of the I/Os generated by all of the nodes in the cluster. The shared disk subsystem is typically a SAN system. With a SAN, the I/O subsystem is automatically shareable because that is what a SAN is designed to do. In addition, a SAN is usually designed to handle a large number of I/Os.

The shared disk subsystem is critical to the performance of the cluster and can easily become a performance bottleneck. The shared disk subsystem has nothing special that makes it more critical that the I/O subsystem in a non-cluster system; however, the fact that multiple computer systems are accessing the storage system can make it more difficult to monitor. Keep in mind RAID overhead, as in any I/O subsystem.

Server Interconnect

The server interconnect is used for communication between the nodes in the cluster. Because of the Cache Fusion architecture, the interconnect is important. Depending on the amount of activity in the cluster and the amount of lock traffic that is being transferred back and forth between the various nodes in the system, the amount of data being transferred across the server interconnect can be quite significant. Thus, the interconnect should be of sufficient bandwidth to handle the lock and block traffic. If the interconnect is not of sufficient bandwidth to handle the traffic, you can experience a severe performance problem. Although you can create an Oracle cluster with an interconnect as slow as a 10baseT (ten megabit) Ethernet network, that is not necessarily a wise thing to do. New technology on the market can be used as an interconnect that is faster than Ethernet networking. Depending on your needs, you might have to invest in this technology. In fact, Oracle highly recommends using a gigabit interconnect of some sort to achieve linear scalability.

Locking

Locking is performed through a process called the Distributed Lock Manager (DLM). The DLM is responsible for locking data that is being modified so that it cannot be modified in another instance. Locking ensures data integrity across the entire cluster. A data block or group of blocks is locked until another instance needs that data. The DLM provides the following functionality:

- Keeps track of resource ownership
- Queues requests for PCM locks
- Notifies an instance that a resource is requested
- Notifies the requesting instance that the resource has been acquired

Because the locks are held until another instance needs them, if you can partition your users so that users who are accessing data in a particular table all use the same instance to access that data, you will reduce lock contention. Performance can be enhanced by carefully partitioning the data and the users. If you partition the data into update-intensive and read-intensive tables, you will also benefit.

BREAKING UP... YOUR DATA

Because the PCM locks are held until the data covered by those locks is requested by another instance, partitioning your data to reduce the amount of data that different nodes in the cluster access can greatly improve performance.

At instance startup, a number of PCM locks are created. PCM locks are used to lock data blocks that are being accessed within each instance to guarantee that multiple instances do not alter the same data. These PCM locks might cover hundreds, thousands, or even millions of data blocks, depending on your configuration.

Locks can be acquired in one of two modes:

Exclusive Lock mode	When a lock is acquired in Exclusive Lock mode, the instance is allowed to update the blocks that the lock covers. If those blocks are already in use, the DLM requests the other instance to release the lock.
Read Lock mode	When a lock is acquired in Read Lock mode, the instance is assured that during the time the lock is active, the data will not change. It is possible for multiple instances to have Read Locks on the same data blocks.

PCM locks can be used to lock data blocks for reading or for updating. If a PCM lock is used as a read lock, other instances can acquire read locks on the same data blocks. You only need to acquire an exclusive lock when you are updating a block.

READ-ONLY PUT TO GOOD USE

Because PCM locks are used to lock data to guarantee data consistency between nodes, you can eliminate the need for PCM locks by taking advantage of read-only tablespaces. Because read-only tablespaces cannot be updated, Oracle does not have to allocate PCM locks for those tables.

When an instance wants to update a data block, it must acquire an exclusive lock on that block. If another instance has a lock that includes that block, the instance holding the lock must relinquish the lock. With cache fusion, the instance then sends the block along with the lock to the node that wants to acquire the lock.

Locking has two modes. The default behavior is to use lightweight locks that individually lock each block. This works well when the interconnect is sufficiently fast to handle all the lock traffic, and involves managing a large number of blocks. In a system where it is feasible, you can run in traditional OPS lock mode when a lock covers several or many blocks. A PCM lock can lock one or more data blocks, depending on the number of PCM locks that are allocated to the data file and the size of the data file. Because an inherent overhead is associated with PCM locks, it is not beneficial to overestimate and configure Oracle for many of the locks.

Because a PCM lock covers more than one block, you might unnecessarily be pinging if you want a block that the other instances is not using. This is why, with active tables, you might want to add more locks; with less active tables, you can reduce the number of locks.

The Parallel Server option can be quite effective if your application can access partitioned data. If all the users in your system must access the same data, however, the Parallel Server option might not be for you. However, if you can partition your workload into divisions based on table access or if you need a fault-tolerant configuration, consider the Parallel Server option.

If you use RAC, take special care to properly configure the system. By designing the system properly, you can take maximum advantage of the scalability.

Cluster Configuration

The individual components previously described must be carefully configured to create an optimal cluster. A diagram of an Oracle9i RAC is shown in Figure 16.1.

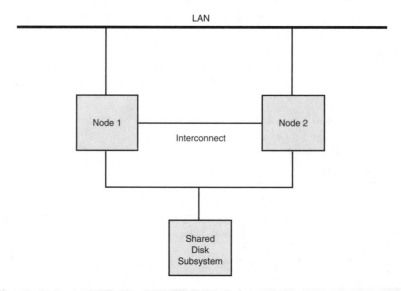

FIGURE 16.1
An Oracle9i RAC system.

Careful sizing, planning, and configuration are essential for an optimal performing system. Several areas can be especially difficult in configuring the cluster. These difficult tasks include the following:

Sizing the system	Sizing is important, especially with the I/O subsystem. See Chapters 9, "I/O Concepts," and 10, "Oracle and I/O," for information on configuring and sizing the I/O subsystem. A poorly sized I/O subsystem can adversely affect system performance.
Configuring the I/O subsystem	In most cases, an Oracle9i RAC system uses a SAN as the shared disk subsystem. Even in a non-cluster configuration, a SAN is difficult to configure. SANs typically require additional software and configuration steps.
Configuring the interconnect	The interconnect is fairly easy if you are using an off-the-shelf component such as an Ethernet controller. In the case of a high-performance proprietary solution, vendor-specific software and configuration steps might be necessary.

As mentioned, a cluster is never easy to configure. Careful planning and good documentation can be a great deal of help.

RAC Design Considerations

The primary way to optimize performance with a RAC cluster is to properly configure the system. By properly configuring the system to avoid contention, you can see good performance by adding nodes. With the Parallel Server option more than any other Oracle feature, it is important to properly design the system for performance.

In a poorly designed Parallel Server cluster, you might not see performance improvement by adding nodes; in fact, you might even see performance degrade. By understanding the basic principles of the OPS and setting good design goals, you can achieve amazing performance from the cluster.

The goals in designing a RAC system are fairly straightforward. Your primary goals are to reduce contention between servers and to reduce the number of PCM locks that must be obtained and released. By reducing contention on specific data areas, you can minimize the use of locks and increase performance.

Assuming that the I/O subsystem can handle the required shared throughput, the only thing that can slow you down is contention between systems. If this contention is reduced or eliminated, the system will show scaleable performance when you add nodes.

You can reduce this contention if you understand how the data is accessed. Only by knowing your application can you most effectively optimize the RAC system.

If you have a system in which some users access only certain tables and other users primarily access other tables, you can benefit from partitioning those users. If the users are spread out in a random fashion, you see a lot of pinging because multiple nodes want to update data in the same table (see Figure 16.2) and often in the same block. When a node requests blocks that the other node is not using, it is not much of a problem; however, when both nodes request the same block, contention occurs.

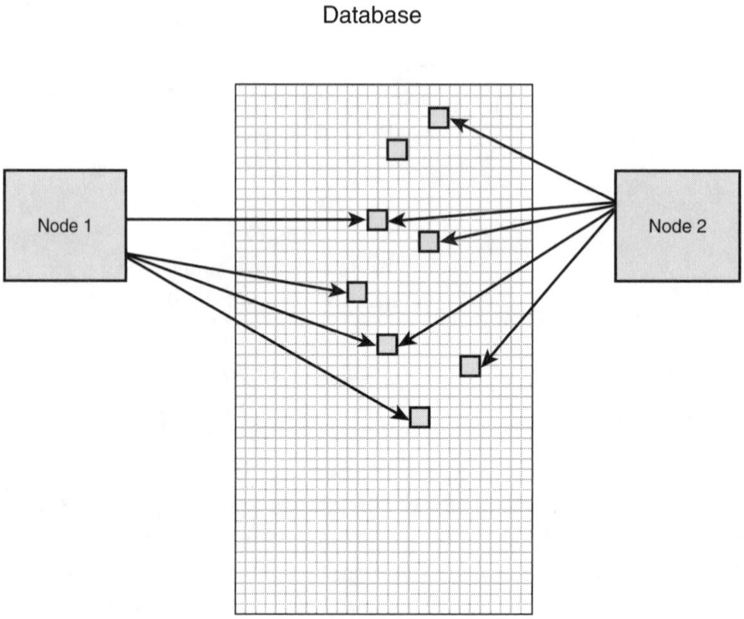

Database

FIGURE 16.2
PCM lock contention.

By segmenting the users so that the users on each node access data in the same tables, you can greatly reduce PCM lock contention because each instance can hold the locks longer. Although you still have some contention, any reduction is useful. This kind of segmentation is necessary to get optimum performance from the Oracle parallel server system. An example of a segmented system is shown in Figure 16.3.

If all users must access all the data, you can still segment this activity by using a transaction monitor (TM). A TM is a class of product, known as *middleware*, that is used to facilitate the communication between the client and the database server.

You can use the TM on many different modes for different functions. Tuxedo has some of the following capabilities:

Multiplexing   You can use the TM as a multiplexer to allow a few Oracle connections to service multiple client processes, thus reducing the connections into the RDBMS.

Queuing	You can use TM as a queuing mechanism to store requests to be serviced either sequentially or at a later time.
Distributed services	Two distributed applications can be supported with the TM to transparently provide distributed services to the application.
Smart routing	The TM can be used to route requests to different servers based on the content of the request. In this way, requests can be segmented.

Database

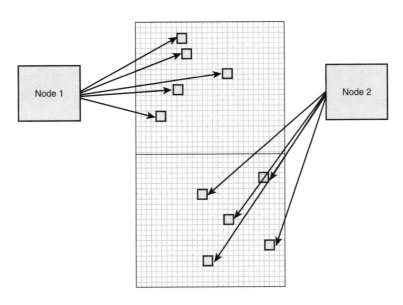

FIGURE 16.3
Reducing contention by segmenting users.

You use the segmentation feature to segment the data among the different servers in a parallel server system. When you use a TM, the segmentation is transparent to the users (see Figure 16.4).

Regardless of whether you use a TM, the main goal of the parallel server system designer is to try to set up the system to reduce lock contention by segmenting tables and users. It is a secondary goal to balance the number of PCM locks based on the amount of contention that remains.

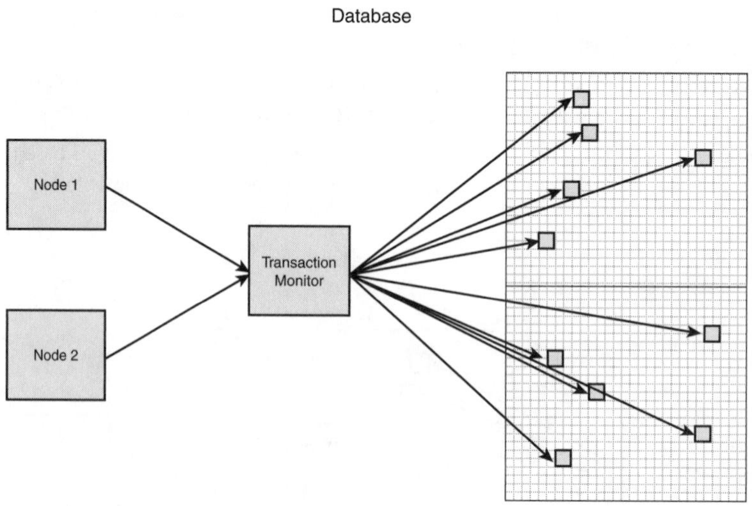

Database

FIGURE 16.4
Segmenting data using a TM.

System Design

By knowing your data access patterns, you can configure your system based on some general rules:

- Partition work between servers. Try to balance the systems so that users who are accessing the same table reside on the same computer. Doing so reduces lock contention between machines. By segmenting the work, you reduce the amount of lock traffic. Remember: After a lock is acquired, it is released only when another system needs to lock that data.

- Put numerous PCM locks on tables with heavy update traffic. If you have many updates, you can benefit from lowering the blocks-per-lock ratio. By increasing the number of locks, you increase overhead, but by having fewer blocks per lock, you might cut down on the percentage of locks with contention.

- Use PCTFREE and PCTUSED to cause fewer rows per block on high-contention tables. By doing this—and decreasing the number of blocks per lock—you reduce the lock contention. However, more locks and more space are required.

- Put fewer locks on read tables. If you have tables that are mostly read, use fewer PCM locks. Read locks are not exclusive; the reduction in locks cuts down on interconnect traffic.

- Take advantage of FREELIST GROUPS. The use of the FREELIST GROUPS storage parameter allows different instances to maintain separate freelists. Use this parameter to cause inserts to occur on different parts of the data files, thus reducing contention.

- Use read-only tables. If a table will not be updated, make it read-only. A read-only table does not require PCM locks because no updates can be made to that table.

- Partition indexes to separate tablespaces. Because indexes are mostly read, you can benefit from needing fewer PCM locks. By segmenting the tables, you can put fewer PCM locks on the index tables and more on the data tables.

By properly designing the system to avoid data block contention, you reduce the number of locks that must be acquired and released, thus reducing overhead and delays.

When to Use RAC

The Oracle9i RAC system is scalable; that is, by adding more nodes to the cluster, you achieve more performance. Therefore, a RAC system can be used when more performance is needed and you cannot (or prefer not to) move to a higher performing standalone system.

In addition, the RAC system can be used to create a high performance, high availability system. With the RAC system, if a node were to fail, the other nodes in the system would continue to function. One of the remaining nodes is chosen to recover the data that was previously owned by the node that failed. These blocks that the failed node had owned must be recovered, and they will be locked until the recovery has completed. All other blocks in the system will still be available for use.

RAC systems are useful when maximum uptime is essential and when extra performance is a plus. Thus, the Oracle RAC system is both a scalable performance cluster and a high availability system. You must weigh the complexity of the RAC system versus the additional benefits that you will receive from it to determine whether RAC is right for you.

Tuning RAC

For those of you who are familiar with the OPS system, you might remember the amount of lock tuning that is involved in an Oracle cluster. With the Oracle9i RAC system, the amount of lock tuning has been reduced. However, much of the same tuning that was necessary with OPS is still required with the RAC system. Tuning RAC can be divided into three areas: hardware tuning (configuration and sizing), instance and lock tuning, and application tuning. The next sections look at these different areas of tuning.

Configuration and Sizing

Configuration and sizing is important. Sizing and configuring the RAC system does not differ much from configuring and sizing a standalone system. Sizing mainly involves the size and number of CPUs, the amount of memory, and of course, the I/O subsystem. Sizing of these components is based on the load that will be put on the system, the number of users, the number of processes, and the size of the database. This subject was covered in Chapter 8, "Oracle and System Hardware."

Instance and Lock Tuning

Lock tuning has been greatly reduced with Oracle9i RAC. With Oracle8 OPS, it was necessary to tune locks, but now it is optional. By default, each block has one lock; however, if the system is mainly read-only, it is possible to reduce lock traffic by using 1:N locks. This allows one lock to cover many blocks.

No tuning is involved with the RAC system if you are using default locking mechanisms. Normal Oracle instance tuning is all that is really required. Many global statistics in V$SYSSTAT pertain to the global locking mechanisms, but you cannot do anything about them.

Application Tuning

Application tuning really goes back to carefully designing your database with contention in mind. Don't design tables that all users access unless you have a way of partitioning the users off into different partitions. Avoid having all users update a single counter or take a single value from a table. This reduces the amount of pinging between the systems. Design the application with partitioning in mind and avoid locking. By understanding the RAC system while you are designing your application, you should be able to reduce locking and increase performance.

Summary

In this chapter, you learned a little bit about how Oracle RAC works and how to best design an Oracle RAC system to reduce locking and increase performance. The most tuning that you can do for a RAC system is to properly design the system and application from the beginning, with RAC in mind. By designing for a RAC system, you should be able to optimize performance.

TUNING BACKUP AND RECOVERY

B acking up your database is one of the most important tasks that you must perform. It is your job as a DBA to make sure that this task is performed well and that the backup is valid. Even though it might not be necessary to restore from the backup, you must be able to restore that backup on a moment's notice. Your business might depend on it.

With most systems, the time that is available for performing backups is limited. Some systems might allow for offline backups, whereas others might require online backups only. In either case, the more quickly you can perform the backup, the better. In this chapter, you will learn techniques for improving backup and recovery performance that might help you reduce the time that it takes to perform these tasks.

Two main methods exist for performing backup and restore operations. You can perform the backup through OS or through third-party backup software, which is known as user-managed backups. In addition, you can back up and restore your system via the Oracle Recovery Manager (RMAN) utility. Regardless of which method you use, the underlying activity and principles are the same. However, some different configuration and tuning options are available if you are using the RMAN utility. This chapter first covers the basic principles to all backup and restore operations, followed by the RMAN tuning options.

BACKUP AND RECOVERY TERMINOLOGY

Following are some of the terms used in backup and recovery and their meanings:

Hot backup	This is officially known as an *online tablespace* backup. This backup occurs while users are connected to the database and executing transactions (even to the table being backed up). Hot backups are performed on a tablespace basis.
Cold backup	This is officially known as an *offline* backup. This backup is done when the Oracle instance is not running. Cold backups can be performed on a database or tablespace basis.
Full backup	A full backup is a backup that is performed on every tablespace in the database. Typically, full backups are done as cold backups.
Export	The Oracle export facility can also be used as a method of performing backups, but it is usually not the preferred option due to performance.

An Oracle backup can consist of either a *hot* backup (while users are connected and running transactions) or a *cold* backup (the database is shut down). In a user-managed backup environment, neither relies on Oracle to perform any functions except to keep the data files from changing during the backup. Using export can be an alternative to traditional methods because it includes the additional feature of allowing the structure of the database to change. However, an export does not provide for the flexibility and recoverability that traditional backups do. Rather than just copying the data as it exists, you can export and import the data to restructure the database and reduce fragmentation.

Although an export can loosely be considered a backup function, the export facility does not provide the same level of recovery as the standard Oracle backup facilities. However, there is more to export/import than just backup and recovery. Export/import can be useful in moving from one version of Oracle to another and for reconfiguration of the database. Export/import can also be used to move data between Oracle databases. Because exports do not allow for instance recovery and because many of the concepts of the export process are similar to those of the traditional backup procedure, this chapter does not address the export process as a backup method.

This chapter consists of a number of hints for how to minimize the effect of the backup and increase its performance. Some of the hints might be directly applicable to you, whereas others might not apply to your configuration. By determining which hints might help you, you can find some useful optimizations for your configuration. This chapter starts by describing some of the characteristics of an Oracle backup and from those characteristics derives methods of improving backup and recovery performance.

Parameters Used in This Chapter

This chapter includes the use of many Oracle initialization parameters. Chapter 1, "Tuning," introduced you to these parameters and explained how to use them. This chapter covers the following initialization parameters:

- BACKUP_TAPE_IO_SLAVES: BACKUP_TAPE_IO_SLAVES specifies that asynchronous I/O be used for tape I/O operations. If this parameter is set to FALSE, synchronous I/O is used.

- DBWR_IO_SLAVES: For systems that do not support asynchronous I/O, this parameter specifies that I/O slave processes are used. This number specifies the number of I/O processes that the DBWR process uses. In addition, if this parameter is set to any non-zero number of I/O processes used by ARCH, LGWR and RMAN are set to four.

Oracle Operational Review

When you make changes to the Oracle database, the changed information is not only eventually written to the database by the DBWR process, but it also is recorded in the redo logs by the LGWR process. When the log file is filled, a log switch occurs, which triggers a database checkpoint.

The checkpoint event ensures that all dirty buffers in the SGA are written out to the data files on a regular basis. The checkpoint can occur more frequently than a log switch for data integrity purposes.

ARCHIVELOG MODE DESCRIBED

ARCHIVELOG mode is used to save or archive the redo log files after a log switch has occurred. This process is essential if you want to perform point-in-time recovery (get the database back to where it was when the problem occurred). If you are not running in ARCHIVELOG mode, you will only be able to restore to the last backup that you have made. If you value your data, run in ARCHIVELOG mode.

When the log switch occurs, the previous log file is copied to an archive log file (assuming that you are running in ARCHIVELOG mode). This archive log file, along with the online redo log file and the last backup, allows for database recovery.

Backup Process

When you perform a backup of the data files, you not only copy the data, but you also copy valuable header information that identifies the data file. The header information tells Oracle when the data file was last backed up and at which point in its operation it was when this backup occurred.

Oracle uses the information from the backup, the archive log files, and the online redo logs to recover the data to where it was when the system failure occurred. The backup feature is one of the things that makes Oracle such a powerful and robust RDBMS system.

As part of your ongoing backup process, it is important to keep all the archive log files safe and available in case a recovery is necessary. The archive log files allow you to restore your system to a point in time should it become necessary to recover the system.

Should you lose an archived log or if one becomes corrupt, recovery can only proceed up to that point in time and no further. That is why if you rely heavily on archived redo logs for recovery, you should take extreme precautions in preserving them. A missing file could mean substantial lost and unrecoverable data.

Recovery Process

If you are not running in ARCHIVELOG mode and a failure occurs, you can reload your database from the last full cold backup and start running from there. Oracle has no facility to recover further if you are not running in ARCHIVELOG mode.

If you *are* running in ARCHIVELOG mode and a failure occurs on a data file, you only have to restore the damaged data file from a recent hot or cold backup. It is not necessary to restore the entire tablespace unless you are not running in ARCHIVELOG mode.

When you bring the tablespace back online, Oracle prompts you to apply various archive log files. Using these files, Oracle restores all the changes made to this data file until the time of the media failure. In this manner, no data is lost, and minimal downtime is incurred.

If you have the Oracle Parallel Query option installed and have enabled parallel recovery, the time it takes to perform instance recovery can be greatly reduced. The Oracle backup and recovery process separates Oracle from its competition.

The Oracle redo log architecture and the archiving processes allow Oracle to recover from almost any failure. These features provide a high level of data integrity and robustness.

Characteristics of the Oracle Backup Process

Before looking at the specifics of the hot and cold backups, you should review a little of the operation of Oracle and how the backup process fits into this operation.

To characterize an Oracle backup, you should first understand how it operates in terms of both a hot backup and a cold backup. Because the cold backup is much simpler, you will learn about it first.

Cold (Offline) Backup Using User-Managed Backups

In a cold backup, the system is in a quiescent stage, the database is shut down, and no Oracle processes are running. The cold Oracle backup is sometimes referred to as an *offline backup*. To perform a backup, each of the data files is backed up as an OS file or raw partition. You can accomplish an offline backup by using an OS function or a third-party utility you might have purchased. It is important that you back up not only the data files, but also the redo log and control files.

In this kind of backup, each data file is read sequentially. Unless another OS function accesses the disks, you get purely sequential I/O. To take advantage of the sequential nature of the cold database backup, isolate the sequential I/Os by avoiding any other I/Os to that disk volume. Because several tablespaces might use the same volume, serialize the backup of those data files.

Hot (Online) Backup Using User-Managed Backups

When performing a hot Oracle backup, also referred to as a *hot backup*, the tablespace to be backed up is taken offline using the Oracle command ALTER TABLESPACE BEGIN BACKUP. The tablespace that is being backed up can still be modified, but all changes are kept in the SGA and are not written to the data files until the backup is complete. After the tablespace is brought offline with this command, the data files that are associated with that tablespace are backed up as OS files or devices. You can accomplish the backup by using an OS function or a third-party utility you might have purchased. You back up the control files in a slightly different manner.

To back up the control file, you use the Oracle command ALTER DATABASE BACKUP CONTROLFILE TO *'filename'* REUSE. This command copies the current control file to the file that is specified by *filename*. Back up the control file any time that the layout of the database changes.

In this kind of backup, each data file is read sequentially. Unless another OS function accesses the disks, you get purely sequential I/O. To take advantage of this sequential nature, isolate the sequential I/Os by avoiding any other I/Os to that disk volume. Compared to a cold backup, it is much more difficult to guarantee that no other I/Os are being done to the disk volumes during a hot backup because the database is still up and running. Because several tablespaces might use the same volume, you should serialize the backup of those data files.

Hot (Online) Backup Using the RMAN Utility

The RMAN utility allows the same functionality as the user-managed hot backup. The tablespace is backed up while users are still allowed to use and even modify the tablespace. Although the end result is the same, the ALTER TABLESPACE BEGIN BACKUP command is not used. RMAN uses its own internal functionality to allow it to perform the online backup.

The RMAN utility checks the footer of each data block while performing the backup. If the data block is in the process of being written to, the RMAN utility rereads the data block until it gets a complete (nonfractured) data block. In this manner, the RMAN utility can perform the hot backup without having to quiesce the tablespace using the ALTER TABLESPACE BEGIN BACKUP command. When you quiesce a database, you place it in a mode in which only DBA transactions, queries, fetches, or PL/SQL statements are allowed.

Hot (Online) Backup Using Storage Area Network Features

Many storage area network (SAN) storage systems include advanced features such as snapshots and cloning. These features allow you to quickly get a consistent picture of the storage system at a specific instance in time. To take advantage of these features, you still must acquiesce the database for the instant in time that you are performing this operation. To perform a snapshot or clone backup, perform the following steps:

1. Prepare the tablespace for backup using the ALTER TABLESPACE *tablespace_name* BEGIN BACKUP command.

2. Perform the snapshot or cloning operation using the SAN utilities.

3. Reset the tablespace to normal mode using the ALTER TABLESPACE *tablespace_name* END BACKUP command.

4. Using your SAN utilities, make the snapshot or clone available to either the same system or another system in your SAN.

5. Back up the tablespace's data files using OS or third-party utilities.

Using SAN utilities such as the snapshot or cloning operation, you can quickly perform the snapshot or cloning operation. You can then offload the actual backup of this data to another system for writing to backup media, or you can save it online in the event that a quick restore is necessary. SAN systems vary. Check the documentation of your SAN to determine the features and limitations of shapshot and cloning operations.

Data Access Patterns During User-Managed Backups

When performing user-managed backups, the actual reading of the database is done externally to Oracle. With both the hot and cold backups, purely sequential access is available to the data files by the backup process. When you isolate the sequential disk access, you can accomplish much higher I/O rates than when you access a disk volume in a random fashion. Because you want to do backups as quickly as possible, the highest I/O throughput is desired. Therefore, try to get as much sequential access as possible.

During a cold backup, you can control how the data is accessed on the disks by carefully designing the backup process. By serializing the backups so that one sequential data access exists per disk volume at a time, you can achieve good backup speeds. The preceding statement assumes that the media to which you back up can handle the load.

During a hot backup, you don't have as much control over how the data is accessed except through the design of the system. Because other tablespaces are active during the backup, if any of them has data files on the same disk volume as the one you are backing up, accesses to that disk volume will be of a random nature. If you can configure your system so that only one tablespace exists per disk volume, you can maintain the sequential data patterns of the backup process.

Data Access Patterns During RMAN Backups

The Recovery Manager actually uses the Oracle RDBMS to access the data to be backed up. Although the I/O operations have been optimized to perform the backup, the data blocks are still being read and processed. This approach has both advantages and disadvantages.

One main advantage of performing the backup using the Oracle RDBMS is that the entire tablespace or database needs to be read. Because RMAN is aware of the data within the database, only used blocks need to be read. In addition, because RMAN is controlling this operation, it can set up its own buffering and I/O operations so that they can be optimized for backup.

A disadvantage of using RMAN is that more processing is done to the data than during the user-managed backup. With the user-managed backup, the main load on the system is simply I/O to the disks that are holding the data. Less CPU is used because the data blocks are not analyzed or even looked at. The file is simply copied.

System Load During Backup

During the backup process, the load on the system is caused primarily by I/Os unless you are using compression for the backup. Compressing the data results in significant CPU usage. In fact, if you do a hot backup and you do not have sufficiently fast processors, you might be CPU-bound during the backup, and the backup might take even longer to perform. RMAN requires some additional CPU load as well, but the load is still primarily I/O.

Because the time it takes to perform the backup depends primarily on how fast you can read the data from the data files, you should minimize any external factors such as compression speed or network throughput if you want to run the backup at its full potential.

Backup Goals

The goal of the backup system is to back up the data files as quickly as possible. For a hot backup, it is important to get the data files back online as soon as possible. The backup operation should be an I/O-bound task. If the performance of the system is limited by the speed of your CPUs or by the throughput of your network, take steps to minimize these bottlenecks. Although speed is important, it is equally important for the backup to run completely without errors. Do not sacrifice completeness for speed. A fast backup that is missing files or has data corruption is useless.

By minimizing factors such as compression speed and network throughput, you can maximize the performance of the backup. The highest backup speed possible is the speed at which the data files are read in a purely sequential fashion. Of course, system overhead prevents you from reaching the theoretical maximum, but by minimizing this overhead and maximizing throughput, you should be able to approach this speed.

Both the hot and cold backup operations involve reading the data files and writing the data to the backup medium. The actual copying of the data is done using OS or third-party utilities. Oracle allows you to back up the system in the most optimal manner for your system.

You access the data in a mostly sequential manner (even for RMAN). If you isolate the I/Os either by serializing the data file backups (for cold backups) or by carefully partitioning data (for hot backups), you can achieve maximum performance. The following section looks at some of the system designs that can help you achieve maximum backup performance.

System Design Considerations

The following sections distinguish between the hot, or online, backup and the cold, or offline, backup and provide several hints on how to design your system for optimal backup performance. Some of these hints might or might not apply to your configuration. It is up to you to determine which ones apply to your system.

Cold Database Backup

In a cold database backup, the database is shut down and no users have access to the system. This situation is the best case for backup because it is up to the database administrator to determine how the database is backed up and how the data is accessed. This control makes it easier to optimize the system than is possible with a hot, or online, backup.

Because you have control over how the disks are accessed in a cold backup, you should design the backup procedure to take maximum advantage of sequential disk I/O to the backup storage device. By making the I/Os sequential, you can achieve a much higher throughput rate. The following sections examine how you can achieve sequential I/O.

Physical Data Access

The way to guarantee sequential I/O is to allow only one backup stream at a time to access a set of disks. If you use Oracle disk striping or RAID arrays, the concept is the same. For each disk drive or volume of disks, serialize the backup of the data files so that only one backup process at a time accesses it. Because multiple RAID volumes might exist on your machine, parallelize the backup operation on these devices by backing up all the disk volumes simultaneously.

For a cold backup, it is not necessary to change the design of the system because you eliminate all other database accesses to the data files by shutting down Oracle. By designing the backup procedure, you should be able to achieve optimal I/O rates.

Hardware/Software Considerations

When choosing hardware and software for backup, make your decisions with the following issues in mind:

- Fast tape device. The speed of the backup is most likely limited by how fast you can write to tape.

- Fast network device. If you are backing up the system through a network, make sure that your network hardware is not a limiting factor.

- Optimal software. Some third-party backup vendors are much faster than others. Make sure that you are getting good software for your platform.

- Optimal tuning. By adjusting values such as the block size you are using, you might be able to optimize disk and tape speeds.

- Compression. If you use compression, make sure that you are using an optimal compression method that has both high performance and a good compression ratio.

By optimizing all these areas, you should be able to achieve an excellent backup rate. Shop around for tape devices; you will find that some of the new tape devices have incredible performance characteristics.

Hot Database Backup

Hot database backup is more complex than cold database backup. In cold database backup, the backup is usually the only disk activity; in hot database backup, significant disk activity is occurring among the other data files in the system. To optimize the backup, you can do several things, all of which happen at the database and hardware design stage.

All the optimizations that you can make have the goal of shortening the amount of time that data files must be taken offline for the backup. These optimizations can include the following:

- Isolate sequential I/O. This might or might not be possible or effective. Put more than one tablespace on a disk volume unless the performance is sufficient during normal operation.

- Use temporary backup volumes (a staging area) to compensate for slower components such as network or tape. If possible, back up your database to local disk. After you bring your users back online, you can begin the task of backing up those files to the network or to tape.

- Use high-speed, isolated links between the database server and the backup server. By backing up the database via an isolated link, performance of the backup can be improved, as well as limiting the effect that the backup has on the network bandwidth.

- Split up backups. It is not necessary to perform the entire backup at one time. If necessary, perform the backup across several days.

These optimizations can help speed the backup process. Not all these hints might apply to your configuration; use the ones you think will benefit your particular system.

Physical Data Access

The following sections describe a few of the ways you can better configure your system to optimize the backup process. Some of the methods described might be impractical for your installation because of the additional hardware requirements. However, by understanding the concepts, you might be able to improvise a method that better suits your particular installation.

Isolating Tablespaces

By isolating data to a single tablespace per disk volume, you can take advantage of the sequential nature of the backup's I/O access patterns (assuming that very little read activity is occurring). Although this might seem to be a good way to get high-speed sequential I/Os from the disks, the system might suffer in the long run.

Because the tablespaces must also be used during the normal operation of the system, it might not be wise to limit the disk volumes to one tablespace. When you do this, you might have disk volumes that are either overutilized (causing an I/O bottleneck) or underutilized (causing some other disk volume to be overutilized).

For many applications, the best way to balance I/Os is to spread the tablespaces over all the available disk volumes. By having all the tablespaces on all the disk volumes, you have the best chance of balancing the I/Os, even if some tablespaces are more active than others.

Isolating the tablespaces so that you have only one tablespace data file per disk volume might help backup performance; however, the overall performance of the system might suffer. It is not recommended that you have only one tablespace data file per disk volume unless backup time is more critical than general RDBMS performance.

MINIMIZE THE IMPACT

Even if you have only one tablespace data file per disk volume, it is not guaranteed that the access to the disks will be sequential. If read activity is present on the tables within the tablespace that is being backed up, the access pattern to the data file changes from sequential to random. This can affect backup performance a great deal. It's best to minimize other activity on the systems while making backups.

Use of Temporary Backup Space or a Staging Area

Because access to the tablespace is deferred to the SGA for updates during the backup, it is essential that you finish the backup as soon as possible to get the table back to its normal state.

If you use a tape drive for the backup media, you might be constrained by the speed of the tape drive. If you use a network to back up the data to a network backup server, you might be constrained by the speed of the network. In both of these cases, you can minimize the time that the tablespace access must be deferred by backing up to a disk drive or set of disk drives that is reserved for this purpose. Even though you might not be able to get purely sequential I/Os out of the data files, you will be able to take advantage of sequential access to this temporary space.

After the data has been written to this temporary space, the tablespace can be brought back online and normal operations resumed. At this point, you can back up the data from the temporary space to the tape or network or even compress the data without significantly affecting performance to that tablespace.

After the data has been transferred off the RDBMS system, you can proceed to back up the next tablespace. In this way, you minimize the time that database operations are affected by the backup. Of course, some extra I/Os are associated with the backup files, but these are isolated to a separate disk volume. Compressing the data while it is still on the RDBMS system can significantly affect performance by taking large amounts of CPU time.

Isolate the Network

When performing backups across the network to another server or a dedicated backup server, it is important to keep in mind the large amount of network bandwidth that this backup can consume. Because large amounts of data are being transferred with large block sizes, the load can be significant.

By isolating the backup to its own network segment, you not only increase the performance of the backup, but you also reduce the effect that your backup has on other users on the network. Confining the backup to its own network segment isolates the effect of the backup to the segment that is used for the backup.

If multiple servers use the same network segment for backups, simple scheduling can reduce the load by spreading out the backups so that each system backs up at different times. If you need fast backups to multiple systems, you might have to segment the network further.

If possible, make this network as fast as possible. The network is often a backup bottleneck and can be eliminated by using faster network hardware. At the time of this writing, Gigabit networking was just becoming popular.

Hardware/Software Considerations

When selecting hardware and software for your backup tasks, try to get the best performing hardware that is currently available. Because backup is such a critical task, it is worth the extra expense to get the very latest hardware and software.

If you can perform only hot, or online, backups, you might want to invest in some extra disks to offload the data to temporary storage so that you can get the data files back online as soon as possible. If you perform your backups over a network, you should get fast network hardware such as Gigabit network hardware.

Your backup media (such as tape or optical storage) should perform at a rate necessary to do the backup in the specified amount of time. Upgrading your backup hardware to a faster tape device is always a good investment because both the speed and the quality of your backup is essential to your system.

BETTER SAFE THAN SORRY

Be sure to periodically test your backups to make sure that they function properly. The time of a failure is the wrong time to realize that your backups have been failing. This can prove to be quite an undertaking, but the results will pay off when you need it most.

REVIEW OF DESIGN CONSIDERATIONS

By carefully designing a backup plan that isolates sequential I/Os on a per-disk-volume basis, you can greatly enhance the performance of the cold backup. With hot backups, it is more difficult to isolate the I/Os because read activity still occurs on the data files during backup and because other data files might share the same disk volume.

By taking advantage of fast backup media (such as fast tape devices, optical storage, and fast network components), you can enhance the performance of the hot backup as well. If you are innovative and use a temporary disk storage device, you can reduce the time that the tablespace is offline and bring the system back to its full performance level as soon as possible.

Determine the Bottleneck

You can determine where the backup bottleneck might be using several methods. The different components that are typically bottlenecks include the following:

The I/O subsystem   The I/O subsystem is frequently a backup bottleneck. However, if the I/O subsystem is a backup bottleneck, it is quite possible that it is also a general performance bottleneck that you should address.

Network   The network is also a common cause for backup slowdowns. By knowing the speed of the network components, you can determine your backup throughput.

Tape drives   The tape drive is typically the slowest component in the backup system. You can use multiple backup devices or staging areas to help alleviate this.

Software overhead   Software in the backup system can also slow things down. Too much software in the path of the backup can add significant overhead.

Table 17.1 shows the throughput of some of the common backup components.

Table 17.1   *Backup Component Performance Characteristics* ———————

Component	Throughput (MBps)	Backup Rate (GB/hr)
Fibre channel bus	100MBps	351GB/hr
SAN controller (typical)	50MBps	175GB/hr
Add SAN overhead;		
file system, OS overhead	25MBps	87GB/hr
Speed per disk	8MBps (random I/O)	29GB/hr
GBit network	1Gbps	360GB/hr
100BASE-T network	100Mbps	36GB/hr
Tape drive (non-compressed)	4MBps	14GB/hr

As you can see, a wide range of performance characteristics exists. Choosing the correct components can drastically change your backup performance.

Tuning Considerations Using User-Managed Backups

When tuning for backups, no particular Oracle parameters can help you because Oracle allows you to use your OS or third-party backup utility to perform the backup; however, you can do a few things to improve the performance of the backup program.

Test various block sizes. Don't stop with the default block size that the backup program uses. By increasing the block size used both to read the data from disk and to write the data to tape, you might find enhanced performance. Increasing the value too high might degrade performance.

The optimal block size for backups varies based on your operating system, disk hardware, tape hardware, and OS. A good starting point is a 64K block size. By varying the block size and timing the backups, you should be able to determine the kind of effect that different block sizes have on your system.

If the time it takes to perform a backup is critical and you are not particularly concerned about the overall affect on the system, you can increase the priority of the backup process. Doing so ensures that the process always runs when it is ready; in some operating systems, increasing the backup's priority ensures that the job is never preempted. Although this might help reduce the time it takes to perform the backup, it is not recommended that you adjust process priorities because doing so might degrade performance.

Tuning Considerations Using RMAN Backups

With the Recovery Manager, you can tune backup and recovery in several ways. These tunables are mainly in the area of setting up additional processing and buffer resources for the Recovery Manager to use. In this section, you will learn how to tune the Recovery Manager as well as how to monitor backups using the Recovery Manager.

The RMAN Buffers

The Oracle RMAN process uses its own internal buffering to improve I/O performance. Both disk buffers and tape buffers are involved in this process. The number of these buffers is fixed to be four buffers per disk file and four buffers per tape channel. This number cannot be changed, but because it is fixed to the number of data files and tape devices, increasing the number of data files backed up at a time increases the number of buffers used for the backup operation. If you have multiple data files and sufficient hardware I/O capacity, you might see some improvement in overall backup and restore performance by doing this. In addition, increasing the number of tape devices that are written to simultaneously improves performance.

RMAN AND THE LARGE POOL

Recovery Manager will first try to get buffers from the large pool (if it is set) and then from the shared pool. Configuring the large pool will help RMAN performance in most cases.

Asynchronous Versus Synchronous I/O

The RMAN process can work in one of two ways. Using synchronous I/O, the operation of each backup process is synchronous; that is, it performs one operation at a time and waits for its completion before moving on to the next I/O operation. With asynchronous I/O, the request is submitted and the process continues. Eventually, it polls the OS to find out if the I/O has completed, and if it has, it finishes performing that particular request.

To set asynchronous I/O on for tape operations, set the Oracle initialization parameter BACKUP_TAPE_IO_SLAVES to TRUE. Doing so sets asynchronous I/O on. For systems that don't support asynchronous I/O within the operating system, Oracle simulates this functionality by setting the parameter DBWR_IO_SLAVES to a number. This number create I/O slaves that simulate asynchronous I/O.

RMAN Tuning Parameters

You can set a few additional parameters in the Recovery Manager to affect how it performs. You should carefully set these parameters to both enhance backup/restore performance as well as reduce excessive resource usage on the system.

RATE	This is the maximum number of bytes per second that RMAN reads on a channel. This can be used to throttle RMAN so that it doesn't use excessive system resources. Remember what happens to I/O performance when you overdrive the disk subsystem.
MAXOPENFILES	This controls the maximum input files that a backup can have open at any given time. Setting this can avoid error messages such as `too many open files` during backups.

Monitoring RMAN

One benefit of the Recovery Manager is that performance information is kept on the backup and restore operations. This information is kept in the performance views V$BACKUP_SYNC_IO and V$BACKUP_ASYNC_IO. These views contain information on what backup/restore operations have been done and how well they performed.

Synchronous I/O

The V$BACKUP_SYNC_IO view contains the column DISCRETE_BYTES_PER_SECOND. This is the average rate that the backup/restore operation took. If this number is less than the performance of the hardware devices, then something in the system should be tuned that might be causing additional overhead. Because synchronous I/O is a single-threaded operation, you don't have much to tune.

Asynchronous I/O

With asynchronous I/O, you can view more statistics. The LONG_WAITS and SHORT_WAITS values should be compared with the IO_COUNT value. Short waits are non-blocking waits and long waits are blocking waits. If these numbers are high in comparison with the total I/O count, then you might be experiencing an I/O or CPU bottleneck.

System Enhancements to Improve Backup Performance

You can enhance the system by adding faster backup devices such as faster tape devices, faster network hardware, or faster software. By using the fastest storage medium, you can significantly reduce the time it takes to perform the backup.

Don't assume that all backup software performs the same. The way that the software reads the data files as well as the algorithms that it uses for compression can greatly affect performance. By choosing a backup software package that performs well and has all the features you need, you can optimize your backup performance.

CPU Enhancements

Enhancing the CPUs on your SMP or MPP system can provide instantaneous performance improvements (assuming that you are not I/O bound). The speed of CPUs is constantly being improved, as are new and better cache designs.

Although the backup process primarily focuses on reading the disk and writing to another device, many backup programs include efficient compression options. Because you are usually limited by the speed of your tape drive and the speed of the network for network backups, compressing the data allows you to increase the performance of the backup by reducing the amount of data that must be transferred. If you have sufficiently fast CPUs, you can perform efficient compression. If you add CPUs to your system, you can reduce the effect that the backup or compression has on other users in the system.

Make sure that the speed of the CPUs is sufficiently fast to compress the backup data at a rate that meets or exceeds the performance of the slowest component in the backup process. Doing so guarantees that the compression process is not a bottleneck in the backup process. Testing this is simple. Back up a typical table both using compression and doing without compression and compare the results.

I/O Enhancements

By enhancing the I/O devices to be optimized, you can see significant performance increases during backup. Disk arrays allow you to perform a hot backup much more effectively than with traditional Oracle striping techniques. Using a sufficiently large block size to cause multiple disks to be active simultaneously can enhance the use of a disk array.

Another benefit of hardware disk arrays is caching. Most disk arrays on the market today offer some type of write or read/write cache on the controller. The effect of this cache is to improve the speed of writing to the disk as well as to mask the overhead that is associated with fault tolerance. Backup activities might see improved performance with disk controllers that take advantage of read-ahead features.

Read-ahead occurs when the controller detects a sequential access, reads an entire track or another large amount of data, and caches the additional data in anticipation of a request from the OS. Because this data can then be accessed almost immediately, having data in the controller cache can be a benefit.

IF YOU ARE BACKING UP TO DISK, TUNE IT

Several years ago, I went on a tuning assignment, and as a side project I was asked to look into backup and restore performance. The company was backing up to disk across the network and performance was slow. Upon further investigation, I found that the company was backing up to an old system that had only a few disk drives running RAID 5. This RAID 5 subsystem did not have a controller cache, and at the rate that the backup was going, the disks were heavily overloaded. In fact, on average, I/Os were taking in the hundreds of milliseconds.

The lesson here is that if you are backing up to disk, which is a good idea, make sure that the disk subsystem to which you are backing up can handle the load.

Enhancements to the I/O subsystem almost always help backups because large amounts of data are read during backups. Be sure that you have a high-speed I/O path that is properly configured. An I/O bottleneck is usually difficult to work around. A good third-party backup program can also be beneficial.

Network Enhancements

If you perform backups over a network, the speed of the network is extremely important, as is the amount of other traffic on the network. By segmenting the network into a production OLTP network and a backup network, you can see a decreased effect on the OLTP users and an increase in backup performance. This network segment should be of a high-performance variety, such as 100BASE-T or fiber optics.

The less time that you spend waiting for the network, the less time that the backup takes. Because it is easy to improve network performance by adding links, it is a good investment to try this.

Split Up the Backup

One way that you can minimize the performance impact due to backups is to split the backup into several portions. You can perform the backup on a tablespace basis; you can back up some tablespaces on one day and back up other tablespaces on other days. Doing so can reduce the amount of time that is required to perform the backup on a daily basis. However, the total time that is necessary to perform the backup remains the same.

When segmenting backups, you can decide which tablespaces have more critical data or are updated most frequently and back up those tablespaces more often than other, less-used tablespaces. In this manner, you can reduce the time it takes to restore your most critical data.

In the event of a system failure, remember that the time it takes to restore your data depends on when the last backup occurred and how much data has been modified or added to that table-space since that backup. By performing backups more frequently on active tables, you can reduce the time it takes to restore the system.

A reasonable schedule would allow you to perform hot backups during non-peak hours. You can split up the backup into several sessions. By doing this, you can perform a backup over several days, thus reducing the time each day that the system's performance is affected. If backup takes several days, you might want to back up the most active, critical data more often.

Following are some recommendations for segmenting backups:

- Perform hot backups in off-peak hours. Because the hot backup affects performance somewhat, you should arrange the backup so that it affects the fewest number of users.

- Make sure that your data is protected. Even if users are affected, you must maintain a level of protection that allows you to get back online as soon as possible in the event of a system failure. Wouldn't you rather have a few users grouse about the inconvenience caused by frequent backups than an entire corporation up in arms because you can't restore its data after a system failure?

- Back up heavily used data more often. The time it takes to recover depends on when the last backup occurred and how much data has been modified since that time.

- Back up critical data more often. If a system failure occurs, it might be important to get some critical tables back online first. If this is true in your implementation, you should back up those critical tables more often.

These recommendations should help you design a reasonable backup schedule to allow you to segment your backups and at the same time achieve reasonable recovery times. Of course, your system might have its own special requirements that must be addressed.

REVIEW OF SYSTEM ENHANCEMENTS

By carefully examining the characteristics of the backup system, you can enhance the performance in several ways:

- Additional CPU power can increase the performance of compression utilities, reducing the amount of data that must be written to tape or network.
- I/O enhancements, such as disk array, can help performance for both hot and cold backups.
- Network enhancements, such as a high-speed link, can reduce the time that it takes to transfer the data between machines.
- Splitting up backups across several days' off-peak hours can reduce the overall effect of the backup on users, while maintaining a reasonable recovery time.
- Other innovative enhancements such as hardware compression devices can be used to improve backup performance.

By taking advantage of enhancements to your system, you can improve the performance of your backup and reduce the time that the backup takes. In a cold backup, this reduces the time that the RDBMS is offline.

Performance Verification

After you design and build your system, you must have a way to verify performance. If you built your system for optimal backup/recovery performance, this task is quite simple.

The simplest method of verifying performance is to test the system using the backup process as the standard. It is not necessary to save a test database to test backup performance; simply measure the time it takes to perform your daily backups. Keep in mind that as the amount of data in your database grows, the time it takes to back up those tables also increases.

By periodically documenting the backup performance of the system and trying new parameters such as various block sizes, you might be able to fine-tune your backup process. I don't recommend that you change parameters on a production system that might put the backup at risk, but values such as block size incur no risk. The following sections look at what should be tested in the RDBMS and the operating system.

What to Test in the RDBMS

Whether you perform hot or cold backups, you cannot tune anything in the RDBMS to increase the performance of the backup. However, this is not the case if you are using the export utility to back up the system.

The export process *does* use the RDBMS to perform its function. The function of the export utility is to read data from the database and output that data to an OS file. An export does not require much tuning except with long rows. (In this case, you might want to increase the BUFFER parameter.)

By increasing the size of the BUFFER parameter, you might see some performance improvement. Perform the same export using different values for the BUFFER parameter and note any differences in performance.

What to Test in the OS

You can perform various tests in the OS to verify and increase the performance of the backup process:

- Data disk read performance. By testing the process of reading from the data disk drives, you can determine an optimal block size. Many disk drives and disk array controllers have a certain block size that is optimal.

- Tape write performance. By writing data to the tape drive using various methods and block sizes, you can determine the optimal configuration.

- Network configuration. It might be possible to tune the network so that you can use larger network packets to cut down on the number of packets to be sent.

- Optimized backup software. By using the most efficient OS facility or third-party utility, you can increase performance of the backup.

- Optimized compression techniques. Using a modern, high-performance compression algorithm can improve performance and efficiency.

An improvement in any of these areas can add an incremental performance improvement to your backup process. The following sections examine some of these areas in more detail.

Disk Block Size

Many disk drives and disk array controllers have a certain block size that is optimal. By reading the data file and discarding the data, you might be able to find the optimal block size for your particular configuration. With some disk array controllers, having a sufficiently large disk request allows multiple disks to service that request simultaneously.

During a backup operation, large block sizes (such as 64K) are not unreasonable. With some devices, a block size even larger than this might be acceptable. When the block size gets too large, performance begins to degrade because internal OS buffers have been overflowed or the request has been split up by the controller's device driver into smaller pieces, causing additional overhead. By testing various block sizes, you can determine what is optimal for your specific configuration.

Tape Block Size

Different types of tape drives have different characteristics. In determining the proper block size for your tape drive, the goal is to keep the tape streaming. When the tape drive is streaming, it is continually moving and writing data to the tape. If the tape drive is not fed data quickly enough, the tape stops, rewinds a short amount, and starts up again when more data arrives.

Even though data might be arriving at the tape device at a certain rate, the rate at which it is written to tape might be degraded because the tape is stopping and starting. This phenomena is known as "shoe-shining" or "rocking" because the tape must move back and forth over the tape head for the data to be written contiguously to the tape.

By feeding data to the tape at a fast enough rate to stream the tape, you can see significant improvements in performance. Any time the tape has to stop and back up, performance is degraded. Providing a large enough block size and buffering data is important in helping improve tape performance.

Try various block sizes when the tape is streaming to see what is optimal for your particular hardware. If the tape is not streaming, this test is not really valid because performance is severely degraded by the shoe-shining effect.

Network Packet Size

By using larger network packets, you can transmit the same amount of data with fewer packets. Because an inherent overhead is associated with each network packet, reducing the number of packets enhances the overall performance. The size of the network packets is typically not an OS issue, but an issue of the backup software you are using. It might be necessary, however, to increase the maximum allowable network packet size to accommodate your backup software.

If you use larger network packets, you can typically use more of the bandwidth of the network. When a typical Ethernet network card wants to transmit on the network, it first checks to see whether a packet is currently being transmitted. If the network is busy, the card waits a specified period of time and then tries to transmit again. If you use many small packets, it is more likely that the network will be busy than if you use a few large packets; with the larger packets, more time usually exists between transmissions.

The efficiency of larger packets provides better performance. If network bandwidth is still an issue, consider adding an isolated segment for backups or going to a faster network controller such as 100BASE-T or fiber optics.

Backup Software

The choice of OS or third-party backup programs can be important. Don't be influenced solely by the flashiness of the GUI or the number of features in the backup software. The features that are included in many of the backup packages are important, but they should not overshadow the product's performance.

The main goal in backing up your database is to protect your data and to disrupt the user community as little as possible. To do this, the backup software should be high performance and reliable. The integrity of your system depends on the reliability of your backups. Measure the performance of your backup software periodically and test the backups to make sure that everything is working properly.

The performance of your backup software can depend on the configurability of the product. Make sure that you can adjust the block size of both data reads and tape writes so that you can optimally tune for your particular devices.

High-Performance Compression

Vast improvements have been made in compression algorithms over the past few years. By using a high-performance compression algorithm in your backup procedure, you can improve the efficiency of the backup. By using a fairly recent version of your backup software, you will most likely be taking advantage of the most optimal compression techniques. Many of the components of the backup (such as the network or tape device) have a maximum data rate. By using compression to reduce the amount of data to be written to these devices, the entire data file can be written to the device more quickly.

Your performance might suffer if the compression causes you to become CPU bound. If you have a sufficient number of CPUs that are fast enough to keep the tape or network device running at maximum efficiency, compression can be a beneficial part of your backup procedure.

You can verify the performance of your CPUs by backing up the same data file both with and without compression and comparing the performance. Keep in mind that many tape devices have hardware compression built in. If you compress the data before sending it to the tape device, the efficiency of the hardware compression might be reduced, nullifying any beneficial effect of OS or software compression.

The only way to know whether compression can be beneficial is to try backing up with and without it. After you have determined the beneficial value of compression, you can concentrate on other areas of enhancement.

Summary

This chapter looked at how backups work in the Oracle system and at some of the ways you can enhance the performance of your backups. With mission-critical systems that must be available 24 hours a day, 7 days a week, backup and recovery performance is crucial. By increasing the performance of the backup, you shorten the amount of time that users see some sort of degraded performance caused by the backup.

CREATING A HIGH-PERFORMANCE DISASTER SURVIVAL SYSTEM

18

Creating a system that can survive a failure or disaster is important to most companies. In the event of a catastrophic failure, it is important that your company has a contingency plan and systems in place to ensure that you can still continue taking orders or processing data. In lieu of this, you might face costly downtime or even permanent loss of data.

This chapter takes you through disaster survival concepts, planning for a disaster, and recovering from a disaster. In addition, it teaches you how to create these types of systems in an efficient and optimally performing manner. By putting together an optimally performing disaster survival system, you will be able to survive a disaster with minimal overhead.

Parameters Used in This Chapter

This chapter includes the use of many Oracle initialization parameters. Chapter 2, "Using the Oracle Configuration Parameters," introduced you to these parameters and explained how to use them. In this chapter, the following initialization parameters are covered:

- RECOVERY_PARALLELISM. RECOVERY_PARALLELISM specifies the number of processes to use for instance recovery. This number can be up to the value of PARALLEL_MAX_SERVERS.

- PARALLEL_MAX_SERVERS. PARALLEL_MAX_SERVERS specifies the maximum number of parallel processes to use in query and recovery processing.

Why Plan for a Disaster?

You might ask why special planning for a disaster is important. You might already be using a RAID disk subsystem and perform regular backups. Why is anything else needed? In many different scenarios, backup tapes and RAID systems won't protect you. These scenarios include the following:

- Weather. A hurricane might cause your entire installation, city, or even county to be closed down for days or even weeks. When your computer center is without power for weeks at a time, it might be impossible to keep that center running.

- Communication outage. With a condition such as weather or a technical difficulty, your computer center might be without network communication for extended periods of time. This might effectively remove your ability to function as a company.

- Fire. You might lose your entire computer center in a disaster such as a fire. Regardless of the type of fire control system that you have, you still might lose your entire center.

In each of these cases, not only might your installation be closed, but the entire area might be closed down, making it impossible for your company's employees to make it to work. In any of these cases, you must have a plan in place to stay in business.

Disaster Survival Concepts

The basic concept behind disaster survival is to have some sort of contingency plan so that your computer system and applications can continue to function in the event of a disaster. This typically involves keeping an additional system at a remote location that can be used to continue operations in the event of a disaster. This can be done in several ways:

- Remote mirroring of data. Using hardware, you can mirror data at remote sites.

- Oracle9i Data Guard. Using Oracle9i Data Guard, you can keep a remote system at an equivalent level to the primary system by using Oracle recovery principles.

- Replication. Using replication, you can keep systems in sync.

Each of these solutions provides some level of disaster survival ability, but each functions in a different way and might or might not be able to provide the solution that you need.

Remote Mirroring

Most storage area network (SAN) systems support remote mirroring functionality. This feature allows data on the local disk subsystem to be automatically mirrored to a remote site. With most of these disk subsystems, the remote site can be several kilometers away if you're using fiber optics, and unlimited distances away if you're using asynchronous transfer mode (ATM) or the Internet for the interconnect.

This SAN functionality allows you to automatically keep an up-to-the-minute copy of your data at a remote site in a different location. However, it has some limitations. The remote mirroring features of most SAN systems do not allow you to access the remote copy while it is in the remote mirroring mode. In the event of a failure, the system can be automatically or manually failed over to a secondary system, but it is not available online during the mirroring process.

It is usually possible, however, to take snapshots or clones of this mirrored disk and then access the snapshot or clone. A snapshot is used to take a current copy of the data at a specific point in time. A clone is similar. With the snapshot, only changed data is copied to the snapshot drive; the clone causes all data to be copied. In either case, the snapshot or clone can be assigned to another system for access.

This method can also be used to produce system backups with little or no downtime on the primary system. A snapshot or clone can be created on the storage system after putting the tablespace into backup mode. After the snapshot has been created and assigned to another server, the Oracle database files can be backed up without affecting the performance of the primary system.

Several hardware vendors support this type of remote mirroring with their SAN systems. Check with your hardware vendor to verify the functionality before investing in this type of system. These systems are complex and require much work to install and configure them to work properly. In most cases, the hardware vendor will offer services to help you configure your system for remote mirroring.

Oracle9i Data Guard

The Oracle9i Data Guard feature is built on the Oracle8i Standby Database and is an excellent option for disaster recovery. This option does not require special hardware, but it does require some type of high-speed link between the primary and standby site. An illustration is shown in Figure 18.1.

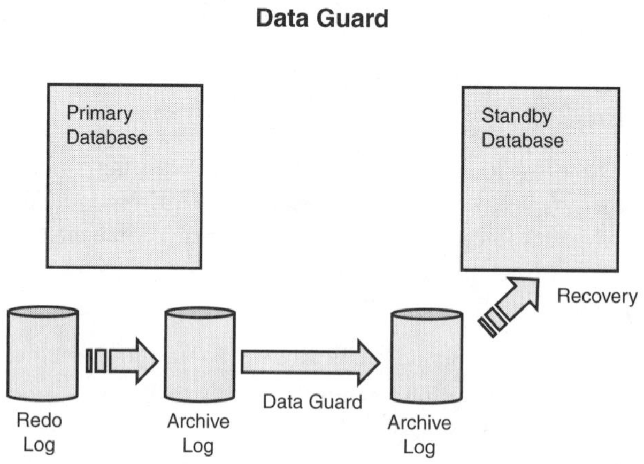

FIGURE 18.1
Oracle9i Data Guard.

The Data Guard feature takes an Oracle backup, restores that backup on a system other than the primary system, and then uses transaction log backups to keep the standby system up-to-date with the latest archive log file. This enables the database to be kept almost up-to-date with the primary database. Because the standby database is using archive log files, it is not exactly up-to-date; it lags by one redo log file, which has both advantages and disadvantages.

The disadvantage of lagging by one redo log file is that in the event of a disaster, you might not be able to retrieve the online redo log file. You must put the standby system into production without the latest changes to the database. This will probably cause some loss of business that has recently been done.

The advantage of the lag is that a human error, such as the deletion of a table or data, can be avoided by not applying those changes to the database. This enables you to recover from human or application errors that might destroy data inadvertently. Because you have the lag of one redo log file, you have a short window to avoid that type of problem.

The Data Guard feature works in one of two modes: Physical Standby and Logical Standby. Physical Standby is more efficient than Logical Standby, but Logical Standby has some additional features that Physical Standby does not. The next section describes Physical and Logical Standby modes.

Physical Standby

Physical Standby is similar to the Oracle8i Standby Database feature. The archive log files are applied to the standby database and the Oracle recovery mechanisms are used to restore the database up to the point of that archive log file. The recovery mechanisms are efficient because they work on the block level. Because of this mode of recovery, the Physical Standby mode allows you to open the database in read-only mode, but not in read/write mode.

Logical Standby

The Logical Standby mode actually takes the archive log files and transforms the log records back into SQL transactions. Because the recovery uses SQL transactions, other processes and users can also work with this database in read-write mode. Therefore, with Logical Standby mode, the database can be open and available to users while it is acting as a standby system.

The Archive Log Files

The Oracle9i Data Guard Broker is used to copy the archive log files from the primary system to the standby system, apply these logs, and initiate failover in the event of a failure. This primary process is performed externally to the Oracle9i RDBMS; as such, it does not have specific tuning parameters. However, the general concept of both Physical and Logical Standby is to copy the online redo log files and then apply them to an Oracle database. Some tuning can be done to enhance this process. Tuning Oracle9i Data Guard is covered in the next section.

Tuning Data Guard

Data Guard is not tuned, but the functions that are involved in the Oracle9i Data Guard process can be tuned. The main areas involved in tuning Data Guard involve the following components:

- The Archivelog process. The Archivelog process on the primary system performs in the same manner as archiving does in a non–Data Guard system. When the redo log file is filled, a log switch occurs. The previous redo log file is archived to the archive log area. By making sure that a disk bottleneck does not occur on either the redo log volume or the archive log volume, you improve Data Guard performance.

- Data transmission. After the Archivelog process has completed, the data must be copied to the standby server. By making sure that your interconnect (network) between the primary and standby servers is of a sufficient bandwidth to keep up with redo log activity, you will have a well-performing system.

- Recovery process. On the standby system, you can tune the recovery process by using the initialization parameter RECOVERY_PARALLELISM (if you are using physical standby). This improves the recovery process performance.

- Database. On the standby system, you might need to tune the database for insert, update, and delete activity. If the I/O subsystem and Oracle cache cannot keep up with this activity, you will experience performance problems. The standby system should be of equivalent performance of the primary system.

You can tune the actual process of the Oracle Data Guard option in a few different ways.

Replication

Replication can also be used to create a standby system. By replicating data among several servers, in the event of a failure or an inability to communicate with one of the servers, the other server can also serve the requested data. Replication is more real-time than Data Guard because data is replicated on an as-needed basis rather than at log switch time. An illustration of Oracle Replication is shown in Figure 18.2.

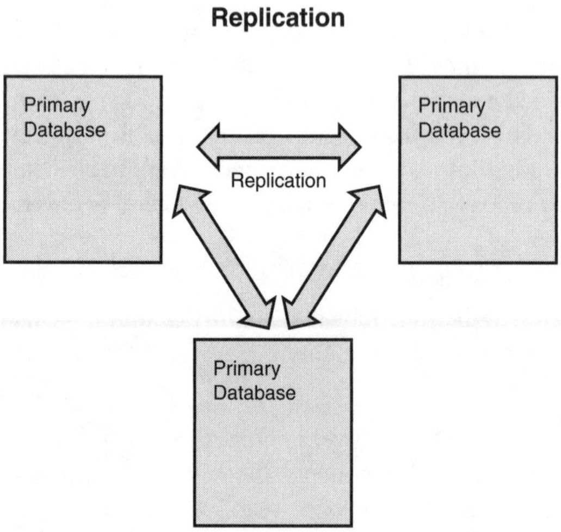

Replication

FIGURE 18.2
Oracle9i replication.

As with Data Guard, the main tuning that is done within replication is to tune the system for the workload as well as to properly size and tune the I/O subsystem and network.

Planning for a Disaster

Probably the most important thing that you can do to prepare for a disaster is to plan and document carefully. Planning and testing of that plan ensure that the disaster recovery scheme will work. Documentation of the disaster survival plan ensures that the plan can be implemented even though the author and designer of the plan might not be present at the time. You must take several steps into account when developing your disaster survival plan. These steps are listed in the next section.

Planning Steps

When planning the disaster survival plan, you must take into account your own needs and system requirements. No two disaster survival plans are alike because everyone's application and database is different. You must take several factors into account:

- The criticality of your data. How important is it to recover every transaction?

- The allowable downtime. The allowable downtime influences the type of disaster survival plan that you implement.

- The makeup of your company. If your company is small and in one location, your options are limited.

- The cost of downtime versus full recoverability. Sometimes, you must choose between getting up and running quickly versus recovering all transactions.

These different requirements influence your options for disaster survival.

Data Criticality

How critical is your data? If you are primarily running reports and do not often update your data, it might be sufficient to restore a new system with your data to recover. If the data can be easily re-entered into the system without an extreme effort, it might be sufficient to ship backups offsite and not even have a standby system. It is also important to weigh the cost of the survival plan versus the benefits.

Allowable Downtime

The allowable downtime is important to your decision on how to implement and plan the disaster survival plan. If you can only be down for a few minutes or an hour at most, some sort of remote mirroring might be the only solution for your requirements. This solution will keep the data up-to-date and can usually bring a failover site up in a few minutes to an hour.

Company Locations

If your company is located in one town and has no satellite locations, it might not be feasible to implement a backup data center. In this case, you might be limited to offsite backups and uninterruptible power supplies (UPSs) as your best hopes to survive a disaster.

Downtime Versus Recoverability

You might also consider whether it is more important to be back up and running quickly or to preserve all transactions. Oracle9i Data Guard can have you up and running in seconds or minutes, but depending on the type of disaster, you might not be able to recover all your data.

These are all ideas that you should consider when planning for your disaster survival scenario.

Documentation

No matter what type of plan you choose, it is important to properly document it. Not only should the documentation include the steps necessary to initiate a failover, but it should also include emergency contact information as well as a complete diagram of the system and its components. Following is a list of what should be included in your documentation:

- System hardware. List all the components that make up the system. This way, if your system needs to be reordered and rebuilt, you know what to get.

- System software. Include versions of the OS, all patches that you have installed, and all the applications that have been installed.

- Failover steps. In the case of failover for disaster survival, include the steps necessary to perform the failover in your documentation.

- Contact list. Include a list of people to notify as well as people to call if you need help.

- Escalation instructions. Include cases where the implementer should call for help. Take the guesswork out of your disaster survival plan.

These ideas should help you develop outstanding documentation for your disaster survival plan.

Scenarios

The following sections offer a few ideas for implementing a disaster survival plan, starting with simple and inexpensive plans and increasing in cost and complexity.

Offsite Backup

Even the most basic and simple disaster survival plan must include offsite storage of backup media. This can be done either by sending tapes offsite or by transmitting the backup data to a remote system via a network connection. If your computer center was to burn down and your backup media was on location, you might lose all of your backups as well as your systems.

Log Shipping via Tape

Oracle9i Data Guard is set up to be automatic and to transfer archive log files for you across the network and automatically apply them on the standby server. If you do not have a network connection fast enough to do this, it is possible to have the same effect by shipping tapes of the archive log files via an overnight carrier. This enables you to have a backup site with yesterday's data ready in the event of a failure.

Oracle9i Data Guard

Data Guard is an excellent way to implement a standby server. However, you must have a link sufficiently fast enough to handle all the archive log traffic. This might mean implementing a T1, T3, or ATM connection between data centers, which can be quite costly. Data Guard allows you to keep these systems almost identical and can quickly be used to bring a standby data center online.

Remote Mirroring

Probably the most costly (and most effective) way to implement a disaster recovery plan is by using SAN features such as remote mirroring of data. Unfortunately, this is a time-consuming and often expensive procedure. In addition to the SAN hardware and software, many of these systems require an ATM connection, which can be expensive.

Recovering from a Disaster

As mentioned earlier in this chapter, recovering from a disaster is really about planning. The better the planning is, the better the implementation will be. If you have a well-documented, well-planned disaster survival plan, you should easily be able to quickly and orderly implement that plan.

Usually, implementing the plan means activating a remote data center and bringing in employees to man it. If your company is large enough you might have a DBA staff at the remote data center. If not, it might be impossible to get people from the main center over to the remote site if weather or other problems are a factor.

The better the plan and the documentation, the more successful the failover will be. This plan should be practiced or at least walked through with the staff of the remote data center so that they will not be surprised by any of the required steps.

Tuning Standby Systems

Not much specific tuning is done in the disaster survival plan. The key performance issues are the capacities of both the interconnect between the main and standby data centers and the network access to the data center from the Internet. Following are a few points to consider when designing, configuring, and tuning the disaster survival system:

- Interconnect bandwidth. If you are using a disaster survival plan such as remote mirroring or Data Guard, you must have sufficient bandwidth to copy the data from the primary site to the remote (standby) site. If you cannot copy the standby data quickly enough, you might not only reduce your ability to survive a disaster, but you might also reduce the performance of your main site. Remote mirroring capabilities within a SAN can often cause performance problems if they cannot keep up with the amount of data that is being changed.

- Site Internet connectivity. If your business is run via the Internet, you must ensure that the path that your customers take to access your system is of sufficient bandwidth that it can keep up with demand. Just because a disaster has occurred does not mean that the amount of orders from your customers has slowed down.

- I/O capacity. Sometimes, the standby server is underconfigured because it will most likely not be used. This is a great cost-savings measure, but in the event that it does need to be used, you will experience performance problems.

- Data Guard usage. With the Data Guard solution, you can use the standby server as a reporting server or for another use. If you intend to do this, you should configure and tune that system for the type of activity for which you will be using it as well as for the type of activity that the main site sees.

- Guard your survival systems. Ensure that your disaster survival systems have the same type of protection that you might put on your main systems. Use a UPS, keep it in a temperature controlled data center, and keep that system secure. Your business might depend on these systems.

- Keep the plan handy. Ensure the availability of several printed copies of your disaster survival plan to whomever might need them. Keep the plan up-to-date and note any changes to the system.

These tips should help you develop, configure, and tune your disaster recovery system effectively.

Summary

This chapter was written to help you develop a working disaster survival plan. It included a number of tips, scenarios, and information on different types of products that can help you. However, each system is different because each hardware vendor's offerings are unique. Decide what is right for you and plan ahead. It is too late to start planning after a disaster has happened.

Depending on your particular needs and your tolerance to downtime, you have many different options. As with most things in life, the better the solution, the more expensive it is. Many of the SAN systems that you can purchase today have nice fault tolerance and business continuance features.

ORACLE NETWORKING PERFORMANCE

One of the most common bottlenecks in the Oracle system is the network. The I/O subsystem and the network are often the slowest components in the system. The problems that are normally encountered within the network are not within the Oracle RDBMS network components, but with the hardware. The network has a finite bandwidth that is shared among many users on the network and can easily be overloaded.

By understanding how the network hardware and software operate, you can understand what affects the performance of the network and why. The chapter starts by looking at the different types of network hardware and software that are available. In addition, this chapter explores the Oracle network components and ways that you can monitor and tune those components.

Network Architecture

The network is made up of many components, both hardware and software, and can vary in function. Several different types of networks are available on the market today, including Ethernet, Token Ring, fiber optics, and some new technologies such as asynchronous transfer mode (ATM). On top of these different hardware layers lies the OS device driver, the network protocol layer, and finally Net9 (see Figure 19.1).

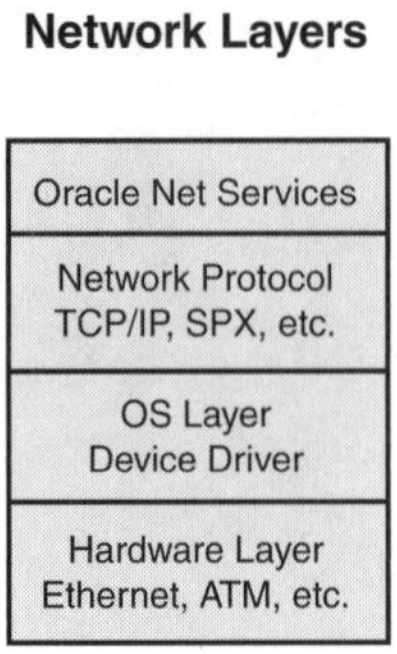

Network Layers

| Oracle Net Services |
| Network Protocol
TCP/IP, SPX, etc. |
| OS Layer
Device Driver |
| Hardware Layer
Ethernet, ATM, etc. |

FIGURE 19.1
Network layers.

For the SQL request to be sent from the client to the server, the request must go through each of these layers on both the client and the server. The following sections describe these components in more detail.

Hardware Components

At the lowest layer of the network subsystem lies the network hardware. This hardware can be of various types that provide different functionality and characteristics. Probably the most popular of these network types are Ethernet and Token Ring.

Ethernet

Ethernet is probably the most popular of the network protocols. Ethernet has been around since the early days of computer networking. The Ethernet standard includes various types of wiring (such as twisted pair and coaxial) and speeds (a standard speed of 100 megabits per second [Mbps] for most Ethernet and 1 gigabit per second [Gbps] for the newer hardware).

Ethernet is standards based, which means that multiple vendors can build Ethernet NICs, hubs, routers, and so on that all work together, regardless of the brand. An Ethernet network is built around the idea that all machines on an Ethernet segment have equal access to the network. As long as the network is available, the NIC can use it (see Figure 19.2).

Ethernet Network

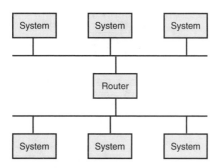

FIGURE 19.2
An Ethernet network.

The NIC sends the data in a structure called an *Ethernet packet* or *frame*. These packets contain not only the data network protocol information, but also information that the NIC has sent concerning the packet and the receiving NIC's address. When a packet is sent, all NICs or routers on the network receive the packet. Each NIC performs a quick check; if the packet is not addressed for that NIC, the packet is quickly discarded. If the packet is indented for the NIC, further processing is done.

The Ethernet packet contains a *network packet* that the network protocol driver generates. Additional Ethernet information is placed around this network packet to create an Ethernet packet. The network protocol being used determines the structure of the packet.

When the device driver sends a network packet to the NIC to be sent across the network, the NIC checks to see whether traffic is currently on the network. If the network is busy, the NIC waits a while and then tries again. The packet is stalled waiting for the network and is referred to as a *deferred packet*.

When the NIC believes that the network is available, it sends out the packet. The NIC ensures during the sending of the packet that no other NIC initiates a transmission at the same time. If another NIC had sent a packet at the same time, a *collision* occurs. When a collision occurs, both NICs must wait a small amount of time and try to re-send their packets. The contents of any sent packets that have experienced a collision are discarded.

When a collision occurs and the packet has to be re-sent, performance is degraded. Although the effect of a single collision is small and hardly noticed, the effect of thousands of collisions *is* noticeable. Collisions prevent the true bandwidth potential of an Ethernet network from being reached. The closer you get to the bandwidth of the Ethernet network, the higher the chance of collision and delays, as shown in Figure 19.3. This figure is the standard queue depth versus utilization relationship that you might have seen before.

Queue Depth vs. Utilization

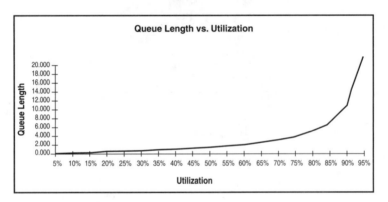

FIGURE 19.3
Queue depth versus utilization.

As the network is driven closer to its maximum bandwidth, the number of collisions increases exponentially. The more traffic that the network has, the more likely it is that your packet will collide with another packet. Therefore, even though your network might be able to theoretically handle 10Mbps, it is unlikely that you will ever achieve this rate. These factors make collisions more likely:

- Numerous connections. If many NICs are on the LAN segment, you are more likely to see collisions because it is almost guaranteed that a NIC will be transmitting.

- Small packet sizes. If the packet size is small, more packets are likely to exist, thereby increasing the collision rate.

Smaller packets have a greater chance of having more wasted time between packets (that is, time during which no network activity exists). With larger packets, the network has more activity. Larger packets are more efficient and perform better.

As you will see later in this chapter, you can avoid collisions and increase the performance of an Ethernet network by segmenting the network and reducing overhead.

Network Protocols

Several popular network protocols are in use today, including Transmission Control Protocol/Internet Protocol (TCP/IP), SPX/IPX, Banyan Vines, AppleTalk, and NetBIOS. This chapter focuses on the two most popular network protocols: TCP/IP and SPX/IPX. TCP/IP has been in use since the early days of computer networking and is probably the most popular of the network protocols.

The network protocol is responsible for the network communication between the different nodes in the network. The network protocol defines how the messages are sent, who receives them, and how or if the data is routed to other machines or networks. The network protocol is also the determining factor about what other applications or protocols can be layered on top of it.

TCP/IP

TCP/IP is the most popular network protocol in use today; it runs on virtually every computer system and operating system. As do the hardware devices, the network protocol wraps the data within a structure called an *IP packet*. This packet contains information such as the machine's IP address, the address to which the packet is being sent, and the routing information.

TCP/IP has an addressing protocol used to facilitate routing of IP packets. The address is in the form www.xxx.yyy.zzz and is a standard. Typically, the first three sets of numbers, www.xxx.yyy, are used to identify the subnet on which the machine is located; the final numbers, zzz, are used to uniquely identify the computer system. Each of the sets of numbers is eight bits and is known as an *octet*.

For machines on the Internet, the first two octets are registered and are unique to your corporation. The last two octets are available for your own use. Having two octets allows you to divide your network into subnets. A *subnet* is an individual isolated portion of your network.

When communicating from a system on one subnet to a system on another subnet, it is necessary to go through a router. It is common for the router to be a bottleneck in the system because the router is an active component that must take data from one subnet, process it, and then send it out on another subnet. On a busy system, this can become a bottleneck and add delays. Although the user will not normally notice this delay, performing operations such as backup over a router might cause a noticeable delay.

SPX/IPX

SPX/IPX are network protocols designed by Novell to support the NetWare operating system. Because NetWare was originally designed around file and print services, it required a high-speed network subsystem. As such, the SPX/IPX protocols are lightweight and have high performance.

Even though SPX/IPX were originally designed for file and print services, they work well with SQL*Net. Not only do they provide compatibility with the NetWare server, but they also are high-performance network transfer protocols. If you operate in a NetWare network, you can easily take advantage of SPX/IPX by using Oracle and SQL*Net as well as NetWare directory services.

Tuning the Network Components

In the first part of this chapter, you learned about the components that make up the physical network. After you have quantified the limitations of the network, you can design a network to function within those limits.

Network performance problems often occur because the bandwidth of the network has been exceeded. The network can only support a certain amount of traffic. After that limit is reached, the network experiences delays. In turn, these delays can cause noticeable increases in response times.

You can do a few optimizations to the OS to tune performance, but these fall into the category of fine-tuning. You cannot really do much to the OS to overcome the limitations of the network.

NETWORK LIMITATIONS

When I talk about the limitations of the network, I am referring to the actual limitations of the medium you are using, usually the bandwidth of the connection. If you use traditional Ethernet, this limitation is 10Mbps. If you use Fast Ethernet, the limit jumps to 100Mbps. If you use gigabit Ethernet, the limitation is an incredible 1000Mbps.

Software and hardware standards and the limitations of the hardware fix the network limits. You cannot increase the limits of these mediums. By knowing your limitations, you can design your network to fit within the bounds. When the application and database need data more quickly than the medium can supply it, the network becomes a bottleneck.

The next section starts by discussing some of the tuning you can do to the network software. The following sections provide some design hints to help you put together a high-performance network. By properly designing the network segments to handle the requested load, you can enhance the performance of the system.

Software Tuning

You can do little or no tuning in the operating system to improve network performance. Hopefully, your operating system vendor has optimized the network components so that they are efficient. Some operating systems don't have tuning parameters. However, you *can* tune a few things in Oracle to improve performance.

Oracle Tuning

The best way to improve network performance in software is to design your application to eliminate the transmission of unwanted and unnecessary data. By using stored procedures, you not only reduce the amount of data transmitted, but you also improve performance by taking better advantage of the shared SQL areas.

Only retrieve useful data from your stored procedures and queries. Any unnecessary data that is transmitted from the server to the client wastes valuable network bandwidth.

Another way to reduce network traffic within Oracle is to take advantage of local tables. If part of your data is never updated and is heavily used locally, you might benefit from replicating the data to your client machine. The replicated data not only reduces network traffic, but it also speeds access to the data. Another way is materialized views (formerly snapshots) of data, which do not have to be completely current and can be one or more days old.

Optimize the amount of data that is transmitted across the network as much as possible. You should also streamline the network subsystem in the operating system to provide optimal performance. If you still have a network bottleneck, your only alternative is to increase the bandwidth of the network.

Network Design

As you have seen, you have only a few options in the operating system and the application to improve network efficiency. The majority of the performance improvements are accomplished by reducing the load on a particular component in the network. Primarily, you can improve performance by subnetting—that is, by segmenting the load among several different segments.

The other alternative to increasing the bandwidth of the network is to purchase faster network hardware. By upgrading from 100BASE-T to gigabit, you instantaneously see substantial improvement in bandwidth. In many cases, your network wiring might already be able to handle the faster gigabit networks.

You should use a network load monitor on a regular basis to determine whether you are near the limits of the network. Do some trend analysis to determine where the majority of network traffic is originating. You might discover that a certain operation (such as backups or loads) uses a large percentage of the network bandwidth and should be segmented off the main network.

If you keep the network usage within limits, the network should not be a bottleneck. As mentioned in Chapter 18, "Creating a High Performance Disaster Recovery System," as you near the limits of an Ethernet network, the number of collisions increases exponentially. It is a good idea to segment these types of networks so that you never exceed 60–70% of the available bandwidth.

Bandwidth Considerations

The *bandwidth* of the network represents the theoretical maximum of data throughput that can be achieved by the network medium. For Ethernet, this is 10Mbps. By using larger packets, you can achieve a maximum throughput that is much closer to the theoretical limit than you can with small packets. The more computers that try to access the network, the less likely you are to reach the maximum throughput because of the increased likelihood of collisions.

When your network load reaches 60–70% of the bandwidth of the network, you will begin to see a fairly high collision rate. At this point, the performance of the network starts to be affected. If possible, try to keep the network usage below 60%. Of course, in peak times, the network will have high usage, but in general, try to keep the load in this range.

The only way to increase the bandwidth of the network is to upgrade to a faster type of network hardware, such as gigabit Ethernet or ATM. The available bandwidth of the network is based on the type of hardware you are using. The speed of the LAN segment is based on standards. By standardizing the speeds, you can add different hardware components supplied by different hardware vendors, and they will all work on your network.

Segmenting the Network

The best way to reduce the amount of traffic on your network is to use subnetting or segmenting. Subnetting involves breaking the network into smaller individual LAN segments. By breaking the LAN into smaller segments, you divide the network load among the segments and reduce the load on individual segments.

By reducing the load on individual segments, you reduce collisions and avoid performance degradation. When the network is segmented, you might have to deploy routers. Routers are used to pass network packets between different subnets.

Although most operating systems can perform routing, doing so uses CPU resources. Avoid routing on your database server. Hardware routers are also available; these routers bypass the operating system and can perform routing tasks with little overhead. Hardware routers can route network packets much more quickly and efficiently than operating systems.

BEWARE OF THE OVERLOADED ROUTER ──────────────────────────────

When subnetting the network, be aware of maintenance functions such as backup and restore operations. Although subnetting is great for keeping local traffic off the networks, the overhead of going through a router can be time consuming. Although the delay going through a router might be unnoticeable to the user, it can add significant time to large operations such as backup and restore.

Bridges, Routers, and Hubs

Bridges, routers, and hubs are all needed to keep a network running. *Routers* are used to route data back and forth between different subnets; *bridges* are used to bridge between networks; and *hubs* are used simply as electrical repeaters. All these elements might be in use in your installation.

Unlike hubs, in which packets go to all ports and therefore dramatically increase the potential for collisions, *switches* are intelligent hubs that learn which MAC address is on each port and send data only to that port. Switches eliminate collisions and, although they are more expensive than hubs, they are well worth the cost on a busy network.

Be sure that your routers and bridges are not a source of delays. Especially if you employ a router or a bridge that uses a general-purpose operating system for routing and bridging functions, you might see substantial delays in these services. A special-purpose hardware router or bridge provides significant performance gains over an operating system-based router or bridge.

Summary

As you have seen, the performance of the network can be affected by hardware and software inefficiencies as well as the load on the network. The most common problem is the one caused by overloading the network. With every type of network, only a certain amount of data can be simultaneously transferred before the network is overloaded.

When an Ethernet network becomes extremely busy, you see many collisions. These collisions cause the network to retransmit the data, wasting CPU and network cycles. As you get closer to the limits of the network, you generate more collisions.

Exceeding the fixed load that the network can handle causes most of the network performance problems. To optimize your network, look at both the software and the hardware. You can't do much to optimize the network. By reducing unnecessary network protocols and applications, you can streamline the operation of the network. You can't do much else to enhance its performance.

You can't do much to optimize the network hardware either. The best thing to do is simply monitor the network load and break the network into smaller segments if necessary. By subnetting the network, you can reduce the load for each segment, thus avoiding network bottlenecks.

Upgrading to more intelligent networking hardware, like network switches instead of hubs, is also an option to explore. It is no substitute for monitoring and knowing your network's performance.

INDEX

Symbols

+ signs, 311

A

accesses, performance view, 117

active processes, 119

aggregation, 92

alert log
    initialization parameter problems, 31-32
    startup troubleshooting, 26-28

ALL_ROWS hints, 313

ALTER SESSION command, 269

ANALYZE command
    capabilities, 277
    chained rows, 277, 280
    estimated statistics, 279
    exact statistics, 278
    integrity of data, 277, 280
    modes available, 278
    obsolete soon, 273
    running, 278
    structural integrity, 280

AND_EQUAL hint, 315

append mode hints, 326

ARCH processes, 170

archive log files
    ARCHIVELOG mode, 346
    Archivelog process, 369
    Data Guard, 369
    LOG_ARCHIVE_DEST initialization parameter, 31
    RAID 10 recommended, 213
    recoveries, role in, 346

asynchronous I/O, 164

Automatic Undo Management mode, 38

B

B*-Tree indexes
    branch blocks, 71, 258
    branch nodes, 70
    composite, 72
    data storage in, 70
    defined, 70
    function-based, 72-73
    IOTs, 73, 258
    leaf blocks, 71-72, 258
    leaf nodes, 70
    nonunique, 72
    root nodes, 70
    search method, 70
    segments, 71
    unique, 72
    using, 258-259

backdoors, creating, 25

background processes, 168-170

background system-wide wait events, 132

BACKGROUND_CORE_DUMP parameter, 31

BACKGROUND_DUMP_DEST parameter, 31

backup and recovery performance, 6

backups
    archive log files, 346
    ARCHIVELOG mode, 346
    asynchronous I/O, 345, 356-357
    BACKUP_TAPE_IO_SLAVES parameter, 345
    block size, 355, 358-359, 362-363

bottlenecks, hardware, 355

buffering, 356

checkpoints, 345

clones, 348

cold, 344, 347, 351

component performance characteristics, table of, 355

compression, 350-351, 362-364

control files, 348

CPUs, enhancing, 358

data access, physical, 352-354

Data Guard, 368-370

DBWR_IO_SLAVES parameter, 345

disaster preparation. *See* disaster survival systems

export, 344-345, 361

full, 344

goals for, 350

hardware considerations, 351, 354-355

header information, 346

hot, 344, 347-349, 352-355

I/O subsystem, 353, 355, 358-359

initialization parameters, 345

isolated links recommended, 352-354

large pool configuration, 356

network bandwidth, 352-355, 359, 362-363

network device speed, 351

network segmentation, 359

offline, 344, 347

online, 344, 347-349

optimizations available, 352

OS performance, 361-362

performance considerations, 350, 355-356

performance verification, 361-363

planning, 354

process of, 346

quiescing databases, 348

RAID, 351, 358-359

recovery from. *See* recovery

remote mirroring, 367-368

replication, 370-371

RMAN, 348-349, 356-357

SANs for, 348-349

scheduling, 360

sequential access, 349, 351-353

snapshots, 348

software for, choosing, 363

software overhead, 355

splitting up, 352, 359-360

staging areas, 352-353

synchronous I/O, 356-357

system enhancements, 358, 360-361

system load during, 350

tablespaces, 347, 352-353

tape device speed, 351, 354-355, 362-363

temporary backup volumes, 352-354

testing, 354, 361-363

workload tuning, 112-113

badly-tuned SQL statements, 288, 294-295

Balanced Tree Indexes. *See* **B*-Tree indexes**

bandwidth, 177

binding variables, 286

bitmap indexes

advantages of, 73-74

defined, 70, 258

design criteria, 75

hints for, 310

selectivity, 75

structure of, 73

using, 262-264

block contention, 121

block size, 229-231

bottlenecks

defined, 16-17

existing application SQL statements, 302

finding, 17

frequently occurring areas, 36

branch blocks, 71, 258

branch nodes, 70

bridges, 385

BSTAT/ESTAT (UTLBSTAT/UTLESTAT)

baselines, 127

buffer busy wait statistics, 133, 135-136

cache buffers LRU chain latch statistics, 135

cache statistics, 128-130

consistent changes, 129

consistent gets, 129

database statistics, 128-129

Db block gets, 130

defined, 126

dictionary cache statistics, 138-139

dirty buffers inspected, 130

enqueue statistics, 128, 130

free buffer wait statistics, 133

free buffers inspected, 130

hot buffers moved, 130

I/O statistics, 139-141

latch statistics, 133-135

library cache statistics, 127-128

logical reads, 130

measurement intervals, 126, 141

output files, 126-127

overall statistics, 127

overhead from running, 127

parameters, listing, 137-138

physical reads, 130

redo statistics, 128, 131, 135

report.txt, 126-127

rollback segments statistics, 136-137

running, 126-127

scripts, 126-127

sort statistics, 128, 131

system-wide wait events statistics, 131-133

TIMED_STATISTICS, 126

UTLBSTAT.sql, 126

UTLESTAT.sql, 126

version information, 141

buffer busy waits statistics, 133, 135, 136

buffer cache

block size, 166

DB_BLOCK_BUFFERS parameter, 48-49

DB_CACHE_SIZE parameter, 48-49, 166

Default Buffer Pool, 52

defined, 47, 166

free buffer wait statistics, 133

hit ratio, 48-49, 122

importance of, 49

Keep Buffer Pool, 50

multiple buffer pools, 49

purpose of, 166-167

Recycle Buffer Pool, 51

statistics, 48

buffer pools, 49, 117

bus design, 176-177

C

cache buffers LRU chain latches, 135

cache fusion, 333, 335

cache hit ratio statistics, 43-44, 48-49, 129, 153

caches

buffer. See buffer cache

buffer parameters, 37

CACHE hints, 325

CPU, 170-171, 174

data dictionary. See data dictionary cache

hints for, 325-326

hit ratio, 43-44, 48-49, 129, 153

importance of, 36

library. See library cache

miss rate, 45-46, 48

performance view, 117

PINS, 43

reloads, 43-44

row, 45

shared pool, 42-47

SQL statements, caching, 42

statistics gathering, 37, 129-130

capacity planning

Capacity Planner, 123

defined, 20

steps in, 21

chaining, 222-223, 225, 227, 277, 280

CHAR data type, 288

checkpoints, 62-63

CHOOSE hints, 313

CISC processors, 172

CKPT processes, 169

clean blocks, 166

cluster buckets, 230

CLUSTER hint, 315

cluster indexes, 304

clustering. *See* **RAC (Real Application Clusters)**

cold backups, 344, 347, 351

columns

indexing, 76-77, 260, 305

views of statistics, 282

comments, 311

COMPATIBLE parameter, 31

composite indexes, 72, 76, 257, 260, 304, 306

composite partitioning, 95-96

configuration parameters. *See* **initialization parameters**

connections

creating, 25

defined, 9

OPEN_LINKS parameter, 32

transaction stage, 282

consistent mode, 243

consumer groups. *See* **resource consumer groups**

contention

data contention, IOPS, 221

disk. *See* disk contention

freelist, 65, 133, 136

parallel execution, 77

CONTROL_FILES parameter, 31

cost-based optimization, 251, 313-314

CPUs

32 bit versus 64 bit, 174-175

caches, 170-171, 174

CISC processors, 172

designs of, 171

MPP (Massively Parallel Processing), 173-174

multiprocessor systems, 173-174

performance of, 170

RISC processors, 172

SMP (Symmetric Multiprocessor) systems, 173

current instance, performance view, 118

current mode, 243

cursors

creation, 284

CURSOR_SHARING_EXACT hints, 327

CURSOR_SPACE_FOR_TIME parameter, 42, 44

OPEN_CURSORS parameter, 39, 41

performance view, 120-121

purpose of, 41

SESSION_CACHED_CURSORS parameter, 39

customer feedback, 7

D

data blocks
buffer busy waits, 136
caching, 166
free space parameters, 225

data contention, IOPS, calculating, 221

data dictionary cache
hit ratio, 122, 139, 156
performance view, 120
purpose of, 44-46
statistics on, 138-139, 156, 167

Data Guard, 113, 368-370, 373-374

data integrity, ANAYLYZE command, 277, 280

data scrubbing, 196

Database Writer (DBWR) write latency, 212

DBMS_STATS package
creating statistics tables, 274
database statistics, 277
DELETE_TABLE_STATS function, 275-276
GATHER_TABLE_STATS function, 274-275
IMPORT_TABLE_STATS function, 276
index statistics, 276
purpose of, 273
restoring statistics, 276
system statistics, 277
table statistics, 276
using, 277

DBWR processes, 169

DBWR_IO_SLAVES parameter, 208, 345

DB_2K_CACHE_SIZE parameter, 208, 231

DB_BLOCK_BUFFERS parameter, 48-49

DB_BLOCK_CHECKING parameter, 208

DB_BLOCK_CHECKSUM parameter, 208

DB_BLOCK_SIZE parameter, 208, 230-231

DB_CACHE_ADVICE parameter, 37

DB_CACHE_SIZE parameter, 37, 48-49, 208, 231

DB_FILES parameter, 32

DB_FILE_MULTIBLOCK_READ_COUNT parameter, 91, 209

DB_KEEP_CACHE_SIZE parameter, 37

DB_NAME parameter, 31

DB_RECYCLE_CACHE_SIZE parameter, 37

DB_WRITER_PROCESSES parameter, 209

dedicated server process, 98-99

Default Buffer Pool, 52

definition of tuning, 6

degree of parallelism, 79-83

deletes, 75

DELETE_TABLE_STATS function, 275-276

determination phase, 10, 12

dictionary cache. *See* **data dictionary cache**

dirty blocks, 62, 166

dirty buffers, 130

disaster survival systems
advantages of, 366
allowable downtime, 371
bandwidth considerations, 374
concepts in, 367
criticality of data, 371

Data Guard, 368-370, 373-374

design factors, 371

documentation, 372

downtime vs. recoverability, 372

hardware documentation, 372

I/O capacity, 374

importance of, 366

initialization parameters for, 366

Internet connectivity, 374

log shipping via tape, 373

offsite backup, 373

physical locations, 372

physical security, 374

planning, 371-373

reasons to use, 366

recovery, 370, 373

remote mirroring, 367-368, 373

replication, 370-371

software documentation, 372

Standby Database, 368-370

tuning, 374

disk bound systems, 215

disk contention

defined, 215

eliminating non-Oracle I/Os, 222

hardware striping, 220

identifying problems, 216-217

index separation, 221-222

isolating sequential I/Os, 218

Oracle striping, 219-220

OS striping, 220

problem solving rules, 218

RAID, 217

random I/Os, 219

random vs. sequential I/O, 217

statistics, 215-216

striping, 219-221

disk drives

components of, 181-182

contention, 215-222

cylinders, 181

disk bound systems, 215

full disk seeks, 183

heads, 181

hot spots, 215

I/O capacity, 185

I/O controller latency, 187

knee of the curve, 187

limitations, designing around, 215

operating mechanism, 180-182

parallel processing considerations, 86

performance measures, 184-187

platters, 181

queuing, 186

RAID. *See* RAID (Redundant Array of Inexpensive Disks)

random I/O, 183, 186-187

read latency, 209-211

rotational latency, 181, 183

sectors, 181

seeks, 181, 183

sequential I/O, 185-186

specification sheets, 184-185

statistics, 141, , 215-216

track-to-track seeks, 183

write latency, 209, 211-212

disk fragmentation, 231, 233-234

disk striping, 188

DISK_ASYNCH_IO, 209

dispatchers, performance view, 118-120

DLM (Distributed Lock Manager), 334-336

Dnnn processes, 170

documentation for disaster recovery planning, 372

drives. *See* disk drives

DRIVING_SITE hints, 320

DSS systems, 230

dynamic extensions, 224-225

Dynamic Performance Views. *See* Oracle
  Dynamic Performance Views

E

elapsed time statistic, 243

elevator sorting, 199

enqueues, 38, 130

ENQUEUE_RESOURCES parameter, 38

Ethernet, 379-381

evaluating tuning achievement, 7

execution plans
    displaying. *See* EXPLAIN PLAN command
    optimization. *See* Optimizer, Oracle
    plan stability feature, 98

execution time, 243

existing applications
    bottlenecks, 302
    broken, 299
    capacity problems, 299
    effects of SQL statements, 302
    EXPLAIN PLAN command, 301
    familiarization phase, 300
    optimizable, 299
    Parallel Query option, 301
    problem analysis, 298-299
    scheduling changes, 298
    SQL statements, 298-302
    SQL Trace analysis, 300-301
    steps for tuning, 300-302

EXPLAIN PLAN command
    existing application SQL statements, 301
    initialization, 249-250
    invoking, 250
    purpose of, 238, 248, 289
    results, extracting, 250-251
    SQL statements covered, 248
    table definition, 249-250
    TKPROF, running from, 241
    using results from, 251

export backups, 344-345

F

FACT hints, 324

Fail Safe, 204

failovers
    controllers, 203
    Fail Safe, 204
    vs. clustering, 332

false pings, performance view, 118-119

fault tolerance. *See also* RAID
    best solution, 213
    budget solution, 214
    cost vs. performance, 212
    defined, 9
    exceptions to guidelines, 214
    goals for tuning, 9
    good solution, 213-214

file I/O performance view, 121

file I/O statistics, 139-141

file pings performance view, 118

FIRST_ROWS hint, 314

fragmentation, 231, 233-234

free buffer waits statistics, 133

freelist contention, 65, 133, 136

full backups, 344

full disk seeks, 183

FULL hints, 80, 316

function-based indexes, 72-73, 258, 264

G

G$ views, 116

goals, tuning
    fault tolerance, 9-10
    instance tuning, 66
    number of users, 9
    operating system tuning, 40
    Optimizer, specifying for, 273
    response time, 8
    setting, 7
    throughput, 7-8

groups. *See* **resource consumer groups**

H

hard drives. *See* **disk drives**

hardware
    busses. *See* bus design
    initialization parameters affecting, list of, 164
    networks, 378, 380-381, 384-385
    processors. *See* CPUs
    RDBMS optimization, 17
    routers, 384-385

hardware striping, 220

hashes
    hash clusters, 89-90
    HASH_AJ, MERGE_AJ, NL_AJ hints, 321

HASH_AREA_SIZE parameter, 38

HASH hints, 316

hash joins, 296-297

HASH_JOIN_ENABLED parameter, 38

Hash Partitioning, 92, 95

HASH_SJ, MERGE_SJ, NL_SJ hints, 321

hashing, bypassed, problem with, 289

HBAs (host bus adapters), 202-203

header information, 346

hints
    + signs, 311
    access methods, 315-317, 319
    advantages of, 288, 310, 328
    ALL_ROWS, 313
    AND_EQUAL, 315
    APPEND, 326
    approaches to optimization, 313-315
    CACHE, 325
    CHOOSE, 313
    CLUSTER, 315
    comment types, 311
    compound queries with, 311
    conditions indicating need for, 310
    conflicting, 311
    cost-based optimization, 313-314
    CURSOR_SHARING_EXACT, 327
    DRIVING_SITE, 320
    errors in, 311
    FACT, 324
    FIRST_ROWS, 314
    FULL, 80, 316
    full table scans, 312, 316
    HASH, 316
    HASH_AJ, MERGE_AJ, NL_AJ, 321
    HASH_SJ, MERGE_SJ, NL_SJ, 321
    implementing, 311
    INDEX, 316-317
    INDEX_ASC, 317

INDEX_COMBINE, 317
INDEX_DESC, 317
INDEX_FFS, 318
INDEX_JOIN, 318
indexes, 264, 306, 310, 315-318, 323
join operations, 319-321
join orders, 319
join predicates, 327
LEADING, 321
MERGE, 324
multiple, 312
NOAPPEND, 326
NOCACHE, 326
NOPARALLEL, 80, 322
NOPARALLEL_INDEX, 323
NOREWRITE, 325
NO_EXPAND, 325
NO_FACT, 324
NO_INDEX, 318
NO_MERGE, 324
NO_PUSH_PRED, 327
NO_UNNEST, 327
ORDERED, 319
ORDERED_PREDICATES, 327
overview of, 290-291
PARALLEL, 80, 321-322
parallel execution, 80
parallel queries, 310, 312, 321-323
PARALLEL_INDEX, 323
PQ_DISTRIBUTE, 322-323
PUSH_PRED, 327
PUSH_SUBQ, 326
query transformation, 323-325
response time, 314
ROWID, 318
RULE, 315
rules-based optimization, 315
STAR, 319
STAR_TRANSFORMATION, 323

subqueries, 326-327
syntax, 311
throughput optimization, 313
UNNEST, 327
USE_CONCAT, 319, 324
USE_HASH, 320
USE_MERGE, 320
USE_NL, 320
views, 324

historical reports, 112

hot backups, 344, 347-349, 352-355

hot buffers, 130

hot spots, 11, 215

hubs, 385

I

I/O (input/output). *See also* **I/O subsystem**
    parallel execution, 81
    random, 217
    reducing using indexes, 74-75
    reduction techniques, 222-229
    sequential, 217
    statistics using BSTAT/ESTAT, 139-141
    statistics using Statpack, 152-153

I/O bound systems, 215

I/O bus, 177

I/O subsystem
    best solution, 213
    budget solution, 214
    chaining, 222-223, 225, 227
    configuring for performance, 212-214
    dependence on, 209
    design considerations, 215
    drives. *See* disk drives

dynamic extensions, 224-225

good solution, 213-214

initialization parameters, 208-209

migrating, 222-223, 227

overloading of, 16

PCTFREE, 225-228

PCTUSED, 225-228

performance vs. fault tolerance and cost, 212

read latency, 209-211

write latency, 211-212

IFILE parameter, 31

immediate-gets latches, 134

index clusters, 86, 304

INDEX hints, 316-317

Index-Organized Tables (IOTs), 73, 258, 262

index segments, 258

indexes

advantages of, 69

analyzing, 265

avoiding, 306

B*-Tree. *See* B*-Tree indexes

back-of-the-book, 69

benefits of, 256-257

bitmap. *See* bitmap indexes

branch blocks, 258

clusters, 86, 304, 341

column selection, 76-77, 260

columns, indexing, 305

compacting, 262

composite, 76, 257, 260, 304, 306

creating, 256, 264

data reduction with, 74-75

defined, 69, 256

deletes, effects of, 75

design considerations, 74-75

disk contention, minimizing, 221

EXPLAIN PLAN command, 301

fragmentation, 262

function-based, 72-73, 258, 264

guidelines for creating, 259-261

hints for, 264, 306, 310, 314-318, 323

inserts, effects of, 75

IOTs, 73, 258, 262

joins, 76

leaf blocks, 258

maintenance, 69, 256, 261-262

monitoring, 265

nodes, 70

NOLOGGING option, 84

nonunique, 72, 257, 304

not used, problem of, 289

OPTIMIZER_INDEX_CACHING parameter, 257

OPTIMIZER_INDEX_COST_ADJ parameter, 257

overhead from, 69, 256, 303

overindexing, 261

Parallel Index Creation feature, 256

parallelism, 84, 303

partitioning, 92, 97-98

purpose of, 303

RAC, 341

rebuilding, 262

reducing I/Os with, 74-75

scans, specifying use, 317, 323

segments, 71

selectivity, 70, 74-76, 262

speeding creation of, 84

statements causing performance penalties, 305

tables, of, 304-305

testing, 76, 306

transparency of, 69

types of, 70, 257-258, 304

unique, 72, 257, 304

updates, effects of, 75, 261-262

views of statistics, 281

when to create, 304

INDEX_ASC hints, 317

INDEX_COMBINE hints, 317

INDEX_DESC hints, 317

INDEX_FFS hints, 318

INDEX_JOIN hints, 318

init.ora. *See* **initialization**

initialization

alert log, troubleshooting with, 31-32

asynchronous I/O, 164

file for, 24, 31-32

resource limiting parameters, 32-33

parameters. *See* initialization parameters

initialization parameters

BACKGROUND_CORE_DUMP, 31

BACKGROUND_DUMP_DEST, 31

backups, 345

block size cache, 164

buffer cache, 164

COMPATIBLE, 31

CONTROL_FILES, 31

DB_2K_CACHE_SIZE, 208, 231

DB_BLOCK_CHECKING, 208

DB_BLOCK_CHECKSUM, 208

DB_BLOCK_SIZE, 208, 230-231

DB_CACHE_SIZE, 48-49, 208, 231

DB_FILE_MULTIBLOCK_READ_COUNT, 91, 209

DB_FILES, 32

DB_NAME, 31

DB_WRITER_PROCESSES, 209

DBWR_IO_SLAVES, 208

disaster survival systems, 366

DISK_ASYNCH_IO, 209

I/O subsystem, 208-209

IFILE, 31

indexing related, 68-69

INSTANCE_GROUPS, 32

LARGE_POOL_SIZE, 47

LICENSE_MAX_SESSIONS, 32

LICENSE_MAX_USERS, 32

listing current, 137-138, 159

LOG_ARCHIVE_DEST, 31

MAX_DISPATCHERS, 68

MAX_DUMP_FILE_SIZEs, 32, 239

MAX_SHARED_SERVERS, 68

MTS, 100-101

MTS_DISPATCHERS, 101

MTS_MAX_DISPATCHERS, 101

MTS_MAX_SERVERS, 101

MTS_SERVERS, 101

OPEN_LINKS, 32

OPEN_LINKS_PER_INSTANCE, 33

Oracle Optimizer, 268-271

parallel execution, 80

PARALLEL_ADAPTIVE_MULTI_USER, 68

PARALLEL_AUTOMATIC_TUNING, 68

PARALLEL_BROADCAST_ENABLED, 68

PARALLEL_EXECUTION_MESSAGE_SIZE, 68

PARALLEL_MAX_SERVERS, 69, 80, 83, 366

PARALLEL_MIN_PERCENT, 69

PARALLEL_MIN_SERVERS, 69, 83

PARALLEL_THREADS_PER_CPU, 69

PARTITION_VIEW_ENABLED, 69

PGAs, 37-38

PROCESSES, 33

RECOVERY_PARALLELISM, 69, 85, 366

RESOURCE_LIMIT, 104

SESSIONS, 33

SGAs, 37, 39

standard block size, 164

STARTUP commands, 25

TIMED_STATISTICS, 239
TRANSACTIONS, 33
UNDO_MANAGEMENT, 53
undos, 38-39
USER_DUMP_DEST, 239
writer processes, 164
workload tuning, 104

INSERT activity, 289

inserts
indexes, effects on, 75
PCTFREE/PCTUSED, setting, 228

instances
activity statistics, 150-152
checking connection, 29
components of, 165
connecting, 25
memory structure, 165
Oracle. *See* Oracle instances
SGA. *See* SGA (System Global Area)
shutting down, 28-30
starting, 24
STARTUP command, 25
startup event sequence, 26
troubleshooting startup, 26-28

INSTANCE_GROUPS parameter, 32

IOPS, calculating, 221

IOTs (Index Organized Tables), 73, 258, 262

J-K

joins
clusters, 86-87
hash, 296-297
hints for, 319-321
indexing, 76

merge, 296
nested loop, 295-296
orders, hints for, 319
read latency, 210

Keep Buffer Pool, 50
key generation, 288

L

L1 cache, 170

L2 cache, 170

large numbers of user, tuning for, 6, 9

large pool
backups, configuring for, 356
defined, 166
LARGE_POOL_SIZE parameter, 37, 47
MTS requirements, 99-100
using, 47

latches
block size, effect on, 229
contention, 50-51
gets, 134
hit ratios, 134
immediate-gets, 134
Keep Buffer Pool, 50
LRU, 135
misses, 134
nowait statistics, 134
performance view, 118-119
Recycle Buffer Pool, 51
redos, 135
sleeps, 134
statistics on, 133-135, 155-156
willing-to-wait, 134

latency, 181-183, 209-212

LCKn processes, 170

LEADING hints, 321

leaf blocks, 71-72, 258

leaf nodes, 70

LGWR (Log Writer) processes, 169, 211, 283

library cache
 components of, 42-44
 defined, 42, 167
 hit ratio, 122, 128, 157
 performance view, 117, 119
 shared SQL area, 42-44
 SQL Trace report on misses, 241, 247
 statistics, 43-44, 127-128, 157

LICENSE_MAX_SESSIONS parameter, 32

LICENSE_MAX_USERS parameter, 32

list buffer busy waits, 136

List Partitioning, 91, 94-95

load time, tuning for, 6, 9-10

local tables, advantages of, 383

lock manager, performance view, 117

locks
 cluster system. See PCM (Parallel Cache Management) locks
 DLM, 334-336
 LOCK_SGA parameter, 37
 performance view, 118-119, 121

log buffer. See redo log buffer

log switches, checkpoint creation by, 62

Log Writer processes (LGWR), 169, 211, 283

LOG_ARCHIVE_DEST parameter, 31

LOG_BUFFER parameter, 39

LOG_CHECKPOINT_INTERVAL parameter, 63

Logical Standby, 369

long-running operations, performance view, 120

LRU latches, 135

M

maintaining indexes, 261-262

Manual Undo Management mode, 38

maximum number of database files, specifying, 32

MAX_DISPATCHERS, 68

MAX_DUMP_FILE_SIZE parameters, 32

MAX_SHARED_SERVERS, 68

memory
 effective use of, 39-40
 hierarchy of speed, 36
 importance of, 18
 insufficient, 16
 OS requirements, 40
 performance view, 121
 persistent areas, 41
 PGA. See PGA (Program Global Area)
 private SQL areas, 41
 runtime areas, 41
 SGA, 40, 165-167
 sorts, required for, 64
 structure of, 165
 system memory architecture, 175
 user processes requirement, 40
 virtual, 176

MERGE hints, 324

merge joins, 296

methodology, tuning. *See* tuning methodology

Microsoft Windows, starting Oracle instances, 25

migrating, 222-223, 227

MPP (Massively Parallel Processing), 173-174

MTS (multithreaded server)
  advantages of, 99
  backdoor, creating, 25
  dispatcher, performance view, 120
  initialization parameters, 100-101
  large pool requirements, 99-100
  memory use, 100
  MTS_DISPATCHERS, 101
  MTS_MAX_DISPATCHERS, 101
  MTS_MAX_SERVERS, 101
  MTS_SERVERS, 101
  performance view, 119
  purpose of, 99
  shared pool use, 47
  tuning, 100-101

multiblock reads, 91

multiprocessor systems, 173-174

multithreaded message queues, 120

multithreaded server (MTS) configuration. *See* MTS (multithreaded server)

N

NAS (network attached storage), 206

need for tuning, 7

nested loop joins, 295-296, 320

networks
  addressing, 381
  architecture of, 378
  bandwidth, 382, 384
  bridges, 385
  collisions, 380-381, 384
  deferred packets, 379
  design considerations, 383-384
  Ethernet, 379-381
  frames, 379
  hardware components, 378, 380-381
  hubs, 385
  limitations, 382
  load monitoring, 383
  local tables, 383
  NICs, 379
  Oracle tuning, 383
  packets, 379
  protocols, 381-382
  reducing unnecessary aspects, 385
  routers, 384-385
  segmenting, 383-384
  slow, 16
  SPX/IPX, 382
  subnets, 381
  TCP/IP, 381

new applications, 303-306

NICs (Network Interface Cards), 379

NOAPPEND hints, 326

NOCACHE hints, 326

nodes, cluster, 332

non-background system-wide wait events, 131

nonunique indexes, 72, 257, 304

NOPARALLEL hints, 80, 322

NOPARALLEL_INDEX hints, 323

NOREWRITE hints, 325

NO_EXPAND hints, 325

NO_FACT hint, 324

NO_INDEX hints, 318

NO_MERGE hints, 324

NO_PUSH_PRED hints, 327

NO_UNNEST hints, 327

numbers of users, tuning for, 6, 9

O

object caches, performance view, 120

OCI procedure, 243

offline backups, 344, 347

OLTP systems. *See* transaction processing

online backups, 347-349

online reports, 113-114

online tablespace backups, 344

OPEN_CURSORS parameter, 39

OPEN_LINKS parameter, 32

OPEN_LINKS_PER_INSTANCE parameter, 33

operating systems
  dependence on, 208
  reason for tuning, 40
  requirements, 40
  resource tuning, 18

OPS (Oracle Parallel Server). *See* RAC (Real Application Clusters)

optimization hints. *See* hints

Optimizer, Oracle
  ALL_ROWS option, 270
  ALTER SESSION command, 269
  CHOOSE option, 270
  cluster views, 281
  column views, 282
  cost-based approach, 271-273
  costs, table of, 271
  FIRST_ROWS option, 270
  goal specification, 273
  hints. *See* hints
  index views, 281
  initialization parameters, 268-271
  join order, 269
  operation of, 269
  OPTIMIZATION_MODE parameter, 269
  OPTIMIZER_FEATURES_ENABLE parameter, 268
  OPTIMIZER_FEATURES_ENABLED parameter, 270
  OPTIMIZER_INDEX_CACHING parameter, 268, 271
  OPTIMIZER_INDEX_COST_ADJ parameter, 268, 270
  OPTIMIZER_MAX_PERMUTATIONS parameter, 268, 271, 273
  OPTIMIZER_MODE parameter, 268
  options, table of, 270
  purpose of, 268
  RULE option, 270
  rule-based approach, 271-272
  statistics, gathering, 272
  table views, 281
  views, 280-282

OR expansions, prohibiting, 325

Oracle bitmap indexes. *See* bitmap indexes

Oracle Dynamic Performance Views
  accesses on objects, 117
  active processes, 119
  analysis, 116
  block contention, 121
  buffer cache hit ratio, 122

buffer pools, 117

cache efficiency, 117

child cursor execution plans, 121

counters, 116

current instance, 118

cursor usage, 120

data dictionary cache ratio, 122

data dictionary usage, 120

data files, 121

defined, 116

dispatchers, multithreaded servers, 118

false pings, 118-119

file I/O, 121

G$ views, 116

global transactions, 118

instancing, 116

latch usage, 118-119

library cache, 117, 119, 122

lock manager, 117

locks, 118-119, 121

memory usage, 121

multithreading (MTS), 119-121

object cache, 120

operations, long-running, 120

parallel processes, 118-119

parameters, session, 119

pings, 117-119, 121

RAC locks, 119

reserved shared pool, 120

resource commerce groups, 120

resource limits, 120

session information, 120

session statistics, 120

SGA cache, 117

shared pool, 119

shared pool free space, 123

shared SQL area, 121

sorts, 121

SQL queries to access, 122

SQL scripts for, 116

statistics names, 121

Statspack, 123

system parameters, 121

system statistics, 121

temporary space, 121

third-party analysis tools, 116, 124

transactions, 121

undos, 121

UTLBSTAT, 123

UTLESTAT, 123

V$ views, table of, 117-121

waits, 118, 120-121

X$ tables, 116

Oracle instances

checking connection, 29

connecting, 25

Microsoft Windows, starting from, 25

order of tuning, 36

shared memory allocation, 37

shutting down, 28-30

starting, 24-25

STARTUP command, 25

startup event sequence, 26

troubleshooting startup, 26-28

Oracle Optimizer. *See* **Optimizer, Oracle**

Oracle Parallel Query. *See* **parallel execution**

Oracle processes

background processes, 169-170

server processes, 168

Oracle Real Application Clusters. *See* **RAC (Real Application Clusters)**

Oracle Recovery Manager. *See* **RMAN (Recovery Manager)**

Oracle striping, 219-220

order of tuning, 36

ORDERED hints, 319

ORDERED_PREDICATES hints, 327

OS striping, 220

P

packages, 288, 290

paging, 40, 176

Parallel Cache Management (PCM) locks. *See* PCM (Parallel Cache Management) locks

parallel execution

    contention, 77

    CPU capacity, 81-82

    defined, 77

    degree of parallelism, 79-83

    design guidelines, 82

    disabling, 322

    FULL hint, 80

    hints, 80, 310, 312, 321-323

    I/O capacity, 82

    I/O configuration, 81

    indexes, 84

    initialization parameters, 80

    loading, 84-85

    memory limitations, 81

    monitoring, 82-83

    negative consequences of, 82

    NOPARALLEL hint, 80, 322

    number of servers, setting, 83

    operations available for, 79

    PARALLEL hint, 80, 321-322

    Parallel Query option, 287, 301

    PARALLEL_MAX_SERVERS, 83

    PARALLEL_MIN_SERVERS, 83

    performance, 79

    performance view, 118-119

    query coordinators, 78-79

    query processing, 78-83

    query servers, 78, 80

    query tuning, 80

    recovery, 85-86

    statistics, 82-83

    storage considerations, 80-82, 86

    striping, disk, 81

    table scans, 77-79, 82

    temporary tablespace, 81

    types of operations, 77

PARALLEL hints, 80, 321-322

Parallel Index Creation feature, 256

parallel loading, 84-85

parallel queries. *See* parallel execution

Parallel Query. *See* parallel execution

parallel recovery, 85-86, 347

PARALLEL_ADAPTIVE_MULTI_USER, 68

PARALLEL_AUTOMATIC_TUNING, 68

PARALLEL_BROADCAST_ENABLED, 68

PARALLEL_EXECUTION_MESSAGE_SIZE, 68

PARALLEL_INDEX hints, 323

PARALLEL_MAX_SERVERS parameter, 69, 80, 83, 287, 366

PARALLEL_MIN_PERCENT, 69

PARALLEL_MIN_SERVERS, 69, 83

PARALLEL_THREADS_PER_CPU, 69

parameters

    initialization. *See* initialization parameters

    resource limiting, 32-33

parity, 195-197

parsing

caching of, 42

criteria for reuse, 284-285

data dictionary accesses, 44

reducing frequency of, 41

statistics on, 149-150

steps in, 285-286

stored procedures, 285

partitions

benefits of, 97

Composite Partitioning, 95-96

defined, 91

Hash Partitioning, 92, 95

indexes, options for partitioning, 97-98

keys, 91

List Partitioning, 91, 94-95

MAXVALUE range, 94

PARTITION_VIEW_ENABLED, 69

Range Partitioning, 91, 93-94

schemes available, 91-92

Sub-Partitioning, 92

when to use, 92-93

PCM (Parallel Cache Management) locks, 332, 334-336

PCTFREE, 225-228

PCTUSED, 225-228

performance snapshot statistics. *See* **Statspack**

Performance Manager, 123

persistent areas of memory, 41

PGA (Program Global Area)

components of, 168

initialization parameters, 37-38

private SQL area, 168

session information, 168

stack space, 168

Statspack statistics, 154

Physical Standby, 369

pings

OPS, 333

performance view, 118-121

PINS, 43

plan stability, 98

platters, 181

PMON processes, 169

PQ_DISTRIBUTE hints, 322-323

predicates, 327

prefetching data, 175

private SQL areas, 41, 168

processes, 168-170

PROCESSES parameter, 33

processors. *See* **CPUs**

profiles, 110-112

PUSH_PRED hints, 327

PUSH_SUBQ hints, 326

Q

queries

execution. *See* EXPLAIN PLAN command; SQL statement execution

parallel. *See* parallel execution

processing, steps in, 286

subqueries, 326-327

transformation hints, 323-325

query coordinators, 78-79

query servers, 78, 80

quiescing databases, 348

R

RAC (Real Application Clusters)
application tuning, 342
balancing, 340
benefits of, 332, 341
cache fusion, 333-335
clusters defined, 332
computer system for, 333
configuration, 342
contention, reducing, 337-338
DB_NAME initialization parameter, 31
defined, 86, 332
design considerations, 337-338, 340-341
disadvantages of, 88
distributed services, 339
DLM, 334-336
Exclusive Lock mode, 335
failover vs. true clustering, 332
FREELIST GROUPS, 341
hardware requirements, 333
hash, 89-90
I/O subsystem configuration, 337
indexes, 341
instance tuning, 342
INSTANCE_GROUPS parameter, 32
locking system, 119, 332, 334-336, 340, 342
multiplexing, 338
nodes, 332
Parallel Server option, 336-337
PCM, 332, 334-336
PCTFREE and PCTUSED, 340
pings, 117, 333
queuing, 339
Read Lock mode, 335
read tables, 340-341
SANs with, 204-205
scalability, 341
segmenting users, 337-338

server interconnects, 333-334, 337
shared disk subsystems, 333-334
single image clusters, 333
sizing systems, 337, 342
smart routing, 339
system diagram, 336
Tuxedo TM (transaction monitor), 338-339
views of statistics, 281
when to use, 86, 88-89

RAID (Redundant Array of Inexpensive Disks)
0 level, 189-190, 197
1 level, 190-191, 198, 212-214
2 level, 192
3 level, 192
4 level, 193-194
5 level, 194, 198-199, 201, 212-214
10 level, 191, 198-199, 212-214
backups using, 351, 358-359
cache, controller, 200
controller performance, 199-201
data guarding, 193-194
data scrubbing, 196
defined, 187
disk contention, 217
disk mirroring, 190-191
disk striping, 188-189, 201
distributed data guarding, 194
drive parity, 193-194
elevator sorting, 199
external, 202-203
fault tolerance, 188
hardware vs. software, 188
HBAs, 202
internal vs. external, 201, 203
levels, 188
parity, 195-197
performance of levels, 197-199
performance vs. fault tolerance and cost, 212

purpose of, 188

read caches, 200

recommended level, 199

SANs, as component of, 203

stripe size, 201

striping, 188-189, 201

virtual drive property, 188

write caches, 201

XOR operation, 201

random I/O, 217

random seeks, 183

Range Partitioning, 91, 93-94, 289

RBU (Rollback Segment Undo Scheme)

circular buffering, 55

creating rollback segments, 57-58

dynamic growth, avoiding, 60-61

extents, 60

number of rollback segments, 58-59

rollback segment operation, 54-55, 57

rules for using, 61

sizing, 59-60

statistics, 59-61

vs. SMU, 52

reads

consistency, 52

disk, statistics on, 243

latency, 209-211

multiblock,, 91

Real Application Clusters (RAC). *See* **RAC (Real Application Clusters)**

RECO processes, 169

recovery

archive log files, 346

ARCHIVELOG mode, 346

Data Guard, 370

disaster survival systems, 373

parallel, 85-86, 347

point-in-time, 346

process of, 346-347

Recovery Manager (RMAN). *See* **RMAN (Recovery Manager)**

RECOVERY_PARALLELISM parameter, 69, 85, 366

recursive calls, 224

recursive SQL statements, 241, 248, 261

Recycle Buffer Pool, 51

redo log files

ARCHIVELOG mode, 346

Archiver process, 170

bottlenecks in, 62

buffer , 62, 166-167

contention, 62

RAID 1 recommended, 213

statistics on, 131

write latency, 211

redos

block statistics, 153

checkpoints caused by, 62

information on

LGWR process, 283

log files. *See* redo log files

registering applications, 251-252

release compatibility

initialization parameter for, 31

OPTIMIZER_FEATURES_ENABLE parameter, 268

reloads, 43-44

remote mirroring, 367-368, 373

replication, 370-371

reporting servers, 112-113

reserved share pool

performance view, 120

using, 46-47

resource consumer groups
adding users, 109-110
advantages of, 105
allocation, 107
configuring, 105
creating plans, 106-107
directives, setting, 107-109
enabling, 105
management software packages, 105
monitoring, 110
performance view, 120
purpose of, 104-105
resource manager plans, 105-109

resource limiting parameters, 32-33

resource manager, 105-109. *See also*
resource consumer groups

resources, performance view, 120

RESOURCE_LIMIT, 104

RESOURCE_MANAGER_PLAN, 104

response time, tuning for
defined, 6
example, 13
goals, 8
hint for optimizing, 314

RISC processors, 172

RMAN (Recovery Manager)
access patterns, 349
advantages of, 349
asynchronous I/O, 356-357
buffering, 356
large pool configuration, 356
MAXOPENFILES parameter, 357
monitoring, 357
operational steps, 348
parameters, 357
RATE parameter, 357
synchronous I/O, 356-357

rollback entries, 55

Rollback Segment Undo (RBU) scheme.
See **RBU (Rollback Segment Undo
Scheme)**

rollback segments. *See also* **RBU (Rollback
Segment Undo Scheme); SMU (System
Managed Undo)**
automatic transaction assignment, 55
circular buffering, 55
contention, minimizing, 58
creating, 57-58
dynamic growth, avoiding, 60-61
extents, 55, 58, 60
hand configuring, 53
large updates, 59
long queries, 59
manual transaction assignment, 55
number, setting, 58-59
OLTP transactions, 59
operation of, 54-55, 57-58
purpose of, 52
shrinks, 137
sizing, 59-60, 137
SMU recommended, 52
statistics, 58-61, 136-137, 154-155
transaction tables, 55
transactions parameter, 39
wraps, 137

root nodes, 70

rotational latency, 183

routers, 384-385

row cache, 45

ROWID hints, 318

rows
chaining, 222-223, 225, 227
migrating, 222-223, 227
specific, updating bottleneck, 289
SQL Trace, number processed, 243

RULE hint, 315

rules-based optimization, 315

runtime areas, 41

S

SANs (Storage Area Networks)
backups using, 348-349
clustering, 204, 334
defined, 203
failover controllers, 203
OPS, 205
RAC, 205
remote mirroring, 367

schema statistics, 277

seeks, 181, 183

segments, 224-225

SELECT statements, 301, 311

sequential I/O, 217

server processes, 168

session information, storage of, 168

sessions, performance view, 119-120

SESSIONS parameter, 33

SESSION_CACHED_CURSORS parameter, 39

SGA (System Global Area)
buffer cache. *See* buffer cache
buffer pools, 37
components, 165
initialization parameters, 24, 31, 37, 39
large pools. *See* large pools
locking into memory, 37
memory requirement, 40
performance view, 117

redo log buffer, 166-167
shared pools. *See* shared pools
statistics on, 145, 157, 159

shadow processes. *See* **server processes**

shared memory, 37, 40

shared PL/SQL area, 42

shared pool
components of, 42-47
data dictionary, 44-46, 167
defined, 166
large pool, 47
library cache, 42-44, 167
performance view, 123
reserved area, 46-47
SHARED_POOL_RESERVED_SIZE parameter, 37
SHARED_POOL_SIZE parameter, 37, 44

shared processes, 121

shared SQL area, 42, 284-285

shutdown, checkpoint creation by, 63

SHUTDOWN ABORT command, 30

SHUTDOWN IMMEDIATE command, 30

SHUTDOWN NORMAL command, 29

SHUTDOWN TRANSACTIONAL command, 29-30

shutting down Oracle instances, 28-30

single image clusters, 333

sites, choosing with hints, 320

sizing systems
defined, 19
for the worst case, 8
steps in, 20-21

SMON processes, 169

SMP (Symmetric Multiprocessor) systems, 173

SMU (System Managed Undo) mode, 52-54

sort-merge joins. *See* **merge joins**

sorts
elevator, 199
memory required, 64
performance view, 121
runs, 64
sort area size, 63-64
SORT_AREA_RETAINED_SIZE parameter 38, 64
SORT_AREA_SIZE parameter, 38
statistics on, 63, 131
temporary tablespaces, 64-65

SPX/IPX, 382

SQL Analyze, 123

SQL area, 121

SQL statement execution
binding variables, 286
cursor creation, 284
execution step, 286
execution plans. *See* EXPLAIN PLAN command
fetching rows, 287
Parallel Query option, 287
parsing statements, 284-286
query processing, 286
steps in, 284-288

SQL statement optimization. *See also*
EXPLAIN PLAN command; SQL Trace
analyzing, 288-289
comments. *See* comments
cost, 301
designing, 290
effects of, 289, 302
existing applications, 297-302
EXPLAIN PLAN. *See* EXPLAIN PLAN command

familiarization phase, 300
goals for optimizing, 294
indexes, 303-306
join optimization. *See* joins
new applications, 297, 303-306
page read statistics, 147
parses, 149-150
problem analysis, 298-299
problems, list of, 289, 294-295
SQL Trace analysis. *See* SQL Trace
statistics on, 147-150
steps for tuning, 300-301
tuning steps, 302
well-tuned, characteristics of, 288

SQL Trace
counts, 240, 243, 247
CPU parameter, 243, 247
current parameter, 243, 247
disabling, 240, 243
disk parameter, 243, 247
elapsed times, 240 243, 247
enabling, 239-240, 243
EXPLAIN PLAN command, 301
guidelines for use, 238
index performance, 306
indications of problems, 301
information gathered, 240-241, 248
initialization parameters required, 239
library cache, 241, 247
MAX_DUMP_FILE_SIZE parameter, 239
optimizer hints, 247
output from, 246-247
parameters, table of, 243, 247
purpose of, 238, 289
query parameter, 243, 247
read statistics, 241
rows parameter, 243, 247
TIMED_STATISTICS parameter, 239

TKPROF for formatting, 238, 241-243, 245-247

USER_DUMP_DEST parameter, 239

SQL*Plus, 24-25

stack space, 168

standardized naming conventions, 43

Standby Database, 368-370

STAR hints, 319

star query plans, 319

starting Oracle instances, 24-28

STARTUP command, 25

STAR_TRANSFORMATION hints, 323

statistics. *See also* BSTAT/ESTAT;
  DBMS_STATS package; Statspack

    creating table for, 274

    database statistics, 277

    DELETE_TABLE_STATS function, 275-276

    disk drive accesses, 215-216

    GATHER_TABLE_STATS function, 274-275

    index statistics, 276

    parallel execution, 82-83

    restoring, 276

    snapshots. *See* Statspack

    system statistics, 277

    table statistics, 276

statistics names, performance view, 121

Statspack

    buffer pool statistics, 153

    cache hits ratio, 153

    defined, 123, 142

    dictionary cache statistics, 156

    general information, 144

    I/O statistics, 152-153

    initialization parameters, listing, 159

    installing, 142

    instance activity statistics, 150-152

    instance recovery statistics, 153

    latch statistics, 155-156

    library cache statistics, 157

    parse statistics, 149-150

    PGA statistics, 154

    redo block statistics, 153

    rollback segment statistics, 154-155

    running, 142, 144

    SGA statistics, 145, 157, 159

    snapshot display, 142

    SQL statement statistics, 147-150

    system load statistics, 145

    truncating tables, 144

    wait event statistics, 146-147

storage. *See also* disk drives

    PCTFREE/PCTUSED, setting, 228

    STORAGE clause options, 225

stored procedures

    benefits of, 290

    caching in shared pool, 42

    shared SQL area benefits of, 285

striping

    costs of, 220

    defined, 189, 218

    hardware, 220

    Oracle, 219-220

    OS, 220

    parallel execution, benefits with, 81

    RAID, 189, 201

    stripe size, 201, 219

structural integrity, 280

Sub-Partitioning, 92

subnets, 381

subqueries, hints for, 326-327

swapping memory, 40, 176

system memory architecture, 175

system parameters performance view, 121

system statistics performance view, 121

system tuning, 18-19

T

table scans
ROWID hints, 318
statistics indicating, 141

tables
data dictionary cache, 44
indexing, guidelines for, 260, 304-305
specific, updating bottleneck, 289

tablespaces
block size, setting, 231
checkpoint creation by, 63
fragmentation, 231, 233-234
I/O statistics, 139-141
sorting with, 64-65
undo parameters, 38

TCP/IP networks, 381

temporary space performance view, 121

threads, 168. See also processes; MTS
(multithreaded server)

throughput, defined, 7-8

throughput, tuning for
defined, 6
goals, 7-8
hint for, 313

TKPROF
optional parameters, 241-243, 245-247
output from, 246-247
recursive SQL statements, 241
sort options, 242
SQL Trace formatted by, 238

Top Sessions, 123

Trace Data Viewer, 123

trace files, maximum size parameter, 32

track-to-track seeks, 183

transaction processing
block size, 230
commitment, 283
completion requirements, 62
connection stage, 282
defined, 282
function reallocation, 112
performance view, 118, 121
processing stage, 282-283
read consistency, 52
redo information, 283
rollback segment sizing, 59
steps in, 282-283
termination stage, 283
TRANSACTIONS parameter, 33
TRANSACTIONS_PER_ROLLBACK_
SEGMENT, 39
user profiles for, 111
workload management, 111

transaction tables, 55

tuning methodology
analysis phase, 12-13
analyzing test results, 15-16
determination phase, 10, 12
examining the problem, 10, 12
existing applications, 298
goal setting, 14-15
response time example, 13
steps in, 10, 21-22
testing solutions, 15

tuning, definition of, 6

U

UGA (User Global Area), 38

undo header buffer busy waits, 136

undos

monitoring tablespace, 54

parameters, 38-39

performance view, 121

rate, determining, 54

RBU, 54-61

retention period, 54

SMU, 52-54

tablespace creation, 53

tablespace size requirement, 53

UNDO_MANAGEMENT parameter, 38, 53

UNDO_RETENTION, 38

UNDO_SUPPRESS_ERRORS, 39

UNDO_TABLESPACE, 38

write latency, 211

UNION operator, 311

unique indexes, 72, 257, 304

UNIQUE integrity constraints, 257

UNNEST hints, 327

updates

chaining rows, 222-223

indexes, effects on, 75, 260-262

migrating rows, 222-223

overhead from, 301

PCTFREE/PCTUSED, setting, 228

USE_CONCAT hints, 319, 324

USE_HASH hints, 320

USE_MERGE hints, 320

USE_NL hints, 320

user processes, 168

user profiles, 110-112

user resources, 110-112

UTLBSTAT. *See* **BSTAT/ESTAT**

UTLESTAT. *See* **BSTAT/ESTAT**

V

V$ views. *See* **Oracle Dynamic Performance Views**

VARCHAR2 data type, 288

views. *See also* **Oracle Dynamic Performance Views**

data dictionary cache, 44

hints for, 324

virtual memory, 176

W

waits

performance view, 118, 120-121

statistics on, 131-133, 146-147

WHERE clauses, USE_CONCAT hints, 319

willing-to-wait latches, 134

Windows NT Fail Safe, 204

workload tuning

Data Guard, 113

function reallocation, 112

goals of, 104

historical reports, 112

initialization parameters, 104

methods for accomplishing, list of, 104

online reports, 113-114

reporting servers, 112-113

resource consumer groups, 104-108, 110

user resource limiting, 110-112

write caches, 201
write latency, 209, 211-212

X-Z

X$ tables, 116